Private and Public Enterpr

This is the first comparative history of the economic organisation of energy, telecommunications and transport in Europe in the nineteenth and twentieth centuries. It examines the role that private and public enterprise have played in the construction and operation of the railways; electricity, gas and water supply; tramways; coal, oil and natural gas industries; telegraph, telephone, computer networks and other modern telecommunications. The book begins with the arrival of the railways in the 1830s, charts the development of arm's-length regulation, municipalisation and nationalisation, and ends on the eve of privatisation in the 1980s. Robert Millward argues that the role of ideology, especially in the form of debates about socialism and capitalism, has been exaggerated. Instead the driving forces in changes in economic organisation were economic and technological factors and the book traces their influence in shaping the pattern of regulation and ownership of these key sectors of modern economies.

ROBERT MILLWARD is Professor of Economic History at the University of Manchester. His previous publications include *Public and Private Ownership of British Industry 1820–1990* (1994) and *The Political Economy of Nationalisation in Britain 1920–1950* (1995).

Cambridge Studies in Economic History

Editorial Board

Cambridge Studies in Economic History comprises stimulating and accessible economic history which actively builds bridges to other disciplines. Books in the series will illuminate why the issues they address are important and interesting, place their findings in a comparative context, and relate their research to wider debates and controversies. The series will combine innovative and exciting new research by younger researchers with new approaches to major issues by senior scholars. It will publish distinguished work regardless of chronological period or geographical location.

Private and Public Enterprise in Europe

Energy, Telecommunications and Transport, 1830–1990

Robert Millward

CAMBRIDGE
UNIVERSITY PRESS

CAMBRIDGE UNIVERSITY PRESS
Cambridge, New York, Melbourne, Madrid, Cape Town, Singapore, São Paulo

Cambridge University Press
The Edinburgh Building, Cambridge CB2 8RU, UK

Published in the United States of America by Cambridge University Press, New York

www.cambridge.org
Information on this title: www.cambridge.org/9780521835244

First published 2005
This digitally printed version 2008

A catalogue record for this publication is available from the British Library

ISBN 978-0-521-83524-4 hardback
ISBN 978-0-521-06828-4 paperback

Cambridge University Press has no responsibility for the persistence or
accuracy of URLs for external or third-party Internet websites referred to in
this publication, and does not guarantee that any content on such websites is,
or will remain, accurate or appropriate.

For Sam, Thea, Flora and Patrick

Contents

Part IV State Enterprise c. 1945–1990

Part V Conclusions

Figures

Tables

Preface

I hope that historians and economists will treat this as a first stab at a subject where cross-European comparisons have been neglected in the past. There does not appear to have been any systematic attempt to analyse and quantify the economic history of regulation and public ownership in Europe. Much remains to be done, especially since my command of languages is limited so that this book is more a research monograph than a text. There are large gaps, set out at the end of chapter 1, in both topics and countries, which I hope others will address. In the meantime let me thank the large number of scholars who have, in one way and another, been most helpful and in particular: Francesca Antolin, Judith Clifton, Francisco Comin, Alexandre Fernandez, Massimo Florio, James Foreman-Peck, Daniel Fuentes, Renato Giannetti, Andre Giuntini, Ingrid Henriksen, Ole Hyldtoft, Gregorio Nunez, Dieter Schott and Richard Tilly.

Thanks are also due to the Leverhulme Trust for the invaluable financial support which gave me time for researching and writing.

Some of the ideas and data in Part II and in chapter 14 (the data on productivity) have appeared in the following publications by Cambridge University Press: 'European Governments and the Infrastructure Industries c.1840–1914', *European Review of Economic History* 8(1) (2004); 'The Rise of the Service Sector', in R. Floud and P. Johnson (eds.), *The Economic History of Britain since 1700*. III. *Structural Change and Growth 1939–2000* (2004); 'The Political Economy of Urban Utilities in Britain 1840–1950', in M. Daunton (ed.), *Cambridge Urban History of Britain*, III (2001).

Glossary and abbreviations

AGIP	Azienda Generale Italia Petroli (1926)
AGTVF	Asociación General de Transportes par Viá Férnea
ASEA	Allmäna Svenska Elektriska AB (Swedish electrical equipment manufacturer)
ASST	Azienda di Stato per i Servizi Telefonici (Italian state enterprise for trunk telephone lines)
BA	British Airways, 1974, merged from British Overseas Airways Corporation (BOAC, 1940) and British European Airways (BEA, 1946)
BERG	Berg u. Hüttenbehieze AG (former Herman Goering works, 1936)
BP	British Petroleum (1914)
BR	British Railways (1962 the successor to the Railways Executive, 1947)
BT	British Telecom (1981)
BTC	British Transport Commission (1947)
CAMPSA	Compañía Arrendetaria del Monopolio de Petróleos (Spain, 1927)
CASMEZ	Cassa per il Mezzogiorno (Italian government development fund for the south, 1950)
CDF	Charbonnages de France (state coal board, 1946)
CEB	Central Electricity Board (Britain, 1926)
CEEP	Centre Européen de l'Entreprise Publique
CFP	Compagnie Française des Pétroles (1926)
CGE	Compagnie Générale d'Electricité (French electrical equipment manufacturer)
CGP	Commissariat Général du Plan (1946, France)
CGT	Conféderation Générale du Travail (workers' association, France)
CNR	Conseil National de Résistance (in France)
CPE	Customer premises equipment (telecommunications)

DB	Deutsche Bundesbahn (Federal West German railway enterprise, 1951)
DBP	Deutsche Bundespost (Federal West German post and telecommunications enterprise, 1951)
DR	Deutsche Reichsbahn (Imperial German railway, 1919)
ECSC	European Coal and Steel Community (1951)
EDF	Electricité de France (1946)
EC	European Community (1965, formed from merger of EEC, ECSC and Euratom)
EEC	European Economic Community (1957)
ELKRAFT	Danish electricity group supplying Zealand, 1978, formerly Kraftimport, established in 1954
ELSAM	Det Jysk-fynske Elsamarbejde (Electricity group supplying Jutland and Funen in Denmark, 1956)
ENDESA	Empresa Nacional de Electricidad (Spain, 1944)
ENEL	Ente Nazionale de l'Energia Elettrica (Italy, 1962)
ENHER	Empresa Hidroelectrica del Ribagorzana (Spain, 1946)
ENI	Ente Nazionale Idrocaruri (1953, Italian state financial company holding shares in AGIP and others)
EU	European Union (1993)
FFSS	Azienda Autonoma delie Ferrovie dello Stato (Italian state railways, 1905)
GDF	Gaz du France (1946)
gigawatt	one million kilowatts
HEP	hydroelectricity
HMSO	Her Majesty's Stationery Office (UK)
IATA	International Air Transport Association (1945)
INI	Instituto Nacional de Industria (Spain, 1941)
IRI	Istituto per la Ricostruzione Industriale (Italy, 1933)
ISDN	Integrated services digital network (telecommunications)
IT	inclusive tour
ITT	International Telephone and Telegraph (USA)
joule	one unit of energy (work done when one Newton moves one metre)
KLM	Koninklijke Luchtvaart Maatschappij (Royal Dutch Airlines, 1919)
km	kilometre
kV	kilovolt (a measure of the strength of electric current on a transmission line)
kW	kilowatt (1000 watts)
kWh	kilowatt hour

MW	megawatt (1000 kilowatts)
NCB	National Coal Board (UK, 1947)
NESCO	Newcastle-upon-Tyne Electricity Supply Company
NTA	Telegrafslyret (National Telephone Authority, Norway)
NVE	Nordvestsjællands Elektriciteit-Værk (Norwegian Waterways and Electricity Administration, 1920, renamed Statkraft in 1960)
OECD	Organisation for Economic Cooperation and Development
OPEC	Organisation of Petroleum Exporting Countries
petajoule	10^{15} joules, equivalent to approximately 27.1 million cubic metres (used in measure of natural gas)
PABX	Private automatic branch exchange (telecommunications)
P-L-M	Paris, Lyons, Mediterranée railway
P-O	Paris-Orleans railway
PSO	Public service obligation
PSTN	Public switching telephone network
PTO	Public telecom operators
PTT	Postes, Téléphone et Télégraphe (in France, similar abbreviation for Denmark and the Netherlands)
RENFE	Red Nacional de los Ferrocarriles Españoles (Spanish state railways, 1941)
RPTV	Reichspost- und Telegraphenverwaltung (1876, German imperial post and telegraph management)
RWE	Rheinisch-Westfalisches Elektrizitätswerk (mixed German enterprise, 1898)
SAS	Scandinavian Airlines System (1946)
SIP	Società Italiana per l'Esercizio Telefonico (1964, financial subsidiary of STET operating non-trunk telephone networks, formerly Società Idrolettrica Piemontese)
SJ	Statens Järnvägar (Swedish state railways, 1888)
SNCF	Société Nationale des Chemins de Fer Français (1937)
Statkraft	See NVE
Statsföretag	Swedish state holding company (1970, renamed Procordia in 1984)
STET	Società Finanziaria Telefonica (IRI financial subsidiary, holding shares in telephone companies, 1933)
Telefónica	Originally Compañía Telefónica Nacional de España established in Spain, 1924, and renamed Telefónica in 1984
Televerket	State telegraph and telephone board in Sweden (1853)

terajoule	10^{12} joules
TFP	Total factor productivity
UN	United Nations
Vattenfall	Statens Vattenfallswerk (Swedish state electricity power board, 1909)
VANS	Value added network services (telecommunications)
VAS	Value added services (telecommunications)
VEBA	Vereinigten Elektrizititäts u. Bergwerk AG (1929, Germany)
VIAG	Vereinigte Industrieunternehmen AG (1923, Germany)

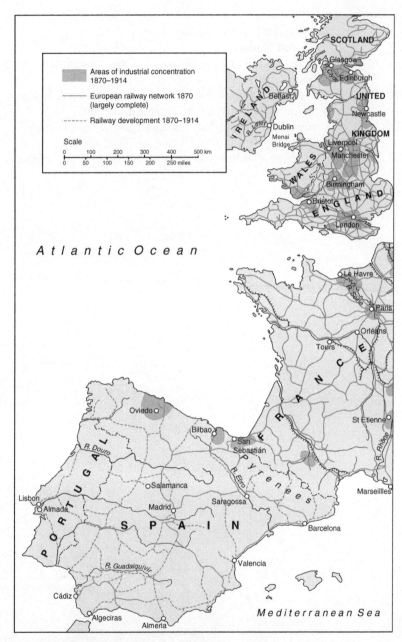

The European economy in 1914.

Source: G. Barraclough (ed.), *Times Atlas of World History* (London: Times Books, 5th edn, 1981), 212–13.

Map xix

Part I

Introduction

1   Ideology, technology and economic policy

How effectively have energy, transport and telecommunications been delivered over the last two centuries? What role was played by ideologies of socialism and capitalism? What has been the role of government? These sectors, sometimes called infrastructure industries, provide services and commodities that meet both a commercial demand (a rail service for tourists, mobile phones) and a public service (road, rail and telephone links for military/strategic aims). They have traditionally been delivered by enterprises that have a commercial orientation. Many are, or were, in complete private ownership like the Electric and International Telegraph Company, Edison, the Berlin Tramways Company, British Telecom. Some, such as the oil distributor British Petroleum, the German electricity utility Rheinisch-Westfalisches Elektrizitätswerk and the Danish telephone enterprise Fyas Communale had mixed private/public ownership. Others were run by local government: the Bologna municipal gas undertaking, the London Metropolitan Water Board. Others were state-owned enterprises: Alitalia, the French railway enterprise Société Nationale des Chemins de Fer Français, the National Coal Board in Britain, the telecommunications enterprises in Spain (Telefónica), Germany (Deutsche Bundespost) and Sweden (Televerket). Some then were privately owned enterprises, many still are, some are public but in all cases their position on the border between the private and the public sector make them of special interest in the economic history of Western Europe. This book analyses the development of energy, transport and communications from the arrival of the railways in the 1830s, through the emergence of large electricity, gas, water and tramways undertakings in the nineteenth century, to the replacement of coal by oil in the mid-twentieth century and the electronic transformation of communications in the 1980s.

One aim is to assess how far common patterns of regulation and ownership emerged across the seemingly different contexts of southern Europe, Scandinavia, France, Germany, the Low Countries and the UK. These regions had different resource endowments and were positioned

3

differently with respect to trading opportunities. There was no coal industry to nationalise in Scandinavia. The British had to travel for sunny holidays and were pioneers in the development of charter airlines in the 1960s but had few mountains suitable for hydroelectricity, which met only a small part of UK energy requirements. Germany had poor access to the sea, saw only limited development of merchant shipping but had excellent rivers and canals for inland waterways. Spain had unreliable rainfall and few canals but its airline flourished from tourism. Italy had a mountain range forbidding for the construction of railways but it proved great for hydroelectricity. Europe as a whole has an array of languages and nation states, which contrasts vividly with the USA. Such differences affected the attitudes of governments, at both state and municipal level, to the industries but do not in themselves mean that similar responses to the same economic pressures could not be expected. The challenge here then is to see how far there was a common pattern of regulatory behaviour and ownership across Europe.

The starting point in the early nineteenth century is a period when isolated villages, manors and cottage industries were giving way to economic activities that were, physically, drawing communities together and in urban areas creating new problems for health and housing. The shift to mass production in manufacturing factories was complemented by a gradual move to mass joint consumption of services – away from the stagecoach, the river and stream for water supply, peat and wood for fuel, the messenger for communications, to the railway train, the distribution networks for gas and water, the telegraph for communications and, later in the century, the spread of electric cables, tramlines and telephones wires. The new means of transport and communications had significant strategic and political potentialities, of which the new nation states of Europe were well aware – breaking down regional enclaves and offering the prospect of new military instruments and political and social unification.

At the beginning, in the 1830s, factory development was well advanced in Belgium and Britain. In France and Germany it followed slightly later, whilst Italy, Norway and Sweden experienced their main industrial spurt at the end of the century. In the 1830s there were wide differences in income per head as may be seen in the first column of Table 1.1. The spread of factory industry and the growth of urban areas were important in providing a demand for better and cheaper energy, transport and communications. A key indicator was how much of the labour force had shifted to industry and how much was still in agriculture. A measure of the extent to which Britain had already been transformed was that only 29% of its male labour force was employed in agriculture in 1840. Britain differed markedly from

Table 1.1 *Income levels and economic structure in the early nineteenth century (contemporary geographic boundaries)*

	Gross Domestic Product per head of population in 1820 in 1985 US dollars	Share of male labour force in agriculture in the year when 1840 British GDP per head was attained[a]	
		%	Year
UK	1405	29[b]	1840
Netherlands	1307	41	1860
France	1052	51	1870
Belgium	1024	49	1850
Denmark	988	48	1870
Italy	960	54	1910
Sweden	947	53	1900
Germany	937	58[c]	1870
Spain	931[d]	56	1890
Norway	856	60	1910

Notes:
[a] Estimated by Crafts (*British Economic Growth*) as 550 US dollars in 1970 prices.
[b] Britain, i.e. excludes all Ireland.
[c] Rough estimate based on Milward and Saul, *Development of the Economies*, 44–6.
[d] Assumed to be 93% of Italy. See Maddison, *Monitoring the World Economy*, 194 and 198.

Sources: N. F. R. Crafts, *British Economic Growth during the Industrial Revolution* (Oxford: Clarendon Press, 1985), Table 3.4; A. Maddison, *Dynamic Forces in Capitalist Development* (Oxford University Press, 1991), Table 1.1; A. Maddison, *Monitoring the World Economy 1820–1992* (Paris: OECD, 1995); A. S. Milward and S. B. Saul, *The Development of the Economies of Continental Europe 1850–1914* (Cambridge, Mass.: Harvard University Press, 1977).

the others, not so much because of income levels or productivity growth, but because of the size of the structural shift of economic activity from agriculture to industry. The income level that Britain had reached by 1840 was attained in Denmark, France and Germany by 1870, but at that date one half or more of their male labour forces was still in agriculture. The full set of corresponding figures for the share of male employees in agriculture is given in the second column of Table 1.1.

When the steam-propelled railways came on the scene in the 1830s, Britain already had a big industrial sector that could benefit from better transport services, but this was very different, as will be seen in chapter 4, from the situation in Italy, Norway, Spain and Sweden and also in eastern Germany, which in the nineteenth century stretched across the vast rural areas of eastern Prussia, that is, present-day Poland and Lithuania (see the map at the front of this book). Perhaps the railways could stimulate economic development by opening up new regions as in the USA? Many Norwegian communities were self-sufficient for fishing and farming. Sweden was also heavily dependent on agriculture but had good resources of timber and iron, exports of which formed the initial response to industrialisation in Britain, Belgium, France and Germany. Shipping was a major infrastructure industry in Scandinavia, especially important in Denmark with its long coastline and easy access to British coal supplies and markets for Danish food products. Spain and Italy were not so fortunate. They were both mountainous countries with few inland waterways, apart from the Po Valley in Italy. The silk industry was well developed in Italy but was not of sufficient size to form an export growth pole in the same fashion as Scandinavia's iron and timber. The same could be said of Spain's rather poor quality coal and other minerals.

Nineteenth-century Europe saw a massive expansion of railway track, telegraph lines, electricity stations and cables, gas and water works and mains, followed at the turn of the century by tramways and telephone lines. Apart from water supply, these infrastructure industries were offering new services based on technological innovations. They exhibited all the classic problems of monopoly. Railways in a given region were often owned by a single company, so also for the electric telegraph, while the towns witnessed bursts of competition between suppliers of gas, electricity and water followed closely by the emergence of a local monopoly or intercompany agreements on districts to be served. These networks had great potential for opening up regions and perhaps stimulating economic growth. The methods of supply were, however, very intrusive, especially in growing urban areas where disease, housing squalor, unsightly cables, mains and drains were common. From an early twenty-first century perspective it is not surprising to find that, notwithstanding the nineteenth-century commitment to free enterprise capitalism and self-help, these sectors were closely regulated and sometimes taken over by local and central governments. Private enterprise was nonetheless pervasive. Almost without exception it was involved in all the initial construction and operation of the new networks and, across Europe, was still the dominant form of undertaking in 1913 on the eve of the First World War.

All countries faced many common economic problems but, by 1913, the pattern of regulation and ownership did vary enormously. Legislative ceilings on fares, tariffs and rates were common, but the use of the concession system, franchises, profit sharing, subsidies and grants varied considerably. Municipal ownership of gas, water and electricity was strong in Germany and Scandinavia but not in Spain and Italy.

Railways were still mainly privately owned in Britain, France and Spain but not in Norway, Italy or Germany. One result of the complex institutional pattern is that the economic history of these sectors has usually been written as a separate story for each country. Despite some recent attempts to draw out common themes,[1] the literature is dominated by the separate stories, and the explanations of the differences, whether implicit or explicit, often invoke socio-political factors: Scandinavian local community life, the orchestrative role of the French state, the pressures for cultural and political unification in Italy, Belgium and Sweden, the addiction to free trade in Britain, Prussian regulation by administration rather than by the legal system. All of these are relevant and important but how do they relate to the economic issues of monopoly and network development? That is the subject of Parts II and III whilst Part IV takes the story on to the era of state enterprise 1945–90.

The analytical framework is as follows. Comparable cross-European data on the different patterns of ownership and regulation are patchy, and assembling such a picture has been the first major task. It was decided to concentrate on Western Europe and to obtain a good spread of experience by covering Denmark, France, Germany, Italy, Norway, Spain, Sweden and the UK, consistently from 1830 to 1990. The experiences of Belgium and the Netherlands are an important part of the story even though quantitative information is not presented consistently for these countries. Secondly, the inherent economic characteristics of the infrastructure industries in terms of their need for rights of way, the monopoly problem, network effects, the potential for stimulating economic growth are identified and the implications for government assessed in relation to the actual experience in each country. How much of the actual pattern of regulation and public ownership do they explain and at what point is it necessary to invoke socio-political issues? Thirdly, the whole of the period c. 1830–1990 is broken up into phases, characterised mainly by technological changes or the discovery of new resources. For each phase, an exogenous force is identified, such as the advent of steam railways in the 1830s, the emergence in the early twentieth century of techniques for long distance transmission of electricity, the discovery of European deposits of oil and natural gas in the 1960s and 1970s. The economic implications are then analysed and some of the likely government responses assessed and then compared with the actual responses. For example, the controls on railway company charges and profits in the nineteenth century followed from the monopoly characteristics of railway technology. Another example is the mushrooming of fax and email in the late twentieth century with a potentially important influence on the structure of the market for customer premises equipment – computers, fax machines and so on. The effect of technological changes will vary in different geographical regions so that similar behavioural responses to technological and economic forces may prompt a different reaction in different settings; the governments of Norway and Sweden, with their scantily populated land masses, were likely to react differently to the advent of railways than the government of densely populated Britain. Discoveries of new resources and technological changes in the infrastructure industries were continuously presenting governments with new instruments of social and economic policy. Indigenous deposits of oil had great strategic significance in the twentieth century in times of war and other crises; railways offered a way of facilitating political unification in Belgium in the 1830s and Italy in the 1860s. The analysis and quantification of these factors will not explain everything but will allow an assessment of how much is left for cultural and ideological influences.

A common characterisation of the economic history of the infrastructure industries over the last 150 years or so is that private enterprise and free trade were dominant in the nineteenth century at the national level whilst municipal socialism paved the way for municipal enterprise at the local level. The vicissitudes of the 1930s' depression and the Second World War then heralded, so the story goes, a period of socialist-inspired state monopolies from the late 1940s followed by a return to the free enterprise creed in privatisation programmes from the 1980s. These ideological shifts were certainly present but it is far from clear that they can account for the timing and incidence of the regulatory and ownership changes since 1830. So far as the nineteenth century is concerned, John Moore claimed that the infrastructure business had 'been founded by the great Victorian entrepreneurs. They would not even have been created, let alone flourished, if there had not been a free market.'[2] He was perhaps unduly influenced by the history of the railways in Britain since, as will be clear from chapter 3, many an enterprise in electricity, gas and water supply and tramways in the nineteenth century was introduced by municipalities in Scandinavia, Britain and Germany whilst the nation state was heavily involved in building up the Belgian railway system and all European governments were deeply involved in regulation. On the other hand, Parts II and III also consider how far the role of socialist ideology has also been exaggerated. The spread of municipally owned and managed enterprises in gas, electricity, water and tramways is often attributed to the supporters of municipal socialism. In Germany 'municipal socialism was identified ... [says Kuhl] ... with efforts ... to provide services ... by municipalisation of private monopoly enterprises ... The rapid reception of municipal socialism is commonly attributed to the activities of a group of economists and sociologists in the Association for Social Policy.' But Kuhl points out that the major initial burst of municipalisation occurred well before the activities of the Association, which are usually dated at the end of the nineteenth century.[3] Similar remarks can be made about the Webbs and the Fabians in Britain. Chapter 3 suggests that hard-nosed shopkeepers, business men and other wealthy elites on town councils encouraged municipal enterprise in the growing industrial towns.

Ideological influences are also an issue in the context of mid-twentieth century changes, about which there is much confusion. Parts II and III show that by the late 1940s most Western European countries had a substantial state enterprise sector. This was true of Italy and Germany but, in these former fascist regimes, it had little to do with socialism; the same applies to Spain. Romano Prodi was keen to emphasise that in Italy 'the major institutional innovations that increased public ownership and public influence ... have not been taken in response to some political demand for state ownership of the means of production as in Britain'.[4] Students of Swedish politics are prone to say something similar. 'It is relatively easy in Sweden ... [says Coombe] ... to justify every example of public ownership according to some specific social or economic policy of government'.[5] This writer and others want to see Sweden as exceptional yet, as is argued in the following chapters, the experiences of Italy and Germany have many similarities. What happened in France and Britain does seem to be different, and certainly these two countries witnessed some dramatic parliamentary legislation in the 1945–8 period when coal, railways, electricity and gas were nationalised. The war-time resistance movement in France (Conseil National de Résistance) was politically influential towards the end of the Second World War and it declared on 15 March 1944 that in order 'to bring about indispensable ... reforms ... in the economic ... sphere ... [there should be a] ... return to the nation of the chief means of production, now monopolies, which are the result of communal labour ... and the participation by the worker in the direction of the economy'.[6] These allusions to neo-Marxist concepts of means of production find echoes in Kelf-Cohen's argument that, in Britain, public ownership was a product of socialism, which itself stemmed from the social upheavals associated with nineteenth-century industrialisation.[7] 'Public ownership was, after all ... [said Cairncross] ... at the centre of the socialist vision of the future in 1945'.[8] Yet socialism seemed to stop at the gates of manufacturing industry (apart from steel in Britain and the Renault car company in France, the latter deemed to have collaborated during the war) and left land and commerce in the private sector. Moreover the cumulative experience of regulation, municipalisation and state ownership over the previous 100 years, ensured, as will be seen in the following chapters, that the central governments of France and Britain had a strong grip on all the infrastructure industries by the end of the 1930s, before the electoral success of social democratic parties in the 1940s. And finally even some of the students of the privatisation programmes of the late twentieth century doubt whether the ideologies associated with the 1980s' Thatcher government in the UK can explain the timing and incidence of the programmes in other Western European countries.[9]

The differences between Europe and the USA are also often portrayed in ideological terms but in some respects this is also misleading. The geography and political fragmentation of Western Europe made for large contrasts with the USA and indeed Eastern Europe, with respect to the regulation and ownership of the infrastructure industries. In the second half of the twentieth century, many in Europe looked over their shoulders to the relatively unregulated free market economy of the USA and to its continuing economic success. The approach to regulation and government has been very different. By the late nineteenth century the USA's huge land area was relatively unencumbered with internal trade barriers and language differences. Western Europe is also a large land mass, but one populated by nations with potentially hostile states on each country's borders. Each had certain social and political objectives, not unlike those of the US federal government, but in Europe this inevitably meant a more fragmented set of infrastructure industries with each country controlling its own airspace, railway system, telecommunications and energy supply. Comparisons of the regulation and ownership of the infrastructure industries that do not allow for these differences are empty of meaning. It is no point arguing that American airlines were more economically efficient in the 1950–80 period than national airlines like Air France and Alitalia and attributing this to the more liberal regime in the USA.[10] When the airline business took off in the late 1940s, each nation wanted to exert some control over its aviation industry (as did the USA), an industry that had great strategic and military significance, so pan-European airlines did not emerge. Unfortunately this was not the most economical way of running airlines – it simply reflected the constitutional and political realities. Similarly it can be misleading to compare enterprise performance in the Third World and Eastern Europe with Western Europe. By the end of the nineteenth century, several Western European states had strong bureaucracies, civil service codes and democratic processes. They were the administrative backup for the regulation and public ownership of the infrastructure industries. Many of the latter were economically efficient. They contrast strongly then with the fledgling public sectors emerging from the 1960s in many Third World countries. The latter's failure to provide efficient public services in transport, telecommunications and energy and the subsequent recourse to privatisation, often to a foreign company, tells us little about the efficiency or otherwise of state enterprise in Western Europe. Statistical regressions over worldwide populations tell us little about the differences and similarities within Western Europe.[11] The benefits of privatisation in late twentieth-century Eastern Europe reflect more on the nature of the communist economies of the 1920–90 period than on the relative performance of public and private enterprise in Western Europe in the nineteenth and twentieth century.

A final note about what is not covered. The aim is to provide, for the first time I believe, a cross-European perspective on regulation and government ownership of the infrastructure industries from the arrival of the railways in the 1830s to the onset of privatisation in the 1980s. This is a huge unexplored area, and I have tried to focus on some central issues, leaving many gaps. Thus for much of the twentieth century the problem facing the railways was one inherited from the nineteenth century and brought to a head with the arrival of competition from road transport in the 1920s. There is much in the book about nineteenth-century railways and a section on road–rail competition in the inter-war period but that issue is not followed through in any detail for the post-1945 period. In turn, the emphasis for that later period is on the regulatory issues associated with the new competitor, the airlines. Similarly, water supplies are at the centre of debates about nineteenth-century urbanisation and public health programmes but are less of an issue in the twentieth century, at least in Europe. They are discussed in chapter 3 but, because of space limitations, not thereafter. The coal industry's problems are discussed in chapter 11, along with the other major post-1945 fuel commodity, oil, and it includes a discussion of the underlying causes of government action, which date from the nineteenth century. Virtually nothing is said about airports, inland waterways, harbours, shipping, nuclear power, roads and road transport, or industrial relations, safety, pollution and other environmental issues. There is nothing on Austria, Portugal and Switzerland and much less than full justice is done to Belgium, Ireland and the Netherlands. I hope this book and its bibliography, limited as it largely is to work in English and French, will be a starting point for others.

Notes

1 N. Lucas, *Western European Energy Policies* (Oxford: Clarendon Press, 1985); F. Cardot (ed.), *1880–1980: Une siècle de l'électricité dans le monde* (Paris: Presses Universitaires de France, 1978); V. Zamagni, *Origins and Development of Publicly*

Owned Enterprises (Bern: Ninth International Economic History Conference, Section B111, 1986); J. Foreman-Peck and J. Mueller (eds.), *European Telecommunications Organisation* (Baden-Baden: Nomosverlagsgesellschaft, 1988); M. Trédé (ed.), *Electricité et électrification dans le monde 1880–1980* (Paris: Association pour l'Histoire de l'Electricité en France, Presses Universitaires de France, 1990); H.-L. Dienel and P. Lyth, *Flying the Flag: European Commercial Air Transport since 1945* (Basingstoke, UK: Macmillan, 1998); L. Andersson-Skog and O. Krantz (eds.), *Institutions and the Transport and Communications Industries* (Canton, Mass.: Science History Publications, Watson, 1999); P. A. Toninelli (ed.), *The Rise and Fall of State Owned Enterprise in the Western World* (Cambridge University Press, 2000).

2 J. Moore, 'Why Privatise?', in J. Kay, C. Mayer and D. Thompson (eds.), *Privatisation and Regulation: The UK Experience* (Oxford: Clarendon Press, 1986), 79.

3 The quotation is my translation. 'Le SM [socialisme municipal] s'identifiait aux efforts déployés ... pour fournir des services ... par la municipalisation des entreprises monopolistiques privées ... La rapide réception du concept de SM ... est attribuée communément aux activités ... d'une groupe d'économistes et de sociologistes qui s'étaient rassemblés dans le 'Verein für Socialpolitik' '. A. Kuhl, 'Le Débat sur le socialisme municipal en allemagne avant 1914 et la municipalisation de l' électricité', in A. Kuhl (ed.), *Der Munizipalsozialismus in Europa* (Munich: Oldenberg Verlag, 2002), 81–2.

4 R. Prodi, 'Italy', in R. Vernon (ed.), *Big Business and the State* (Cambridge, Mass.: Harvard University Press, 1974), 45.

5 D. Coombe, 'State Enterprise in Sweden', in *State Enterprise: Business or Politics* (London: Allen and Unwin, 1972), 183.

6 J. Moch, 'Nationalisation in France', *Annals of Collective Economy*, 24 (1953), 97–8.

7 R. Kelf-Cohen, *Nationalisation in Britain: The End of a Dogma* (London: Macmillan, 1958), ch. 1.

8 A. Cairncross, *Years of Recovery: British Economic Policy* (London: Methuen, 1985), 463.

9 J. Clifton, F. Comin and D. D. Fuentes, *Privatisation in the European Union: Public Enterprises and Integration* (London: Kluwer, 2003).

10 As does M. Baily, 'Competition, Regulation and Efficiency in Service Industries', *Brookings Papers in Microeconomics* 2 (1993), 71–159. See the discussion below in chapter 14.

11 See, for example, S. Littlechild, 'The Effect of Ownership on Telephone Concentration', *Telecommunications Policy* 7 (1983), 246–7.

Part II

The Construction of the New European Infrastructure c. 1830–1914

2 Infrastructure development and rights of way in the early nineteenth century

During the nineteenth century, a complex infrastructure of railway and tramway track, water reservoirs and distribution systems, gas works and pipes, electricity stations, cables and grids, telegraph and telephone systems was constructed. The first developments were in the country that was the first to shift to factory industry, Britain. The early decades of the century witnessed a huge increase in the industrial demand for water and in household needs arising from rapid urbanisation. The construction of water distribution systems goes back at least to the Romans, but the first decades of the nineteenth century saw a major discontinuity, and in several Western European countries this took the form of the growth of large joint stock water companies, tapping rivers and later constructing reservoirs. Gas was a new industry supplying lighting in streets and factories, and gas street lighting spread to all the European capitals from Oslo to Lisbon in the first half of the century. Investment in roads, canals, rivers and other inland waterways was also important and very well developed in France, the Low Countries, Germany and the Po Valley in Italy. All was changed, however, by the railway, whose expansion is illustrated in Figure 2.1 for eight European countries. Led by Britain and Belgium from the 1830s, the others were initially slow to follow, but the length of track open in Britain was overtaken by Germany in the 1870s and by France in the 1880s. Relative to population, but especially relative to geographic size, the networks of Britain and the Low Countries remained the densest and most intensively used systems throughout the century, with Germany and Denmark next in line. The same can be said for gas production in which Britain, well endowed with the key raw material coal, maintained a massive lead when measured against population. To some extent this accounts for its relatively slow initial development of electricity supply in the 1880s and 1890s when it was Germany that forged ahead with new generating plants and electric trams and where Sweden, Norway and Italy developed strongly in the twenty years or so up to the First World War, escaping their poor endowments of coal (and therefore gas)

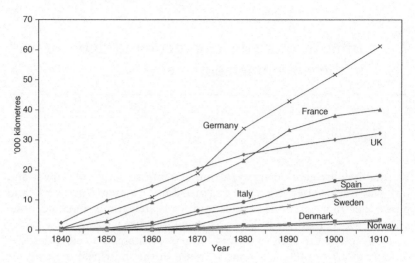

Figure 2.1 Length of rail track open, 1840–1910 ('000 kilometres).

Source: B. R. Mitchell, *International Historical Statistics: Europe 1750–1993* (London: Macmillan, 3rd edn, 1981).

as hydroelectricity schemes mushroomed in the Norwegian fjords, the Swedish waterways, the Alps and the Apennines.

From Sicily to Scotland, from Portugal to Norway, private enterprise and capitalism in their full flow played a central role. Yet by the early years of the twentieth century the tentacles of government were spread everywhere. Figure 2.2 and Table 2.1 provide a picture of one crude dimension of government involvement: the proportion of undertakings owned by municipal or state or national governments. Some of this is well known and there are also some standard explanations for the pattern. Government involvement was high in Germany, whose long tradition of active municipal government is often invoked by historians – also in Sweden, Norway and Denmark – and where states like Prussia siphoned off some of the railways' profits as a supplement to state taxation. Both the French and German governments came to see their rail networks as important for military strategy and here, as in Belgium, Italy, Norway and Sweden, the railways could help unify relatively new nations or mitigate regional cultural differences, and in many cases this appears superficially to have been important in state takeovers. The telegraph was nationalised in many countries as a key element of communications for both civil and military purposes.

Why then did telephone systems show a very mixed pattern of ownership? Why the mixed pattern for gas and electricity systems? Some writers claim that the railways were taken over by the Prussian state to achieve economies of scale and simplify the hated rate structure. A common feature of municipally owned enterprise in Germany, Britain and Denmark and a big incentive for municipalisation was the use of trading profits to relieve local taxes. How then did municipalities survive in France where there was little municipal trading? If in some sectors, like the railways, Britain matched American laissez-faire, why in others, like electricity and trams, was government ownership so high? Spanish governments in the nineteenth century were keen to use the railway system as an engine of industrialisation and economic growth. Why then was state and municipal ownership so limited? France is renowned for the power of the Grand Ecoles and the Corps of Engineers in the planning of the infrastructure in canals, roads and railways. Why then was government ownership so limited?

Finally, how far can the role of government be linked to the pace at which both the economy and the infrastructure developed? By 1870 about one half of the labour force was still in agriculture in many of these countries. The exceptions, as Table 2.2 shows, were Britain where it was less than one quarter and, at the other extreme, the southern European countries; in Spain agriculture was still employing nearly 80% of the labour force. Income per head was highest in Britain but Denmark, France and Germany were catching up, and if life expectancy is taken into account the best place to live by 1913 was probably Denmark. How far was this ranking of countries paralleled by the relative size of their infrastructures and what were the links with ownership patterns?

One important theme of Part II is therefore to explain the economic organisation of transport, communications, fuel and water supply industries as they had developed by the early years of the twentieth century. In most cases they involved networks of tracks, cables, mains and overhead lines, connecting different geographic points. The nineteenth century was the period when many of these networks were laid out. Rights of way were needed, and it was this issue which more than anything accounted for the initial involvement of government. Unless land or space was in great abundance there were transaction costs in buying, hiring or otherwise gaining access to uninterrupted rights of way. To take a classic example from the horse-drawn railway age, in 1823 the Compagnie de Chemin de Fer wanted to build a railway from the Loire through the St Etienne coalfield to Pont de l'Ane on the Furens River. The company felt it could not 'count on the unanimous co-operation of the interested [land] proprietors' and sought help from the state.[1] Once the rail track, tramlines, gas mains and water pipes had been laid, the value of the land was highly 'specific' to these activities; there were

Table 2.1 *Ownership patterns in the infrastructure industries at the start of the twentieth century*

	(% owned by state or local government)								
	UK	Denmark	France	Germany	Sweden	Italy	Norway	Spain	USA
(1) Rail mileage in 1906	0	56.2	5.9	92.8	32.3	77.1	85.4	0	0
(2) Tramway undertakings 1905	56.2	0[a]	2.0[b]	3.4[c]				5.0[d]	2.0[e]
(3) Telegraph lines in 1913	100.0	100.0	100.0	100.0	100.0	100.0	100.0	100.0	0
(4) Telephone exchanges in 1913	100.0	1.2	100.0	100.0	68.0	64.7	50.7	5.0	0
(5) Electricity supply undertakings 1900/18	71.6 (1900)	15.4[f] (1905)	2.0[b] (1900)	17.9[g] (1908)	37[h]	10[i]	80.0 (1918)	10.0[j] (1900)	13.1[e]
(6) Gas supply undertakings 1890–1908	28.8 (1900)	84.1 (1905)	2.4[k] (1905)	30.8[c] (1908)	94.5 (1910)	2.0 (1910)	50.0 (1890)	2.5[l] (1901)	2.0[e]
(7) Water supply undertakings 1897–1913	80.4 (1900)	100[m] (1905)	75.0 (1913)	53.6[c] (1908)	100.0 (1909)	90.0[n] (1913)	–	5.0[d]	53.2 (1897)

Notes:

[a] Information from O. Hyldtoft that there were tramway undertakings in Copenhagen and Aarhus, all private.

[b] Estimates based on the claim that, although municipal management of electricity could be found in Grenoble from 1882, St Etienne from 1890 and Tourcois from 1900, 'elle fut exceptionelle' and that 'ce genre d'institution ne se développe que très peu en France' (Caron and Cardot (eds.), *Histoire générale*, 399 and 299). See also A. Fernandez, 'Les Lumieres de la ville: L'Administration municipale a l'épreuve de l'électrification', *Vingtieme Siècle Revue d'Histoire* 62 (1999), 115.

[c] Relates to 2309 urban districts in Germany in 1908.

[d] Estimate based on Nunez's description ('Spanish Cities', 6–7) of the dominance of the private companies.

[e] Based on Keller's summary (*Regulation and the New Economy*, 56): 'Only 20 out of 981 cities … had a municipal gas works in 1900; only 193 out of 1471 urban electricity systems were publicly owned. Almost all municipal transit was privately owned.'

[f] Information supplied by O. Hyldtoft; sixteen electricity works in towns of which five were municipal; twenty-six in countryside, one owned by the state, the rest private.

[g] Note that R. Messager states that 47.3% of electric power in 1913 in Germany was supplied by plant entirely owned by municipal undertakings, 26.7% by mixed enterprises and the rest (20%) by private companies. According to Kuhl, the proportion of works that were municipally owned fell by over a quarter 1897–1913 whilst their share of output rose from 31% to 37%. See 'Municipalities and Managers: Heat Networks in Germany', in J. A. Tarr and G. Dupuy (eds.), *Technology and the Rise of the Networked City in Europe* (Philadelphia: Temple University Press, 1988), 288. A. Kuhl, 'Le Débat sur le socialisme municipal en allemagne avant 1914 et la municipalisation de l'électricité', in A. Kuhl (ed.), *Der Munizipalsozialismus in Europa* (Munich: Oldenberg Verlag, 2002), 94.

[h] Based on Kaijser's statement ('Controlling the Grid', 34), that one third of all Swedish output was produced by the State Power Board in 1920. A further 4% has been added for the urban municipalities.

[i] Municipal undertakings in Italy produced 0.7 gigawatt hours in 1928, that is 8% of the 8.74 gWh total whilst a further 2% is assumed to have been produced by the state railways. These proportions are assumed to hold for the pre-1914 period (Schiavi, 'Municipal Services in Italy', 35; Galasso *Storia dell' industria eletrica in Italia*, 1236; Einaudi, Byé and Rossi, *Nationalisation in France and Italy*, 223.

[j] Estimate based on Antolin's view ('Public Policy', 20) that the few municipal electricity supply undertakings which existed in the late nineteenth century disappeared or restricted themselves to distribution on the advent of hydroelectricity.

[k] Of 844 gas works in 1905, 20 were municipally managed.

[l] Estimate based on the fact that, of the list in Sudria, *Notas sobre la implantacion*, of 81 gas works in 1901, only San Sebastian and Bilbao appear to have municipal ownership of gas supply.

[m] Information from O. Hyldtoft based on the 1906 Industrial Census, which recorded 42 towns with waterworks and 2 in the countryside, all municipal.

[n] Estimate based on Fenoaltea's statement ('The Growth of the Utility Industries', 619) that 'most water supply systems appear to have been built and operated by the local authorities'.

Sources by row:

(1) J. Foreman-Peck, 'Natural Monopoly and Railway Policy in the 19th Century', *Oxford Economic Papers* 39 (1987), Table 5.

(2) R. Millward, 'The Political Economy of Urban Utilities in Britain 1840–1950', in M. Daunton (ed.), *Cambridge Urban History of Britain*, III (Cambridge University Press, 2001), Table 11.2. Information on Denmark supplied by O. Hyldtoft. The German data are from W. H. Dawson, *Municipal Life and Government in Germany* (New York: Longman Greens, 1916), 186. The French figure is based on F. Caron and F. Cardot (eds.), *Histoire générale de l'électricité en France. I. 1881–1918: Espoirs et conquêtes* (Paris: L'Association pour l'Histoire de l'Electricité en France, Fayard, 1991), 299, 399. US data from M. Keller, *Regulation and the New Economy: Public Policy and Economic Change in America 1900–1933* (Cambridge,

Sources to Table 2.1 (*cont.*)

Mass.: Harvard University Press, 1990), 56. For Spain, see G. Nunez, 'Spanish Cities in a Forgotten Modernising Process', in M. Morner and G. Tortella (eds.), *Different Paths to Modernisation* (University of Lund, Sweden, forthcoming), 6–7.

(3) It is assumed that only the USA, in the form of Western Union, had privately owned telegraph lines.

(4) J. Foreman-Peck and R. Millward, *Public and Private Ownership of British Industry 1820–1990* (Oxford: Clarendon Press, 1994), Table 3.7.

(5) See n. 2. Danish data from O. Hyldtoft based on the 1906 Industrial Census and published in *Statistiske Meddelesler* 4.30.7 (1907), 27–31. For Sweden, A. Kaijser, 'Controlling the Grid: The Development of High Tension Power Lines in the Nordic Countries', in A. Kaijser and M. Hedin (eds.), *Nordic Energy Systems: Historical Perspectives and Current Issues* (Canton, Mass.: Science History Publications, 1995). For Italy, A. Schiavi, 'Municipal Services in Italy', *Annals of Collective Economy* 5 (1929), 35; G. Galasso (ed.) *Storia dell' industria elettrica in Italia. III. Espansiove e oligopolio 1926–45* (Roma-Bari: Laterza & Figli, 1993), 1236; M. Einaudi, M. Byé and E. Rossi, *Nationalisation in France and Italy* (Ithaca, N. Y.: Cornell University Press, 1955), 223. For Norway see L. Thue, 'The State and the Dual Structure of the Power Supply Industry in Norway, 1890–1940' in M. Trédé (ed.), *Electricité et électrification dans le monde 1880–1980* (Paris: Association pour l'Histoire de l' Electricité en France, Presses Universitaires de France, 1990), 229–31. For Spain see F. Antolin, 'Public Policy in the Development of the Spanish Electric Utility Industry', Paper presented at European Historical Economics Society Conference on *A Century of Industrial Policy in Europe*, Oxford, Worcester College, 1992, 20.

(6) See n. 2 above. Danish data from O. Hyldtoft based on the 1906 Industrial Census and published in Statistiske Meddelesler, 4.30.7 (1907),14–27. Also O. Hyldtoft, 'Making Gas: The Establishment of the Nordic Gas systems, 1800–1870', in Kaijser and Hedin (eds.), *Nordic Energy Systems*, 91; O. Hyldtoft, 'Modern Theories of Regulation: An Old Story: Danish Gasworks in the 19th Century', *Scandinavian Economic History Review* 42(1) (1994), Table 1. For France, see Caron and Cardot (eds.), *Histoire Générale de l'électricité en France*, 399 and 500. The entry for Italy is a guess based on the frequent assertion that there were few municipal undertakings in this period. For Norway, see Thue, 'The State and the Dual Structure of the Power Supply Industry in Norway', 239. For Sweden, see M. Hietalla, *Services and Urbanisation at the Turn of the Century: The Diffusion of Innovations* Studia Historica 23 (Helsinki: Finnish Historical Society, 1987), 239. For Spain, see appendix of C. Sudria, 'Notas sobre la implantacion y el desarrollo de la industria del gas en España 1840–1901', *Revista de Historia Economica* 1(2) (1983) and F. Antolin, 'Las empresas de servicos publicos municipales', in F. Comin and P. M. Acena (ed.), *Historia de la empresa publica en España* (Madrid: Espasa Calpe, 1991), 310.

(7) See fn. 2 above. Danish data from O. Hyldtoft based on the 1906 Industrial Census and published in Statistiske Meddelesler 4.30.7 (1907),7–13. See also for France G. P. Goubert, *The Conquest of Water: The Advent of Health in the Industrial Age* (Princeton University Press, 1989), 186–7. For USA, see L. Anderson, 'Hard Choices: Supply of Water to New England Towns', *Journal of Interdisciplinary History* 15(12) (1984), Table 1. For Sweden, see Hietalla, *Services and Urbanisation at the Turn of the Century*, 207. For Italy, see S. Fenoaltea, 'The Growth of the Utility Industries in Italy 1861–1913', *Journal of Economic History* 42 (1982), 619.

Table 2.2 *Income levels and living standards in 1913*

	UK	Denmark	France	Germany	Sweden	Italy	Norway	Spain	USA
(1) GDP per head in 1913 in 1985 US dollars	4024	3037	2734	2606	2450	2087	2079	1504	4854
(2) Population in 1910 in millions	44.8*	2.8	39.5	64.6	5.4	35.5	2.4	19.9	92.4
(3) Area in 1911 in thousand square miles	121*	15	207	207	173	111	124	196	3663
(4) Percentage employees in agriculture 1870	22.7	51.0	49.2	49.5	54.0	62.0	53.0	78.4	50.0
(5) Life expectancy in 1913 in years	53	58	50	49	57	45	57	42	52

*Excluding all Ireland, the British figures are 40.0 million population and 89 thousand square miles.

Sources by row:

(1) A. Maddison, *Dynamic Forces in Capitalist Development* (Oxford University Press, 1991), Table 1.1. The entry for Spain was obtained by multiplying the UK figure by the ratio between Spain and the UK in the figures of GNP per head in 1960 US dollars and prices in 'The Main Trends in National Economic Disparities since the Industrial Revolution', in P. Bairoch and M. Levy-Leboyer (eds.), *Disparities in Economic Development since the Industrial Revolution* (London: Macmillan, 1981), 10.

(2) Maddison, *Dynamic Forces in Capitalist Development*, Table B-2. Spain and Britain interpolated from census data in B. R. Mitchell, *International Historical Statistics: Europe 1750–1993* (London: Macmillan, 3rd edn, 1998).

(3) *Whitaker's Almanack* (London: Whitaker and Sons, 1911).

(4) Maddison, *Dynamic Forces in Capitalist Development*, Table C-5. The entry for Denmark relates to 1880 and is taken from A. S. Milward and S. B. Saul, 'The Economic Development of Scandinavia', in *The Economic Development of Continental Europe 1780–1870* (London: Allen and Unwin, 1979), 510. The figure for Spain relates to 1877 and is derived from Mitchell, *International Historical Statistics: Europe 1750–1993*, 169.

(5) N. Crafts, 'The Human Development Index and Changes in Standards of Living: Some Historical Comparisons', *European Review of Economic History* 1(3) (1997).

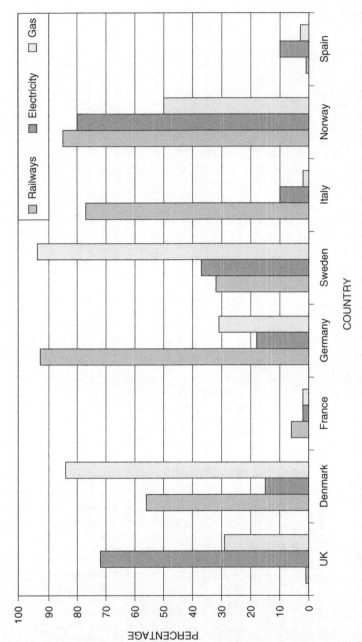

Figure 2.2 Ownership patterns in railways, electricity and gas in the early 1900s (% owned by state or municipalities).

Source: See Table 2.1

considerable costs, that is, in converting the land back to general usage. Hence, unless the land was already in the public domain, the owners were not inclined to rent it out but rather preferred to sell outright to the companies building the infrastructures. At the same time, these networks usually harboured the condition of natural monopoly: one firm could supply services more cheaply than two or more firms. That is, it was usually expensive to duplicate networks. An economic role for government emerged then in granting rights of way, that is, in enforcing the sale or access to land – what many have regarded as the greatest infringement of private property rights in the nineteenth century. As a quid pro quo, all governments usually attached certain conditions as to how and who could use the rights of way.

Taking the question of rights of way as a springboard, Part II explores and explains the various ways in which governments regulated the infrastructure industries and assesses how far there were common patterns across Western Europe. We shall do this by exploring the following themes:

1. the extent to which government involvement can be explained by the desire to facilitate rights of way and to control the natural monopoly problem;
2. the role of fiscal pressures, local government structure and municipal socialism in explaining the complex pattern of private concessions and municipal enterprise in the local networks for gas, electricity, trams and water;
3. the use by state governments of subsidies, interest guarantees and public ownership of railways and telegraph systems to encourage economic growth and political unification and to exercise controls over the movement of people, goods and information.

There was actually one part of the infrastructure where rights of way were definitely not an issue and that was in merchant shipping, where the basic 'track' was available free. Here there were no economies of scale from lumpy track investments, as in gas and railways, and no spillover effects in the form of congestion and health as in tramways and water supply. Even by the late twentieth century, use of the sea involved no major congestion problems (contrast fishing) and few environmental effects apart from oil spills. Economies from increases in ship size were present but, in relation to the size of the market, were small, and shipping could and did operate like a classic competitive industry, almost like the later road freight transporters in scantily populated areas of Australia and America. The key resource was coal, and Britain's coal resources, its early industrialisation and the development of its shipbuilding industry proved decisive. By the 1860s it had nearly 3000 steam ships – more than twice the rest of Europe put together – and accounted for one third of the world's merchant shipping tonnage. It faced rising competition from Sweden, Norway and Germany in the latter part of the nineteenth century. Many British contemporaries thought these other countries benefited from state subsidies. Certainly in countries like Spain, the central government in the late nineteenth century supported shipping and the navy programme such that its merchant fleet tonnage, relative to population, grew to the level of France and Germany by 1913, if not Britain and the Scandinavian countries. The Danish government subsidised shipping services to Britain to promote its growing export trade in butter and bacon. In Britain, shipping subsidies were restricted to support for postal services and for aiding the admiralty. Aldcroft's study of Anglo-German rivalry suggests that the impact of subsidies by the imperial German government was small and any gains that Germany achieved were genuinely competitive gains. The subsidy per ton in 1901 was bigger in Germany, at 4 shillings and 6 pence (4s 6d), than in the UK, 2s 2d, but dwarfed by that in France, 34s 6d, which, however, favoured the building of inexpensive sailing vessels, and the growth of France's mercantile marine was consequently quite modest.[2] By 1913 the British steam ship fleet had risen to 12602 – still more than the rest of Europe put together. Its tonnage was still one third of the world total and, relative to population, was, in Europe, exceeded only by Norway. British ship-owners (as well as shipbuilders) clearly held their own in this period.

Denmark and Sweden had long traditions of shipbuilding, and the former developed shipping services to its colonies as well as to other European countries and their colonies. Shipping tonnage in Denmark increased rapidly from the 1860s to the First World War, and the associated earnings were important ingredients of the balances of payments. Whilst the period up to 1880 saw a large growth in the number of steam ships in Denmark, a significant part of the total fleet was sail, and so by 1913 its tonnage per head of population was, like Sweden, higher than France but much less than Norway. In the latter, tramp shipping and fishing had for long been part-time complementary occupations to self-subsistent farming. Much timber was exported, and as trade regimes liberalised in the nineteenth century, Norway came to be heavily engaged in shipping grain, timber and coal all over Europe and largely independent of its own transport needs. It used a lot of second-hand ships, some as boilers for whaling, and the average size of the ships constructed in Norway was less than those in Sweden and Denmark, partly reflecting its limited access to iron and steel. Norway's strengths were in tramping, and it lost out in the development of tanker fleets. Nevertheless, by the end of the nineteenth century it had the third largest fleet in the world, generating one half of its export earnings and, relative to population, was way ahead of the rest of Europe in its total tonnage, even in 1913.[3]

Rights of way and natural monopoly

Was it inevitable, when land or space were scarce, that governments became involved in the development of the infrastructure industries? After all, Demsetz did ask 'Why Regulate Utilities?'.[4] When the enterprise building and operating the network already owned all the relevant land and space, governments obviously did not intervene. Railways were first used in mines, while gas lighting in the early nineteenth century first appeared in manufacturing firms, often textile producers, and was fed by a gas supply produced within the factories. The first railway in Russia was built in 1838 from St Petersburg to Pavlovsk, the imperial summer residence, soon supplemented by a resort hotel and amusement park (the Vauxhall) to promote passenger traffic.[5] Presumably the tsar did not need a government to establish rights of way. Where, however, the property rights were fragmented, it does not seem that simple market solutions emerged. Whilst rail lines within the St Etienne coal mines would not occasion problems, they did when, as we have seen, in 1823 the Compagnie de Chemin de Fer wanted to build a railway from the Loire to Pont de l'Ane and the company had to apply to the state for the 'privilege of expropriation'.[6] It is possible, of course, that, in some cases, issues other than the natural monopoly problem drew in government forces. In 1818 the Manchester Police Commissioners established a municipal gas undertaking to provide the first public lighting system in Manchester, and no doubt safety considerations were paramount. Otherwise it would appear that the land markets never worked expeditiously enough to satisfy the infrastructure entrepreneurs or their governments. Nor, in the case where the routes were already public rights of way, as in streets for gas and water mains and later tramlines, when local Town Councils granted access, sometimes for a fee, were such approvals made without the imposition of conditions.

In other words, the suppliers of infrastructure services were never left to simply compete for land and rights of way as if they were using land for farming or the exploitation of coal and other mineral resources. Governments intervened to expedite rights of way. In some countries the state or sovereign claimed rights to all surface soil, and in the debates of the 1830s and the 1840s some contemporaries hailed this as the case for significant government involvement. In Prussia the railway companies held a 'regalia', a royal privilege that could be withdrawn at will by the state which could siphon off revenue or run the system itself.[7] In France the Napoleonic code 'extended public property to the subsoil and ground transport infrastructures... This meant that during the early industrial period coal, iron and other minerals, railroads, shipping, armaments production and postal services were publicly operated or awarded by the state to private interests.'[8] It is not clear, however, that the presence or absence, across European countries, of such legal provisions made any difference to the scale of government involvement. Rather, they reflected the varying attitudes to government planning of the infrastructure – more positive in France and Germany than Britain but unable to account for the huge differences in government ownership between France and Germany.

The important point is that governments did intervene to expedite the establishment of rights of way and at the same time attached *three* conditions that were inextricably linked to the award of rights of way. These conditions related to the soundness of the companies, the control of profits and the configuration of routes. Firstly, municipal or state governments did some sort of check on the financial and engineering soundness of the companies. If they were to be given rights of way, they should at least show signs of being able to benefit from that privilege. Parliaments, executives, their agencies and sub-committees in Britain and France closely scrutinised the promoters and their proposals. The process was open to abuse, with many accusations that Members of Parliament in Britain took bribes and that the parliamentary costs added significantly to the mounting construction costs per mile. In addition, in these countries the companies had to be legally incorporated with some sort of limited liability status (like the *sociétés anonymes*), which was another privilege requiring a check on their financial and engineering soundness.[9] Where the main concern was the commercial riskiness of a project, like a new railway line in Spain and Italy, and a need to attract capital, monitoring of foreign companies was limited, though local politicians often sat on the boards of management or directors.[10] In other cases the scrutiny of companies increased over time as governments gathered experience. The 'yardstick competition' by which Copenhagen and other Danish cities weighed the proposals of the Danish Gas Company against performance standards elsewhere had elements of the monitoring function.[11] The scrutiny of companies is seen most clearly and perhaps most strongly in the work of the French government's Corps des Ponts et Chaussées, which saw itself as the technical authority in these matters.[12] It vetted rail, gas and water companies, assessing their proposals, claimed a right to work inside the companies and exercised a continuing technical supervision even after the railway, waterworks and gas plants had been constructed. In a classic early example in the 1830s in the proposal for the Paris St Germain railway, traffic forecasts were made both by the promoter (Emile Pereire) and the Corps, and then compared.[13]

Secondly, governments attempted to control profit levels by encouraging multiple bids for the construction of tracks and by setting ceilings on prices and profits. Thus we see governments, early on, insisting on a public adjudication of the contract; that is, ensuring there were several enterprises bidding. Some powerful entrepreneurs like the Pereire brothers tried to dissuade the French government in the 1830s and 1840s from insisting on this in relation to the early railway lines like the Paris St Germain. Where the risks were high it was not always easy to attract more than one company, but even in Spain from the middle of the century, the government offered sections of track for franchise bidding. Profits could also be held down by promoting competition between different companies using the same track at different times. This was actually permitted by the Prussian railway law of 1838 though never implemented. In Britain a Parliamentary Select Committee of 1839 said it was dangerous, on safety grounds, advised against it, and its recommendations were integrated in the 1840 Railway Act.[14] In contrast to the late twentieth century, this form of competition was rare in nineteenth-century Europe. The chief medium for controlling profits was the regulation of fares, rates and tariffs in tune with the older practice for canals and turnpike roads. In addition, governments took a share in excess profits. In Britain the main legislation for the infrastructures in gas, water and the railways was introduced in the 1840s with an emphasis on setting maximum prices (for municipal as well as private enterprises) rather than on rates of return on capital. The Danish Parliament, the Rigsdag, shied away from anything like this for gas supply so the onus fell on local town councils, who initially exercised a control over gas prices through the contracts made with companies like the Danish Gas Company for town gas lighting. In the first such case in 1853 that company secured a twenty-year concession with the town of Odense at an agreed charge for street lighting.[15] From the 1870s, as gas supplies in Denmark spread to households and businesses, town councils increasingly incorporated maximum prices in their contracts with the private companies. The Prussian 1838 railway law made explicit provision for the control of passenger fares and freight rates and control over profits by securing a right to 25% to 50% of any profits above stated thresholds. Fremdling has suggested, however, that these powers were not used very diligently, and the excuse that the 1838 law allowed competition between operating companies carried little weight since, as we have already noted, such competition was not encouraged.[16] In France there is clear evidence, even from the horse drawn railways era, that the General Highway Council was setting rates to limit excess profits (as on the Loire/Pont de l'Ane line mentioned before). For the lines opened in the 1830s – such as that for the line from Montbrignon to Montrand – leases were often for ninety-nine years.[17] But concern over monopoly profits reduced this in the 1840s to an average of forty-six years, and leases were shorter the greater were expected revenues. Some of these leases proved quite restrictive, and after 1851, as part of a more general standardisation of conditions, the ninety-nine-year lease became the norm. On the other hand, when rates of return exceeded 8% half of the excess was to go to the Treasury. These provisions, according to an Act of 1859, were to apply to all new lines. The state had the option of re-purchase after fifteen years quite apart from the automatic reversion after ninety-nine. Such controls on excess profits were finally standardised in the 1883 conventions, though, as we shall see later, by that stage the concern about monopoly profits was much less important than a desire to underwrite the continuing expansion of the railway system in France.[18]

So far we have identified two consequences of government grants of rights of way: monitoring the financial and engineering soundness of the companies and curbing excess profits by public adjudication of contracts and regulating prices and profits. A third consequence related to the configuration of the distribution networks. Here there was a dilemma. If duplication was allowed, it could constrain profits, but that would undermine the benefits of the natural monopoly position, that is, the achievement of economies of scale. In practice in the early days, competition between duplicate networks was sometimes allowed (or eyes were closed), but by the end of the nineteenth century governments were exercising control over the configuration of networks. In the early decades of the century, many British towns like Birmingham, York and Edinburgh had more than one gas supplier, and tales abounded of the way London streets were strewn with the gas mains of different companies.[19] Private joint stock companies were granted rights in the same period to supply water in London in overlapping areas. The construction of the telegraph in Britain in the years before nationalisation in 1868 was left, largely unregulated, to the market, and there were tariff wars between different companies.[20] There were two railway lines for Paris–Versailles, but both companies failed. In Prussia the 1838 railway law explicitly forbade the granting of a charter to parallel routes, but it would seem this came to be ignored by the state. One explanation of why governments secured rights of way and then allowed the natural monopoly advantages of a single supplier to be partly dissipated may be that they hoped to get some of the incentive gains from competition between enterprises without losing all the benefits of a small number of suppliers.[21]

In 1859 Edwin Chadwick thought that this kind of competition was futile and attributed the low profits, high costs and poor quality of the water supplies of English towns to the prevalence of 'competition in the field'.[22] In the second half of the century governments came to be more actively involved in the alignment of routes, the impact on competitors like canal companies and in the avoidance of duplicate facilities. The state built the trunk rail network in Denmark and Sweden, and in the latter all private railway construction had to be approved by the government to ensure it fitted in with the national plan. In Denmark there was no legal provision for granting of exclusive franchises to private companies so the initiative in gas lighting lay with the municipality in its contract with the gas supplier. In Helsingør and Århus in the 1870s, the local council came very close to approving competition in gas supply between a private and a municipal enterprise but drew back at the last moment.[23] In Britain a strict parliamentary procedure was followed for each new utility or any extension of an existing network, and a similar scrutiny operated in Prussia where, however, the encouragement for parallel railways lasted longer (and in the Netherlands) than elsewhere – until the 1870s and the onset of nationalisation. In Spain, from the middle of the century the central government played a strong role in the alignment of the railway network, offering sections of track for franchise bidding.[24] Dobbin suggested that the state in France wanted to 'orchestrate' if not manage.[25] As early as 1833 the Corps was granted half a million francs to mount a study of the development of the rail network. An Act of 1842 set out nine arteries, and, although little followed, it has been seen by some writers as clinching the state's right to control the layout of the system and the companies involved in its construction. For Lefranc, this was the basis of future success. 'The immediate result was the postponement of everything, but the very postponement made possible the subsequent establishment in France of a co-ordinated system, in a free field, such as exists in no other country.'[26] A plan for six regional networks to absorb twenty-eight independent companies was agreed in 1850 and became effective during the imperial enthusiasm of the 1850s. Concessions were open to public adjudication. In effect in the design of the network, competition between different parallel tracks ('in the field') was not approved. Competition 'for the field' was encouraged.[27] Competition over the same track between different operating companies, paying access charges, was not precluded by any of these particular government initiatives, but this kind of competition, as we have seen, seems to have been very limited.

None of these matters, however, seem able to explain the onset of state or municipal ownership, since they are consistent with the continuation of the system of granting concessions to private companies. A fortiori, they do not appear able to explain the pattern of public and private ownership across countries or within such countries as Germany, Britain and the Scandinavian countries. To do this it is necessary to look more closely at specific networks. We do this by first examining what determined the regulatory pattern in the networks for gas, water, electricity and tramways. Then we turn to the nation state and examine how the needs of economic growth, military strategy and pressures for political unification affected the railway and telegraph systems.

Notes

1 G. Lefranc, 'The French Railroads 1823–42', *Journal of Economic and Business History* 2 (1929/30), 303–4.
2 D. Aldcroft, 'British Shipping and Foreign Competition: The Anglo-German Rivalry, 1880–1914', in D. Aldcroft, *Studies in British Transport History* (Newton Abbott: David and Charles, 1974), 53–99. For France, see J.-P. Dormois, 'France: The Idiosyncrasies of *Voluntarisme*', in J. Foreman-Peck and G. Federico (eds.), *European Industrial Policy: The Twentieth Century Experience* (Oxford University Press, 1999), 58–97.
3 See the following articles in *Scandinavian Economic History Review* 28 (1980): M. Fritz, 'Shipping in Sweden, 1850–1913', 147–60; O. Gjolberg, 'The Substitution of Steam for Sail in Norwegian Ocean Shipping, 1866–1914: A Study in the Economics of Diffusion', 135–46: O. Hornby and C. A. Nilsson, 'The Transition from Sail to Steam in the Danish Merchant Fleet, 1865–1910', 109–34.
4 H. Demsetz, 'Why Regulate Utilities?', *Journal of Law and Economics* 11 (1968), 55–65.
5 J. Blum, *Lord and Peasant in Russia: From the Ninth to the Nineteenth Century* (Princeton University Press, 1961), 284.
6 Lefranc, 'French Railroads', 304.
7 J. C. Bongaerts, 'Financing Railways in the German States 1840–60. A Preliminary View', *Journal of European Economic History* 14 (1985), 351.
8 E. Chadeau, 'The Rise and Decline of State Owned Industry in France 1900–50', in P. A. Toninelli (ed.), *The Rise and Fall of State Owned Enterprise in the Western World* (Cambridge University Press, 2000), 192. See also F. Dobbin, *Forging Industrial Policy: The United States, Britain and France in the Railway Age* (Cambridge University Press, 1994), p. 125.
9 C. Freedman, 'Joint Stock Business Organisation in France 1807–67', *Business History Review* 39 (1965), 184–204; J. H. Clapham, *The Economic History of Britain: Vol. I* (Cambridge University Press, 1964), ch. 9; C. I. Savage, *An Economic History of Transport* (London: Allen and Unwin, 1966), ch. 3; R. W. Rawson, 'On Railways in Belgium', *Journal of the Royal Statistical Society of London* 2 (1839), 47–62; J. Foreman-Peck and L. Hannah, 'Britain: From Economic Liberalism to Socialism – and Back?', in Foreman-Peck and Federico (eds.), *European Industrial Policy*, 23.

10 R. Cameron, *France and the Economic Development of Europe 1880–1914: Conquests of Peace and Seeds of War* (Princeton University Press, 1961), p. 251.

11 O. Hyldtoft, 'Modern Theories of Regulation: An Old Story: Danish Gasworks in the 19th Century', *Scandinavian Economic History Review*, 42 (1994), 40–1.

12 A. L. Dunham, 'How the First French Railways were Planned', *Journal of Economic History* 1 (1941), 12–25; C. O. Smith, Jr, 'The Longest Run: Public Engineering and Planning in France', *American Historical Review* 95 (1990), 657–92.

13 B. Radcliffe, 'The Origins of the Paris-Saint Germain Railway', *Journal of Transport History* 1(4) (1972), 197–219; B. Radcliffe, 'The Building of the Paris-Saint Germain Railway', *Journal of Transport History* 2(1) (1973), 20–40; B. Radcliffe, 'Railway Imperialism: The Example of the Pereires' Paris-St. Germain Company', *Business History* 18 (1976), 66–84.

14 Cameron, *France and Economic Development*, p. 252; R. Fremdling, 'The Prussian and Dutch Railway Regulation in the 19th Century', in L. Andersson-Skog and O. Krantz (eds.), *Institutions and the Transport and Communications Industries* (Canton, Mass.: Science History Publications, Watson, 1999), 61–92; Radcliffe, 'The Origins of the Paris-Saint Germain Railway'; Clapham, *Economic History of Britain*, ch. 9; Savage, *Economic History of Transport*, ch. 3.

15 O. Hyldtoft, 'Making Gas: The Establishment of the Nordic Gas Systems, 1800–1870', in A. Kaijser and M. Hedin (eds.), *Nordic Energy Systems: Historical Perspectives and Current Issues* (Canton, Mass.: Science History Publications, 1995), 84.

16 Fremdling, 'The Prussian and Dutch Railway Regulation'.

17 Lefranc, 'French Railroads'.

18 F. Caron, 'The Evolution of the Technical System of Railways in France', in R. Maintz and T. P. Hughes (eds.), *The Development of Large Technical Systems* (Boulder, Colo.: Frankfurt and Westview Press, 1987); F. Caron, 'French Railway Investments 1850–1914', in R. Cameron (ed.), *Essays in French Economic History* (Georgetown, Ontario: R. D. Irwin, 1970); K. Doukas, *The French Railroads and the State* (New York: Columbia Press, 1945).

19 D. Matthews, 'Rogues, Speculators and Competing Monopolies: The Early London Gas Companies, 1812–1860', *The London Journal* 2 (1985), 39–50.

20 J. Foreman-Peck, 'Competition, Co-operation and Nationalisation in the Early Telegraph Network', *Business History* 31(3) (1989), 81–102; 'L'Etat et le développement du réseau de télécommunications en Europe à ses débuts', *Histoire, Economie, Société* 4 (1989), 383–402.

21 V. J. Primeaux found a similar practice in 60 American cities in the 1960s with municipal and private electricity suppliers allowed to compete in the same town area with duplicate cables. See 'An Assessment of X-Efficiency Gained through Competition', *Review of Economics and Statistics* 59 (1977), 105–8. For Paris-Versailles, see Dunham, 'First French Railroads'. For Prussian railway law, see Fremdling, 'The Prussian and Dutch Railway Regulation'.

22 E. Chadwick, 'Results of Different Principles of Legislation and Administration in Europe: Of Competition for the Field, as Compared with Competition within the Field, of Service', *Journal of the Royal Statistical Society* 22 (1859), 381–420.

23 J. Bohlin, 'Sweden: The Rise and Fall of the Swedish Model', in Foreman-Peck and Federico (eds.), *European Industrial Policy*, 152–76; Hyldtoft, 'Nordic Gas systems', 37–8.
24 Cameron, *France and Economic Development*, 252.
25 Dobbin, *Forging Industrial Policy*, 96.
26 Lefranc, 'French Railroads', 324.
27 Caron, 'The Evolution of the Technical System of Railways in France'; M. Blanchard, 'The Railway Policy of the Second Empire', in F. Crouzet, W. Chaloner and W. Stern (eds.), *Essays in European Economic History 1789–1914* (London: Arnold, 1969), 98–111.

3 Local supply networks, private concessions and municipalisation

The technology of gas, electricity and trams in the nineteenth century allowed economies of scale in production and delivery over a spatially limited area. It is argued here that the initial developments were dominated by the private sector but that the pace of expansion thereafter was not affected decisively one way or the other by whether the utilities remained in private ownership or were taken over by municipalities. It is also argued that an ideological commitment to municipal socialism was not the prime determinant of the ownership pattern. Rather, it was the set of fiscal problems facing local authorities. These issues will be illustrated initially by the case of gas and water, which have a longer history than electricity and trams, which we will consider later.

Gas was produced from coking coal and was used initially for lighting, later for heat and power. It could be stored only for short periods and was expensive to transport. Here was a technology that yielded small local networks, most effective when each undertaking supplied one densely populated urban area. Not until the second half of the twentieth century, and especially with the discovery of deposits of natural gas, was there a real push for regional and national grids. This simple setting nonetheless demonstrates some of the central puzzles of public ownership at the local level in the nineteenth century. The countries like Germany, Denmark and Britain, which saw the most rapid development of gas supply, also witnessed the most extensive involvement of local governments, and in many cases it appears that this was motivated in part by town council interest in transferring some of the gas trading profits to relieve local tax levels – that is, to use them as 'cash cows'. Sweden and Norway had, like Denmark, a tradition of strong local communities and also saw considerable municipalisation, yet managed only a modest development of gas supplies. Finally France, Spain and Italy relied heavily on the private sector and also experienced fairly slow growth.

Two dimensions of the nineteenth-century gas infrastructure should be noted. One relates to the timing of expansion and of the rise of municipal socialism. The other is the way private and municipal enterprises

33

Table 3.1 *Coal, gas and shipping 1890–1913*

	UK	Denmark	France	Germany	Sweden	Italy	Norway	Spain	USA
(1) 1912 Coal output in metric tons per 100 pop.	581	0	103	386	na	2	1	21	508
(2) No. of merchant ships in 1913 per million pop.	458	1286	460	73	500	155	1375	30	2079
(3) 1913 Merchant ships in '000 tons per million pop.	265	179	40	49	161	33	708	45	70
(4) 1900 Gas supplied in cu. metres per head of pop.	115[a]	34	16[a]	24[a]	9	6	15[a]	6	31[a]
(5) % Gas supply undertakings in municipal ownership 1890–1908	28.8 (1900)	78.6 (1890)	2.4[b] (1905)	30.8[c] (1908)	94.5 (1910)	2.0 (1910)	50.0 (1890)	2.5[d] (1901)	2.0[e] (1900)
(6) % Gas supply undertakings in 50 largest towns in municipal ownership 1908/9	42.0	88.5[f]		100.0					

Notes:

[a] The UK figure relates to Britain (excludes all Ireland) and to the 1897/8 financial year. The French figure relates to 1888 and the Norway figure to 1913.

[b] Of 844 gas works in 1905, 20 were municipally managed.

[c] Relates to 2309 urban districts in Germany in 1908.

[d] Estimate based on the fact that, of the list of 81 gas works in 1901 in Sudria, 'Notas sobre la implantacion', only San Sebastian and Bilbao appear to have had municipal ownership of gas supply.

[e] 'Only 20 out of 981 cities had municipal gasworks in 1900 . . .' M. Keller, *Regulation and the New Economy: Public Policy and Economic change in America 1900–1933* (Cambridge, Mass.: Harvard University Press, 1990), 56.

[f] Estimate supplied by O. Hyldtoft. 54 out of 61 town gasworks were in municipal ownership.

Sources by row:

(1) B. R. Mitchell, *International Historical Statistics: Europe 1750–1993* (London: Macmillan, 3rd edn, 1998). US data from B. R. Mitchell, *International Historical Statistics: The Americas: 1750–1993* (London: Macmillan, 4th edn, 1998). Population data from A. Maddison, *Dynamic Forces in Capitalist Development* (Oxford University Press, 1991), Tables B-2 and B-3. Population for Spain and Britain interpolated from census data in Mitchell, *International Historical Statistics: Europe 1750–1993*. Denmark was a 'country devoid of coal resources . . .' (A. S. Milward and S. B. Saul, *The Economic Development of Continental Europe 1780–1870* (London: Allen and Unwin, 1979), 515).

Sources to Table 3.1 (*cont.*)

(2) As for (1).

(3) As for (1).

(4) Population data as in (1) with Great Britain population interpolated from census data in Mitchell, *International Historical Statistics: Europe 1750–1993*. Gas data from R. Millward, 'The Market Behaviour of Local Utilities in Pre-World War I Britain: The Case of Gas', *Economic History Review* 44 (1991), Table I; for Denmark and Sweden, O. Hyldtoft, 'Making Gas: The Establishment of the Nordic Gas Systems, 1800–1870', in A. Kaijser and M. Hedin (eds.), *Nordic Energy Systems: Historical Perspectives and Current Issues* (Canton, Mass.: Science History Publications, 1995), 85; for France, F. Caron and F. Cardot (ed.), *Histoire générale de l'électricité en France. I. 1881–1918: Espoirs et conquêtes* (Paris: L'Association pour l'Histoire de l'Electricité en France, Fayard, 1991), 386; C. Sudria, 'Notas sobre la implantacion y el desarrollo de la industria del gas en España 1840–1901', *Revista de Historia Economica* 1(2) (1983), 108; for Italy, S. Fenoaltea, 'The Growth of the Utility Industries in Italy 1861–1913', *Journal of Economic History* 42 (1982), Table 3; German and US data interpolated from the chart in D. Matthews, 'Technology Transfer in the Late 19th Century Gas Industry', *Journal of Economic History* 47 (1987); information for Norway supplied by O. Hyldtoft and based on Norske Gasverkers Forenings (Gasteknikeren: 1915), 257–8.

(5) See Table 2.1.

(6) See Table 2.1.

co-existed within countries. The industry's birth is associated with classic early British industrialisation such that, even by the First World War, Britain's production was many times larger than the rest of Europe. Those countries, like Denmark, that were able and willing to draw on British coal exports also raced ahead, and Germany was not far behind when its coal reserves were brought into play. At the same time, the limited size of economies of scale in production and the high transport costs meant that the natural monopoly advantages of a single supplier had a limited range. Everywhere the introduction of gas supply was initiated by private enterprise, and municipal ownership seems to have flourished only when the technology and systems had settled down. The Gas, Light and Coke company started public lighting in London in 1814, Brussels opened in 1819, Rotterdam and Berlin 1826, Amsterdam 1833 and Lyons 1834. British equipment, engineers and coal were imported wholesale with English companies, like the Imperial Continental Gas Association, heavily involved in the construction of gasworks in Hanover, Berlin, Ghent and Rotterdam. The process was spread over the whole of the first half of the nineteenth century. The other 'first towns' were Barcelona 1841, Vienna 1842, Gothenburg 1845, and Oslo 1846, and in 1853 Odense was the first town in Denmark with a public lighting system, built, as we have noted, by an English company, 'The Danish Gas Company'.[1] Spain and Italy also relied on foreign companies like the Credit Mobilier in Madrid and entrepreneurs like Charles Lebrun who was extensively involved in Barcelona.[2]

In terms of sheer growth rates, the most rapid development was in the period 1850–1870, as public lighting systems spread to smaller towns and in Britain gas lighting entered middle-class households.[3] But growth did continue strongly in the last part of the century as gas came to be increasingly used for heating and power, whilst the introduction of the incandescent mantle and the pre-payment meter eased the extension to working-class homes, at least in the more industrially advanced nations. Even in France, where urbanisation was slow and coal supplies not generous, gas accounted for 75% of lighting in 1895 and was still dominant by 1910.[4] If the British evidence is any guide, the real price of gas was falling very rapidly. Relative to the general movement in all retail prices in the period 1882–1914, coal prices in Britain rose by 30% and gas prices fell by 12%. Electricity prices were falling even faster, but they had a long way to go before doing any damage in the gas market.[5] Table 3.1 shows how far ahead Britain was in gas supply, and it is as well to bear this in mind when, later, we record the sluggish early developments in electricity. Relative to population, British gas supplies were three to four times the level in Germany and Denmark. In France, but especially in the other countries, coal supplies were the limiting factor. Spain's coal was of poor quality and at its ports could not compete with British exporters, who had the benefit of iron ore and other minerals as return cargoes. By 1861 gasworks were to be found only in the main cities, and there were only eleven gasworks outside Catalonia.[6] By 1900 gas supplies were less, per head of population, than in all the other countries we are studying. Even though gas supply in Italy grew very rapidly from 25 million cubic feet in 1861 to 358 in 1913 (a vitality that even Fenoaltea could not explain),[7] Italy was not particularly better off than Spain, and its industrial development was constrained by its limited resources, a position that was relieved only when Alpine hydroelectricity came on the scene at the very end of the nineteenth century.

Municipal ownership spread quite extensively, though accounting for its incidence is not easy. In Germany it started in earnest in the 1860s; half of all gasworks were in municipal ownership by the 1880s, and by 1908 this was true of works in all the fifty largest towns.[8] In Scandinavia the movement commenced only slightly later: by 1870 half of the gasworks in Sweden and 71% in Denmark were municipally owned; by the end of the century it was 75% in Sweden and Denmark and 50% in Norway. In the Netherlands the big surge was in the 1880s and 1890s.[9] In Britain in 1874 there were already 104 municipally owned undertakings but the private sector remained large, holding on to more than 60% of the undertakings from the 1870s onwards up to the Second World War. There is evidence, as we shall see later, from Britain and Germany, that the trading profits of municipally owned enterprises were transferred across into the municipal accounts and thereby reduced local taxes, especially in those towns where pressing urbanisation problems meant costly public health programmes. Private enterprise therefore escaped unchallenged in towns where population growth was small or where the local government structure was fragmented (as in London and in rural areas) or where the ability to draw on non-tax revenues (dockside property income in Liverpool, Southampton and other ports) dulled the quest for securing trading profits from municipal enterprises.[10]

Much of the drive to municipalisation predated the rise of socialism as a force in elections and predated the propagation of municipal socialism as an ideology. Thus it was in the middle decades of the century, and not at the end of the century, that municipalisation first flourished in Britain in newly incorporated towns like Oldham and West Bromwich. The population faced mounting public health problems from rapid urbanisation, and the potential monopoly profits of single town suppliers were not curbed by the parliamentary legislation on prices (where the monitoring mechanisms were weak), or by municipal control of prices, but by the municipalities expropriating the trading profits of enterprises they owned, as a relief to the main local tax (that on property, the 'rates'). In Germany, a tradition of strong local government is often invoked as the reason for the spread of municipal enterprise.

> On the continent, and especially Germany ... [claimed Hughes] ... a city was idealised as a great family, organised for economic, political and social ends and its government was seen as the means of achieving these ends. Among the means were public utilities, industry, transportation, water and gas, waste disposal and lighting.[11]

However, this tradition seems to have died out by the middle decades of the nineteenth century, and more bread-and-butter issues seem to have driven municipalisation. Prussian towns had a limited, privileged electoral roll, and the councillors made sure the finance of local government expenditure fell less on direct income taxes than on indirect taxes, supplemented by trading profits from the municipal gas, electricity and tramways undertakings. The transfer of trading profits in this way needed no vote in council or electoral support, so that Kuhl characterises the whole process as a bourgeois electorate seeking efficient services and tax relief.[12] In Scotland such practices were barred.[13] Mutters of disapproval were being aired in the early 1900s in England when a Joint Select Committee of the House of Commons and the House of Lords discussed the practice.[14] Nonetheless, these transfers were an important source of revenue. In the financial year 1910/11 in the seventy-two German towns with a population of 50000 or more, £2.6 million of gas trading profits accrued to the municipalities. For the thirty-one towns with populations ranging from 100000 to 200000 this worked out at 3s per head of population; the comparable figure for the thirty-seven British towns in that category was only 1s 3d[15] – a difference that may be linked to how far overheads were budgeted separately (cf. the later discussion of water supply). Use of municipal undertakings as cash cows was important in Denmark, though Hyldtoft's research suggests that other factors – such as the ability of the municipalities to raise capital – were present.[16]

The local communities have always been viewed as a vital part of social and economic life throughout Scandinavia, and municipal ownership was extensive in Sweden and Norway. Indeed, more generally in Europe, a necessary condition for municipal ownership was strong, economically active local government. Where local government was fragmented, as in London, or where the units were very small, as in Belgium, or had limited powers, as in France, Spain and Italy, municipal management of trading enterprises developed only feebly not only for gas, but also, later, as we shall see, for electricity and tramways. Of the 844 gasworks in France in

1905, only 20 were municipally owned; of 81 gasworks in Spain in 1901, only San Sebastian and Bilbao were owned by the municipality.[17] Here the concession method was common, and English and French techniques and capital spread to Spain and Italy, where the cost of coal imports and the limited technical and administrative power of local government rendered the establishment of gas supply an uncertain venture. It was better left to the private sector, at least until local government was strengthened by an Act of 1903, which gave legal status to municipal enterprises and allowed town councils like Bologna to bring gas supply under their control.[18] The key unit of local government in France, the commune, had little power to initiate economic activity. An 1884 law invoked the communes to regulate the affairs of the community, but there was no mention of involvement in industry or commerce, and at least one outside contemporary observer suggested that what was not mentioned was forbidden.[19] Fernandez's recent analysis of local utilities confirms that the communes were subjugated to the tutelage of the central government via the prefect system, with engineering and financial parameters laid down by the Conseil d'Etat.[20] How then could French municipalities survive without the non-tax revenues from municipal trading profits? One answer is that in many rural areas (as in Britain), the pressure for financing public health programmes was absent – and urbanisation was very much delayed in France. Moreover, there was the 'octroi', the duty levied on commodities entering the commune, which accounted for about one third of all communal revenues in the early 1900s and more than one half for some towns like Dijon and Lyon.[21]

If Paris is any guide, the larger communes may have had more scope and ability for independent economic activity and earned a good revenue from the private gas companies operating under concessions. The Paris Gas Company emerged in 1855 from a fusion of eight companies that had been supplying Paris on a district basis. Under its charter, which was renewed in 1870, the company paid the Council 200000 francs per annum for the right to lay pipes and 2 francs for each cubic metre of gas produced – in lieu of the payment of the local tax, the octroi, on coal consumption. By the 1890s, these revenues had become an important part of the council's budget, 20 million francs per annum. This does raise the question of how far the extraction of revenues from local utilities was decisive in the shift to municipal ownership. Quite apart from the case of Paris, there are, as we shall see later, examples such as the Berlin electricity supply, which was provided by a concessionaire for many years with the Berlin town council siphoning off a significant revenue, and this was not uncommon in other towns. In Denmark, supplies from the private sector were dominated by the Danish Gas Company, which came to a similar deal, with the Copenhagen City council, of payments for the 'droit de concession'.[22] In Britain, in contrast, a clear line was drawn between the private and public sectors. When gas, water and railways were left in the private sector, they were taxed in the same way as any other business in Britain. There was nothing analogous to the profit-sharing found on the Continent. When municipally owned utilities were used as cash cows in Germany, this was done to circumvent the normal electoral and democratic process, which would have required a parliamentary or council debate.

Several conclusions are warranted at this point:

(1) There was no simple correlation between the pace of development of gas supply and the institutional setting. Extensive municipal ownership was found in countries with very well-developed systems – Britain, Germany, Denmark – but also in countries with only limited development – Sweden and Norway. In fact, Britain had a large private sector, and detailed studies suggest there was no difference in efficiency between the private and public sectors.[23]

(2) Private enterprise predominated where the risks were greatest. The early gas supplies were found in private-sector manufacturing firms (as in textiles) producing their own gas as well as in private companies specialising in gas production and servicing the new public lighting in all the European capitals. In Spain and Italy indigenous coal supplies were limited, coal imports costly and local technical expertise limited; the way was open for foreign private companies – English, French, Dutch and Belgian.

(3) Once gas systems were well established they became attractive as sources of non-tax revenues to nineteenth-century town councils dominated by middle- and upper-income social groups. In most cases this was closely associated with the municipal ownership of gas undertakings and such revenues were especially important in Germany, with its limited local electoral franchise. It seems to have acted as a strong spur to municipalisation, though more research is needed on its incidence. The English evidence suggests that municipalisation occurred where there were strong pressures to find revenues, which on the one hand hit a wider spectrum than direct taxes on property or income and on the other financed public health programmes in rapidly growing towns. It therefore did not occur in rural areas or sleepy, wealthy towns.

(4) A necessary condition was the presence of a municipal authority with a good structure, a mandate for initiative and a fair amount of independence, and this was the case in many of the growing towns of Britain, Germany and Scandinavia. In France the central government was,

paradoxically, strongly interventionist in planning the infrastructure, but favoured the concession system. Local communes had limited powers for economic activity, but did have the octroi as an important indirect tax. In addition, big town councils like Paris could cream off some of the private company's profits as a useful non-tax revenue.

(5) Finally, it would appear that ideology was important only in the freedom it gave local authorities. Municipal socialism as an ideological weapon did not have much of a role and it flourished towards the end of the century after the great initial surge in municipal ownership had occurred. Where local authorities had some degree of independence from central government, they seem to have been driven more by business and middle-class pressure for efficient services, low income tax and low property taxes, than by socialist idealists.

Urban water supplies and public health

How far do these conclusions hold for the economic organisation of water supply in the nineteenth century? Water supply is the oldest utility, and by the early nineteenth century many villages and towns in Europe still relied on the village pump or on aqueducts and other distribution systems, which dated from Roman times. The nineteenth century then saw a major break with the past as huge new reservoirs were constructed, steam pumps introduced, iron pipes laid, water meters installed in factories and, eventually, constant pressure systems emerged, including flushing toilets. Industrialisation was the driving force, and where this was accompanied by rapid urbanisation, it created severe problems of water pollution, increases in mortality levels and pressures for collective action for public health programmes, including schemes for raising the quality of water. Rapid urbanisation in Britain put terrific pressures on town councils to develop new systems for water supply and waste disposal. The number of statutory water supply undertakings rose from 100 in the 1840s to 500 by the 1870s and to 1020 by 1915. Some writers have argued that the abundance of wells and aqueducts for domestic drinking water in France reduced the need to use rivers and, in conjunction with the slow rate of urbanisation, made water pollution less of a problem than in Britain. Only 4 new systems were built in France in the first decades of the nineteenth century, 34 in the 1830s and 1840s, and then 315 between 1850 and 1892. In 1900 more than half of the 691 towns with populations of 5000 or more had a water system, but not many people were actually connected – 17.5% of dwellings in Paris as compared to 90% in London. Germany also lagged, but only slightly. By 1895 86% of its towns with 10000 population or more had a central water system.[24]

The public health problem drew in government, especially when cholera epidemics throughout Europe in the nineteenth century showed the governing middle class that they were not immune, even when residing well away from town slums. Moreover, once water consumption started to rely less on open access to wells, springs and rivers and more on supply from the new reservoirs and artificial distribution networks, significant economies of scale arose in storage and distribution. This was a classic natural monopoly, that is, it became cheaper to supply one area from one enterprise rather than from two or more enterprises. Government legislation on prices and profits became common, as we have seen, for railways, gas supply, electricity and tramways. What distinguished water supply from the rest, as may be seen in Table 2.1, was that by the eve of the First World War, government ownership, in the form of municipal enterprise, was pervasive.

Of course, one retort is to simply say that water supply attracted more government ownership because, unlike gas, electricity, trams and railways, there were health issues of great significance. This is not an adequate answer since governments, local or national, could set standards for water quantities and quality and then regulate the industry by legislation and/or operate concession systems or franchises, as clearly the French did in other sectors. The same point applies to the natural monopoly argument: in principle, that issue can be dealt with, as was the case of the railways in Britain and France, by the regulation of fares, freight rates and profits. One has to look elsewhere, as we shall do in the next chapter, for explanations of why trunk railways came to be state owned in Sweden, Italy and Germany before the First World War. In water supply similarly one has to look elsewhere for explanations of why municipal ownership was so pervasive.

Much of what follows relates to Britain, on which my research has focused. However, as the most rapidly industrialising and urbanising country in the nineteenth century, the development of water supplies there does have some general significance for what came later in other countries. The context is that of the expansion of storage and distribution systems in the nineteenth century. Of course in earlier centuries, local government in Britain had been active in the development of supplies, with authority stemming from Royal Warrant, Charter, Statute and latterly Private Act of Parliament. This was a common feature of the domain state drawing its revenues from scarce resources or rights of way. But by the late eighteenth century, these powers had been allowed to lapse, and even where the water source was owned by a local council, as in Gloucester, Leicester, Leeds and Plymouth, it had been leased out to private contractors.[25] In this earlier period, springs, lakes, rivers and rain were all significant sources of untreated water, access to which was fairly easy in a country with the UK's climate and geography. In contrast, what I am trying to explain is the government activity that accompanied the huge increase in storage and distribution capacity, which started in the first half of the nineteenth century. The main dynamic elements were private joint stock companies. Indeed, Hassan has characterised the period as one of partial privatisation. Of his sample of eighty-one large towns in Britain in 1801, joint stock companies were involved in the water supply of five towns. By 1851 this had risen to forty-five.[26] In this period, and especially before the Municipal Corporations Act of 1835 that established new standards and structures, much local government was inefficient or corrupt, and capital raising powers were limited. The main local taxpayers (paying 'rates' on their property) were opposed to municipal initiatives, seeing joint stock finance with limited liability as a much more attractive option.[27]

Nonetheless, government was drawn in, and for two reasons. The first was that the huge capital requirements of these enterprises meant that local sources of finance would not be enough. 'Blind capital' would be attracted only if there were limited liability and, since that was regarded as a great privilege, there would have to be a Parliamentary Act with appropriate scrutiny of the financial soundness of the company. The investment expansion in the nineteenth century was therefore largely financed by borrowing approved under the relevant Parliamentary Act. Both private and, later, municipal undertakings came to issue their own stock quoted on the London and provincial stock exchanges. There is no doubt that the whole process favoured the large companies and municipalities – only they could deal with the administrative costs of securing stock issues and parliamentary bills. Indeed over the whole range of urban developments, including investment in the sanitary infrastructure, it was the large local authorities like Leeds and Glasgow, rather than small ones, that flourished, since the finance available from other sources, such as the Public Works Loan Board, involved high interest charges and short repayment periods.[28] The second reason why governments were drawn into the operations of utilities relates to the question of rights of way, that is, the securing of access to land for the laying of water mains. Local authorities sometimes had sufficient powers of approval, but in the early years of the century this was less likely and the central government was drawn in. By an Act of Parliament, an undertaking was permitted to lay pipes and supply water, if necessary by compulsory expropriation of the land.

Exclusive franchises were never awarded, but whoever was first in the field clearly had some advantages. In recognition of this, Parliament imposed ceilings on water charges, in line with the previous practice for canals. That was the limit of government involvement in the early days of the nineteenth century. The consumer interest was to be protected by the encouragement of competition. For example, in the first decade of the century in London, there were three water companies, but, as a Parliamentary Select Committee reported, subsequently the 'East London, West Middlesex and Grand Junction Company were formed under ... several Acts of Parliament ... The principle of the Acts under which these companies were instituted was to encourage competition.'[29]

By the middle of the century, however, things looked different in three ways. Competition between companies did exist, either in overlapping areas or as contested markets with the incumbents threatened by new entrants. The financial return on equity of the water companies was well below the rate of return in railways, manufacturing and commerce, and the famous Chadwick Report of 1842 suggested that the low dividend rate of 4% to 6% for the London companies was due to the duplication of facilities.[30] The technology of water supply at the time was such that the provincial towns of industrial Britain appeared to be ideal units, in economic terms, for supply by a single enterprise – the classic natural monopoly case. Small wonder then that by the middle of the century many towns had only one supplier, and in the very large towns like London each company kept, by agreement, to its own district; the town was 'districted'. The potential for monopoly profits was therefore increasing and was reinforced by the fact that Parliament was refusing to sanction new companies if this created competition. The ceilings on water charges specified in many of the companies' Parliamentary Acts had not been done in a systematic way. A stronger approach now seemed appropriate. The second factor was water pollution in the rapidly growing towns – on which endless volumes have been written. Suffice to note that the link between cholera and poor water supplies was not surprising given that some 'methods of collecting water ... represented no more than a transfer of pollution from houses and streets to streams and rivers'.[31]

The third factor was the limited quantitative extension of supplies. The companies, it was argued, had concentrated their distribution systems on supply to factories and the streets of the wealthy, and constant high-pressure systems had not yet emerged. The reasons behind this reluctance have perhaps not been given their due weight in the literature. Although districting came to be encouraged, Parliament never granted exclusive franchises nor gave legal endorsement to exclusive suppliers, so that the threat of entry remained. Official investigations in the 1840s and 1850s suggested that this threat inhibited the incumbent companies.[32] A number of arguments may be advanced to explain why this threat contributed to the unsatisfactory nature of urban water supplies. Firstly, each company did not necessarily have a natural monopoly over all the area in which it was located, and hence it could never be certain, as the single firm, that it would undercut entrants supplying only a part of the market. In Manchester and Salford the water company supplied only 20% of the industrial and commercial firms. In Bath in 1875 there were eight undertakings supplying different groups. Everywhere there were springs, wells and even ditches for the desperate. Secondly, the natural monopoly feature arose as much from the distribution network as from 'production' and hence it was vital to catch all the customers in a given area. But when this required an investment by industrial customers in meters and by households in sinks, the company could not be certain that it would capture all the market and hence enjoy all the economies of customer contiguity. The 1840s official reports contained many complaints about the absence of proper water supplies to small towns and the heavy costs of connection pipes to small groups of consumers.[33] Customer costs were especially important when the companies wanted to develop constant-pressure piped supplies, since residents then faced the prospect of expenditure on drains and sinks. Finally, it is worth emphasising, and we shall come back to this later, that companies were trying to expand supplies in a context where average costs were rising. This was in part because of the need, as in Manchester, Liverpool and Glasgow, to look for supplies from distant locations in mountains and hills. In addition, the development of constant-pressure systems would require increased monitoring of customer premises to guard the companies' service pipes against leakage and misuse. Matters were very complicated in households with landlord and tenants.[34]

The government response was weak. As much as anything this was due to a fear of central authority undermining local authorities, the latter including Highway Surveyors, Poor Law Commissioners and Sewerage and Water Commissioners, as well as municipal boroughs and other units of local government. They argued amongst themselves but were united in opposing central interference. The government measures that emerged were therefore permissive rather than mandatory. There had certainly been lots of complaints about services and many were authoritative. The 1840 Select Committee on the Health of Towns, the 1842 Chadwick Report and the two reports of the Commissioners on the State of Large Towns in 1844 and 1845 contained strong critiques of the water industry.[35] Moreover the 1847 Gasworks and Waterworks Clauses Act spelled out maximum prices and a 10% limit on dividends. However, this was very much a tidying-up operation setting out what should appear in the acts for individual towns and undertakings. The sheer numbers of applications coming forward during the mid-century Victorian economic boom are sufficient explanation. The data are poor for the early years of the century, but it seems that, whilst there were only ten municipal boroughs in England and Wales operating their own water system in 1845, there were already sixty-seven joint stock companies. In the next ten years the number of municipal borough systems quadrupled and increased by a further 50% in the subsequent ten years reaching sixty-one in 1865, by which time there were 147 joint stock water companies.[36] The legislation appeared to have no teeth. It only applied to new undertakings, there was no inspectorate, complaints had to be taken up at the Quarter Sessions and the companies in particular were adept at 'watering' the capital base in various ways to produce nominally lower rates of profit.[37] However, we shall return to consider the effects of price controls later, since the experience of the water industry may have been rather different from gas supply, railways and the other infrastructure industries.

So far as water quality was concerned, the mid-century legislation was fatally flawed. The cleanliness of the water supply was at the heart of the 1840s' health reports mentioned above. The 1848 Public Health Act gave local authorities powers to facilitate an improvement in the quality of supply but they were not mandatory. It was compulsory to establish a local board of health only when mortality exceeded 23 per 1000; otherwise it depended on whether at least 10% of ratepayers petitioned for one. The local boards had enabling powers to secure adequate water supplies, to erect free public cisterns and pumps, and to establish their own water-works, but none of this was mandatory and required the agreement of the local water company. Progress towards clean water supplies at constant high pressure was slow. Even the laws that specified that the companies should supply fireplugs were weak because they failed to specify the minimum distance between the plugs. In 1871 a Royal Commission noted that promoters of water bills were still being allowed to escape the obligation to provide a constant high-pressure supply.[38]

Concessions and franchise systems differ from the above regulatory arrangements in so far as the land or water resource or access right resides with some body other than the water undertaking, usually the local or national government. The use of such facilities is then granted to a water supply undertaking for a specified period of years under strict conditions with respect to areas to be supplied, prices charged, quantities delivered and quality level. In the UK such systems never developed in the nineteenth century. In the 1840s Edwin Chadwick saw water supply and sanitation as strongly interrelated problems and envisaged new companies supplying a range of services to towns. He was behind the establishment of the Town Improvement Company to enter into contracts for water supply as well as drainage, sewerage and refuse collection. Part would be financed by local taxes and part from customer charges. Nothing emerged, and more generally in the nineteenth century such companies never flourished in Britain.

So arms' length regulation had proved weak. In historical time, municipalisation followed, but the inadequacies of regulation do not appear to be the whole story. After all, it was a big step for a local community to supervise the management of waterworks and distribution systems. Many town councils in Britain and continental Europe, as we have seen, appear to have been content to continue with arm's length regulation of gas supply, leaving their regulation to Parliament. Water supply does look different. Concession systems for water supply could be found all over continental Europe though they seem to have been limited to the larger towns. In Spain the contractual terms for the private companies were fairly liberal, symptomatic of the physical difficulties in organising supplies in southern Europe; the concessions were often for an unlimited period, and an 1879 law allowed them to be bought and sold. In Italy, with its great heritage of Roman water supply projects, it seems that many of the local authorities operated their own water-supply system, though such undertakings tended to be small. Municipal ownership was extensive in Germany and Sweden. By 1908 in Germany, thirty-eight out of the forty-one large towns with populations of 100000 or more had municipally owned waterworks, whilst in Sweden by 1909 all eighty-one waterworks were municipally operated. In Britain 60% of the undertakings were in municipal hands by the 1870s and this rose to 80% by 1914, and most of the private undertakings that remained were distributing only small quantities of water. Even in France, the home of the concession system, municipalisation was rife. The concession for Paris was held from 1857 by the Compagnie Général des Eaux, but elsewhere municipal systems grew rapidly from the middle of the century, and by 1913 three-quarters of all communes ran their own system.[39]

It is not obvious that the ideology of municipal socialism was instrumental in initiating municipal enterprise, if only because the main initial surge in municipalisation predated the spread of socialism as an electoral force. The data are patchy for the UK, and the best series, as Table 3.2 shows, is for those towns (usually large towns) that attained the status of municipal boroughs. It is the case that the number of statutory water undertakings owned by municipal boroughs rose from 195 in 1885 to 306 by 1905, coinciding with the debates in London about gas and water

Table 3.2 *Number of statutory water supply undertakings in the UK, 1845–1956*

	Municipal Boroughs	Other local gov.	Total	Private	TOTAL
1845	10			67[a]	
1855	39				
1865	61			147[a]	
1871					250
1875	127				
1885	195				
1895	237				
1905	306				
1914	326	494	820	200	1020
1934			878[b]	173[b]	1051[b]
1956			925[b]	90[b]	1015[b]

Notes:
[a] England and Wales only.
[b] Excludes Southern Ireland.

Sources: A. L. Dakyns, 'The Water Supply of English Towns in 1846', *Manchester School* 2(1) (1931), 21–25.
M. E. Falkus, 'The Development of Municipal Trading in the Nineteenth Century', *Business History* 19(2) (1977), Table III.
H. Finer, *Municipal Trading* (London, Allen and Unwin, 1941), 41.
J. Hassan, 'The Water Industry: A Failure of Public Policy?', in R. Millward and J. Singleton (eds.), *The Political Economy of Nationalisation in Britain 1920–50* (Cambridge University Press, 1995), Table 9.1.
W. A. Robson, 'The Public Utility Services', in H. J. Laski, W. I. Jennings and W. A. Robson (eds.), *A Century of Municipal Progress: The Last One Hundred Years* (London: Allen and Unwin, 1935), 316–19.

socialism, associated with the Webbs and Fabians, and with the growing power of political movements on the left.[40] However, there had been a huge surge in municipal ownership well before this, with the numbers of such undertakings rising from 10 in 1845 to 127 as early as 1875. The number of all local government undertakings probably overtook that of the statutory private companies by the end of the 1880s, if not earlier. Total investment by the water sector averaged, at constant 1900 prices, some £1.7 million per annum in the 1850s rising to £2.8 million by the 1870s. Throughout these decades it was the largest component of local infrastructure investment, bigger than gas, sewerage, street maintenance, docks, electricity or tramways.[41]

In fact the chief sources of political power on town councils were businessmen and other ratepayers like shopkeepers. In Birmingham, for example, 55% of councillors in the period 1860–91 were businessmen.[42] The fortunes of their factories were often contingent on good local water and transport, and if that required municipal operations, so be it. To take one example of business influence, Wakefield Council wished to avoid some of the health problems in taking their water supply from the local polluted rivers by drawing on the good clean water in deep local wells. This option was eventually dropped because the water was hard and therefore unsuitable for use in textile mills, whose owners were well represented on the council. In all towns businessmen had a vested interest in a good water supply for fire fighting, and the American literature shows that fire insurance premiums were noticeably less in towns with good water systems.[43] Indeed, the heavy industrial demand for water actually worsened the public health position in the middle decades of the century. The water schemes developed under municipal ownership in the industrial towns of northern England were designed to benefit industry. The contemporary, inadequate system of waste removal based on the privy and cesspool became strained by flooding from the increased supply of water to factories and the household closets of the affluent. More water was being produced, but appropriate methods of drainage lagged far behind.[44] A recent study of thirty-six towns in England and Wales revealed that the annual capital expenditure on water supply in the middle of the 1880s was just below £20000 per town. This was equivalent to the total of all capital expenditure on sewers, streets and other sanitation. As an indication of the early priority given to water supply, the value of outstanding financial loans associated with past investment in water supply by these same towns amounted, by the mid 1880s, to some £275000, as opposed to £50000 for sewers, £12000 for streets and £100000 for other sanitation. Even by the early 1900s annual capital expenditure on sewers was only one half that on water supply.[45]

The other key group on the town councils, sometimes overlapping with businessmen, was ratepayers. The last quarter of the century saw town councils in the rapidly expanding industrial boroughs faced with immense financial burdens as they struggled to overcome the terrible living and working conditions that industrialisation had brought. All were investing heavily in sewerage, drainage systems and roads and also had responsibility for the growing bill for policing and education. In the last quarter of the century, population in Britain rose by 37% and local taxes (the rates) by 141%.[46] One response, as we have seen, was to take over private gas enterprises, or start new ones (also electricity and trams later), using their profits as a useful non-tax source of revenue. There are examples of water supply undertakings being used as cash cows but not as systematically as gas and electricity, and it is doubtful whether municipal undertakings did earn profits. Dawson argued that while 'the water service is not usually regarded in England as a legitimate source of profit, the large German towns levy charges which yield a very considerable contribution towards the general funds'.[47] He quoted a rate of return of 7.7% on capital for sixty-two large towns in 1913. This, however, was before deducting interest and depreciation, and water resource development was very capital intensive. For France, Goubert's analysis of the finances of water undertakings for 1894 suggests that income exceeded operating expenses for most of the municipal enterprises. However, 'loan repayments were settled by members of the local community ... through the levying of new taxes ... [so that the capital expenditure] ... was not a burden upon the finances of the water authorities'.[48] British evidence indicates that, when loan charges are included, municipal water undertakings made a financial loss, whereas municipal gas, electricity and tramways made a profit. For a sample of twenty-five towns in England and Wales for the ten years 1904–13, water supply revenues exceeded operating expenditures to yield an annual average operating surplus per town of £37300, but loan charges averaged £40700.[49] This is confirmed by the data in Table 3.3, which covers all municipal water undertakings in Britain. Whilst in every year for which we have data revenues tended to exceed operating costs and generate positive gross profits, the source data (in the local taxation returns) do not identify loan charges for the water undertakings before 1903. They are all lumped together with loan charges for gas, electricity, tramways, docks, roads, hospitals, schools and so on. From 1903, however, when separate figures start appearing, it is clear that the water undertakings' gross profits were less than their loan charges. In this they were different from gas, electricity and tramways, each of which, for most of the years, earned positive net profits.[50]

It would appear, therefore, that water supply was viewed differently from the other local infrastructure industries in the nineteenth century. It was a halfway house between on the one hand programmes financed by taxes like public health and education and on the other hand the more commercially orientated services of electricity, gas and tramways. The 1875 Public Health Act *required* local governments to ensure that adequate water supplies existed. The water undertakings generally made a financial loss, as we have seen, so that if the object was to generate profits, the achievements were poor. More likely, the aim was to expand supplies of clean water for residents, as the 1875 Act required, and to develop soft water and a firefighting capability for factory owners. Why, though, was water municipalised?

Table 3.3 *Income and expenditure of water supply undertakings of all local authorities in Britain, 1883–1948 (£ million)*

	Operating costs	Total costs	Revenues	Gross profits	Net profits
1883[a]	0.8		1.6	0.8	
1894[a]	1.1		2.8	1.7	
1902	2.5		4.8	2.3	
1903		5.4	5.0		−0.4
1906		9.5	8.5		−1.0
1908		9.1	8.7		−0.4
1910		9.4	9.0		−0.4
1913		10.1	9.5		−0.6
1922		18.4	14.6		−3.8
1925		17.0	17.2		−0.7
1928		19.8	19.2		−0.6
1930		21.2	19.6		−1.6
1938[a]		24.9	23.8		−1.1
1948[a]		35.4	33.5		−1.9

Notes:
[a] Excludes Scotland. For 1938 and 1948, Scotland is excluded from the revenue and net profit entries but not those for costs.

Definitions: Revenue includes all receipts, grants, tolls and fees. Operating costs comprise annual labour, fuel, maintenance and other operating costs. Total costs comprise operating costs plus annual loan charges. Gross profit is revenue less operating costs as defined above. Net profit is revenue less total costs as defined above. Before 1903 the cost figures for England and Wales exclude loan charges as do the data for Scotland before 1893. The post-1902 data do not identify loan charges separately. The coverage of the cost data for England and Wales changes in 1929, but this has a very small quantitative impact.

Source: B. R. Mitchell, *British Historical Statistics* (Cambridge University Press, 1988), 609–29.

Some of the explanations in the literature are not convincing. Hassan and, much earlier, Shaw and Knoop, argued that the large scale schemes for taking water supplies to the large urban conurbations involved levels of finance and a degree of planning beyond the scope of private enterprise.[51] The investment requirements of the Rivington Pike scheme for Liverpool in the 1840s and the later one for Vyrnwy in Wales, the Loch Katrine project for Glasgow in the 1850s, and the Thirlmere and Longdendale schemes for Manchester in the 1870s and 1880s were certainly substantial. But private enterprise had laid a route network for railways in the 1830s and 1840s equivalent to the modern British motorway network, and the later work on lines linking the outer reaches of

Wales and Scotland involved even more costly outlays on bridges, viaducts and tunnels.

Rather, one might point to the institutional difficulties in the way of water companies earning sufficient profit to expand supplies at a rate demanded by town councils. For one thing, the price controls established by parliamentary legislation probably had little effect in gas supply, electricity and tramways because these industries witnessed great technological changes, which saw costs falling for much of the period 1850–1914.[52] For water supply, matters were different. That is, water supply is obviously dependent on natural resources and hence, like agriculture, is liable to diminishing returns. Unless significant technical progress in storage and delivery takes place, expansion will lead to rising real unit costs. Clearly there were important technological changes in the nineteenth century. One was the introduction of steam-driven pumps, which affected the elevation, distance and speed at which water could be carried and was important for firefighting once pumps became reliable. There is evidence that steam engines were being used in Liverpool in 1847, and it was probably only from the middle of the century that they spread. A second technical development was the replacement of wood and stone pipes by iron, which seems to have been significant from early in the century. Finally, there were the purification facilities such as sand filters. On the other hand, the demands from rapid urban population growth and industrialisation exhausted the more obvious local supplies, and towns had to look further afield, a factor raising costs. Data on the cost of water is actually quite meagre, but Cavalcanti collected information on the costs of the London companies and Table 3.4 is derived from his data. It shows the pattern for one of the larger companies (the New River Company) as well as for all the London companies combined. The broad message is that costs per gallon rose by 30% in the nineteenth century, from 3d to 4d. Relative to the prices of all other goods and services, most of which were falling absolutely, the real cost of water may have risen by about 50% in the nineteenth century. For the companies to make a normal rate of return, water charges would have had to rise accordingly and large numbers of customers captured in order to exploit the economies of scale and contiguity required to hold down costs. This is where the maximum prices specified in the 1840s' legislation did appear to bite. Households were not metered, and water charges were in the form of a water rate linked not to the volume of consumption, but to a proxy measure, the value of the property. A contemporary authority, Silverthorne, suggested that, in the 1880s, the maximum water rates allowed in the 1847 Clauses Act were never high enough for the companies and so

Table 3.4 *London water supplies, 1820–1900*

	New River Company		All London companies	
	1820	1900	1820	1900
Output in million gallons per annum	4218	131311	8947	73766
Number of houses ('000)	52	161	135	850
Supply per house (in '000 gallons)	81	81	61	86
Total costs (£'000)	48	316	103	1223
Costs per thousand gallons in pence	3	6	3	4
Revenue in £'000	67	593	193	2348
Revenue per '000 gallons in pence	4	11	5	8

Source: Derived from J. Cavalcanti, 'Economic Aspects of the Provision and Development of Water Supply in Nineteenth Century Britain', PhD Thesis, University of Manchester, 1991, Tables 4.3, 4.10, 4.12, 5.7.

they, instead, engaged in protracted legal battles over the valuation of property to which the water rate was applied.[53] Most business customers were metered, and many town councils dominated by manufacturers had meter schedules that were very generous, as were the volumes of 'compensation' water. The latter refers to situations where the development and alignment by water companies of rivers and reservoirs affected the free access that manufacturing factories had to nearby water supplies. The water companies then had to provide free 'compensation' water for the factories. None of this meant profit for the water companies. Similarly, it was important for the companies to capture large numbers of customers given the 'lumpiness' of the investment required in water resource development. Ideally such customers should be geographically concentrated in order to take advantage of the economies of contiguity inherent in distribution networks. A major problem the companies therefore faced, as we have already noted, was that for constant high-pressure supply to be introduced – which all parliamentary reports were promoting – it was essential for customers themselves to invest in pipes, sinks and drains in their own homes. A great deal of uncertainty therefore surrounded the operation of companies dealing on a one-to-one basis with households, some of whom would be reluctant to make the necessary investments. A great attraction of municipal operation was that it involved the finance of water services to households by a water rate, that is, a price related not directly to the volume of household water consumption, but to the value of local property, a method analogous to all local taxation in this period. By such a uniform levy, councils automatically enrolled all ratepayers on to the water undertakings' books.[54]

For municipal enterprise to succeed it was of course vital that local government was reasonably honest and efficient, and structured in a way that could accommodate the management of utilities. In the late eighteenth century and early nineteenth century, local government in Britain was sometimes unrepresentative or corrupt or inefficient. Ratepayers shied away from municipal initiatives. Later in the century, rural areas often proved unsuitable for municipal undertakings because the number of customers was uneconomically low. They were left to the private companies who straddled local government boundaries. The best example of unsuitable government structures was London. For much of the century it was a hotchpotch of local vestries, poor law unions, sewerage boards and road authorities. Large private utilities flourished, as we have seen, in gas supply as well as in water supply. All this changed after the 1894 Local Government Act, which established a London County Council and numerous urban district councils alongside twenty or so metropolitan boroughs. The Metropolitan Water Board then emerged in 1902 as a large metropolitan water undertaking to set alongside the new LCC Tramways Corporation and the metropolitan boroughs' electricity corporations.

Notes

1 O. Hyldtoft, 'Making Gas: The Establishment of the Nordic Gas Systems, 1800–1870', in A. Kaijser and M. Hedin (eds.), *Nordic Energy Systems: Historical Perspectives and Current Issues* (Canton, Mass.: Science History Publications, 1995), 76–99; O. Hyldtoft, *Den lysende gas: Etablerinjen af det danske gassystem 1800–1890* (Herning, Denmark: Systimes Teknologihistorie, European Educational Publishers Group, 1994), (English summary pp. 173–90); V. Duchene, *150 jaar stadsgas te Leuven* (Deurne, 1995), p. 21; H. J. S. Peterson, 'Diffusion of Coal Gas Technology in Denmark 1850–1920', *Technological Forecasting and Social Change* 38(1) (1990), 37–48.

2 C. Sudria, 'Notas sobre la implantacion y el desarrollo de la industria del gas en españa 1840–1901', *Revista de Historia Economica* 1(2) (1983), 97–118; F. Antolin, 'Las empresas de servicos publicos municipales', in F. Comin and P. M. Acena (eds.), *Historia de la empresa publica en España* (Madrid: Espasa Calpe, 1991), 283–330; G. Tortella, *The Development of Modern Spain* (Cambridge, Mass.: Harvard University Press, 2000).

3 D. Matthews, 'Laissez-faire and the London Gas Industry in the Nineteenth Century: Another Look', *Economic History Review* 39(2) (1986), 244–63.

4 F. Caron and F. Cardot (eds.), *Histoire générale de l'électricité en France.*
    I. 1881–1918: Espoirs et conquêtes (Paris: L'Association pour l'Histoire de
    l'Electricité en France, Fayard, 1991), 526. See also M. Levy-Leboyer, 'The
    French Electrical Power System: An Inter-Country Comparison', in R. Maintz
    and T. P. Hughes (eds.), *The Development of Large Technical Systems* (Boulder,
    Colo.: Frankfurt and Westview Press, 1978), 245–62.
5 R. Millward, 'The Economic Organisation and Development of Electricity
    Supply in Britain in the 20th Century', in A. Giuntini and G. Paolini (eds.), *La*
    Citta elettrica: Esperenze di elettrificazione urbana in Italia e in Europa fra ottocento
    e novecento (Rome: Gius, Laterza & Figli and ENEL, 2003).
6 Sudria, 'Industria del gas en España 1840–1901'; J. Nadal, 'Spain 1830–1914',
    in C. Cipolla (ed.), *The Fontana Economic History of Europe: The Emergence of*
    Industrial Societies, 2 parts (Glasgow: Fontana/Collins, 1973), part 2; Tortella,
    Modern Spain; A. Milward and S. B. Saul, 'The Economic Development of
    Spain and Italy', in *The Economic Development of Continental Europe 1780–1870*
    (London: Allen and Unwin, 1979), ch. 4.
7 S. Fenoaltea, 'The Growth of the Utility Industries in Italy 1861–1913',
    Journal of Economic History 42 (1982), 601–28.
8 W. H. Dawson, *Municipal Life and Local Government in Germany* (London:
    Longmans, Green and Co., 1916), 186; D. Schott, 'Electrifying German Cities:
    Investment in Energy Technology and Public Transport and their Impact on
    Urban development 1880–1914', Paper presented to the International
    Economic History Conference, Madrid, 1998, p. 3.
9 Hyldtoft, 'Nordic Gas Systems'; J. L. van Zamdem, 'The Netherlands: The
    History of an Empty Box', in J. Foreman-Peck and G. Federico (eds.),
    European Industrial Policy: The Twentieth Century Experience (Oxford
    University Press, 1999), 177–93.
10 R. Millward and R. Ward, 'From Private to Public Ownership of Gas
    Undertakings in England and Wales, 1851–1947: Chronology, Incidence
    and Causes', *Business History* 35(3) (1993), 1–21.
11 T. P. Hughes, *Networks of Power: Electrification in Western Society 1880–1930*
    (Baltimore: Johns Hopkins Press, 1983), 178. See also F. Howe, *European Cities*
    at Work (New York: Charles Scribner's Sons, 1913) and U. Wengenroth, 'The
    Rise and Fall of State Owned Enterprise in Germany', in P. A. Toninelli (ed.),
    The Rise and Fall of State Owned Enterprise in the Western World (Cambridge
    University Press, 2000), 103–27.
12 U. Kuhl, 'Le Débat sur le socialisme municipal en allemagne avant 1914 et la
    municipalisation de l'électricité', in U. Kuhl (ed.), *Der Munizipalsozialismus in*
    Europa (Munich: Oldenberg Verlag, 2002), 81–100. See also R. Tilly,
    'Municipal Enterprise, Tax Burden and Municipal Socialism in German
    Cities 1870–1914', and J. C. Brown, 'Who Paid for the Sanitary City?:
    Issues and Evidence c.1910', both papers presented to the Eleventh
    International Economic History Conference, Milan, 1994.
13 H. Fraser, 'Municipal Socialism and Social Policy', in R. J. Morris and
    R. Rodger (eds.), *The Victorian City: A Reader in British Urban History:*
    1820–1914 (London: Longman, 1993), 258–80.

14 Joint Select Committee of the House of Lords and the House of Commons, *Report on Municipal Trading*, Parliamentary Papers 1900 VII and 1903 VII (London: HMSO). See also R. Millward, 'The Political Economy of Urban Utilities in Britain 1840–1950', in M Daunton (ed.), *Cambridge Urban History of Britain*, III (Cambridge University Press, 2001), 334.

15 Dawson, *Municipal Life in Germany*, 190.

16 O. Hyldtoft, 'Nordic Gas Systems' and 'Modern Theories of Regulation: An Old Story: Danish Gasworks in the 19th Century', *Scandinavian Economic History Review* 42(1) (1994), 29–53.

17 Sudria, 'Industria del gas en España'; Caron and Cardot, *Histoire de l'électricité en France*, 399 and 500; for Belgium, see L. Hens and P. Solar, 'Belgium: Liberalism by Default', in Foreman-Peck and Federico (eds.), *European Industrial Policy*, 194–214.

18 R. Balzani and A. Giuntini, 'Urban Infrastructure and the Hygiene Question in Liberal Italy (1880–1915)', Paper presented to International Economic History Conference, Madrid, 1998; V. Zamagni, *The Economic History of Italy 1860–1990* (Oxford: Clarendon Press, 1993), 186.

19 Maurice Felix, quoted by A. Fernandez, 'Les Lumières de la ville: L'Administration municipale a l'épreuve de l'électrification', *Vingtième Siècles Revue d'Histoire* 62 (1999), 116.

20 Ibid. See also C. Freedman, *The Conseil d'Etat in Modern France* (New York: Columbia University Press, 1961), 105–6, 160–1.

21 P. Ashley, *Local and Central Government* (London: John Murray, 1906), 100–1.

22 For Paris, see A. Shaw, *Municipal Government in Continental Europe* (New York: Fisher Unwin, 1895), chapter 1. For Denmark see Statens Statistiske Bureau, *Statistisk Aarbog* (Copenhagen: Thiels Bogtrykken, 1912), Table 135.

23 R. Millward and R. Ward, 'The Costs of Public and Private Gas Enterprises in Late Nineteenth Century Britain', *Oxford Economic Papers* 39 (1987), 719–37.

24 J. A. Tarr and G. Dupuy, 'Sewers and Cities: France and the US Compared', *Journal of the Environmental Engineering Division, Proceedings of the American Society of Civil Engineers* 108 (1982), 327–38; J.-P. Goubert, *The Conquest of Water: The Advent of Health in the Industrial Age* (Princeton University Press, 1986), 195–6; J.-P. Goubert, 'The Development of Water and Sewerage Systems in France 1850–1950', in J. A. Tarr and G. Dupuy (eds.), *Technology and the Rise of the Networked City in Europe* (Philadelphia: Temple University Press, 1988), 116–36; P. Hennock, 'The Urban Sanitary Movement in England and Germany 1838–1914: A Comparison', *Continuity and Change*, 15(2), 2000, 269–96; R. Millward 'Privatisation in Historical Perspective: The UK Water Industry', in D. Cobham, R. Harrington and G. Zis (eds.), *Money, Trade and Payments* (Manchester University Press, 1989), Table 10.1

25 W. A. Robson, 'The Public Utility Services', in H. J. Laski, W. I. Jennings and W. A. Robson (eds.), *A Century of Municipal Progress: The Last One Hundred Years* (London: Allen and Unwin, 1935), 311–12.

26 J. A. Hassan, 'The Growth and Impact of the British Water Industry in the Nineteenth Century', *Economic History Review* 38(4) (1985), 531–47.

27 A. L. Dakyns, 'The Water Supply of English Towns in 1846', *Manchester School* 2(1) (1931), 22.

28 J. F. Wilson, 'The Finance of Municipal Capital Expenditure in England and Wales', 1870–1914', *Financial History Review* 4 (1997), 31–50.

29 Select Committee on the Supply of Water to the Metropolis, Report May 1821, 3.

30 E. Chadwick, *Report on the Sanitary Conditions of the Labouring Population of Great Britain: 1842* (ed. M. W. Flinn; Edinburgh University Press, 1965), p. 144. For data on rates of return, see M. Edelstein, *Overseas Investment in the Age of High Imperialism: The United Kingdom 1850–1914* (London: Methuen, 1982), chs. 5 and 6.

31 W. M. Stern, 'Water Supply in Britain: Development of a Public Service', *Royal Sanitary Institute Journal* 74 (1954), 999.

32 Commissioners on the State of Large Towns and Populous Districts, *Second Report 1845* (London: HMSO, 1945), 45; General Board of Health, *Report on the Supply of Water to the Metropolis* (London: HMSO, 1850), 296.

33 Commissioners on the State of Large Towns and Populous Districts, *First Report 1844* (London: HMSO, 1844), xi, xii; H. W. Dickinson, *The Water Supply of Greater London* (London: Courier Press, 1956).

34 A. Shaw, 'Glasgow: A Municipal Study', *Century* 39 (1890), 721–36; W. Smart, 'Glasgow and its Municipal Industries', *Quarterly Journal of Economics* 9(2) (1895), 188–94.

35 Select Committee on the Health of Towns, *Report* (London: HMSO, 1840); Chadwick, *Report on Sanitary Conditions*; Commissioners on the State of Large Towns and Populous Districts, *First Report 1844* and *Second Report 1845*.

36 Dakyns, 'The Water Supply of English Towns in 1846', 21–25; M. E. Falkus, 'The Development of Municipal Trading in the Nineteenth Century', *Business History* 19(2) (1977), Table III; H. Finer, *Municipal Trading* (London: Allen and Unwin, 1941), 41.

37 R. Millward, 'The Emergence of Gas and Water Monopolies in Nineteenth Century Britain: Contested Markets and Public Control', in J. Foreman-Peck (ed.), *New Perspectives on the Late Victorian Economy* (Cambridge University Press, 1993), 109–15.

38 Royal Sanitary Commission, *Report* (London: HMSO, 1871), 42.

39 G. Nunez, 'Spanish Cities in a Forgotten Modernising Process', in M. Morner and G. Tortella (eds.), *Different Paths to Modernisation* (University of Lund, Sweden, forthcoming); F. Antolin, 'Public Policy in the Development of the Spanish Electric Utility Industry', Paper presented at European Historical Economics Society Conference on *A Century of Industrial Policy in Europe*, Oxford, Worcester College, 1992; Fenoaltea, 'The Utility Industries in Italy', 619; Dawson, *Municipal Life in Germany*, 186; M. Hietalla, *Services and Urbanisation at the Turn of the Century: The Diffusion of Innovations*, Studia Historica 23 (Helsinki: Finnish Historical Society, 1987), 207; Millward, 'The UK Water Industry'; Goubert, *The Conquest of Water*, 186–7.

40 Cf. Fraser, 'Municipal Socialism and Social Policy'.

41 C. H. Feinstein and S. Pollard (eds.), *Studies in Capital Formation in the UK, 1750–1920* (Oxford University Press, 1988); F. Bell and R. Millward, 'Public Health Expenditures and Mortality in England and Wales, 1870–1914', *Continuity and Change* 13(2) (1998), 221–49.

42 L. J. Jones, 'Public Pursuit and Private Profit: Liberal Businessmen and Municipal Politics in Birmingham, 1845–1900', *Business History* 25(3) (1983), 240–59.

43 C. Hamlin, 'Muddling in Bumbledom: On the Enormity of Large Sanitary Improvements in Four British Towns', 1855–1885', *Victorian Studies* 32(1) (1988), 57–81; L. Anderson, 'Hard choices: supplying water to New England Towns', *Journal of Interdisciplinary History*, 15 (2) (Autumn 1984), pp. 211–34.

44 Hassan, 'Growth and Impact', 36–7.

45 Bell and Millward, 'Public Health Expenditures', Figures 1 and 2.

46 M. Daunton, 'Urban Britain', in T. R. Gourvish and A. O. Day (eds.), *Later Victorian Britain, 1867–1900* (London: Macmillan, 1988), 37–67; R. Millward and S. Sheard, 'The Urban Fiscal Problem 1870–1914: Government Expenditure and Finances in England and Wales', *Economic History Review* 48(3) (1995), 501–35.

47 Dawson, *Municipal Life in Germany*, 189–90.

48 Goubert, *The Conquest of Water*, 186.

49 Millward and Sheard, 'The Urban Fiscal Problem', Table 2.

50 See Millward, 'Political Economy', Table 11.6.

51 Hassan, 'Growth and Impact'; D. Knoop, *Principles and Methods of Municipal Trading* (London: Macmillan, 1912); Shaw, 'Glasgow: A Municipal Study'. See also J. A. Hassan, *A History of Water in Modern England and Wales* (Manchester University Press, 1998).

52 See, for example, D. Matthews, 'Laissez-faire and the London Gas Industry' and 'Technology Transfer in the Late 19th Century Gas Industry', *Journal of Economic History* 47(4) (1987), 967–80.

53 A. Silverthorne, *London and Provincial Water Supplies* (London: Crosby, Lockwood & Co., 1884), 10, 12, 38. See also W. Sherratt, 'Water Supply to Large Towns', *Journal of the Manchester Geographical Society* 4 (1888), 58–71.

54 Royal Commission on Water Supply, *Report of the Commissioners* (London: HMSO, 1869).

4 Railways and telegraph: economic growth and national unification

The economic problems arising in Europe's growing industrial towns were treated as a local issue in the nineteenth century. Central government kept out of it, especially if there were likely to be demands on the public purse. It was different for railways and telegraph, which involved regional and national networks and, by joining up different parts of the country, offered economic and political benefits at a national level. In all countries, except Belgium, the initial development of the new nineteenth-century railway infrastructures was undertaken by the private sector. The risks were large and the benefits, in the early decades, far from clear. In some regions even sovereigns could be unhelpful. In the Kingdom of the two Sicilies, 'Ferdinand II would allow no tunnels, thinking them immoral, attached a chapel to every station, and allowed no trains to run at night or on holidays'.[1]

The attitudes of most governments, however, were more supportive. They were strongly affected by the experience of Britain. It was the first industrial nation and successfully developed the trunk network of its railway system in the 1830s and 1840s under private ownership, and there seems little doubt that central governments in continental Europe wanted to encourage railway development. Everywhere they provided guarantees of interest on railway investment projects. In France and Germany the intervention of the government was initially hesitant. France, a country still with a large peasantry and a middle class seemingly more interested in government bonds and property, was short of capital for railways. Hence the large bankers like Rothschilds and financiers/entrepreneurs such as the Pereire brothers were drawn in. Emile Pereire argued that to attract a large number of small investors government guarantees were essential; in Britain it was felt that granting the companies limited liability status was enough. From the 1830s what we therefore see in France is government guarantees of 4% return on railway capital. By the 1850s the norm was 4% plus 1% for amortisation, with the guarantee taking the form that any deficits would be met by treasury loans, which were to be redeemed from future profits.[2] The wrangling over terms and the securement of banker support, together with the various planning schemes of the Corps du Ponts et Chaussées, meant a fairly slow initial expansion and, as may be seen in Figure 2.1, only 4000 km were open by 1850. Some writers like Tilly have characterised the initial railway development in Prussia also as very slow. In the 1830s and 1840s the king was unwilling to go to the Diet to seek funds for supporting railway development because the Diet was likely to ask for electoral reform. Nonetheless, the 1838 law made explicit provision for government guarantees of interest and the very liberal granting of charters, which we have already noted, was instrumental, argues Fremdling, in achieving a growth in rail track higher than in France.[3] From the 1850s the strong commitment of Napoleon raised the pace of development in France, whilst in Prussia a common interest between the middle class and the Junkers in railway development, which would help both the army and the economy, made for strong government commitments to expansion.

In Scandinavia, Spain and Italy, government guarantees of railway returns were pervasive, but the difficult terrain prompted even greater government involvement in railway development. In Sweden and Norway early investments were quite risky, and several British and Swedish companies failed. The state then stepped in to develop the trunk network, though, as we shall see later, the desire to link up disparate regions was very important, as in Italy. In Spain a scanty population and difficult terrain made railways problematic, even with government guarantees, but the central government had continuous budget problems of its own so that foreign capital was essential.[4] The experiences of Spain and Italy will now be examined in more detail, since they provide a good indication for the mid-nineteenth century of how far governments in less developed countries were able and were prepared to promote economic growth. They looked in part to emulate Britain's success with free trade and railways, though when world food supplies increased and prices fell towards the end of the century a more protectionist stance emerged, as it did elsewhere in Europe.

In the Po Valley in Italy, inland navigation was good and experienced something of a golden age in the early nineteenth century, but elsewhere in Italy, rivers and roads were poor, and the same was true for Spain where there were only two canals.[5] Traditional transport was therefore very costly, yet railways made little headway until the late 1850s. By then state governments were keen to promote railway expansion – the Progressives in Spain and the new national government in Italy from 1860. State initiatives took the form of special privileges for private rail companies, the granting of subsidies, guaranteeing financial returns and direct state ownership, though the last was used only in Italy. The 1855 railway law in Spain permitted the government to grant subsidies to foreign-owned companies who were allowed to import rails, rolling stock and other equipment free of duty.[6] Sections of projected track were offered for franchise bidding with the lowest bidder getting the concession. In some cases a direct subsidy was seen to be a better incentive than an interest guarantee. Thus in 1860, for the Manzana–Cordoba line, 40% of the annual costs were met by the government – a method that Cameron felt promoted cost escalation and generally unscrupulous behaviour.[7] In the case of the North Spain Company, a cash subsidy was raised by the Credito Mobiliano Español in 1858 on the credit of the Spanish government.[8] In Italy, the governments (state and later national) guaranteed interest (for example, for the Livourian Railway Company), and in other cases, to avoid paying too many cash subsidies 'up front', guaranteed revenue returns per kilometre of completed track.[9] In addition to state ownership in Piedmont, the central government subsidised the Mediterranean network and bought out the Sicily/Calabria network in 1868 – construction was then subcontracted to the Vitali Co. and railway operations to the Meridionale Co. Whether these subsidies and state takeovers were prompted solely by questions of economic growth is a matter to which we will return in the next section, when we examine the role of political unification and military strategy.

In the meantime we may note that the inducements provided were enough to allow considerable expansion of the railway systems in the 1860s with the basic trunk network complete in Spain and a four-network plan in place in Italy. By the end of the decade there were 5000 km open in Spain and 6000 in Italy. The whole venture was, however, financially disastrous and provided, in the immediate term, only modest economic benefits. None of the traffic expectations were realised in Spain, or in Italy outside the northern network. The main traffic in Spain was coal and other minerals to the ports, and in Italy it was coal and cereals. In neither case was there enough business to make a profit. The failure of traffic to live up to expectations had several causes. There was not the same demand for railways as in the highly industrialised sectors of Britain, Belgium and later France and Germany. The railway in Britain was not really 'developmental', opening up new territories; it was simply a cheaper and faster transport facility for manufacturing firms and for travellers.[10] Secondly, the network in Spain was designed to radiate out from Madrid to the ports and the French frontier. It was not planned for connecting economic centres within Spain but, as one contemporary put it, reflected 'more the belief that wealth can only come to us from abroad'.[11] In Italy the aim was to join up the disparate states that had come to form the new nation state. This weakened the ability of the rail systems to open up and develop regions, even assuming that there was the same potential in Spain and Italy as there was in the USA and Canada with their vast wheatlands and minerals. A third factor was the level of fares and rates, which were high because a difficult terrain made for high operating costs – quite apart, according to Fenoaltea, from the levies, in Italy, of the central government on railway returns.[12] Moreover, backward economic linkages were limited because, initially at least, rails, rolling stock and other equipment were all imported, whilst engineers and even relatively unskilled labour ran the systems.[13] The contrast is with 1830s' Belgium where, after a short infusion of English capital, local finance and industry took over – Belgium was, in other words, already industrialising. Foreign companies in Spain and Italy had links with expatriate and indigenous engineers in government and with engineering companies in north-western Europe. Domestic industry seems to have been limited in the 1860s and 1870s to producing sleepers and wagons. Indeed, several writers have suggested that the railway systems were overexpanded since the imports of railway equipment created balance of payments problems – certainly an issue in Spain, less so in Italy because of emigrant repatriated earnings – whilst capital funds were diverted from manufacturing industry, especially from Catalonian manufacturing.[14] On the other hand, it does not seem that Spanish industry could have supplied railway equipment in this period so that, in so far as calculations do suggest there were some social returns to railway investment, a protectionist policy might have been damaging.[15]

The overall outcome was that by the late 1860s many networks were running into financial difficulties and sought loans from government. Indeed, the creditworthiness of railway companies was linked closely to that of their governments, so that when Italian government bonds fell on the Paris Bourse in 1866, both Spanish and Italian rail bonds also fell and the Credito Mobilario Español collapsed.[16]

National unification and military strategy

For the governments of the nineteenth-century nation states, railways and telegraph were important instruments for promoting social and political unity and for facilitating defence against external and internal enemies. Both the civil and military arms of government had an interest in the alignment of routes and methods of operation for the despatch of troops, messages and supplies, for connecting disparate regions by cultural and physical links, and for the control of information, movement of people and of goods – immigrants, new books, new ideas, news of insurrections and invasions. What was often decisive for government policy was timing – the horizon over which an infrastructure had to be developed and the speed of response in operating the systems. It is no accident that, following the formation of new nation states in Belgium in 1830, Italy in 1860 and Germany in 1870, the new national governments were impatient to forge railway and telegraph links to the new borders and to connect the erstwhile separate regions. State ownership and management of the infrastructures featured strongly in that process. The Minister of Public works, Stefano Jacini, stressed in his speech to the Italian Parliament on 31 January 1867:

In the past few years, we have had to give urgent attention to the question of making up for the inaction of past governments in the sector of public spending. This has involved the building of new roads . . . [and] . . . introducing that wonderful instrument of civilisation, the locomotive, into the most remote corners of the land . . . [as well as the telegraph] . . . All of this . . . had to be achieved in Italy's case in the space of a few months . . . as a result of the nation's need to ensure its independence and to build a solid foundation for national unity and strong government.[17]

The central issue here for us is to ascertain what elements of government involvement can be ascribed to the promotion of social and political unity and national defence as opposed to the promotion of economic growth and the control of natural monopolies. The huge expansion of the railway in North America, after all, was fuelled by the potential economic gains, whilst the large distances between cities gave highly remunerative returns to investments in the electric telegraph. In 1847, 33000 messages were sent by telegram between Toronto and Quebec alone; in contrast, by 1851 there were only 9000 telegrams sent within the whole of France, 14000 in Belgium, 40000 in Germany and 99000 in the UK, with several countries – Sweden, Switzerland and the Netherlands still without any electric telegraph offices.[18] Private enterprise in the form of Western Union dominated the telegraph system in the USA, whilst in the UK a private market flourished up to the late 1860s. What made continental Europe different was the contiguity of different nation states in the same land mass.

There was one dimension of the configuration of routes for which governments clearly felt state ownership was unnecessary. Whilst duplicate railway routes and the presence of several gas and water suppliers in overlapping areas were not uncommon early on, eventually governments exercised control, as we have seen, through the way charters were granted and for which they had powers in the 1838 Prussian railway law, the 1842 and 1859 acts in France, and in the 1840 and 1844 acts in Britain. Nor was state ownership used to control the natural monopolies that emerged from such legislation. Effectively, as a quid pro quo for rights of way, bidding for franchises was encouraged, while the fares, rates and tariffs of the enterprises were usually regulated; and this was the case whether or not an enterprise was in public ownership. Where private companies were involved in the development of telegraph systems, as in Britain, rights of way were readily granted alongside railway track, and roadways could also be used so that competition did emerge. The electric telegraph took off in Britain in the 1840s, and the market was initially served only by the Electric and International Telegraph Company (EITC). It does not appear in this instance that tariffs were regulated, but a stronger constraint came from the threat of competition for the field (if not in the field – that is, only limited direct competitive lines) from companies like the United Kingdom Telegraph Co., which caused the EITC to make market agreements with its rivals. It had been incorporated in 1849 and had 257 stations in 1851 and revenue of 0.5 shillings per message. By the late 1860s the number of stations had risen to 1249, but its market share had fallen below 60% and revenue to 0.1 shillings per message. Notwithstanding this growth of market and of competition, the industry was nationalised in 1868. To understand this we need to look at the general development of telegraph in Europe.

What seems decisive was the interest of governments in the control of information for military and civil purposes. State ownership of telegraph was not needed for facilitating rights of way, avoiding duplicate facilities, controlling monopoly profits or providing incentives for system growth. Other instruments were available and were being used for all utilities – regulations, price controls, interest guarantees, and subsidies. Governments, however, effectively wanted to operate the telegraph system themselves in order to control the flow of information. Symptomatic of whose interests were at stake was the way in which the visual telegraph by arms and flags (the Chappe Telegraph) was established in France in 1797. It was incorporated into the government administration and financed through the budgets of the army, the navy and from the proceeds of the national lottery. State monopoly of the telegraph was confirmed in an act of 1837, which became the basis for all future state claims to exclusive rights in telecommunications. For the government, 'the instantaneous transmission of news ... [was similar] ... to poison and explosives, the swift diffusion of news to insurrection and disorder'.[19]

The visual telegraph was very secure since the Chappe telegraph signalling towers could be protected against subversion more easily than the lines of the electric telegraph, whose introduction, at least in France, was delayed for that very reason.[20] By 1844 the number of telegraph stations had grown only to 534, with Paris linked to 29 centres, a very sluggish growth, as we have seen, when compared to America.[21] In Austria, Metternich, the Chancellor, viewed telegraph as a threat to the military, and he persuaded the emperor to declare in 1847 that electrical commu-nications would be a state monopoly. Belgium saw rapid expansion, conscious as the new government was of their dependency on external links, and by the early 1850s three telegrams per annum were being sent per 1000 population, about the same as Britain. German expansion was not much faster than the French. The Prussian government opened its first electric telegraph in 1849, though some private commercial lines were allowed initially elsewhere in Germany, such as those along the Taunus, Saxony and Silesia rivers. Denmark, Sweden and Norway were very slow to start but then picked up rapidly. In all three countries a State Telegraph Board was established with a monopoly, the only exception being the Great Northern Telegraph Company established in Denmark in 1869 with a concession to operate international telegrams from west-ern to eastern Europe. In Sweden the Televerket was set up in 1856 and financed by the Merchant and Shipping Foundations as well as by par-liamentary subventions.[22] The telegraph proved a valuable means of communications in the difficult terrain of both Norway and Sweden, where governments were keen to cement regional links. Starting with nothing in the early 1850s, the number of telegrams in Sweden rose to thirty-seven per hundred population by 1890 and eighty-six by 1913, comparable to Germany (Table 4.1). The figure for Denmark was 133 and for Norway 155, levels that were exceeded only by the UK and the Low Countries. In its island setting the liberal British regime had perhaps less need to be concerned about the military and regional dimensions of telegraph development, but Ireland and the control of the news were important. The newspapers resented the companies' monopoly of fast-breaking news, whilst in the increasingly complex market of the 1860s, Chambers of Commerce felt the service was 'expensive, inaccurate and insufficiently widespread geographically'.[23] On nationalisation in 1868, telegraph business was merged with postal services, a common practice in Europe. Many governments pushed for low tariffs so that business grew very rapidly in the second half of the century. By 1880 there were eighty-six telegrams sent per head of the population in the UK, now ahead of Western Union at sixty, and Germany (thirty-eight) and France (forty-five) were not far behind, though, as we shall see, some of this was very much a reflection of slow telephone expansion. Economic efficiency does not seem to have been a central concern in the state telegraph systems. Foreman-Peck's studies suggest that whatever gains accrued from the merger of post and telegraph were offset by the rising administrative costs of operating like government departments.[24]

This analysis of the telegraph sheds considerable light on state owner-ship of railways. It was not needed and not used for facilitating rights of

Table 4.1 *Railway, post and telegraph development by 1906–1913*

	UK	Denmark	France	Germany	Sweden	Italy	Norway	Spain	USA
(1) Rail track mileage open in 1910: per mill. popul.	499[a]	754	630	588	1587	317	776	458	2595
Per 1000 sq. mls.	225[a]	143	120	183	49	101	15	47	66
(2) Train miles per 10000 pop. (p.a. 1902–6).	94	na	65	63	52	15	22	na	128
(3) % rail track mileage owned by state in 1906	0	56.2	5.9	92.8	32.3	77.1	85.4	0	0
(4) Telegrams per 100 pop. in 1913	191	133	128	78	86	58	155	37	81[b]
(5) % telegraph lines owned by state in 1913	100.0	100.0	100.0	100.0	100.0	100.0	100.0	100.0	0
(6) Post in 1913: total mail items per head of pop.	127	69	94	105[c]	49	42	52	23	185[c]

Notes:

[a] Britain, i.e. excludes all Ireland.

[b] Number of telegrams per 100 population handled by Western telegraph in 1910.

[c] The German figure excludes registered mail and the US figure relates to 1912.

Source: Rail track, telegram and postal data derived from B. R. Mitchell, *International Historical Statistics: Europe 1750–1993* (London: Macmillan, 3rd edn, 1998). US data from B. R. Mitchell, *International Historical Statistics: The Americas: 1750–1993* (London: Macmillan, 4th edn, 1998). Population data from A. Maddison, *Dynamic Forces in Capitalist Development* (Oxford University Press, 1991), Tables B-2 and B-3. Population for Spain and Britain interpolated from census data in Mitchell, *International Historical Statistics: Europe 1750–1993*. Area data from Whitaker and Sons, *Whitaker's Almanack* (London: Whitaker and Sons, 1911). Train miles and railway ownership data from J. Foreman-Peck, 'Natural Monopoly and Railway Policy in the 19th Century', *Oxford Economic Papers* 39 (1987), Table 5. It is assumed that only the USA, in the form of Western Union, had privately owned telegraph lines.

way, avoiding duplicate facilities, controlling monopoly profits or lowering the risks of capital investment. Something extra was needed, to be sure, when the routes identified were not the ones that would have been chosen by the railway companies. Here subsidies could be used, and it is useful to look at this in more detail. The aim in France was to provide a 'universal service, accessible over all French territory'.[25] In each of the six networks that emerged in the 1850s there was one dominant company, but outside the basic trunk routes were 'secondary lines', which did not always prove financially viable. The 1859 act distinguished between the old network (the 'ancien reseau', basically the trunk lines) and the new network. The interest guarantees were more generous on the new network and, in addition to subsidies per kilometre of line, the French state expected that such lines, if unprofitable, would be subsidised by the profits on the trunk network. Traffic grew healthily in the 1860s, but many of the secondary lines were not being merged successfully into the six basic networks. It was *only when* such lines were unprofitable and *had military value* that the state stepped in – specifically first for lines in the Paris–Orleans and Western networks. The Franco–Prussian War of 1870–1 was decisive in convincing the French government 'that an adequate system of communications was indispensable to the successful pursuit of military operations'.[26] The law of 1878 made provision for the finances of the new state lines to be incorporated in the budget of the Ministry of Works and financed through government bonds ('rentes').[27]

In France in the nineteenth century the strategic factor was therefore decisive in prompting state ownership, but note that this was the solution only when the lines could not be sustained by subsidies. The government subsidised a number of small companies especially in the west and southwest. The scale of the subsidies throughout the system in the latter part of the nineteenth century caused one cynic, later, to claim that the 'tremendous increase in trackage and rail traffic was to a very large extent due to the lavish contributions made by a bountiful state'.[28] Moreover, in what came to be called the 'scoundrelly' conventions of 1883, the government committed itself, for new lines, to building the substructure and part of the superstructure with companies doing the rest (in the form of paying to the government a number of francs per kilometre).[29] This was a massive subsidy – the substructure was to be effectively provided free, like highways. But it was not a state takeover as in the cases of the Paris–Orleans and Western lines.[30] It would seem that supporting unprofitable lines that were not of significant military value took the form of subsidies, and there was some (unspecified) level of subsidy at which the government would let the line close. In the case of France before the First World War, the situation was one where some parts of the railway system could not be sustained without a subsidy. Thus the whole of the Western network was taken over in 1906 because it was not proving financially viable yet was important militarily.[31] Under the 1883 conventions, lines that were perceived to contribute to national defence 'could not be discontinued even though unprofitable without the approval of the Minister of War'.[32] As early as 1882, 26.4% of railway capital was being supplied by the state, with only 16% accounted for by equity shares – the rest were railway bonds. By 1913, 90% of company capital was in the form of bonds, and close to 9000 kilometres of track were in public ownership.[33]

Much of the basic trunk network was still in private ownership, so that the French government must have felt that it could, during a war, take control of these lines and commandeer resources sufficiently to achieve its military objectives. In the case of Belgium and Sweden, even the trunk networks were, at least initially, built and operated by the state. In the former case this reflected the urgency that the new government of the 1830s attached to establishing links across the country. Soon after 1830, a scheme was devised for a system with two axes: one from the coast near Ostend to the German frontier past Liège, and the other from the Dutch frontier in the north, running south-west through Brussels to the French frontier near Mons. What is significant in the Belgian case is that this trunk network was quite consistent with a set of lines designed on economic criteria. The aim, as one contemporary said, 'was to unite the principal commercial towns on one side with the sea, and on the other with the frontiers of France and Prussia'.[34] The north–south line did go through Brussels, but it was not the crossing point because 'the line selected through Malines ... [the chosen crossing point] ... passed by more large towns...'.[35] The configuration made economic sense: 'the network tapped all major centres of population and economic activity'.[36] The route to Germany was designed to avoid Holland, whose market had been closed following the break-up of the United Provinces. So the new system was planned and did make for a 'Unité Expérimentale', but its initiation by the state arose from the desire for speed.[37] After the first ten years, private companies, both English and Belgian, were allowed to expand the system on a concession basis and, by 1870, fifty companies had actually constructed 2500 km of track. In the late nineteenth century, several lines were becoming unprofitable as in France, and the state repurchased them underlining their strategic significance.

Early railway development in Sweden and Norway was slow, and several British and Swedish companies failed in the hostile physical environment. It would seem, however, that the Swedish government regarded a basic network as essential for forging strategic links and binding the different regions, though economic gains were expected. The first railways were not built until the 1850s. Private capital seemed unable to do it in the time horizon demanded by the state.[38] The state stepped in. Indeed it was actually built by military personnel. The state railway board was set up in 1854 to run the system, and any surplus was to be turned over to the Treasury – it was not encouraged to set fares and rates to make large profits but to meet the needs of business and passengers.[39] The trunk network, therefore, as in France and Belgium, generated economic as well as strategic benefits, but the terrain was so difficult and the economic prospects sufficiently meagre that even with subsidy the system would not have been built in the time required by the state, conscious as it was of how railways were forging ahead in other countries. The government was concerned to avoid 'vacillation and planlessness'.[40] The state railways connected the capital, Stockholm, with the economically most advanced regions, the two largest cities in the south, and there was a line to the Norwegian frontier. By the end of the century, one third of the track was state owned, though the municipalities also held shares in some of the private companies.[41] Subsidies were used for the subsidiary networks. That is, local and regional lines were left to private companies and, after a parliamentary act of 1871, were aided by state subsidies. Clearly the state railway board was not prepared to let them go to the wall and agreed to some element of subsidy. Later, the rail tariff for freight traffic to Norrland was subsidised as a means of keeping down food prices and living costs.[42] It is not clear, for this period, whether secondary lines that struggled even with subsidies would have been allowed to close – an issue in all the other countries – and therefore whether the secondary lines had strategic value, though Andersson-Skog characterises the non-trunk network as one where the 'government considered that business and industry were in the best position to decide'[43] implying that a state take-over would *not* have materialised if private enterprise failed to proceed. A similar situation applied in Norway, where the first line, between Oslo and Eidswold, did not open until 1854. The railways were built by the state, sometimes in conjunction with local authorities. Despite much in-fighting between urban pressure groups and rural groups with no interest in railways, the length of track rose to very high levels, relative to population, by the early years of the twentieth century, by which time most of the capital was owned by the state (Table 4.1). In Denmark, the first line was built by private enterprise in 1847 from Copenhagen to Roskilde, but in 1861 the Parliament approved state construction of lines that connected the largest cities and regions with European markets. Interestingly, in some cases the operation of the trains was franchised to private companies. Some of the privately run lines, like the Odense–Svenbrg Banen, were highly profitable, but in other instances the state bought up shares of companies who were increasingly subsidised towards the end of the century.[44]

Thus the argument so far is that the state took over when there seemed to be no subsidy system that would induce the private sector to operate the lines in question or build and operate them quickly enough. In Spain, the strategic considerations were not as decisive, and the government simply relied on subsidies, which were less of a problem in the closing stages of the century as political and budgetary stability followed the restoration of the Bourbon monarchy in 1875.[45] The subsidy system was never enough to secure the urgent demands of the Italians for unification. We have already noted how there was state ownership in Piedmont, Sicily and Calabria. From the late 1860s onwards the new national government pressed ahead with rail construction to ensure it had a joined-up network and to promote economic links between the south and the rest of Italy. During a fiscal crisis in 1865, some of the state-owned lines in Liguria, Campania and Piedmont had to be relinquished, and the system changed to one of subsidising private companies. However, even with subsidies, these lines did not prove viable and, by a law of 1885, the state took over complete responsibility for the entire network, leading eventually to nationalisation of a large part of it in 1905.[46] Fenoaltea's research raises doubts about whether there were any significant economic benefits from the trunk network. By 1913 there were 1900 km of track, which, relative to area, was a denser network than Spain (Table 4.1). The railways provided a good market for Terni steel and helped machine and metal manufacture, but Fenoaltea argues that it did not 'lead to' industrialisation as some had argued nor was its growth at all indicative of the importance of banks as Gershenkron would have it.[47] There was a boom in the construction of trunk lines in the 1860s and of secondary lines in the 1880s, but these surges could not have been the cause of industrial growth in the 1880s. There is no evidence either that the trunk lines integrated the south economically. 'The trunk lines built in the immediate aftermath of unification seem to have done little to lower transport costs ... their cost had to be justified at least as much by military and strategic benefits'.[48] By 1906, 77% of track was in public ownership. The trunk lines plus the non-trunk lines in the south proved to be the most unprofitable parts of the system.

In turning finally to Germany, we have something of a paradox. In Prussia in the early part of the century there was, as we have seen, a very liberal attitude taken to the granting of charters, and private enterprise was allowed to flourish. By the early years of the twentieth century, the proportion of rail track in state ownership was larger than in any other country – larger even than in Belgium (see also Table 4.1). Of course, the hotchpotch of German states and boundaries before 1870 meant that political factors were ever present, and in the 1840s some of the smaller states like Bavaria and Würtemburg took over their railways, reflecting the strong need for a quick resolution of their strategic needs; so also in Hanover, where every line was bought out by the state prior to its annexation by Prussia in 1866. In the 1870s, Prussia, like France, became more and more conscious of the strategic role of the railways. An important factor was the rapprochement between Russia and France, which raised for Prussia the prospect of wars on two fronts, and one of the main features of the 1870–1914 period was the considerable expansion of track in eastern Prussia.[49] In 1879, the railways were nationalised, and 92% of all German track was in state ownership by 1906.

Why did Germany not opt for subsidies like France? They had been used before and there were still great chunks of track to be constructed and for which the optimal routes on economic grounds could be considered. Some contemporaries in the 1870s expected economies of scale from nationalisation, but why this should have been more important in Germany is not clear.[50] It has also been argued that the railways were operated as cash cows by some of the German states. These revenues were useful but sometimes quite modest. The Royal Hanoverian Railway Company generated revenue of the order of 4.2% of the state budget in 1849/50; for the Electorate of Hesse it was 3.7% in 1850.[51] Big money was, however, involved in Prussia, and Fremdling puts a strong case for the role of railway profits as a non-tax revenue for the state.[52] In the period 1880–1913 the railways' rate of return on capital was in the range 5% to 7%, well above the rate on government bonds – 3.4% to 3.9%. The railways' operating surplus net of investment outlays varied from 60% to 190% of the Prussian state's tax revenue. For Bismarck this was an immensely important non-tax revenue, which did not need the approval of the legislature. Its size on the eve of nationalisation in the 1870s was, however, not expected to be anything like the amounts that accrued later and cannot have been wholly decisive in prompting nationalisation, even if it subsequently proved a strong disincentive for privatisation.[53] Many contemporaries also thought nationalisation might relieve some of the problems associated with the rate structure.[54] There were constant complaints of complex rate structures and price discrimination, which hit German industry and agriculture. The eastern Junkers, for example, complained about the 'penetration rates' that allowed Russian grain imports to move easily through Germany.[55] But complaints like these were common throughout Europe in the second half of the nineteenth century. The opening up of European markets, by rail and steam ship, to the cereal farms of the prairies in USA and Canada and of the Russian steppes, made for a huge increase in food supplies on world markets and a fall in food prices. In Britain, farmers protested at the low freight rates offered by the railway companies to importers of American meat, transferring their shipments from Liverpool by rail across England. This undercut the shipping journey by sea but often implied a lower rail freight rate than was being offered to farmers in, for example, Cheshire. French hops were imported through Folkestone and took advantage of cheap rail rates to London, again to undercut those shipping direct by sea from France to London.[56] Why should this cause nationalisation in Prussia and not elsewhere?

In Germany, the shift to state ownership in the decades from the 1870s reflected a strong desire to exercise direct control over the railway system, analogous to that exercised over the post and telegraph and, as we shall see later, the telephone. 'Under Moltke, [Prussia's] War Staff thoroughly understood what use the army could make of a properly controlled railway system.'[57] There was a huge expansion in the track, doubling between 1880 and 1913, and in absolute terms the increase in rail kilometres exceeded that of France and Britain combined. By 1913, Germany had over 60000 km of track open. In terms of area covered, Germany was more densely settled by track than was France (Table 4.1). More pointedly, 'the German through routes were much further advanced than in France'.[58] It was not only the control of the configuration of routes, but also control over train operations that was regarded as important. American scholars like Keller have observed that, in general, regulation of industry and the infrastructure in Germany was by administrative means rather than by the legal system and acts of Congress as in the USA. The railways in Germany came to be regulated not by the law, but as part of the administrative state.[59] Railway directors were often army generals, and there was no trade union or comparable labour movement. As Sombart said, 'Post and railways were only the civil sections of the army'.[60]

Notes

1 R. E. Cameron, *France and the Economic Development of Europe 1880–1914: Conquests of Peace and Seeds of War* (Princeton University Press, 1961), 285, n. 2.
2 F. Caron, 'The Evolution of the Technical System of Railways in France', in R. Maintz and T. P. Hughes (eds.), *The Development of Large Technical Systems* (Boulder, Colo.: Frankfurt and Westview Press, 1978), pp. 69–73; K. Doukas, *The French Railroads and the State* (New York: Columbia Press, 1945).
3 R. Fremdling, 'The Prussian and Dutch Railway Regulaton in the 19th Century', in L. Andersson-Skog and O. Krantz (eds.), *Institutions and the Transport and Communications Industries* (Canton, Mass.: Science History Publications, Watson, 1999), 61–92. On the King and the Diet, see R. Tilly, 'The Political Economy of Public Finance and Prussian Industrialisation 1815–60', *Journal of Economic History* 26 (1966), 484–97.

4 J. Nadal, 'Spain 1830–1914', in C. Cipolla (ed.), *Fontana Economic History of Europe: The Emergence of Industrial Societies*, 2 parts (Glasgow: Fontana/Collins, 1973), part 2, pp. 532–626; G. Tortella, *The Development of Modern Spain* (Cambridge, Mass.: Harvard University Press, 2000), ch. 5.

5 A. Giuntini, 'Inland Navigation in Italy in the 19th Century', in A. Kunz and J. Armstrong (eds.), *Inland Navigation and Economic Development in 19th Century Europe* (Mainz: Verlag Philipp von Zabem, 1995), 147–57. In the same volume, A. Gomez-Mendoza, 'Europe's Cinderella: Inland Navigation in 19th Century Spain', 131–45.

6 Nadal, 'Spain 1830–1914'. See also R. J. Harrison, *An Economic History of Modern Spain* (Manchester University Press, 1978).

7 Cameron, *France and Economic Development*, 258.

8 Ibid., 251.

9 Ibid., 297.

10 B. R. Mitchell, 'The Coming of the Railway and UK economic growth', *Journal of Economic History* 24 (1964), 315–36.

11 F. J. Orellana quoted in Nadal, 'Spain 1830–1914', 552.

12 S. Fenoaltea, 'Italy', in P. O'Brien (ed.), *Railways and the Economic Development of Europe* (Oxford: Macmillan, 1983), 48–120.

13 L. Cafagna, 'Italy 1830–1914', in Cipolla (ed.), *The Emergence of Industrial Societies*, part 1, 279–328.

14 Nadal, 'Spain 1830–1914' and A. S. Milward and S. B. Saul, *The Development of the Economies of Continental Europe 1850–1914* (Cambridge, Mass.: Harvard University Press, 1977), ch. 4. For a pessimistic view of railways in Portugal, see J. Confraria, 'Portugal: Industrialisation and Backwardness', in J. Foreman-Peck and G. Federico (eds.), *European Industrial Policy: The Twentieth Century Experience* (Oxford University Press, 1999), 268–94.

15 A. Gomez-Mendoza, 'Spain', in P. O'Brien (ed.), *Transport and the Economic Development of Europe* (Oxford: Macmillan, 1983), 148–69.

16 Cameron, *France and Economic Development*, p. 297.

17 Quoted in V. Zamagni, *The Economic History of Italy 1860–1990* (Oxford: Clarendon Press, 1993), 162. See also A. Schram, *Railways and the State in the 19th Century* (Cambridge University Press, 1997) and A. Wingate, 'Railway Building in Italy before Unification', Centre for the Advanced Study of Italian Society, Occasional Papers no. 3, University of Reading, Department of Italian Studies, 1970.

18 J. Foreman-Peck, 'L' Etat et le développement du réseau de télécommunications en Europe à ses débuts', *Histoire, Economie, Société* 4 (1989), 383–402.

19 J. Attali and Y. Stowdze, 'The Birth of the Telephone and Economic Crisis: The Slow Development of Monologue in French Society', in I. de Sola Pool (ed.), *The Social Impact of the Telephone* (Cambridge, Mass.: MIT Press, 1977), 97–111.

20 J. Foreman-Peck and R. Millward, *Public and Private Ownership of British Industry 1820–1990* (Oxford University Press, 1994), 54.

21 Attali and Stowdze, 'The Birth of the Telephone'.

22 J. M. Bauer and M. Latzer, 'Telecommunications in Austria', in J. Foreman-Peck and J. Mueller (eds.), *European Telecommunications Organisation* (Baden-Baden: Nomosverlagsgesellschaft, 1988), 53–85. L. Andersson-Skog, 'The

Making of the National Telephone Networks in Scandinavia: The State and the Emergence of National Regulatory Patterns 1880–1920', in L. Magnusson and J. Ottoson (eds.), *Evolutionary Economics and Path Dependence* (Cheltenham, UK: Edward Elgar, 1996), 138–54; L. Andersson-Skog, 'Political Economy and Institutional Diffusion. The Case of the Swedish Railways and Telecommunications up to 1950', in Andersson-Skog and Krantz (eds.), *Institutions and the Transport and Communications Industries*, 245–66.

23 J. Foreman-Peck, 'Competition, Cooperation and Nationalisation in the Early Telegraph Network', *Business History* 31(3) (1989), 81.

24 Foreman-Peck, 'L' Etat et le développement du réseau de télécommunications'.

25 J.-P. Dormois, 'France: The Idiosyncrasies of *Voluntarisme*', in Foreman-Peck and Federico (eds.), *European Industrial Policy*, 64.

26 Doukas, *French Railroads and the State*, 37, 52.

27 Ibid., 41.

28 Ibid., 25.

29 J. H. Clapham, *The Economic Development of France and Germany 1815–1914* (Cambridge University Press, 1921), 340–1.

30 Doukas, *French Railroads and the State*, 45.

31 Ibid., 52.

32 Ibid., 55.

33 Caron, 'Evolution of the Technical System in France', 91.

34 R. W. Rawson, 'On Railways in Belgium', *Journal of the Royal Statistical Society of London* 2 (1839), 47.

35 Ibid., 48.

36 Cameron, *France and the Economic Development of Europe*, 208.

37 M. Laffut, 'Belgium', in O'Brien (ed.), *Railways and the Economic Development of Europe*, 203–26. See also G. Kurgen van Hentenryk, 'Les Chemins de fer belges ou les ambiguités de l'entreprise publiques en économie capitaliste au XIX siècle', in V. Zamagni (ed.), *Origins and Development of Publicly Owned Enterprises* (Bern: Ninth International Economic History Conference, Section B111, 1987), 47–53.

38 L.-E. Hedin, 'Some Notes on the Financing of the Swedish Railways 1860–1914', *Economy and History* 10 (1967), 3–37; E. F. Soderlund, 'The Placing of the First Swedish Railway Loan', *Scandinavian Economic History Review* 11 (1963), 43–59.

39 L. Andersson-Skog, 'Swedish Railways and Telecommunications' and 'National Patterns in the Regulation of Railways and Telephony in the Nordic Countries to 1950', *Scandinavian Economic History Review* 47(2) (2000), 30–46.

40 L. Andersson-Skog, 'From State Railway Housekeeping to Railway Economics: Swedish Railway Policy and Economic Transformation after 1920 in an Institutional Perspective', *Scandinavian Economic History Review* 49 (1996), 28.

41 Hedin, 'Some Notes on the Swedish Railways'.

42 T. Pettersson, 'Institutional Rigidity and Economic Change: A Comparison between Swedish Transport Subsidies', in Andersson-Skog and Krantz (eds.), *Institutions and the Transport and Communications Industries*, 281–300.

43 Andersson-Skog, 'From State Railway Housekeeping to Railway Economics', 28.

44 Andersson-Skog, 'National Patterns'.

45 Nadal, 'Spain 1830–1914'.

46 G. Federico and R. Giannetti, 'Italy: Stalling and Surpassing', in Foreman-Peck and Federico (eds.), *European Industrial Policy*, 125; Zamagni, *Economic History of Italy*, p. 163.

47 Fenoaltea, 'Italy'; A. Gershenkron, *Economic Backwardness in Historical Perspective* (Cambridge, Mass., Harvard University Press, 1967).

48 Fenoaltea, 'Italy', 94.

49 U. Wengenroth, 'The Rise and Fall of State Owned Enterprise in Germany', in P. A. Toninelli (ed.), *The Rise and Fall of State Owned Enterprise in the Western World* (Cambridge University Press, 2000), 106; C. W. Heinze and H. K. Kill, 'The Development of the German Railroad System', in Maintz and Hughes (eds.), *Large Technical Systems*, pp. 105–34.

50 R. Fremdling, 'Freight Rates and the State Budget: The Role of the Nationalised Prussian Railways 1880–1913', *Journal of European Economic History* 9 (1980), 25.

51 J. C. Bongaerts, 'Financing Railways in the German States 1840–60: A Preliminary View', *Journal of European Economic History* 14 (1985), 331–45.

52 Fremdling, 'Freight Rates and the State Budget'; Fremdling, 'The Prussian and Dutch Railways', 80. See also R. Fremdling and G. Knieps, 'Competition, Regulation and Nationalisation: The Prussian Railway System in the 19th Century', *Scandinavian Economic History Review* 41 (1993), 129–54, and Foreman-Peck and Federico (eds.), *European Industrial Policy*, 432.

53 Fremdling, 'Freight Rates and the State Budget', 21; D. E. Schremmer, 'Taxation and Public Finance: Britain, France and Germany', in P. Mathias and S. Pollard (eds.), *Cambridge Economic History of Europe. VIII. The Industrial Economies: The Development of Economic and Social Policy* (Cambridge University Press, 1989), 456–7.

54 Fremdling, 'Freight Rates and the State Budget', 23–4.

55 J. H. Clapham, *The Economic Development of France and Germany 1815–1914* (Cambridge University Press, 1921), 347.

56 P. J. Cain, 'Private Enterprise or Public Utility? Output, Pricing and Investment in English Railways', *Journal of Transport History* 1 (1973), 9–28; G. R. Hawke, 'Pricing Policy of Railways in England and Wales before 1881', in M. C. Reed (ed.), *Railways in the Victorian Economy: Studies in Finance and Economic Growth* (Newton Abbott: David and Charles, 1969), 76–110.

57 Clapham, *France and Germany*, 155.

58 Ibid., 151.

59 M. Keller, 'Public Policy and Large Enterprises: Comparative Historical Perspective', in N. Horn and K. Kocka (eds.), *Recht und Entwicklung der Grossunternehmen im 19. und frühen 20. Jahrhundert* (Göttingen: Vandenhoeck and Ruprecht, 1979), 515–34. See also in the same volume, D. Vagts, 'Railroads, Private Enterprise and Public Policy – Germany and the Unter State', 604–17.

60 Clapham, *France and Germany*, 349.

5 Electricity supply, tramways and new regulatory regimes c. 1870–1914

As a new resource, electricity was in competition with gas for lighting, but it never achieved any dominance before the First World War. It was more adaptable and successful as a source of power and in the form of hydro-electricity relaxed a major energy constraint in countries like Sweden, Norway, Spain and Italy, namely their dependency on coal supplies. Initially, the networks were limited spatially, so the economic organisation of electricity had many of the features found in gas supply, and local government was critically involved. There were differences and they arose firstly from the strong role played by manufacturers of electrical equipment like turbines, generators and tramcars. Such companies produced large quantities of electricity for their own usage and were often closely involved in contracts with town councils for electricity supply and tramways. In Germany, for example, 'big manufacturing industry' preferred to generate its own supplies, and it was not until the 1920s, with the development of transmission grids, that utility supplies of electricity came to exceed industry's own production of electricity.[1] A second feature was the desire of both local and central government for tighter regulation of fares, tariffs, rates, supply conditions and environmental effects, experienced as many of them were from dealings with the railways, gas and water companies.

Electricity supplies started in the 1870s but the main initial spurt came in the 1880s and 1890s. Most undertakings that were selling electricity were vertically integrated concerns engaged in generation, transmission and distribution. The capacity of coal-fired generating stations was determined largely by peak demand during the year, since electricity could not be stored, and with, initially, transport limited to small distances, the networks were essentially local, rather than regional or national. This was also true of the early hydroelectricity schemes. The private sector was dominant in most countries in the initial stages for two reasons. The first was a repeat of the experience of all nineteenth-century utilities, namely that initial uncertainties persuaded most governments to leave development to the private sector. It was a new product but with competing interests in town councils with municipal gas supply.[2] Publicly available supplies of electricity spread very rapidly in the 1880s and 1890s. Even in Spain and Italy, where consumption per head was relatively low, in part because of very high tariffs, the number of connections was large. The first public supply in Italy was by the Edison company in Milan in 1883, and in Spain it was in Barcelona by the Sociedad Español de Electricidad.[3] By the 1890s, all Andalousian towns had public electric lighting.[4] Electrification of tramways started in Spain in 1896, and the undertakings were financially controlled by foreign, often Belgian, companies.[5] The very high level of self-consumption reinforced this early role for the private sector by the electrical equipment manufacturers. In 1898, there were 2286 electricity 'installations' in Italy, of which 80% were for self-consumption by manufacturing firms.[6] In France, firms like Thomas Houston found the manufacture of equipment more profitable than distributing electricity supply and operating trams, but the strategic position of such firms made for a heavy involvement of the private sector.

Thereafter, as long as technology continued to favour small networks, the municipalities started to take over. In Denmark, as for gas, the urban areas were often served by municipally owned enterprises and the rural areas by co-operatives. Municipalisation also developed strongly, again as for gas, in Germany and Britain. The trend was weakest in sectors where local government was weak. France relied heavily on the concession system. Although municipal management of electricity could be found in Grenoble from 1882, St Etienne from 1890 and Tourcois from 1900, these were exceptions. In Belgium, publicly owned undertakings accounted for only 2% of electricity supplies in 1914.[7] There were few municipal works in Spain, where the municipalities were short of capital,[8] whilst in Italy, despite the large municipal works in Turin, Milan and Merano, municipalities in this period generally lacked 'technical knowledge, entrepreneurship and professional personnel'.[9] In contrast, London, from 1894, had an integrated local government, which included twenty metropolitan boroughs, most of which owned electricity works, whilst London County Council developed its own tramways. There were 39 municipal electricity enterprises in the UK in 1895 and this shot up to 164 by 1900; in the same period the number of municipal tramways rose from 38 to 99.[10] As Table 5.1 shows, by the early 1900s municipal enterprise accounted for 72% of all electricity supply undertakings and 56% of all tramways. Many of the private companies were in rural areas where, as for gas, the boundaries of local government units were not conducive to the development of utilities. A similar pattern emerged in Germany, where by 1908 forty-two out of the fifty largest town councils had their own electricity supply and twenty-three their own tramways.

Table 5.1 *Electricity supply and trams, 1898–1920*

	UK	Denmark	France	Germany	Sweden	Italy	Norway	Spain	USA
(1) 1920 electricity supplied in kWh per head of pop.	154	97	149	246	441	110	2304	47	531
(2) Percentage of electricity supply undertakings municipally owned 1900–18	71.6 (1900)	15.4[a] (1905)	2.0[b] (1900)	17.9[c] (1908)	3.7[d]	10[e]	80.0 (1918)	10.0[f] (1900)	13.1[g]
(3) Percentage of electricity supply undertakings in 50 largest towns municipally owned in 1908–9	88.0	31.2[h]	2.0[b]	84.0					
(4) Electric Tramway track km per 1 mill. pop. 1898	5.9[j]		12.6	25.8		4.5		5.7	
1905	84[i]	58[j]	51	56					599[i]
(5) Percentage of tramway undertakings municipally owned in 1905	56.2	0[h]	2.0	3.4[b]				5.0[l]	2.0[m]
(6) Percentage of tramway undertakings in 50 largest towns municipally owned in 1908–9	84.0	0[k]	2.0[b]	46.0					

Notes:

[a] Information supplied by O. Hyldtoft. Sixteen electricity works in towns of which five were municipal; twenty-six in countryside, one owned by the state, the rest private.

[b] Estimates based on the claim that municipal management of electricity 'fut exceptionelle' and that 'ce genre d'institution ne se développe que très peu en France' (Caron and Cardot (eds.), *Histoire générale de l'électricité en France. I. 1881–1918: Espoirs et conquêtes* (Paris: L'Association pour

L'Historie de L'Electricité en France, Fayard, 1991), 299 and 399). See also A. Fernandez, 'Les Lumières de la ville: L'Administration municipale à l'épreuve de l'électrification', *Vingtième Siècles Revue d'Histoire* 62 (1999), 115.

[c] Related to 2309 urban districts. Note that R. Messager states that 47.3% of electric power in 1913 in Germany was supplied by plant entirely owned by municipal undertakings. 26.7% by mixed enterprises and the rest (20%) by private companies. According to Kuhl, the proportion of works that were municipally owned fell by over a quarter 1897–1913, whilst their share of output rose from 31% to 37%. See 'Municipalities and Managers: Heat Networks in Germany', in J. A. Tarr and G. Dupuy (eds.), *Technology and the Rise of the Networked City in Europe* (Philadelphia: Temple University Press, 1988), 288; U. Kuhl, 'Le Débat sur le socialisme municipal en allemagne avant 1914 et la municipalisation de l'électricité', in U. Kuhl (ed.), *Der Munizipalsozialismus in Europa* (Munich: Oldenberg Verlag, 2002), 94.

[d] Based on Kaijser's statement that one third of all Swedish output was produced by the State Power Board in 1920 (A. Kaijser, 'Controlling the Grid: The Development of High Tension Power Lines in the Nordic Countries', in A. Kaijser and M. Hedin (eds.), *Nordic Energy Systems: Historical Perspectives and Current Issues* (Canton, Mass.: Science History Publications, 1995), 34). A further 4% has been added for the urban municipalities.

[e] Municipal undertakings in Italy produced 0.7 gigawatt hours in 1928, that is, 8% of the 8.74 gWh total, whilst a further 2% is assumed to have been produced by the state railways. These proportions are assumed to hold for the pre-1914 period (A. Schiavi, 'Municipal Services in Italy', *Annals of Collective Economy* 5 (1929), 35; G. Galasso (ed.), *Storia dell'industria elettrica in italia. III. Expansiove e oligopolio. 1926–45* (Roma-Bari: Laterza & Figli, 1993), 1236; M. Einaudi, M. Byé and E. Rossi, *Nationalisation in France and Italy* (Ithaca, N. Y.: Cornell University Press, 1955), 223).

[f] Estimate based on Antolin's view that the few municipal electricity supply undertakings that existed in the late nineteenth century disappeared or restricted themselves to distribution on the advent of hydroelectricity (F. Antolin, 'Public Policy in the Development of the Spanish Electric Utility Industry', Paper presented at European Historical Economics Society Conference on *A Century of Industrial Policy in Europe*, Oxford, Worcester College, 1992, 20).

[g] Based on Keller's summary, 'only 193 out of 1471 urban electricity systems were publicly owned. Almost all municipal transit was privately owned' (M. Keller, *Regulation and the New Economy: Public Policy and Economic Change in America 1900–1933* (Cambridge, Mass.: Harvard University Press, 1990), 56).

[h] 5 out of 16 towns.

[i] For 1898 the UK figure relates to Britain. For 1905 the UK figure includes light railways and the US figure relates to 1903.

[j] The Danish data were based on information supplied by O. Hyldtoft that 90.4 km were in operation in Copenhagen in 1905 and that the only other town with track was Aarhus. If the total was 150 km and the Danish population was 2.56 million, track per million pop. was 58.

[k] Information from O. Hyldtoft that there were tramway undertakings in Copenhagen and Aarhus, all private.

[l] Relates to 2309 urban districts in Germany in 1908.

[m] Estimate based on Nunez's description of the dominance of the private companies (G. Nunez, 'Spanish Cities in a Forgotten Modernising Process', in M. Morner and G. Tostella (eds.), *Different Paths to Modernisation* (University of Lund, forthcoming), 6/7).

Sources to Table 5.1 (*cont.*)

Sources by row:

(1) Electricity supply quantities from B. R. Mitchell, *International Historical Statistics: Europe 1750–1993* (London: Macmillan, 3rd edn, 1998). US data from B. R. Mitchell, *International Historical Statistics: The Americas: 1750–1993* (London: Macmillan, 4th edn, 1998). Population data from A. Maddison, *Dynamic Forces in Capitalist Development* (Oxford University Press, 1991). Population for Spain and Britain interpolated from census data in Mitchell, *International Historical Statistics: Europe 1750–1993*.

(2), (3), (5), (6) See Table 2.1.

(4) Tramways kilometre data from J. P. Mackay, *Tramways and Trolleys: The Rise of Urban Transport in Europe* (Princeton University Press, 1976), Tables 5 and 7 and pp. 50–82. Danish data from O. Hyldtoft based on *Statistiske oplysninger om Kepenhavn og Fredericksberg 1903–77* (1908), 110.

The smaller towns and rural areas were largely private; only 413 out of 2309 urban districts had municipally owned electricity supplies and only 18% their own tramways. Access to the trading profits of such enterprises seems again to have been a potent factor. In the towns in 1910/11 with populations of 50000 or more, the transfer of trading profits from municipally owned electricity supply undertakings worked out at 2s 3d per head of population; for tramways it was 10d. The comparable figures for Britain were 3d and 9d.[11]

Again, however, even in Germany a large powerful town council such as that in Berlin could so contract with concessionaires to accumulate profits in the same way as other councils did with their own undertakings. Both electricity and tramways in Berlin were developed by subsidiaries of a leading manufacturer of electrical equipment. In 1883, the Siemen and Hawke company helped to found Deutsche Edison Gesellschaft, which held Edison patents and which came to an agreement in 1884 with the Berlin town council about the supply of electricity. The council was to monitor tariffs, to receive 10% of gross income and 25% of any profits after payment of a 6% dividend to shareholders. The concession was for thirty years – the council could take over earlier, though at a punitive price. Hughes argued that the council did not municipalise the works because electricity was then a speculative venture, but this does not sit well with the fact that other German towns like Mainz, Mannheim and Darmstadt developed their municipal electricity works confident of earning a profit for their council.[12] Perhaps the issue was rather that the big town councils had enough strength to bargain with the large equipment manufacturers. In the next few years Deutsche Edison Gesellschaft had metamorphosed into Allgemeine Elektrizitäts-Gesellschaft which, in turn, founded the Berliner Elektrizitäts-Werke in 1887.[13] Two years later, a new contract was arranged with even better conditions for the town council, including a 50% share in profits after dividends. On the other hand, the power of Berliner Elektrizitäts-Werke was such that it was able to secure that all tramway franchisees, such as the Berlin Tramways Company, would buy electricity from Berliner Elektrizitäts-Werke. The industrial load together with tramways were the main consumers of the output of Berliner Elektrizitäts-Werke, since domestic lighting was still dominated by gas. Eventually negotiations between the council and the owner of Berliner Elektrizitäts-Werke, Allgemeine Elektrizitäts-Gesellschaft, led to a municipal takeover in 1915, but for all the pre-war period this was essentially a concession system which delivered revenues for the town council.

The regulatory regimes for electricity and tramways were tougher than the ones established earlier for gas, water and railways. Some contemporary

American scholars like Hugo Meyer argued that regulation, together with municipal ownership, slowed development.[14] Municipal ownership in Germany and Britain was, however, restricted, as we have seen, to the larger towns and cannot account for the big contrasts in the scale of development in different parts of Europe. The impact of the early cables and tramway lines in many of Europe's winding streets was perhaps environmentally more damaging than in the USA, where the city councils, in any case, appear not to have attached the same weight to such considerations.[15] Electricity output per head of population in Europe was well below that in the USA, even as late as 1920 (cf. Table 5.1). On the other hand, the European countries, and especially Britain, Denmark and Germany, were well endowed with gas supplies (cf. Table 3.1) so that the attraction of electricity was less. The development of electric tramways was also slow by American standards. By 1898 there were only 6 km of track per one million population in Britain and 13 km in France. The situation had markedly improved by as early as 1905, but, as Table 5.1 shows, the USA was in a completely different ball game.

In the case of France, its coal supplies were poor and it urbanised very slowly – in 1902 there was still only one fifth of the population in towns of over 20000. With all these qualifications it is nevertheless the case that the regulatory regime in France and elsewhere in Europe may have had some deleterious effect. The regulatory regime in France was tough. Initially the concession periods were very short, and in 1887 there were only seven public electricity systems (and none in Paris) with total output only one third of Germany.[16] Even by 1889, the six concessionaire companies in Paris were on eighteen-year leases. At Le Havre the leases were only for five years, and even the cables had to be submitted for the approval of the mayor.[17] The regulatory regime in the UK was set out in the 1882 Electric Lighting Act and the 1870 Tramways Act. Apart from controlling tariffs and guarding the interests of highway authorities and frontagers (like shopkeepers), the sting was in clauses that allowed takeovers by the town councils after twenty-one years. Since many of the franchises were coming to fruition in the 1890s when the switch from horse-drawn trams was just taking off, investment was inhibited.[18] The horse-drawn tramways had developed strongly from the 1850s and especially from the 1870s as the world price of fodder fell. In Paris, there were six horse-drawn omnibus companies in the early 1850s, but in 1855 the Compagnie Général d'Omnibus (linked to the Pereire financial empire) was awarded a fifty-year concession, and horse-drawn trams flourished, although there were criticisms that they kept to the most profitable routes.[19] By the 1890s, electric trams were operating in many large towns throughout Europe – Turin in 1891, Düsseldorf in 1892, parts of

Tuscany later. By 1896, however, in France only 2.5% of the tram network was electric. The main operators were equipment manufacturers like Thomas Houston, which was one of ten companies granted concessions in Paris in 1899 after that of the Compagnie Général d'Omnibus had been revoked.[20] Fares and routes had been closely regulated from the 1890s. Even in Germany, which exhibited the fastest growth, regulation and profit-sharing have been viewed by some writers as retarding development. Hugo Meyer was especially critical of the contracts in Berlin, which included what he classed as unrealistic requirements for road maintenance, free travel for some employees and the ability of the town council to take over after forty years.[21] The Berlin Tramways Company paid 8% of its gross receipts over to the town council and, like Berliner Elektrizitäts-Werke, half of its profit in excess of a 6% return on capital. The elevated and underground railway companies were liable for 2% of gross revenues and, again, 50% of any excess profit.[22] Another American observer took a different stance. F. C. Howe suggested that 'regulation touches only the evil of over-capitalisation, excessive charges and obviously bad service. Private ownership does not permit the city to build in a far-sighted way.'[23]

In summary, the duration of franchises in some cases probably did have some inhibiting effects on the initial development of electricity supply and tramways in the period 1880 to 1905, but it was in a context where development was very rapid. The stricter environmental regulation in Europe, whilst not allowing the even faster development witnessed in the USA, could be defended in economic terms. Major changes in economic organisation were to come when the development of transformers allowed transmission of electricity over longer distances and the development of regional and national grids. This was very much a story of the twentieth century and will be considered in detail in chapter 8. Long-distance lines were, however, emerging before the First World War, and nowhere was this more noticeable than in hydroelectricity (HEP). The year 1909 saw the completion of a 250 km line to Madrid, a European record.[24] Because HEP required access to waterfalls and rivers, it raised new issues and uncertainties, and in this respect was like the risky environment of a new infrastructure. Private enterprise therefore dominated, and this was reinforced by the high capital requirements and by the technical status of the designers of the equipment, reservoirs and generating plants. This new energy source provided a powerful boost to manufacturing, especially in Sweden, Norway and Italy, because it released them from heavy dependence on imported coal supplies and, in the case of Sweden and Norway, enabled them, as Table 5.1 shows, to achieve levels of electricity consumption per head well above those in Britain, France and Germany.

A thorny issue was the property right over watercourses, and government attitudes often affected the pace of development. The regulatory regime was very loose in Spain. Private enterprise was dominant, and most supplies came from a small number of regionally based companies. The firms who gained concessions were often those with a licence to import electrical equipment or to manufacture foreign company models in Spain. Spanish banks and entrepreneurs were heavily involved – as in the company Hydroelectrica Iberia – except for Catalonia where there were many foreign companies. Government regulation was so light that companies did not have any 'obligation to supply', so that capacity was often less than the demand emanating from connected consumers.[25] Although the number of connected consumers was high, consumption per head of population was amongst the lowest in Europe (Table 5.1). In Italy access to water supplies was facilitated by an 1894 law which 'granted power line easements analogous to those for aqueducts'.[26] Sixteen HEP plants were built in the period 1900–4 and a further twenty-seven in 1905–9 in the Alps and the Apennines. Banks were often involved with large private undertakings, like the Valdona Company, which promoted the development of electricity supply and tramways in Florence, Ligure and other parts of Tuscany. By 1913, Italy had a capacity of 1.15 million kW of which 70% was HEP and largely in the north. The first large HEP plant in the south was in 1905 and located near to Naples. It typified the pattern of HEP plants in this period in that they thrived only where there was an industrial customer nearby to absorb excess electricity supplies when the water supply was abundant.[27] Total Italian electricity output per head by the First World War was still behind Britain and France, and well below Germany.

Although the development of HEP was successful in both Sweden and Norway, the economic organisation of these infrastructures reflected key geographic differences. Norway had a great variety of waterfalls, large and small, spread through the country but often at high altitude, so that there was not much conflict with rural interests with respect to land, water property rights and water flows. There was no need for long transmission lines because of the wide spread of the suitable sites, and much of the development could remain local. Municipalities had a long tradition in Norway, as we have noted, and they were heavily involved, especially as regards supply for 'general consumption' – that is, non-industrial supplies to Norwegian cities; eighty-five out of eighty-eight electricity works involved in general consumption were municipally owned by 1918.[28] By 1918, 80% of all undertakings were still municipally owned (Table 5.1). In the case of HEP for power, a law of 1880 treated high waterfalls as private property, and this eased the entry of large private companies supplying manufacturing firms and inducing a buoyant export trade in nitrogen, aluminium, carbide and ferro alloys. Concessions were for sixty to eighty years, the rights and assets thereafter to accrue to the state. By 1909, the Norwegian government was asserting its rights over all water-falls with more than 1000 horsepower. The law was reinforced in 1917, and some observers have felt that this inhibited HEP development. Nonetheless, by then Norway was producing much more electricity per head of population than any other western European country (Table 5.1).[29]

In Sweden, in contrast, the waterfalls were less spread out, were at lower altitudes and intruded therefore much more into farming areas. The farming lobby was able to promote heavy state regulation. Moreover, the longer transmission distances meant heavy capital requirements. The 1880 Water Rights Decree restricted the variation in the levels of reservoir water and stream flow, and this appears to have slowed down HEP growth. On the other hand, during the 1900–10 period many joint stock companies were allowed to develop distribution networks, carrying electric power to industry and to local companies and municipalities for retail distribution. Tension between the state and the private sector came to a head in 1904–6 in the long-running dispute over the Trollhattan falls, which led to the establishment of the State Power Board (Vattenfall) in 1906 to manage that waterfall. Not until the passage of a law in 1918 were HEP producers able to encroach on waterfalls with relative freedom. Nevertheless, Sweden was, by 1920, producing 441 kWh per head of population (much of it retailed by municipalities linked to their respon-sibility for public lighting), and this was more than double the level in Britain, France and Germany (Table 5.1) and provided considerable support for the general industrial expansion in the period 1890–1914.[30]

Notes

1 H. Ott, 'History of Electricity in Germany', and U. Wengenroth, 'The Electrifi-cation of the Workshop', both in F. Cardot (ed.), *1880–1980: Une siècle de l'électricité dans le monde* (Paris: Presses Universitaires de France, 1987), 135–50, 357–66.

2 A. Fernandez, 'Production and Distribution of Electricity in Bordeaux, 1887–1956: Private and Public Operation', *Contemporary European History* 5(2) (1996), 159–70; A. Fernandez, 'Les Lumières de la ville: L'Administration municipale à l'épreuve de l'électrification', *Vingtième Siècle Revue d'Histoire* 62 (1999), 107–22; L. Magee, 'Electricity Railway Practice in Germany', *Street Railway Journal* 19 (1899), 647–62.

3 F. Antolin, 'Public Policy in the Development of the Spanish Electric Utility Industry', Paper presented at European Historical Economics Society Conference on *A Century of Industrial Policy in Europe*, Oxford, Worcester College, 1992.

4 G. Nunez, 'Développement et intégration régionale de l'industrie électrique en Andalousie jusqu'en 1935', in M. Trédé (ed.), *Electricité et électrification dans le monde 1880–1980* (Paris: Association pour l'Histoire de l'Electricité en France, Presses Universitaires de France, Paris, 1990), 169–201.

5 G. Nunez, 'Spanish Cities in a Forgotten Modernising Process', in M. Morner and G. Tortella (eds.), *Different Paths to Modernisation* (University of Lund, forthcoming), 7.

6 F. Conti, 'The Creation of a Regional Electrical System: Selt Valdarno Group and the Electrification of Tuscany', in Trédé (ed.), *Electricité et électrification dans le monde*, 155–68.

7 F. Caron and F. Cardot (eds.), *Histoire générale de l'électricité en France*. I. 1881–1918: *Espoirs et conquêtes* (Paris: L'Association pour l'Histoire de l'Electricité en France, Fayard, 1991), 399; G. Kurgen van Hentenryk, 'La Régime économique de l'industrie électrique belge depuis la fin du XIX siècle', in Cardot (ed.), *Une siècle de l'électricité*, Table 2.

8 Antolin, 'Public Policy' .

9 R. Balzani and A. Giuntini, 'Urban Infrastructure and the Hygiene Question in Liberal Italy (1880–1915)', Paper presented to International Economic History Congress, Madrid, 1998, 3. See also G. Galasso (ed.), *Storia dell' industria elettrica in Italia. III. Expansiove e oligopolio. 1926–45* (Roma-Bari: Laterza & Figli, 1993), 1257.

10 R. Millward, 'The Political Economy of Urban Utilities in Britain 1840–1950', in M. Daunton (ed.), *The Cambridge Urban History of Britain, III* (Cambridge University Press, 2000), 315–49.

11 W. H. Dawson, *Municipal Life and Local Government in Germany* (London: Longmans, Green and Co., 1916), 191.

12 T. P. Hughes, *Networks of Power: Electrification in Western Society 1880–1930* (Baltimore: Johns Hopkins Press, 1983), chapter on Berlin; D. Schott, 'Electrifying German Cities: Investment in Energy Technology and Public Transport and their Impact on Urban Development 1880–1914', Paper presented to International Economic History Conference, Madrid, 1998.

13 Hughes, *Networks of Power*, chapter on Berlin; B. C. Brooks, 'Municipalisation of the Berlin Electrical Works', *Quarterly Journal of Economics* 30 (1916), 188–94.

14 H. R. Meyer, 'Municipal Ownership in Germany', *Journal of Political Economy* 14 (1906), 553–67.

15 J. P. Mackay, *Tramways and Trolleys: The Rise of Urban Transport in Europe* (Princeton University Press, 1976); J. P. Mackay, 'Comparative Perspectives on Transit in Europe and the USA 1850–1914', in J. A. Tarr and G. Dupuy (eds.), *Technology and the Rise of the Networked City in Europe* (Philadelphia: Temple University Press, 1988), 3–21 and, in the same volume, A. Sutcliffe, 'Street Transport in the Second Half of the 19th Century: Mechanisation Delayed?', 22–39.

16 M. Levy-Leboyer, 'The French Electrical Power System: An Inter-Country Comparison', in R. Maintz and T. P. Hughes (eds.), *The Development of Large Technical Systems* (Boulder, Colo.: Frankfurt and Westview Press, 1978), 245–62.

17 Caron and Cardot (eds.), *Histoire générale de l'électricité en France*, 400. See also P. Lanthier, 'The Relationship between State and Private Electric Industry, France 1880–1920', in N. Horn and K. Kocka (eds.), *Recht und Entwicklung der Grossunternehmen im 19. und frühen 20. Jahrhundert* (Göttingen: Vandenhoeck and Ruprecht, 1979), 590–603.

18 L. Hannah, 'Public Policy and the Advent of Large Scale Industry: The Case of Electricity Supply in the U.S.A., Germany and Britain', in Horn and Kocka (eds.), *Recht und Entwicklung*, 577–89; V. Knox, 'The Economic Effects of the Tramways Act of 1870', *Economic Journal* 11 (1901), 492–510.

19 D. Larroque, 'Economic Aspects of Public Transit in the Parisian Area', in Tarr and Dupuy (eds.), *Technology and the Rise of the Networked City in Europe*, 40–66.

20 Larroque, 'Public Transit'.

21 Meyer, 'Municipal Ownership in Germany'.

22 Dawson, *Municipal Life in Germany*, 204.

23 F. Howe, *European Cities at Work* (New York: Charles Scribner's Sons, 1913), 179.

24 Antolin, 'Public Policy'.

25 Ibid. See also Nunez, 'Spanish Cities'; M. de Motes, ' L'Electricité, facteur de développement économique en Espagne: 1930–36', in Cardot (ed.), *Une siècle de l'électricité*, 57–67; P. F. Balbin, 'Spain: Industrial Policy under Authoritarian Politics', in J. Foreman-Peck and G. Federico (eds.), *European Industrial Policy: The Twentieth Century Experience* (Oxford University Press, 1999), 235, 245–6.

26 S. Fenoaltea, 'The Growth of the Utility Industries in Italy 1861–1913', *Journal of Economic History* 42 (1982), 615–16; R. Giannetti, 'Resources, Firms and Public Policy in the Growth of the Italian Electrical Industry from the Beginnings to the 1930s', in Cardot (ed.), *Une siècle de l'électricité*, 41–50, and, in the same volume, G. Bruno, 'L'Utilisation des resources hydroliques pour la production d'énergie électrique en Italie du Sud: 1895–1915', 44.

27 Conti, 'The Creation of a Regional Electrical System'.

28 L. Thue, 'The State and the Dual Structure of the Power Supply Industry in Norway, 1890–1940', in Trédé (ed.), *Electricité et électrification dans le monde*, p. 30.

29 See also B. R. Mitchell, *International Historical Statistics: Europe 1750–1993* (London: Macmillan, 3rd edn, 1998).

30 E. Jakobsson, 'Industrialised Rivers: The Development of Swedish Hydro-Power', in A. Kaijser and M. Hedin (eds.), *Nordic Energy Systems: Historical Perspectives and Current Issues* (Canton, Mass.: Science History Publications, 1995), 55–74; in the same volume A. Kaijser, 'Controlling the Grid: The Development of High Tension Power Lines in the Nordic Countries', 31–53; and also in the same volume, L. Thue, 'Electricity Rules: The Formation and Development of the Nordic Electricity Regions', 11–29.

Part III

Nations and Networks c. 1914–1945

6 Infrastructure development from the nineteenth to the twentieth century: an overall perspective

Two World Wars and the biggest depression of the twentieth century: these momentous events dominated the 1914–45 period, but did they have a lasting impact on the economic organisation of the infrastructure? How important were political and ideological factors? A common characterisation of the late 1940s is that it was a period where the apparent success of administrative planning during the Second World War and the rise of social democratic parties since the 1920s made for a massive spread of public ownership in the infrastructure industries and in some countries in manufacturing. Was it the case that the presence of a large number of public sector industries by the late 1940s reflected what the resistance movement in France (Conseil de Résistance) had demanded: the 'return to the nation of the great monopolies of the means of production'?[1] The thesis of the next few chapters is that long-term technological developments and economic problems were more important than all these factors and that there was a broad political consensus on the direction of change if not on the detail.

To put this in proper perspective, it is useful to start with a résumé of our findings from Part II with respect to the development of the infrastructure industries up to 1914. First of all is the proposition that in the nineteenth century there was no simple link between government intervention in the infrastructure industries and either the pace at which these industries developed in a particular country or the level of income per head in that country. Private enterprise was to be found extensively in countries like Britain with high income levels as well as in less developed countries like Spain and Italy. Municipal ownership was to be found in infrastructures that had grown strongly – Norwegian electricity, gas in Denmark and in large towns in Germany and Britain – as well as in some that, relatively, did not grow so quickly – tramways in Britain, telephone in France, gas in Sweden and Norway. Shipping was largely private but its development was high in Scandinavia and low in France and Germany, without any obvious connection with income levels. Private enterprise was common in some sectors that had developed strongly (railways in Britain and France) as well as in some where growth was relatively sluggish (gas and electricity in France, telephones in Spain). State ownership was common in all the telegraph and telephone systems, yet telephone development was very slow in France and very rapid in Sweden and Norway. In the Appendix, a statistical analysis is undertaken of the effect on the level of infrastructure services of some of the likely determinants identified so far in this book: income levels, population density, military spending, coal resources and public ownership. Three sectors (railways, gas and telephones) are examined for a cross section of European countries in the early 1900s. The penetration levels (rail track, gas supplies etc. all expressed per head of population) showed significant statistical association only with GDP per head, but otherwise no simple links emerged. In particular, there are no obvious deleterious effects of public ownership on the spread of railways, the volume of gas supplies or the penetration rates for telephones.

A second conclusion from Part II is that government ownership in the nineteenth century was not strongly associated with the kind of ideological positions found in twentieth-century Europe. On the one hand state ownership was not based on any strong distrust of capitalism, but rather on more pragmatic matters like the control of information flows, speeding up the construction work, ensuring social and political unification. On the other hand, municipal socialism as an ideology cannot account for the main initial surge of municipalisation that occurred for gas and water in the period 1850–70 and electricity and trams from the 1880s, predating the debates on municipal socialism in the 1890–1914 period.

The key to understanding the initial forging of links between governments and infrastructure industries is *rights of way*, but they brought government intervention in the form of arm's length regulation of prices, routes, finances and engineering conditions. Similarly, government attempts to promote economic growth took the form of interest guarantees and route subsidies. None of this implied state or municipal ownership or management. In gas supply, electricity and trams it did, however, become common in the nineteenth century. Municipal enterprises flourished most strongly when they were used as cash cows, so that municipalisation was common in rapidly growing urban areas and where profit transfers to finance public health programmes were welcomed by middle-class councils as a form of non-tax revenues, which had the virtue of not requiring approval by the legislature. Private enterprise was dominant in the early growth of all new networks when risks were high and in settings like Spain and Italy where coal supplies were limited. It remained dominant where municipal government was fragmented or weak or had limited powers as in London, Belgium, Spain, France and rural areas generally. Where the local community was wealthy or was growing only slowly there was neither a need for large sanitary and housing investments nor a shortage of funds so that tax sources were not stretched. Finally, when the local council was able to secure a share in the profits of gas or electricity undertakings, without having to take them over (as in Copenhagen, Berlin and Paris), here again there were no pressures for municipalisation.

When therefore state ownership was chosen in the nineteenth century, it was in a context where interest guarantees and subsidies were common. Central governments were interested in connecting disparate regions by cultural and physical links and also in having infrastructures that facilitated the despatch of troops, messages and military supplies. Both objectives could be achieved by the use of subsidies, but state ownership had to be used when speed in the construction of the infrastructure was required (the trunk railways in Belgium in the 1830s, in the southern German states in the 1840s, in Sweden in the 1850s, in Italy in the 1870s) or when the routes were so unprofitable that no subsidy could with credibility sustain a company (parts of France and Italy in the 1880–1913 period).

A final government interest in the alignment of routes and methods of operation arose from a desire to directly control information and the movement of people and goods. For this, state ownership was unavoidable and seems to explain the widespread state ownership of telecommunication systems and of the railways as part of the 'administered state' of Prussia in the period from 1870. One harbinger of an additional issue that would be common in the twentieth century was the telephone. On the one hand, there were significant economies of scale from having an integrated national network, which would have prompted tariff and/or profit regulation. On the other hand, social and political unification was important for many states, but the provision of telephones to the remotest parts of each country was likely to be unprofitable. Subsidies would be required. The dilemma of subsidising a regulated private monopoly may have been an additional ingredient in the nationalisation of telephone networks and of the other national networks that emerged in the twentieth century.

Wars and depression

The wars and depression of the 1914–45 period had significant short-term effects on national outputs though varying across countries as Figures 6.1 and 6.2 illustrate. Figure 6.1 includes three countries in the Western world that were less directly damaged by the depredations and destruction of the wars – the USA, Norway and Sweden. The UK and Denmark were more directly affected but, with relatively mature

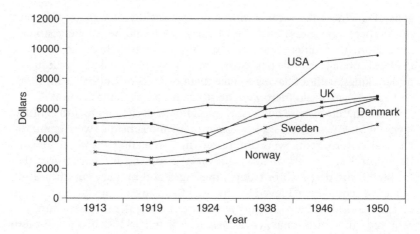

Figure 6.1 GDP per head 1913–1950 in UK, Scandinavia and USA (in 1990 dollars).

Source: A. Maddison, *Monitoring the World Economy 1820–1992* (Paris: Organisation for Economic Cooperation and Development, 1985).

economies, had the resilience and adaptability to shift resources away from traditional civilian uses without reducing aggregate output.[2] In fact the major depressing impact on UK aggregate output in this period was the loss of export markets in Europe, the Far East and South America in part as a product of the First World War, which gave openings for third parties like Japan and the USA as well as encouraging import substituting industrialisation in countries such as Poland and Spain. The UK was the only economy whose national output per head actually fell over the years 1919–24. The big effect of the Wall Street crash and the 1929–32 depression on the USA is reflected in its being the only country to record a fall in national income per head in the period 1924–38. These experiences may be contrasted with those of the western European country most affected by invasion, France, and of the two losers in the Second World War, Germany and Italy, and the other fascist government, Spain (Figure 6.2). Italy was extremely vulnerable because of its dependency on coal imports, and in World War I this was a keystone of Italy's diplomatic accord with Britain and the USA, who accounted for the bulk of its coal imports.[3] In the Second World War it was reliant on Germany, which had its own resource problems so that total Italian imports of energy declined, even when oil is included – at the end Italy had only Romania as a source.[4] Germany's maritime imperialism before and during the First World War

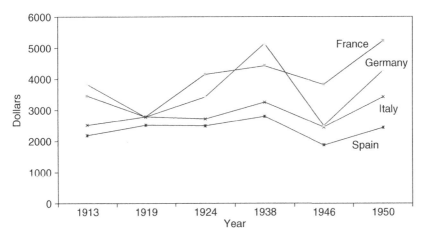

Figure 6.2 GDP per head 1913–1950 in France, Germany, Italy and Spain (in 1990 dollars).

Source: A. Maddison, *Monitoring the World Economy 1820–1992* (Paris: Organisation for Economic Cooperation and Development, 1985).

was a failure, and led to a shift of attention to eastern Europe as a source of raw materials and energy.[5]

Both World Wars had the potential for changing the economic organisation of the infrastructure industries. One factor was their use as tools of military operations. Most railway systems were placed under state control in the First World War, even in laissez-faire Britain, where the government was initially slow to react but later took direct control and fixed maximum profit levels for the railway companies.[6] In war, speed in the execution of orders and in allocating resources was vital, and the strong state controls in transport and communications were echoes of the state takeovers recorded in chapter 4 in Belgium in the 1830s, Sweden in the 1850s and Italy in the 1860s. Unfortunately, the powers and influence of the military were invariably such that fares, rates and tariffs were not allowed to keep up with rising costs, investment was minimal, equipment destroyed and most systems emerged from the wars with a run-down capital stock and huge debts. The other short-term effect of war was to highlight the strategic significance of certain key resources like coal, oil and other minerals, as well as chemical processes linked to the production of explosives. The British and French governments took an active part in developing these resources and in the search for new sources, a policy that continued into the 1920s.

Notwithstanding these two common factors, the policy aftermath of the Second World War was very different from the First World War. It was 'business as usual' in the early 1920s – back to the gold standard and free market forces. The years after the Second World War saw state planning, nationalisation and the suppression of market forces. The wars did of course have long-term effects, and there has been much debate about whether the experiences after the wars – the surges in America's economic dominance, the breakdown of class barriers, the cohesion of national policies – were as much continuations of long-term trends as a direct effect of the wars. Other factors technological, economic and ideological were emerging and played a strong role throughout the 1914–50 period. The main question for us is how much of the restructuring that had emerged in the infrastructure industries by 1950 was a product of the inherent technological and economic problems of transport, communications and energy as opposed to the effects of two World Wars and the depression and of the influence of political and ideological changes. That is the broad subject matter of Part III.

The major regulatory change in the period 1914–45 was the increased role of the central state, especially in the form of state ownership. It is true that by 1913, as we saw in chapter 4, the telegraph was already state owned in most countries as were railways in Italy, Prussia and several other German states and the telephone systems in Britain, France and Germany. The Dutch government had established a state coal mining undertaking, Staatsmijnen, in 1901 and the Prussian state-owned coal mines in the Saar and Silesia.[7] By 1950, however, railways, gas, electricity, coal mines and the central banks had been nationalised in France and Britain. The railways and telephone systems were virtually or actually nationalised in Sweden, Spain and Norway, as were airlines in all countries. The central governments of Spain, Italy and the Federal Republic of Germany owned undertakings with extensive and often dominant holdings in electricity and gas supply, coal and manufacturing companies, while the state electricity power boards in Sweden and Norway were dominant institutions in their sector. Central governments had complete or partial ownership of the major companies supplying oil.

Much of what could be seen in 1950 was, however, well advanced by the end of the 1930s.[8] Railways had already been nationalised in Germany (Deutsche Reichsbahn in 1919), Sweden (Statens Järnvägar in 1939) and France (Société Nationale des Chemins de Fer Français in 1937), while two private companies in the Netherlands had merged in 1917 to form a new undertaking, NV de Nederlandsche, with the Dutch state a major shareholder. The Swedish and Norwegian state electricity power boards had been established in 1909 and 1920, and the Central Electricity Board for the British national transmission grid in 1926. The major state holding companies in Italy and Germany were created in the inter-war period: the Istituto per la Ricostruzione Industriale (IRI) in 1933; the Vereinigten Industrie Unternehmungen AG(VIAG) in 1923; the Vereinigten Elektrizititäts u. Bergwerk AG(VEBA) in 1929; the Berg u. Hüttenbehieze AG(BERG), Herman Goering works, in 1936. The airline companies set up in the inter-war period were mixed enterprises or state owned (Air France, Lufthansa, Sabena, KLM), while the British Overseas Airways Corporation was established in 1940. Central government holdings in oil companies were arranged early in the century: British Petroleum in 1914, Azienda Generale Italia Petroli in1926. In 1924 the French government set up the Compagnie Française de Raffinage and the Compagnie Française des Pétroles, and by 1939, 88% of France's oil requirements were in the hands of the state.[9] The Spanish government was also active in the oil industry, establishing the Compañía Arrendetaria del Monopolio de Petróleos in 1927. Otherwise, the central government in Spain was to take to public ownership rather later than other countries. The state holding company, Instituto Nacional de Industria started in 1941, the railways were nationalised in the same year (the Red Nacional de los Ferrocarriles Españoles) and Telefonica in 1944. Spain's civil war and absence from the Second World War merits special consideration, and we shall do that later. For the rest, governments had taken decisive steps by the end of the 1930s, and I have not even mentioned local and regional government initiatives, such as the London Passenger Transport Board and the continuing involvement of municipalities as well as co-operatives in countries like Denmark.

It will be argued in the next few chapters that these developments were very much a product of technological and economic forces, rather than being due simply to political and ideological forces and the effects of two World Wars and the depression. The key technological and economic forces that will thread through the analysis that follows are:

(1) the moves to system integration in electricity supply and telephones;
(2) the problems in adapting the nineteenth-century economic organisation of the railways to new socioeconomic pressures and to the advent of the internal combustion engine as a prime competitor;
(3) the state's increasing participation in the ownership of key strategic resources like coal and oil (discussed in detail in chapter 11).

The rise of social democratic and other left-wing parties, reinforced by the calamitous effects of the depression, did play a role in the economic organisation that emerged by the late 1940s. I shall argue that they did affect the *form* that public ownership took in many countries. They also had long-term effects outside the boundaries of the infrastructure industries, narrowly defined, and led to a strong state grip over central banks and other financial institutions. But land, commerce and much of manufacturing remained in the private sector. This was hardly a socialist takeover of the means of production. The emphasis in the following chapters of Part III will be on the infrastructure and on the common approaches across different countries and political parties taken to the problems in 1, 2 and 3 above. A résumé of the whole argument is presented at the end of chapter 9.

Notes

1 M. Einaudi, M. Byé and E. Rossi, *Nationalisation in France and Italy* (Ithaca, N.Y.: Cornell University Press, 1955), 74.

2 Cf. M. Harrison (ed.), *The Economics of World War II: Six Great Powers in International Comparison* (Cambridge University Press, 1998), 18–19.

3 F. L. Galessi, 'Hanging off the Windowsill: Italy at War 1915–18', Paper presented at Warwick University Economic History Workshop, July, 2002, 4.

4 V. Zamagni, 'Italy: How to Lose the War and Win the Peace', in Harrison (ed.), *The Economics of World War II*, Table 5.5 and surrounding text.

5 A. Ritschl, 'The Pity of Peace: German Economy at War 1914–18', Paper presented at Warwick University Economic History Workshop, July, 2002.

6 S. N. Broadberry and P. Howlett, 'The UK during World War I: Business as Usual?', Paper presented at Warwick University Economic History Workshop, July, 2002.

7 M. Davids and J. L. van Zandem, 'A Reluctant State and its Enterprises: State-Owned Enterprises in the Netherlands in the "Long Run" 20th Century', in P. A. Toninelli (ed.), *The Rise and Fall of State Owned Enterprise in the Western World* (Cambridge University Press, 2000), 255–6.

8 For all these details see the chapters on Italy, Spain, France, Germany, the Netherlands and the UK in Toninelli (ed.), *Rise and Fall*.

9 J. P. Dormois, 'France: The Idiosyncrasies of *Voluntarisme*', in J. Foreman-Peck and G. Federico (eds.), *European Industrial Policy: The Twentieth Century Experience* (Oxford University Press, 1999), 67.

7   The development of telecommunications

The economic organisation of telephones in the thirty years or so up to
the First World War reflected a set of tensions between local, regional and
national interests that was to characterise most infrastructures in the
1920s and 1930s. The first concessions in each country were London in
1879, Rotterdam, Berlin and Vienna in 1881, Prague, Helsinki and Rome
in 1882, and Stockholm, Ghent and Madrid in 1883. The radius of many
networks was less than 5 miles, and capital cities accounted for a large
share of telephone installations. Longer distance lines were slowly coming
in, bringing the prospect of national networks subject to the kind of
government pressures that had affected the telegraph and railways. In
terms of institutions, there were local companies and municipal enterprises developing local, sometimes regional networks, while trunk lines
were being developed by large nationwide companies like the Société
Générale de Téléphone in France and the National Telephone Company
in the UK or by agencies of the central government like the state boards in
Scandinavia and the Reichspost in Germany.

National joined-up networks were feasible and desirable, as for the
railways, but reinforced in the case of the telephone by the fact that,
once a national network was established, the cost of increasing the number of connections was very low and there were spillover benefits to all
existing subscribers. The main question was whether the initial set of
institutions would facilitate the merger of local, regional and national
networks. In some countries like Britain, competition between overlapping systems was allowed because of the fear of monopoly profits. If,
instead, a national monopoly was encouraged in order to avoid the
costs of duplication, would governments tolerate a private regulated
monopoly?

Alongside this has to be set the other interests of the nation state and its
organs. In some countries like Sweden and Norway, there was a desire to
forge national networks as an arm of social and economic unification.
This might involve unprofitable lines and, at the very least, subsidies for
private firms. A second interest of the state and its agencies arose from the

Table 7.1 *Telecommunications, 1913–1950*

		UK	Denmark	France	Germany	Sweden	Italy	Norway	Spain	USA
(1) Telephones per 1000 population	1913	16[a]	42	7	19	39	2	31	2	91
	1932	46	98	30	46	93	12	70	12	143
(2) Telephone calls per head of population	1938	47	185	23	46	177[b]	1	na[c]	na[c]	
(3) Percentage of telephone exchanges publicly owned	1913	100	1	100	100	68	65	51	5	0
	1920	100	3	100	100	93	na	58	0	0
	1950	100	5	100	100	100	52[d]	84	100	0
(4) Telegrams per 100 population in	1938	122	79	86	33	79	64	138	112 (1935)	156
(5) Mail items per head of population in 1938		171	88	136	116[e]	124[f]	64[f]	66	40 (1935)	200
(6) Radio licences per 1000 population	1938	181	176	112	146	195	22	126	13	

Notes:

[a] Britain only, i.e. excludes all Ireland.

[b] Excluding international calls.

[c] The data available refer to trunk calls only, which were six per head of population in Norway and one in Spain.

[d] Refers to the late 1930s and is based on the statement by Amatori ('Beyond State and Market', 131) that by the late 1930s IRI owned assets supplying 52% of subscribers. This may be an underestimate since Einaudi; Byé and Rossi (*Nationalisation in France and Italy*, 223) record that the state retained throughout, separately from INI, all the national trunk long distance lines. Note also that Zamagni (*The Economic History of Italy*, 301) states that, after its inception in 1933, IRI owned 'most of the telephone companies.'

[e] Unregistered mail.

[f] Excludes newspapers.

Sources by row:

(1) 1913 data from American Telegraph and Telephone (AT&T), *Telephone and Telegraph Statistics of the World (1913)*, bulletin no. 2, and 1932 data from W. H. Gunston, 'Telephone Development of the World at the End of 1932', *The Telegraph and Telephone Journal* 56 (1933), 56–8.

(2) B. R. Mitchell, *International Historical Statistics: Europe 1750–1993* (London: Macmillan, 3rd edn, 1998). Population from A. Maddison, *Dynamic Forces in Capitalist Development* (Oxford University Press, 1991), Table B-3 with population for Spain and Britain interpolated from census data in Mitchell, *International Historical Statistics: Europe 1750–1993*.

(3) 1913 data from AT&T, *Telephone and Telegraph Statistics of the World*, Bulletin no. 2. For 1920 onwards for Scandinavia, see L. Andersson-Skog, 'National Patterns in the Regulation of Railways and Telephony in the Nordic Countries to 1950', *Scandinavian Economic History Review* 47(2) (2000), Table 3. For Italy, see M. Einaudi, M. Byé and E. Rossi, *Nationalisation in France and Italy* (Ithaca, N.Y.: Cornell University Press, 1955), 223–4; F. Amatori, 'Beyond State and Market: Italy's Futile Search for a Third Way', in P. A. Toninelli (ed.), *The Rise and Fall of State Owned Enterprise in the Western World* (Cambridge University Press, 2000), 131 and V. Zamagni, *The Economic History of Italy 1860–1990* (Oxford: Clarendon Press, 1993), 311. For Spain, see A. Calvo, 'El teléfono en España antes de Telefonica (1877–1921)', *Revista de Historia Industria* 13 (1998), 74 and G. Tortella, *The Development of Modern Spain* (Cambridge, Mass.: Harvard University Press, 2000), 134.

(4), (5) and (6) as for (2).

fact that the telephone postdated the telegraph, and in all countries the telegraph was state owned by the 1870s. All the state agencies in France (Postes, Téléphone et Télégraphe), Belgium and the Netherlands and the Post Office in the UK, claimed rights over all telecommunications. One result was that the telephone was often treated as a foreign body in the nest, certainly as long as the post and telegraph were able to give the appearance of efficient comprehensive services. A third issue was the state's desire to control information, as for the telegraph. Initially, the possibilities of the telephone were not always appreciated. Some saw it simply as a transmitter of messages, a perspective reinforced by the fact that many of the early circuits were limited in scope. Since the telephone could not be used for written messages, it would, said those in the know, have only limited uses, mainly for local calls. The Telephone Society in France felt it had to advise: 'While you ring someone, you can also talk to the person who has been called'.[1] Later as its potentialities became more apparent, the state took a close interest. Even in late nineteenth-century Italy, where the network was tiny, the state owned two-fifths of the exchanges and played a major role in the first phase of construction because of its strategic and military significance.[2]

Institutional change was therefore prompted by these two factors: the economic gains from developing national networks and the various sociopolitical aims of the nation state. An important performance indicator was telephone penetration – the number of telephones or telephone calls per head of population. An important institutional change was the rise of public ownership. Let us therefore, first of all, review the pattern of development and see how far it was linked to the degree of public ownership. The scale of development of the telephone was less impressive than in North America, though, as in many such Europe/North America comparisons, the higher equipment costs, scarcer availability of land and related resources all tended to raise costs, whilst demand was lower in part as a function of lower and more unequal income levels.[3] The damage during the First World War widened the gap. By 1932, however, the number of telephones per head within Europe was double the 1913 figure, and the proportionate gap with America had fallen (Table 7.1). The largest proportionate increases were in France, Spain and Italy, but by the 1930s they still had the lowest penetration levels, for which low income levels can only be part of the explanation.[4] Many contemporaries linked low telephone availability to public ownership. For Henry Fayol, an engineer, the French telephone service 'was living proof of the government's incompetence in industrial matters'.[5] The issue is more complicated than that. By 1913, telephone systems were nationalised in Austria-Hungary, Belgium, Bulgaria, France, Germany, Britain, Greece,

Romania, Serbia and Switzerland (not to mention Australia and Japan).[6] By 1950, the systems were completely nationalised in Sweden and Spain, 84% publicly owned in Norway, and in Italy all the trunk lines had, almost from the start, been in the hands of the state. Thus public owner-ship was strong in Sweden and Norway and even in Denmark, since the data in Table 7.1 mask the extensive shareholdings of the state and municipalities in regional systems. Yet it was these countries that showed very high numbers of telephones per head of population and calls per telephone. In Spain, developments were slow in a regime where the Compañía Telefónica Nacional de España (Telefónica) had effectively a private monopoly until the 1940s.

Thus the success in raising penetration levels was not linked in any obvious way to the pattern of ownership. I shall show that it depended rather more on the way the state allowed or encouraged the merging of local, regional and national telephone systems; this process occupied the period before the First World War, by which time the more successful countries had attained a lead, which remained throughout the inter-war period. Central governments used two instruments. The first was sub-sidies to the private sector, especially in the initial stages when the profit-ability of the systems were in doubt. However, as national networks emerged, the desire to avoid subsidising private telephone monopolies proved strong. This was an important element in the trend to state own-ership, which was crucially reinforced by the desire of many governments to control information flows. Although this was a common pattern, there were many nuances, so some account of the experiences of each country is warranted.

In Germany and Britain the pace and level of development over the period 1880–1950 was at about the European average. Post and telegraph were merged in 1875 in Germany into the Reichspost and came to be regarded as an efficient part of the new German state. Telephone sub-scriber networks were developed from the 1880s, but strictly by the Reichspost only. The Rathenau and Bell companies were refused con-cessions. The Reichspost monopoly was confirmed in 1892, but it did cater for local and regional interests effectively, fending off the pressures from the municipalities and achieving the same level of telephone pene-tration as in Britain. Peripheral regions of the Reich were subsidised through a system characterised by low standard tariffs and low profits.[7] A new long-distance underground cable network was laid in the 1920s, and a good national network had emerged by the 1930s. Even during the Second World War, a telecommunications system at the strategic level was maintained throughout. After the war, technical systems had to be reconstructed, but personnel, organisation and procedures were largely intact.[8] In Britain, the first telephone exchanges had opened in 1879 in Glasgow and in London, where the Edison company was given a concession. The Post Office issued the licences, including one in 1889 for the National Telephone Company, which started to develop long-distance trunk lines, but these were taken over by the Post Office in 1892. Companies involved in local networks flourished, and though the Post Office refused to allow them to develop long-distance links, many, like the Lancashire Telephone Company, were able, in Britain's densely settled urban areas, to circumvent this by providing links between the numerous contiguous local exchanges.[9] The market was, however, fairly chaotic, with disagreements within the Post Office on whether competition should be encouraged, and in 1912 all systems were absorbed by the Post Office.[10] Why these systems finished up as integral parts of government departments, rather than autonomous state enterprises, is something we shall consider later, after looking at the other countries.

In France, the telegraph had always been seen by some as a symbol of Bonapartism, so the Third Republic regarded it as one of its key instruments of social control, along with railways and schools.[11] The state claimed rights to all telecommunications, so the telephone was simply added to the telegraph, which had been merged with post in 1878. Local post offices were careful to guard their interests against the telephone newcomer, who was regarded with suspicion. In the municipalities it was initially seen as a simple one-way extension of the telegraph, and links, such as those between the town hall and the excise office together with the 'wire to Paris', dominated attitudes.[12] Business firms, including vineyards, had connections with the major cities – often close-circuit with no external links. During the Belle Epoque, the telephone had a rather licentious image for its non-professional uses. The writer Colette is supposed to have said: 'Why the telephone? . . . It is only used by men for business or by women who have something to hide'.[13] Parliament refused to grant funds. Since it appeared to be mainly a short-distance means of communication, it was treated like gas, electricity and water, with concessions granted to firms such as the Société Générale de Téléphone for Paris. Municipalities who wanted approval for telephone connections had to advance funds to the central government – a practice similar to that which had applied earlier in the nineteenth century, in the mainly private telegraph system. Nor were local leaders eager to extend the number of telephone subscribers, concerned as those leaders were to avoid congestion on the wire to Paris. The result was that telephone development was very slow, and the whole system was nationalised in 1889. Some have ascribed the slow development partly to France's low rate of urbanisation, but this cannot explain the lag behind Scandinavia (cf. Table 7.1). There were lots of exchanges in France, indeed more than in many other European countries, but the number of telephones per exchange was very small.[14] The telephone was simply not treated very seriously in France: the 30000 telephones in 1900 might be compared with 27000 in New York hotels alone. In 1913 there were seven telephones per 1000 population, well below Britain, Scandinavia and Germany. By 1932, as Table 7.1 shows, that figure had risen to thirty, but it was still among the lowest in Europe. Even by 1967, the French network was no bigger than that in Chicago or New York.[15]

The tensions between local, regional and national interests were confronted most clearly and resolved, one way or another, most expeditiously in Scandinavia, where the number of telephones per head by 1913 was well ahead of the rest of Europe, and that lead was maintained throughout the inter-war period (Table 7.1). State boards were established in the mid-nineteenth century and took responsibility for the development of trunk lines, leaving local networks initially to private companies, co-operatives or municipalities. In this early phase, it would seem that governments were concerned that, like the railways, no subsidy system would induce the establishment of a national network, something that was felt essential for social and political unification and for strategic needs. In the long run, as the telephone came to be a potentially profitable activity, other factors must account for the continuance of state ownership.

In Sweden, it was argued in the early days that there was no 'public need', the exchanges were left to the co-operatives and private companies to develop and 200 private companies had emerged by the late nineteenth century.[16] The state board, the Televerket, was in the process of developing a national network, outside Stockholm, which was completed by 1900, and of forging a close relationship with the leading Swedish equipment manufacturer, the Ericsson company. It was also competing in local and regional markets and became embroiled, in 1903, in a famous telephone war with the private company Stockholm Allmanna AB. The company was taken over in 1918 and thereafter, with over 90% of the exchanges under its control, the Televerket dominated the market and proceeded in the 1920s to standardise tariffs throughout the country.[17] Since subsidies for utilities were, as we have seen, common in this period, and technical manpower international, it is not clear why, in the long run, nationalisation of the whole network in Sweden was necessary if the only issue was, as Andersson-Skog suggests, to achieve a network with connections for the sparsely populated areas in the north.[18] The Swedish state rail board's subsidy for freight traffic to keep down living costs in Norrland is a classic counterexample.[19] Similarly, the Telegrafslyret, the

National Telephone Authority (NTA), in Norway claimed that it alone had the technical personnel to develop the system, but the skills of companies like Edison were available throughout Europe.[20] From early on, private companies in Norway were restricted to town boundaries. The NTA developed trunk lines, though a national network did not emerge until the 1920s. Over a long period, the NTA gradually dominated the national scene by buying up private companies and multiplying their trunk exchanges (often assuaging the municipalities by allowing them to run the exchanges). Private companies found it difficult to expand. By the 1930s, NTA had made three attempts to nationalise the whole network. It was not until 1948 that the Parliament (the Storting) decreed that the last remaining fifty-four companies should be purchased.

In Denmark, an 1883 law had circumscribed mergers of private companies, but the state started the development of a trunk network in the 1890s. The concession system was common with twenty-year leases, the exchanges then reverting to the state. Denmark looked different from Sweden and Norway in that regional groups proved strong, and by 1900 the whole country was dominated by four regional companies who had managed to evade the restrictions on mergers. On the other hand, the state held shares in these companies so that the figure of 1.2% public ownership in Table 7.1 reflects only the state involvement in the trunk lines. Later on, it absorbed the telephone exchanges in South Jutland after that region had been regained at the end of the Second World War. By restricting the number of permits for private companies throughout the period 1900–39 but allowing the large companies to provide inter-urban links despite the state trunk system, the Danish government facilitated the emergence of a well-ordered system. 'In 1947 the number of semi-private companies had been reduced to three. Since 1940 the State owned the majority of shares in these companies without exploiting the power they represented.'[21] National integration had been achieved by preventing the fragmentation of the networks, something that in Norway had led to the rather heavy-handed approach of the NTA.[22]

In summary, initially what triggered state involvement in all three Scandinavian countries was the inability to sustain a trunk network by subsidies. In the long run, the continuing state presence seems to have reflected more a desire to avoid a regulated but subsidised private monopoly. Another and more understated motive, as for the telegraph, was to have close control over the flow of information. That power was exercised early, since the Scandinavian state telegraph boards had been established in the 1850s and all later claimed rights over telephones. It is significant that the first meeting of the joint telecommunications administration of Denmark, Norway and Sweden in 1916 was concerned with censorship of information about merchant shipping.[23] A similar control was exercised by the Italian government over its small network, which was nationalised in 1907. The 1920s saw a temporary privatisation process, which was reversed in the 1930s when the Istituto per la Ricostruizione Industriale (IRI) placed three telephone companies into one of its subsidiaries, STET, thereby controlling one half of the telephone exchanges. More significant is that, throughout all these tribulations, the state retained ownership of all trunk lines in the form of the Azienda di Stato per i Servizi Telefonici (ASST).[24] This was an administrative unit, an *azienda autonoma*, under the direction of a government minister. Elsewhere in western Europe, the desire for control was clearly reflected in the way that the typical telecommunications undertaking was often, as in Italy, a closely integrated part of a government department. Even in the 1920s, when such undertakings were encouraged to produce separate accounts, real autonomy was limited. In this respect the telecommunications agencies were treated differently from many other more autonomous public enterprises established in the inter-war period like IRI, INI, the (British) Central Electricity Board, the Port of London Authority, the London Passenger Transport Board, the Preussische Elektrizitäts AG and the publicly owned parts of the French railways.

The exercise of control did vary. It is significant that in Spain, after the Civil War and the advent of Franco, a new autarkic policy saw Telefónica, which had been run as a subsidiary of the (American) International Telephone and Telegraph Company since 1924, taken over by the state in 1944. It was not even allowed to be part of the new national industrial agency INI, which typically acted as a holding company of state enterprises and, as we shall see for electricity, co-existed with private companies in the sector in question. Rather, Telefónica was nationalised outright, so that a state monopoly was created under direct ministerial control.[25] In the case of France, postal services, significantly, had been part of the Ministère de l'Intérieure since 1849. They were merged in 1878 with telegraph and telephone in PTT, which was an integral part of state administration, adding the radio to its claim over telecommunications property rights in 1919. From 1923, it was given a separate budget and some borrowing powers but not a separate capital fund, which it wanted. A separate telecommunications administration was established in 1941 under the Vichy government, but this was closely controlled as was its postwar successor, the Directorate Générale des Télécommunications.[26] In the case of the Netherlands, the PTT controlled all the Dutch network except for the municipal exchanges in Amsterdam, Rotterdam and The Hague. Under the Company Act of 1915 it had become a 'state enterprise', supposedly separate from government, though not financially autonomous.

From 1928, it was encouraged to budget in a more businesslike way, but Parliament still exerted very strong control.[27] Paradoxically, during the Second World War it was given more formal independence from the Dutch government in that it was 'incorporated' as a separate company. However, this was welcomed by the German occupying forces, since they felt more able to exert clear direct authority. It was to return to the state enterprise format in 1952. In Germany itself the Reichspost budget law of 1924 established the Deutsche Reichspost. Its assets, income and expenditures were to be separately identified and it could issue its own bonds. It remained under close supervision; the Reich Minister had explicit 'operational control'. Where authority was really located was apparent in the (unpublished) Reich Defence Act of 1938, which placed the Reichspost as well as the Reichsbahn and the Autobahn under the Supreme Military Command.[28] In the UK, the Bridgeman Committee of 1932 criticised the centralisation of authority in the Post Office and the expropriation of profits by the Treasury. Little changed apart from the shift to a fixed annual payment of £10.75 million, which proved onerous in the troubled depression years. It was to be several decades before telecommunications obtained an independent public corporation status comparable to the likes of the Central Electricity Board and granted even to the fuel and transport industries when they were nationalised in the late 1940s.[29]

Notes

1 J. Attali and Y. Stowdze, 'The Birth of the Telephone and Economic Crisis: The Slow Development of Monologue in French Society', in I. de Sola Pool (ed.), *The Social Impact of the Telephone* (Cambridge, Mass.: MIT Press, 1977), 103.

2 G. Federico and R. Giannetti, 'Italy: Stalling and Surpassing', in J. Foreman-Peck and G. Federico (eds.), *European Industrial Policy: The Twentieth Century Experience* (Oxford University Press, 1999), 130.

3 S. N. Broadberry, 'Manufacturing and the Convergence Hypothesis: What the Long-Run Data Show', *Journal of Economic History* 53(4) (1993), 772–95; J. Foreman-Peck and R. Millward, *Public and Private Ownership of British Industry 1820–1990* (Oxford: Clarendon Press, 1994), 251–8.

4 A. Calvo, 'El telefono en España antes de Telefonica (1877–1921)', *Revista de Historia Industria* 13 (1998), 62.

5 J.-P. Dormois, 'France: The Idiosyncrasies of *Voluntarisme*', in Foreman-Peck and Federico (eds.), *European Industrial Policy*, 66.

6 Foreman-Peck and Millward, *Public and Private Ownership*, Table 3.7.

7 F. Thomas, 'The Politics of Growth: The German Telephone System', in R. Maintz and T. P. Hughes (eds.), *The Development of Large Technical Systems* (Boulder, Colo.: Frankfurt and Westview Press, 1978). See also U. Wengenroth,

'The Rise and Fall of State Owned Enterprise in Germany', in P. A. Toninelli (ed.), *The Rise and Fall of State Owned Enterprise in the Western World* (Cambridge University Press, 2000), 105.

8 Thomas, 'The Politics of Growth', 202.

9 C. de Gournay, 'Telephone Networks in France and Great Britain', in J. A. Tarr and G. Dupuy (eds.), *Technology and the Rise of the Networked City in Europe* (Philadelphia: Temple University Press, 1988).

10 A. N. Holcombe, 'The Telephone in Britain', *Quarterly Journal of Economics* 21(1) (1906); C. R. Perry, 'The British Experience 1876–1912: The Impact of the Telephone during the Years of Delay', in de Sola Pool, *The Social Impact of the Telephone*, 69–96; J. Foreman-Peck, 'Competition and Performance in the UK Telecommunications Industry', *Telecommunications Policy* 9 (1985), 215–27; Foreman-Peck and Millward, *Public and Private Ownership*, 97–111.

11 Attali and Stowdze, 'The Birth of the Telephone'. See also Dormois, 'The Idiosyncrasies of *Voluntarisme*', 65 for the view that the desire for government control was important in the move to nationalisation.

12 C. Bertho-Lavenir, 'The Telephone in France 1879–1979: National Characteristics and International Influences', in Maintz and Hughes (eds.), *Large Technical Systems*.

13 Ibid., 163.

14 De Gournay, 'Telephone Networks in France and Great Britain'.

15 Bertho-Lavenir, 'The Telephone in France', 167–70.

16 L. Andersson-Skog, 'National Patterns in the Regulation of Railways and Telephony in the Nordic Countries to 1950', *Scandinavian Economic History Review* 47 (2000), 30–46.

17 Andersson-Skog, 'National Patterns'; A. Kaijser, 'From Local Networks to National Systems: A Comparison of the Emergence of Electricity and Telephony in Sweden', in F. Cardot (ed.), *1880–1980: Une siècle de l'électricité dans le monde* (Paris: Presses Universitaires de France, 1978), 7–22.

18 L. Andersson-Skog, 'The Making of the National Telephone Networks in Scandinavia: The State and the Emergence of National Regulatory Patterns 1880–1920', in L. Magnusson and J. Ottoson (eds.), *Evolutionary Economics and Path Dependence* (Cheltenham, UK: Edward Elgar, 1996), 145; L. Andersson-Skog, 'Political Economy and Institutional Diffusion. The Case of the Swedish Railways and Telecommunications up to 1950', in L. Andersson-Skog and O. Krantz (eds.), *Institutions and the Transport and Communications Industries* (Canton, Mass.: Science History Publications, Watson, 1999), 245–66.

19 T. Pettersson, 'Institutional Rigidity and Economic Change: A Comparison between Swedish Transport Subsidies', in Andersson-Skog and Krantz (eds.), *Institutions and the Transport and Communications Industries*, 281–300.

20 H. Espeli, 'From Dual Structure to State Monopoly in Norwegian Telephones, 1880–1924', Working Paper, Norwegian School of Management, Scandvika, Norway, January 2002, 2.

21 Ibid., 12. See also S. E. Jeppson, K. G. Paulsen and F. Schneider, 'Telecommunications Services in Denmark', in J. Foreman-Peck and J. Muller (eds.),

European Telecommunications Organisation (Baden-Baden: Nomosverlagsgesellschaft, 1988), 109–29.

22 Ibid. Also on Denmark, see Andersson-Skog, 'The Making of the National Telephone Networks', 'National Patterns', 'Political Economy and Institutional Diffusion'.

23 Andersson-Skog, 'National Patterns'; Kaijser, 'From Local Networks to National Systems'. See also C. Jeding, J. Ottosson and L. Magnusson, 'Regulatory Change and International Co-operation: The Scandinavian Telecommunications Agreements, 1900–1960', *Scandinavian Economic History Review* 47 (1999), 63–77.

24 M. V. Posner and S. J. Woolf, *Italian Public Enterprise* (London: Duckworth, 1967), 21; J. Foreman-Peck and D. Manning, 'Telecommunications in Italy', in Foreman-Peck and Mueller (eds.), *European Telecommunications Organisation*, 181–201; M. Einaudi, M. Byé and E. Rossi, *Nationalisation in France and Italy* (Ithaca, N. Y.: Cornell University Press, 1955), 223.

25 A. Carreras, X. Tafunell and E. Torres, 'The Rise and Decline of Spanish State-Owned Firms', in Toninelli (ed.), *Rise and Fall*, 133–4. For the fortunes of Telefonica as a private monopoly, see D. J. Little, 'Twenty Years of Turmoil: The ITT, the State Department and Spain 1924–44', *Business History Review* 53(4) (1979), 449–72.

26 Bertho-Lavenir, 'The Telephone in France', 170; E. Chadeau, 'The Rise and Decline of State-Owned Industry in Twentieth Century France', in Toninelli (ed.), *Rise and Fall*, 194–5.

27 M. Davids, 'The Relationship between the State Enterprises for Postal, Telegraph and Telephone Services and the State in the Netherlands: A Historical Perspective', *Business and Economic History* 24(1) (1995), 194–205.

28 Thomas, 'The Politics of Growth', 194; Wengenroth, 'The Rise and Fall', 110–1.

29 Foreman-Peck and Millward, *Public and Private Ownership*, 252 and ch. 8.

8 Network integration in electricity supply: successes and failures

There are two reasons for viewing the development of electricity as one of the key issues of economic organisation in the 1914–50 period. In the late nineteenth century, electricity suppliers found the gas industry a tough competitor, and electricity was characterised in chapter 5 as a largely local affair, involving municipalities and small companies, albeit with signs of major developments in industrial uses. By the early decades of the twentieth century, long-distance electricity transmission lines were being constructed, and by the end of the First World War, the potential economic and strategic benefits of interconnected supply systems, stretching over whole regions and countries, had become a key technological reason for government involvement in industrial organisation. A new infrastructure track was being built, which carried even bigger economies of scale than the railways. Once a transmission line was laid, the actual business of transmitting electricity involved hardly any operating costs; the main running 'costs' were energy losses. The benefits from interconnection seemed huge. A second factor was the extension in the use of electricity. In the first half of the twentieth century, coal was still king as an energy source. New sources – oil, natural gas and water power – were emerging, and nuclear was to follow in the near future. They accounted for 3% of Europe's consumption of primary energy in 1920. By 1938 this figure had risen to only 5%.[1] The rest was coal, and those countries with good coal resources (Britain and Germany) and those with ready access to coal imports like Denmark remained in a strong position. But more and more of that coal was being transformed into intermediate energy forms of which electricity was the fastest growing. The development of electro-chemical and electro-metallurgical processes in manufacturing industry, as well as the electrification of tramways, railways and other modes of traction, made electricity the most dynamic element in the economy, reminiscent again of the railway mania of the 1830s and 1840s. Electricity consumption per head of population in western Europe rose threefold at a time when coal supplies were starting to level out, classically in Britain where an industry with old seams was experiencing diminishing returns.

111

Whereas in western Europe industrial production in the 1920s and 1930s was typically growing at no more than 2% per annum, electricity was expanding at 6%–7%. The exceptions, which will be considered later, were Spain, whose consumption per head was growing at 5.1% and Norway (2.1%), which had already, in 1920, achieved consumption levels well above the rest. No wonder Lenin famously reported to the All-Russian Congress of Soviets in the 1920s: 'Communism is the Soviet power plus the electrification of the whole country, for without electrification progress in industry is impossible.'

In several countries the electricity supply industry was eventually nationalised. In France and Britain it was in the form of Electricité de France and the British Electricity Authority respectively, both set up in 1946. Italy had to wait for the establishment of Ente Nazionale de l'Energia Elettrica in 1961. But governments had earlier become deeply involved in this industry.[2] Quite apart from the municipal electricity undertakings, which were still flourishing, several state-owned, albeit relatively autonomous, institutions emerged, often involved, like the Preussische Elektrizitäts AG, in only a part of a country or part of the process of generation, transmission and distribution. State production and/or transmitting boards were established in the form of a state power board in Sweden in 1909 (the Vattenfall, cf. chapter 5), the Norwegian Waterways and Electricity Administration (NVE) in 1920, the Central Electricity Board in Britain in 1926, the Empresa Nacional de Electricidad in Spain in 1944 and the Empresa Hidroelectrica del Ribagorzana in 1946, whilst several electricity companies in Italy were taken over by the state industrial agency, Istituto per la Ricostruzione Industriale, in the 1930s. The exception was Denmark, though here a public interest and collective effort manifested itself in the leverage effects afforded by the complex shareholdings of the municipalities and rural co-operatives in large regional power groups. A similar phenomenon could be seen in Germany, where a majority of enterprises, by the 1930s, had some element of Reich or state or municipal involvement.

Several questions follow and form the leitmotif for this chapter. How and to what extent did interconnection occur? What role did governments play in that process? Finally, how were the progress of interconnection and the scale of government intervention linked to the pace at which electricity consumption grew in this period?

A good indication of the ability of electricity to exert a profound economic influence in this period was the way cost reductions from technological change allowed its price to fall relative to other commodities and services. Antolin has shown this for Spain, Kaijser for Sweden and Levy-Leboyer for France.[3] Here I have chosen to illustrate with UK

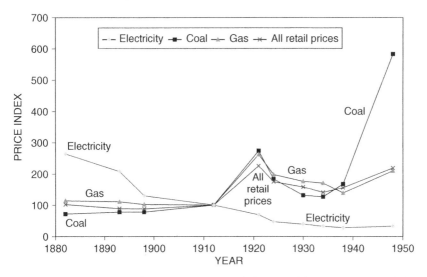

Figure 8.1 Price indexes (1912 = 100) for electricity and other goods in the UK, 1882–1948.

Notes:
The electricity price index is derived from data on average revenue per kilowatt hour in L. Hannah, *Electricity before Nationalisation* (London: Macmillan, 1978), 429–31. The coal entries are based on coal export prices per ton, free on board in London (B. R. Mitchell, *British Historical Statistics* (Cambridge University Press, 1988), 748–9). The entries for gas are an average for all the authorised undertakings and relate to revenue per cubic foot of gas sold. The sources are D. Matthews, 'Laissez-faire and the London Gas Industry in the Nineteenth Century: Another Look', *Economic History Review* 39(2) (1986), Table 1 and interpolations of Figure 1; P. Chantler, *The British Gas Industry: An Economic Study* (Manchester University Press, 1938), 19–35 using his 1920 data for 1921 and 1935 data for 1934; J. F. L. Sleeman, 'Municipal Gas Costs and Revenue', *Manchester School* 21 (1950), using his 1939 data for 1938 and his 1947 data for 1948. The all retail prices plot was derived by splicing Bowley's cost of living index for 1846–1914 on the Ministry of Labour's working-class cost of living indexes for 1915–38 and 1938–52 as given in Mitchell, *British Historical Statistics*, 738–40.

data that stretch over a very long period and provide a useful contrast with the price of British coal, a key fuel for Western Europe. Figure 8.1 shows the trend from the 1880s to the late 1940s. Thereafter the pattern changed, but during the first half of the twentieth century the price of electricity showed a continuous downward trend, and its real (relative) price fell substantially. The severe demands imposed on coal during the two World

Wars and that industry's inability to expand manifested itself in some huge price increases. Additional pressures arose in those countries reliant on imports, blocked during the wars. No wonder the development of hydroelectricity – 'l'houille blanche', the white coal – was hailed as a saviour and seen as of vital strategic significance in France, Italy and Spain. Two key technical developments paved the way for a continuous fall in the cost of electricity and the spread of networks. First was an increase in the technical efficiency and capacity of generating plants such that 25 megawatt (MW) stations became more common and produced electricity at half the cost of a 1 MW plant.[4] Throughout the period we hear claims about the biggest plant in Europe, and they tell us more about the pride in achievement than about the scholarly basis of the claim. All the following were at some point claimed to be the biggest in Europe: the 270 MW Goldenbergwerke plant near Cologne, started in 1914, which came by the mid-1920s to be a key part of the 475 MW capacity of the Rheinisch-Westfalisches Elektrizitätswerk enterprise; the Zshornewitz 128 MW plant built near Bergkemnitz in 1918 to supply war industries; the Gennevilliers plant in Paris owned by Union d'Electricité started operations in 1922 with a capacity of 200 MW extended to 350 MW in 1930; the 105 MW Battersea plant in London (1933).[5]

The second and perhaps even more important technological change was the introduction of alternating current, which, by allowing a flow of current both ways with low energy losses, rendered the development of long-distance transmission lines a potentially economic proposition. In Sweden, for example, a line of 50 kV (kilovolts, a measure of the strength of the electricity current), was built before the First World War. By the 1920s, 120 kV lines were introduced, 220 kV in the 1930s and 400 kV in the 1950s. In France, the first 60 kV line was completed between Grenoble and the Loire in 1909, 120 kV from St. Etienne in 1920, the Union des Producteurs des Pyrénées Occidentales introduced a 150 kV line in 1923 and the Chemin de Fer de Paris–Orleans a 220 kV line in 1932.[6] At the same time, the voltage level could be varied in such a way that, near to final consumers, it would be lowered to match the require-ments of lighting, heating, motors and other power appliances.

The lower unit costs of the new large generating plants heralded the closure of smaller plants and a concentration of production in the large plants. But it was the ability to transmit over long distances that was decisive in expanding the use of electricity. At a minimum, it meant the access of wider markets to the new plants. Supply from the Zshornewitz station near Bergkemnitz, which used brown coal of low calorific value and was therefore costly to transport, was transmitted over a 100 km line to Berlin and was cheaper than using local electricity. So also for the supply from the coal-fired station in Copenhagen over most of eastern Denmark (Zealand) in the 1920s.[7] The lower cost of transmission effectively speeded up the process of concentration of generation in large plants. This kind of network expansion was common in the first three decades of the century. The Newcastle-upon-Tyne Electric Supply Co. built a 6 kV line as early as 1903 and thereafter increased its area of supply from 16 square miles in 1900 to 1400 by 1914.[8] Apart from concentrating production on plants with low operating costs, network expansion offered the prospect of savings in capital costs. Since, as I emphasised in chapter 5, electricity cannot be stored, the capacity of a network that aimed to avoid power cuts to connected consumers was effectively determined by the peak demand – say a cold February morning. The percentage of capacity in use varied throughout the day and the year and the annual number of kilowatt hours produced in the 1920s in many systems was no more than one quarter of that which would have been produced if the system had operated at full capacity throughout the year. Such 'load factors' could be improved when a system latched on to an industrial load (especially one with overnight shift work) and added it to a standard household and shop load, which carried traditional morning and evening peaks.

Even more enticing was the prospect of linking mountainous areas supplied by hydroelectricity (HEP), like the Alps, with areas dominated by thermal production such as Paris and the Ruhr. HEP plants had very high capital costs associated with the construction of dams and reservoirs but very low running costs. Programmes to export electricity from such sites carried with them also the capital costs of transmission lines and energy losses during transmission. There was the great attraction, however, that HEP could substitute for electricity produced in thermal stations with high operating costs, especially attractive on cold February mornings when old high-cost coal plants would otherwise have to be brought into use. Once installed, the marginal costs of HEP were quite low but its value was considerable – the saving in operating costs on marginal coal plants in thermal areas.[9] Indeed, HEP producers would sometimes be willing to practically give away electric power: capacity was determined by rainfall and there were sometimes excess supplies of water to be disposed of. The presence of electro-chemical and electro-metallurgical manufacturing factories near to the HEP sites was of great value. In fact in the first two decades of the twentieth century, when networks were spatially limited, HEP stations in the Massif Central in France were not viable because there was no local industry to absorb excess supplies. High tension lines to Paris in the 1920s made the difference. There was a reciprocal benefit here as well in that, when rainfall was low in the HEP areas, electricity might be shipped from the thermal zones.

The characteristics of a connected network of this kind are shown in Table 8.1 for Paris, where in 1936 the average cost of electricity per kilowatt hour was 14.8 centimes – clearly a lot of averaging over the year is involved in the table, but the general message is clear. For both thermal and HEP to be used, in a given period in a given town, the cost of supply would have to be roughly the same – on the basis that in competitive conditions, the 'law of one price' operates. Electricity supply from thermal plants in the Paris area involved relatively high operating costs, especially from coal, and indeed the net saving in operating costs from using HEP in the example in Table 8.1 is $5.4 + 4.0 - 2.7 - 2.6 = 4.1$ centimes. Thermal, however, had no high tension transmission costs and, coupled with the high capital costs of the HEP plants, meant that thermal showed a net saving on these items of the order also of 4.1 centimes.

On the face of it, the issues involved in the setting up of such integrated networks would appear to be similar to the laying down of the railway track in the nineteenth century, which was achieved fairly expeditiously if not always honestly. The problems then were finance and the extent to which railway track in the relatively under-populated parts of Spain, Italy, Sweden and Norway was uneconomic yet important for strategic and political reasons. Some of these issues were present for electricity. Transporting electricity for distances up to 500 km involved massive capital outlays and often doubled the unit cost.[10] But the analogy with railways is not altogether appropriate. In a technical sense, supplying electricity over long distances was more like telecommunications, water and gas, or even better, highways. The transmission line or road had high capital construction costs but could simultaneously carry many flows from different origins at very low marginal cost – at least up to the point when the network was congested. A high tension line could be uneconomic for one undertaking but it might be worthwhile for three or four.[11] This required harmonisation of electricity currents and agreement on usage and tariffs. At the same time, customers had to be found. Many customers had interests that did not coincide with those of the electricity suppliers. Large companies in manufacturing industry were self-sufficient in electricity in the early decades of the twentieth century, and the available evidence, for Belgium and Germany for example, is that the public sale of electricity to industry did not overtake industry's own in-house production until the 1920s.[12] Other potential customers were small private or municipal electricity supply undertakings already retailing electricity from their own local thermal or HEP plants. Thus in the 1920s, Energie Electrique du Sud-Ouest, a company in the Thomson-Houston group, supplied electricity to the Bordeaux area on a high tension line from its HEP plants in the Pyrenees. Bordeaux town council had recently taken over the old small

Table 8.1 *Costs of electricity in Paris, 1936 (centimes per kilowatt hour)*

	Thermal	HEP
Coal	5.4	–
Wages etc	4.0	2.6
Energy losses in transmission	–	2.7
Capital costs of transmission	–	2.1
Capital costs of generation	5.3	7.5
TOTAL	14.7	14.9

Source: M. Levy-Leboyer, 'The French Electrical Power System: An Inter-Country Comparison', in R. Maintz and T. P. Hughes (eds.), *The Development of Large Technical Systems* (Boulder, Colo.: Frankfurt and Westview Press, 1978), Table 4.

private company producing locally so that retailing was in the hands of a municipal undertaking that continued to produce some electricity of its own.[13] Such small plants were no longer competitive, but by the 1920s many were still in entrenched positions. Could institutions adapt to encourage retailers to take supplies from the high tension networks carrying electric current originating from the large generating plants?

Private sector electricity networks in France, Italy and Spain

If there were, objectively, economic gains to be made from integration, reluctant parties might be seduced by profitable mergers. This is what we would expect to see in regimes dominated by private companies, typified by France, Belgium, Spain and Italy and parts of power production in Scandinavia, Germany and Britain. Municipal and state undertakings would not have the same profit incentives nor was merger so easy. Here inter-municipal agreements and mixed private-public partnerships might emerge. For much of the inter-war period, the integration process often took the form of private sector expansion, that is:

(1) The growth of large companies by investment in plants and grids and/or by merger. In some cases such companies grew to dominate whole regions so that regional networks emerged, monopolistic or at best oligopolistic in nature.
(2) Agreements between the large companies, sometimes from different regions, on pooling arrangements for high tension transmission.

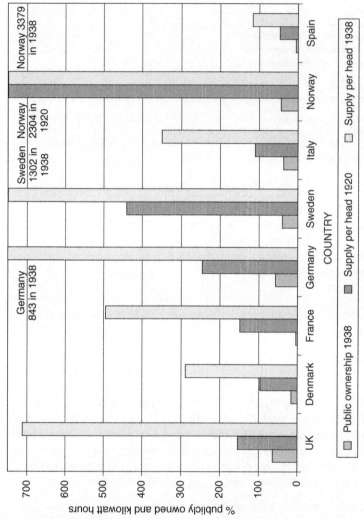

Figure 8.2 Electricity supply and ownership 1920–1938.

Note:
Supply is measured in kilowatt hours per head of population. Ownership as % output from publicly–owned firms.

Source: Table 8.2

The prospective monopoly status of these networks brought complaints and calls for government intervention. Any intransigence by municipalities, in coming to agreements or blocking interconnections, also led to a clamour for central government action. Thus the state was dragged in one way or another, and the essence of the economic organisation problem in the inter-war period was not rights of way but one of establishing the interconnection of towns, rural areas and regions. National networks did not, as a rule, emerge in this period. Even when they did, as in Sweden in the mid-1930s, they were not necessarily integrated networks; there was no guarantee that the least cost method of supply was used in every hour in every town. Only in a managed national grid, like that of the Central Electricity Board in Britain, was there any chance of that occurring and even there, as we shall see, a huge number of inefficient retailers remained at the end of the 1930s. Put otherwise, there was in many countries, by the 1930s, a tension between the private companies and organs of government, which, at the industry level, mirrored the state's problems in the macroeconomy.[14]

In analysing the process of system development, it is as well to recognise from the start that a nationally integrated network was not necessarily an economic proposition. This may be illustrated by the cases of Spain and Norway. Both were heavily reliant on HEP. One finished up with very low levels of electricity consumption; the other with very high levels, as Figure 8.2 and Table 8.2 show. Norway was well endowed with both large and small waterfalls (cf. chapter 5). It did not develop a national network until 1980.[15] Within any given region the need for imported supplies was limited. In contrast, Spain was poorly endowed with coal, and rainfall was unreliable. Demand often exceeded capacity and in all regions there was little available for export. Shortage of capacity rather than an integrated network was the priority, manifest in the fact that from the 1950s a drive to thermal plants fuelled by oil and coal was undertaken to move away from the unreliable supply of water for HEP.

In certain respects Spain exhibited a form of expansion found in other countries where the private sector was dominant. As we saw in chapter 5, the municipalities in Spain were not involved much in the early development of electricity and gas. From 1924, electricity, gas and water were declared by the state to be public services that could be supplied by municipalities, and supply conditions would be regulated by the state.[16] By that stage, however, the large private companies were well entrenched. Established in 1901, Hidroelectrica Iberia, for example, expanded supplies in the Madrid and Basque areas, whilst Saltos de Dureo (established in 1905) developed the Portuguese boundary. This involved Spanish, especially bank, capital. In the industrialised Catalonia, foreign capital, linked to the electrical equipment manufacturers, was more common as in the Barcelona Traction, Lighting and Power Company (with capital from AEG and General Electric). South-east Spain came to be dominated by the Sevillana de Electricidad (established in 1894), which initially had thermal stations.[17]

By the 1930s, the country was supplied by a small number of private company networks, many of them monopolies. Fourteen major groups came to dominate the Spanish scene for the rest of the twentieth century. In 1930 the ten largest firms in the Basque and Catalan areas accounted for 72% of the nation's capacity. By the early 1940s, seven companies produced a half of all output. The potential for state intervention was large yet unrealised. Consumption levels more than doubled from 47 kWh per head of population in 1920 to 117 kWh in 1938, but this change was actually below the European average so that the relatively low absolute level of consumption remained. There is the suspicion that some of this reflected the monopoly power of the major firms. The price of electricity remained unchanged relative to coal in the inter-war period, though this was perhaps not too much out of line with other Western countries, at least for the years 1924–34 (cf. Figure 8.1). The loose regulation of the industry which had characterised early developments continued after the First World War. Although a decree of 1921 specified fixed periods for concessions and those for 1931 and 1935 extended state power over the prices in concession agreements, a 1918 decree had paved the way for private-sector expansion by giving priority in the use of public water supplies to large producers of electricity.[18] State subsidies and loans for river basin development became available from 1926 through the Confederaciones Hidrografica. From the 1920s, the state also pushed for a national network, but most observers have judged that nothing materialised. An advisory body, the Consejo de Energéa was created in 1929 to organise and structure the electricity sector, and after the Civil War, the Unidad Electrica was established as an agreement amongst the companies to organise electricity into a national network.[19]

Rather more decisive, albeit with not much more success in the end, was the new government after the Civil War. Coal and oil imports were cut off during the Second World War so that electricity took on an added significance. Following the Industrial Regulation and Defence Law of 1939 autarky was the dominant theme; foreign capital was not protected and industries like electricity were treated as having key strategic value and were to be naturalised (put into Spanish ownership) and in some cases nationalised. Tariffs were frozen from 1935 to 1957, and the prospects for profits for the private companies looked bleak and expansion out of the question. The state then took the stage in the form of the

Instituto Nacional de Industria (INI), which had been established in 1941 and which set up a new advisory council, the Consejo Tecnico de Electricidad, with a target of increasing electricity output. Indeed, under strong state direction and with prices frozen, consumption rose by 9.1% per annum in the period 1940–3, as compared to 5.1% in 1931–5.[20] Then in 1944 INI established a new state-owned thermal electricity undertaking, the Empresa Nacional de Electricidad, followed by the Empresa Hidroelectrica del Ribagorzana in 1946. However, they only produced 8% of all electricity in 1950 and did not reach their peak of 33% until 1970.[21]

By the 1950s, Spain consumed less electricity than anywhere else in Europe and did not have a national network. The latter was not as important as the sheer shortage of capacity, which was a product of a poor resource endowment, in rainfall and coal, and insecure government institutions at the local and national level. Norway was at the other end of the spectrum. The rich variety of its waterfalls allowed the proliferation of many local networks, while the abundance of good waterfalls at high altitudes reduced the clashes between big electricity producers and farming interests, in contrast to Sweden (cf. chapter 5). Strong local governments developed municipal undertakings, while the big private foreign companies exploited the larger waterfalls, feeding power supplies to the growing manufacturing base. By 1935, one half of all consumption was by 'big industry' (as Thue calls it) and the rest was 'general consumption': households, commerce and small industry.[22] Big industry was supplied mainly by big electricity suppliers (including self production by manufacturing companies). Most of the general consumption came from public utilities, the majority of which were municipalities. Overall, agencies of government were producing 44% of total output by 1935 (cf. Table 8.2 and footnotes). The state power board, Nordvestsjællands Elektriciteit-Værk (Norwegian Waterways and Electricity Administration, established in 1920 and renamed Statkraft in 1960), was mainly concerned to overcome the inability or unwillingness of the municipalities and small companies to extend supplies and develop network links. Interconnection was confined to the Østlandet, the region around Oslo. This had been prompted in part by the completion in 1924 of a 100 km 60 kV power line from an HEP plant at Rjusken to Buskerund county, south of Oslo. It was the work of NVE, which also completed in 1928 a 130 kV line, this time from an HEP plant at Nore, some 100 km from the Oslo region. The network in that region had been the product of bilateral agreements until 1932, when a regional power pool was established.[23]

But that was the limit of national interconnection until the 1950s, when four more regional pools were established. Municipalities proved

Table 8.2 *Energy supply patterns, 1900–1938*

		UK	Denmark	France	Germany	Sweden	Italy	Norway	Spain	USA
(1) Electricity supplied in kWh per head of pop.	1920	154	97	149	246	441	110	2304	47	531
	1938	712	289	495	843	1302	350	3379	117	1092
(2) Percentage of electricity output from hydroelectric plants	1938	4	5	53	10	90	92	95	92	
(3) Percentage of electricity output produced in publicly-owned undertakings	1938	64	16 (1925)	4	57 (1928)	40	37	44 (1935)	5	4 (1917)
(4) Percentage of rail track electric in	1938	5.3	1.6	7.8	5.0	42.4	28.2	9.2	6.2 (1935)	
(5) Gas supplied in cu. metres per head of pop.	1900	115[a]	34	16	24	9	6	15	6 (1913)	31
	1935	249	65	40	51		20		8	
(6) Percentage of gas supply undertakings in municipal ownership 1890–1910		29 (1900)	84 (1905)	2 (1905)	31[b] (1908)	95 (1910)	2 (1910)	50 (1890)	3 (1901)	2 (1900)
(7) Coal output in metric tons per 100 pop.	1912	581	0	103	386	na	2	1	21	508
	1938	486	0	113	581	6	5	10	24	275

Notes:

[a] The UK figure relates to Britain (i.e. excludes all Ireland) and to the 1897/8 financial year.

[b] Relates to 2309 urban districts in Germany in 1908.

Sources by row:

(1) B. R. Mitchell, *International Historical Statistics: Europe 1750–1993* (London: Macmillan, 3rd Edition, 1998) and *International Historical Statistics: The Americas: 1750–1993* (London: Macmillar, 4th edn, 1998). Population from A. Maddison, *Dynamic Forces in Capitalist Development* (Oxford University Press, 1991), Table B-3 with Spain and Britain interpolated from census data in Mitchell, *International Historical Statistics: The Americas*.

(2) R. Millward, 'New Solutions to Old Problems: The Economic Organisation and Development of Electricity Supply in Britain in the 20th Century', in A. Giuntini (ed.), *The Electric City: A Century of Electrification* (Rome: Ente Nazionale de l'Energia Elettrica, 2004), Table 2. The Scandinavian data are rough estimates based on the general descriptions in three chapters of A. Kaijser and M. Hedin (eds.), *Nordic Energy Systems: Historical Perspectives and Current Issues* (Canton, Mass.: Science History Publications, 1995): L. Thue, 'Electricity Rules: The Formation and Development of the Nordic Electricity Regions', 11–29; A. Kaijser, 'Controlling the Grid: The Development of High Tension Power Lines in the Nordic Countries', 31–53; E. Jakobsson, 'Industrialised Rivers: The Development of Swedish Hydropower', 55–74. See also L. Thue, 'The State and the Dual Structure of the Power Supply Industry in Norway, 1890–1940', in M. Trédé (ed.), *Electricité et électrification dans le monde 1880–1980* (Paris: Association pour l'Histoire de l'Electricité en France, Presses Universitaires de France, 1990), 227–34. The French figure is from M. Levy-Leboyer and H. Morsel (eds.), *Histoire de l'électricité en France. II. L'Interconnection et le marché, 1919–46* (Paris: L'Association pour l'Histoire de l'Electricité en France, Fayard, 1994), Table 26. The German figure is a rough estimate based on the general descriptions in T. P. Hughes, 'Technology as a Force for Change in History: The Effort to Form a Unified Electric Power System in Weimar Germany', in H. Mommsen (ed.), *Industrielles System und politische Entwicklung in der Weimarer Republik* (Düsseldorf: Droste Verlag, 1977), 153–66 and T. P. Hughes, *Networks of Power: Electrification in Western Society 1880–1930* (Baltimore: Johns Hopkins Press, 1983). For Italy, see V. Zamagni, *The Economic History of Italy 1860–1990* (Oxford : Clarendon Press, 1993), 282. For Spain, see C. Sudria, 'Les Restrictions de la consummation de l' électricité en Espagne pendant l'après guerre 1944-54', in F. Cardot (ed.), *1880–1980: Une siècle de l'électricité dans le monde* (Paris: Presses Universitaires de France, 1987), 426 and F. Antolin, 'Public Policy in the Development of the Spanish Electric Utility Industry', Paper presented at European Historical Economics Society Conference on *A Century of Industrial Policy in Europe*, Oxford, Worcester College, 1992, 11.

(3) The UK and Danish entries refer to the number (not output) of local authority undertakings as a percentage of the total. See Thue, 'Electricity Rules' fn. 16 and R. Millward, 'The Political Economy of Urban Utilities in Britain 1840–1950', in M. Daunton (ed.), *The Cambridge Urban History of Britain*, III (Cambridge University Press, 2000), Table 11.2. The entry for France is an estimate based on the frequent references in the literature to the small number of publicly-owned undertakings. The figure is higher than the pre-1914 level because of the inclusion of Alsace and Lorraine with stronger German municipal traditions. Fernandez reports G. Roux as claiming that, before nationalisation, '250 régies facé aux 200,000 concessions privées; de plus ces régies étaient quasi exclusivement rurales'. In correspondence, Fernandez tells me that the figure should be 20000, so the proportion would be 1.25%; either way 4% may be too high; see A. Fernandez, 'Les Lumières de la ville: L'Administration municipale à l'épreuve de l'électrification', *Vingtième Siècles Revue d'Histoire* 62 (1999), 115, fn. 4. See also K. Doukas, 'Ownership, Management and Regulation of Electric Undertakings in France', *The George Washington Law Review* 6(2) (March 1938), 306 and P. Schwob, 'Relations between the State and

Source to Table 8.2 *(cont.)*

the Electric Power Industry in France', *Harvard Business Review* 13(1) (1934), 95. The figure for Germany is for 1930 and is from O. Mulert, 'The Economic Activities of German Municipalities', *Annals of Collective Economy* 5 (1929), 233. The Swedish figure is an estimate based in part on the statement by Kaijser ('Controlling the Grid', 34) that the state power board plants produced one third of all electricity in 1920. Thue ('Electricity Rules', 14), suggests rural municipalities were not allowed to produce electricity before 1945. This still leaves the urban municipal undertakings and some allowance for a trend increase by the state board. For Italy, Amatori suggests that IRI in the late 1930s accounted for 27% of all electricity energy output (F. Amatori, 'Beyond State and Market: Italy's Futile Search for a Third Way', in P. A. Toninelli (ed.), *The Rise and Fall of State Owned Enterprise in the Western World* (Cambridge University Press, 2000), 131); see also Zamagni, *The Economic History of Italy 1860–1990*, 301. A further 10% should be added as follows. Municipal electricity undertakings produced 0.7 gigawatt hours in 1928, that is 8% of the 8.74 gWh total. See G. Galasso (ed) *Storia dell'industria elettrica in Italia. III. Expansiove e oligopolio. 1926–45* (Roma-Bari: Laterza & Figli, 1993), 1236 and 1257 and A. Schiavi, 'Municipal Undertakings in Italy', *Annals of Collective Economy* 7 (1931), 35. In addition there may have been 2–3% produced by the state railways (as stated for 1953 in M. Einaudi, M. Byé and E. Rossi, *Nationalisation in France and Italy* (Ithaca, N. Y.: Cornell University Press, 1955), 223). The Norway figure is calculated from data in Thue, 'The State and the Dual Structure of the Power Supply Industry in Norway, 1890–1940', 230–1. 51% of all consumption was 'general' and the rest was 'big industry'. 97% of general consumption was supplied by public utilities of which 84% was accounted for by municipal and state undertakings so that 41.5% of all consumption took the form of supply from these undertakings to general consumers. Since public utilities also supplied 6% of the consumption of big industry, a further 2.5% of total output should be credited to the public sector yielding the figure of 44.0%. The entry for Spain is also an estimate reflecting the fact that Antolin and Balbin stress that private enterprise was dominant in production and distribution: see Antolin, 'Public Policy in the Development of the Spanish Electric Utility Industry', 19–20, and P. F. Balbin, 'Spain: Industrial Policy under Authoritarian Politics', in J. Foreman-Peck and G. Federico (eds.), *European Industrial Policy: The Twentieth Century Experience* (Oxford University Press, 1999), 235, 241. For the USA, see C. D. Thompson, *Public Ownership: A Survey of Public Enterprises* (New York: T. W. Crowell, 1925), 269. Municipal plants accounted for 33% of all undertakings in 1917 but they were often in small towns.

(4) J. Foreman-Peck and R. Millward, *Public and Private Ownership of British Industry 1820–1990* (Oxford: Clarendon Press, 1994), Table 7.2. The entry for Spain was derived from the figure of 1075 km of electric track in 1935 given by L. Segreto ('Aspetti e problemi dell'industria elettrica in Europa tra le due guerre', in Galasso (ed.), *Storia dell'industria elettrica in Italia*, Table 10) and related to an average of the total rail track figures for 1930 and 1940 given in Mitchell, *International Historical Statistics: Europe 1750–1993*.

(5) Population data as in (1).

1900 gas data: R. Millward, 'The Market Behaviour of Local Utilities in Pre-World War I Britain: The Case of Gas', *Economic History Review* 44 (1991), Table I; O. Hyldtoft, 'Making Gas: The Establishment of the Nordic Gas systems, 1800–1870', in Kaijser and Hedin (eds.), *Nordic Energy Systems*, 85; F. Caron and F. Cardot (ed.), *Histoire générale de l'électricité en France. I. 1881–1918: Espoirs et conquêtes* (Paris: L'Association pour l'Histoire de l'Électricité en France, Fayard, 1991); Sudria, 'Les Restrictions de la consummation de l' électricité en Espagne', 108; S. Fenoaltea, 'The Growth of the Utility Industries in Italy 1861–1913', *Journal of Economic History* 42 (1982), Table 3; German and US data were interpolated from the chart in D. Matthews, 'Technology Transfer in the Late 19th Century Gas Industry', *Journal of Economic History* 47(4) (1987), 967–80; information for Norway supplied by O. Hyldtoft and based on Norske Gasverkers Forenings (Gasteknikeren, 1915), 257–8. 1935 data: for Britain, Foreman-Peck and Millward, *Public and Private Ownership of British Industry*, 203; data for Denmark supplied by O. Hyldtoft from Table 19 of Statistiscke Departement, *Danmarks Energiforsyning 1900–51* (Copenhagen, 1959); L. Jouhaux, 'Nationalisation in France', *Annals of Collective Economy* 20 (1949), 219; O. Mulert, 'The Economic Activities of German Municipalities', *Annals of Collective Economy* 5 (1929), 227. For Italy the figure of 339 million cu.m. of consumption for 1923 in Zamagni, *The Economic History of Italy*, 224, was projected forward to 1935 using the index of gas production on p. 273. For Spain, see Sudria, 'Les Restrictions de la consummation de l'électricité en Espagne', 115.

(6) Millward, 'The Political Economy of Urban Utilities in Britain', Table 11.2. Danish data from O. Hyldtoft based on the 1906 Industrial Census and published in *Statistiske Meddelesler*, 4.30.7, pp. 27–31. See also Hyldtoft, *Nordic Gas Systems*, 91 and 'Modern Theories of Regulation: An Old Story: Danish Gasworks in the 19th Century', *Scandinavian Economic History Review* 42(1) (1994), Table 1. The French figure is based on Caron and Cardot (eds.), *Histoire générale de l'électricité en France*. 399, 499–500. The German data are from W. H. Dawson, *Municipal Life and Local Government in Germany* (London: Longmans, Green and Co., 1916), 186. For Sweden, see M. Hietalla, *Services and Urbanisation at the Turn of the Century: The Diffusion of Innovations*, Studia Historica 23 (Helsinki: Finnish Historical Society, 1987), 239. The Italy figure is a guess based on the frequent assertion that municipal gas was a marginal activity. The Norway entry is a rough estimate based on the statement by Thue that in the second half of the nineteenth century 'the local authorities were responsible for about half the investment in infrastructure like roads, schools, gas works and telephone networks' ('The State and the Dual Structure of the Power Supply Industry in Norway, 1890–1940', 229). C. Sudria lists 81 gasworks in Spain in 1901 and only those of San Sebastian and Bilbao were under municipal ownership. See 'Notas sobre la implantacion y el desarrollo de la industria del gas en España 1840–1901', *Revista de Historia Economica* 1(2) (1983), 97–118, and also F. Antolin, 'Las empresas de servicos publicos municipales', in F. Comin and P. M. Acena (eds), *Historia de la empresa publica en España* (Madrid: Espasa Calpe, 1991), 310. M. Keller states that only 20 out of 981 cities in the USA had municipal gasworks in 1900 (*Regulation and the New Economy: Public Policy and Economic Change in America 1900–1933* (Cambridge, Mass.: Harvard University Press, 1990), 56).

(7) Mitchell, *International Historical Statistics: Europe 1750–1993* and *International Historical Statistics: The Americas: 1750–1993* (London: Macmillan, 4th edn, 1998). Population data as in (1). It assumed there was no coal mining in Denmark.

obstinate when invited to merge, and there were many unsuccessful attempts in the 1930s to develop better links.[24] This intransigence does not seem to have been a big issue economically until the 1960s. Norway's electricity output per head of population, by the end of the First World War, was much higher than that of all the other countries of western Europe. In the inter-war period, its output rose only modestly by European standards, but by 1938 it was still nearly as large, per head, as the rest of Europe combined (Table 8.2). For the time being, it seems its institutions had adapted well enough to the new technology.

Expansion by the private sector with very little direct involvement of either municipal or state governments was to be seen most vividly and extensively in France and Italy. Both witnessed the emergence of strong regional private monopolies or oligopolies. Interconnection was achieved by inter-company agreements and joint ownership of transmission lines, the strongest developments of which were in France. Consumption per head of electricity grew quickly, rising threefold in the inter-war period, in many respects a transformation of the energy scene, especially for business users in manufacturing industry. By the late 1930s, however, progress was seen by some customer groups as unsatisfactory, manifest in parliamentary debates in France about the continued dependence on coal and the poor electricity connections in rural areas.

There are three main issues that concern us here. A brief outline of each will show the way this part of the chapter will proceed. Firstly, the growth of production and consumption in the period 1920–38 was large by the standards of the pre-First World War period, but no more than the European average (Figure 8.2). The potential for HEP seemed huge, especially in France, where it came to account for over one half of all supplies, making a big saving in coal usage in thermal plants. In Italy, the very low marginal costs of transmitting HEP from the Alps promised relief down the 'backbone' to the central and southern regions. Secondly, the strategic significance of electricity in countries with limited coal and gas had been recognised during the First World War and was never far off the agenda in the 1918–50 period. During war conditions, coal and oil imports would likely be cut off; the saviour could be HEP, the white coal. The third point is that governments had little influence on the structure of the industry in a period when complaints about the role of private-sector monopolies increased. Macroeconomic considerations linked to inflation, the exchange rate and the banking system certainly brought state action that affected electricity. In Italy in the 1930s, several electricity supply undertakings were taken into public ownership, but this reflected financial and banking problems such that the undertakings remained simply financial holdings of the new national industrial agency, Istituto per la Ricostruzione Industriale (IRI). An interconnected national electricity network did not materialise until the post-1945 period. For France, a contemporary outside observer suggested in 1934 that the regional private sector networks that had emerged constituted a 'system of large islands, established for themselves, which are afterwards to be joined together'.[25] The HEP areas were connected to Paris during the 1930s, but nothing decisive was done about an integrated national network until 1938 with war looming, when a plan for the expansion of capacity and system integration was agreed.

The full story starts with the undoubted expansion of generating capacity, as private companies merged and production came to be concentrated in large plants. In France in the 1920s, the capacity of HEP plants grew rapidly – at 9.1% per annum in the period 1925–32 such that it overtook thermal capacity, which was growing at 7.1%. By the early 1930s, the three major plants in Paris had an average capacity of 300 MW (which may be compared to 5 MW for St Denis in 1905), whilst the HEP plants at Kembs, Brommart and Marèges averaged 140 MW. By this stage five major holding companies had emerged, each dominating generating capacity in their region. In Paris the Union d'Electricité (the Mercier group) had built the large Gennevilliers plant in 1922. It came to control, in conjunction with the Empain Company, most of the thermal supplies in Paris and became the largest public utility in France. Energie Electrique du Littoral Méditerranéen (the Cordier group) was created in 1900 with the backing of Thomas Houston. The others were Loire et Centre (the Giros group), Pechiney et Ugine (the 'electrochemists') and Energie Industrielle (the Durant group). These five groups controlled three-quarters of all French capacity by 1938, and the situation had not changed by the end of the war.[26] In Italy, three companies dominated in the 1930s: Edison (which had taken over Ettore Conti in the 1920s and was prominent in the north), Società Adriatia di Elettricá, linked to AEG and supreme in Tuscany and Emilia, and SIP (Società Idroelettrica Piemontese), which had strong ties in the south with Società Meridionale di Elettricità.[27] There were other companies of significant size: Salt Valdano (cf. chapter 5), which was based in Florence but spread outwards rapidly and came to agreements with Ligure Toscana in 1913; Unione Esercizi Elettrici, Tridentia (near the Austrian border) and Adamello.[28]

Each of these companies in France and Italy commanded regional networks of considerable size within which there was extensive, albeit variable, degrees of interconnection. A different matter was that of joining up the regional networks. This required agreements between the companies or perhaps state intervention when there was intransigence. In both countries the state had taken powers (a 1919 bill in Italy and a 1922 law in France) that enabled them to influence the structure of the national networks. Little progress was made, and the governments largely accepted what emerged from the bargaining process of the companies. In Italy, SIP made some attempts to construct a national network, but Edison opposed state intervention. In the 1920s the large electro-technical manufacturing firms were battered by competition from big American companies like General Electric and Westinghouse. Problems in the banking system and from inflation delayed inter-company agreements further, and SIP and Edison were actually taken over by IRI in the early 1930s, only to be privatised shortly afterwards.[29]

In France, pooling agreements between companies and the development of long-distance high tension lines proceeded much more successfully. The importance of interconnection can be gauged from the fact that HEP in the Massif Central would only be viable if long-distance links were established, since it had no local industry. In the early 1920s, it still awaited such links. By the 1930s, there were six major groups transporting electricity over long distances. From 1926 the Union des Producteurs des Pyrénées Occidentales acted as transporter for its six constituent companies, including the railway company for the Mediterranean area (Chemin de Fer du Midi). The Union de l'Energie Electrique was financially linked to the Paris based company Union d'Electricité, and had established Paris–Alps lines by the mid-1930s. Other transport groups were Société de Transport d'Energie des Alpes, STAD (for the Alpes-Durances) and TERA (for the Auvergne).[30]

It is not easy to assess quantitatively how successful different countries were in achieving system integration. The length of the high tension transmission network, even when allowing for population and area covered, may not be an adequate reflection of system integration, especially when, as in France and Italy, the distribution of population was very uneven geographically. In both of these countries, the scale of construction was quite impressive. By 1930, there were already some 4000 km of high tension transmission lines in France and 7000 km in Italy. The next eight years saw the system double in size in France and rise by about 60% in Italy to the levels recorded in Table 8.3. Expressed per head of population, this measure of network spread shows France and Italy in a better position, by 1938, than Britain, whose system development has usually been seen as a success story. The British data refer only to the national grid, so there may be some high tension lines not included. On the other hand, almost one third of the British lines were less than 70 kV and the total length of the grid network was only 152 km per million population, significantly less than France and Italy. In terms of reaching out to a scattered population, the length of line per square kilometre may be a better guide and Table 8.3 shows that, by that measure, France was less successful than Britain. Italy again scored high marks, so that those writers, like Giannetti, who have criticised the Italian performance would have to argue that the nature of its terrain required a more ambitious pattern of construction for system integration.[31]

The distinctive feature of Britain's network, as we shall see later, was that it was managed as an integrated system, so that the benefits of low-cost sources could be passed through the country as low prices. This was not the case in France and Italy, whose average consumption levels remained low. In France consumption was 197 kWh per head of population in 1924, rising rapidly to 327 kWh in 1930, but then there was stagnation in the depression years, and the 1930 figure was not achieved again until 1936.[32] In truth, the French network had served industry and traction well, since the consumption levels in these sectors were equivalent to those in the same sectors in other parts of Europe, as Table 8.4 shows. By the end of the 1930s, Paris consumption levels attained the levels in Berlin. Only when Paris was fully connected was a national network seriously considered.[33] It was the household sector, especially in rural areas, which lagged behind with consumption levels in the centre-west as low as 28 kWh per inhabitant, some of which was public lighting. In Italy, similar low levels could be found in households, commerce and the small business sector, with relative prices favouring big industry: 'an excessive development of power intensive industries and the adoption of power intensive technologies [in manufacturing industry]'.[34]

Giannetti suggests that the outcome of the rapid growth of the 1920s and 1930s in Italy was 'not an integrated network of large plants but a system which was fragmented at the industry level and unstable from a financial point of view'.[35] The state was not actively involved in regulating the structure of rates, the import of electrical equipment, the establishment of technical standards or the promotion of better industry structures.[36] In the 1920s, the state had floated the idea of a unified electricity system linking the thermal zones with HEP in the north via a backbone ridge line.[37] The national industrial agency IRI was established in 1933 and its financial holdings gave it leverage over 27% of all electricity output by the late 1930s.[38] But IRI was simply a financial institution replacing the banks, and the Fascist government, although talking about a unified system, left the matter to the private companies. During the war, Marco and Anglese were assigned to ensuring adequate electricity supported the war effort, and in 1942 there was an agreement between the main companies to open up the centre and develop the south.[39] Nothing of substance emerged until after the war, when harmonisation of frequencies

Table 8.3 *High tension transmission lines in France, Italy and Britain in 1938 (length in kilometres)*

	France	Italy	Britain
220 kV	2062	505	0
120–150 kV	5325	11263	4818
Less than 120 kV	1325	0	2227
Total	8712	11768	7045
Per million population	207	267	152
Per '000 square kilometres	16	38	30

Sources: M. Levy-Leboyer, 'Panorama de l'électrification: De la Grande Guerre à la nationalisation' in M. Levy-Leboyer and H. Morsel (eds.), *Histoire de l'électricité en France. II. L'Interconnection et le marché, 1919–46* (Paris: L'Association pour L'Historie de l'Electricité en France, Fayard, 1994), Table 2; Central Electricity Board, *Annual Report for 1938* (London: Whitchurch Morris, 1939), 3; Italian electricity data kindly supplied by R. Giannetti and based on his book, *La conquista della forza* (Milan: Angeli, 1989). Population and area data from *Whitaker's Almanack* (London: Whitaker and Sons, 1938).

was achieved. Criticism of the private companies continued in the 1950s and focused on the failure to create a single transmission network and capillary distribution system. Tariffs still varied considerably across the country, and their harmonisation in 1961 was the preface to full nationalisation of the industry in the form of ENEL (Ente Nazionale de l'Energie Elettrica).

Schemes for a unified network abounded in France in the 1920s. Initially, the focus was a plan for connecting the liberated territories in the north-east coal mining area and the iron regions in Lorraine. It was soon learnt that the main likely benefits from interconnection lay elsewhere and involved HEP. The hopes for 'houille blanche' in easing the dependency on coal had already prompted the 1919 law which separated riparian rights in rivers from the energy associated with water flows, which were vested in the state and thereby obviated the burden on HEP producers of buying out such riparian rights. Then the 1922 law stipulated that all new high tension lines had to be approved by the state.[40] This prompted a state commission to propose a national plan ensuring that the Paris and Lyons urban areas would be joined to the HEP regions of the Pyrenees, the Alps, the Massif Central and Alsace, and all joined to the coal region in the north-east.[41] Another plan was devised by engineers with a five-network scheme envisaged, including proposals for closing all thermal plants in HEP areas.[42]

Table 8.4 Electricity consumption by sector, 1937/8 (kWh per head of population)

	Europe[a]	Italy		France				
						(1937)		
	(1938)	(1938)	(1938)	Paris	East & north	South-east	South-west	Centre-west
Domestic[b]	137	31	77	107	45	65	47	28
Industry	333	237	314	254	529	592	336	121
Traction	32	34	32					
Total	502	302	423	361	574	657	383	149

Notes:

[a] Comprises Germany, England, Belgium, Norway, Holland, Sweden and Switzerland.

[b] Assumed to cover the same as the Italian entries viz. public and private lighting, households, commerce and communal services.

Sources: M. Levy-Leboyer, 'Une réussite inachevée, 1919–46', in M. Levy-Leboyer and H. Morsel (eds.), Histoire de l'électricité en France. II. L'Interconnection et le marché, 1919–46 (Paris: L'Association pour l' Historie de l'Electricité en France, Fayard, 1994), Table 1; R. Giannetti, 'Dinamica della domanda e delle tariffe', in G. Galasso (ed.), Storia dell'industria elettrica in Italia. III. Espansione e oligopolio. 1926–45 (Roma-Bari: Laterza & Figli, 1993), Table 1.

The state, however, did not impose a national plan. It did intervene and invest in specific areas. It had set up the mixed enterprise Compagnie Nationale du Rhone to develop water supplies and electricity in the Rhone valley. In other regions, the electricity supply companies were expanding supplies to the railways, many of whose networks were subsidised or owned by the state. Then in the 1919–39 period, the government subsidised the electrification of certain rail tracks and the spread of electricity to rural areas. It was not however until 1937 that anything decisive happened about an integrated system. A revamped Conseil Supérieur de l'Electricité produced a 3000 million franc plan for expansion of capacity. It envisaged new HEP dams, a 220 kV line to Paris and the completion of integrating lines.[43] Re-armament diverted the funds, but during the war, the Vichy government's Comité de l'Organisation de l'Electricité made some progress.[44] Most important it recognised a role for the state in securing a firm link between the HEP and thermal areas. Thus, in seeming contrast to the case of the railways and the activities of the Corps du Ponts et Chaussées, the French government's involvement in planning the electricity infrastructure seems weak. Tension between the powerful private companies, the trade unions and the state were one of the ingredients of the move to nationalisation in 1946. During the war and after, the Confédération Générale du Travail and the resistance movement (Conseil National de Résistance) were very critical of the role of the companies, though some economic historians have seen this as misdirected and have argued that the lack of national focus was more a function of the hesitancy of the central government.[45] After the war, electricity was one of the industries deemed to have a strategic value, whose reconstruction could not be left in the hands of the private sector.[46] The legislation in 1946 setting up Electricité de France withdrew most of the concessions, thereby 'degranting' the whole of the network.[47] All generating capacity, except that less than 12 MW capacity, was taken over, and six regional networks were established. Nationalisation, as Morsel has emphasised, was not something that sprang out of the blue; it did follow a long history of arm's-length regulation by the state.[48] The arm does seem to have been particularly long in the inter-war period and was an important ingredient in nationalisation.

States and municipalities in electricity supply in Germany, Scandinavia and the UK

By the early 1900s, in several European countries, direct management of electricity undertakings was still in the hands of municipalities. This was the case in forty-two of the fifty largest towns in Germany and forty-four in Britain. Five of the sixteen largest towns in Denmark had municipally owned undertakings, including Copenhagen. In Sweden, before 1945, the rural co-operatives, unlike the urban municipalities, were not allowed to produce electricity; for the urban municipalities, merger with large private companies was neither easy constitutionally nor so obviously attractive economically. Nevertheless, all these countries witnessed a growth in consumption at least as big as the European average; for Germany it was significantly above the average, and Britain saw a fivefold increase over the years 1920–38 (Figure 8.2). Sweden's rise was proportionately the same as the European average, but because it had already attained very high absolute levels by 1920 (441 kWh per head), its rise was the largest of all in absolute terms (to 1032 kWh per head). An integrated national network and one that was managed nationally emerged before 1939 only in Britain. In Sweden, a national network was achieved by the mid-1930s and a managed system shortly after the Second World War. Each of the two halves of Denmark attained their own system integration, and one of them secured sea links to Swedish HEP. In Germany, the benefits of interconnection between the thermal north and HEP in the Alps were potentially large, but a central co-ordination of networks only appeared from 1935 after the Nazis had started to exert a centralising force. The key question is how the municipalities were accommodated in the drive to system integration. Private-sector expansion was important especially in the 1920s, but eventually government institutions adapted and facilitated the changes to a new regime. The initiative was taken by agencies of the central government in Britain (the Central Electricity Board created in 1926) and in Sweden (the Vattenfall, the state power board, created in 1909, cf. chapter 5). Germany saw many forms of governmental leverage via inter-municipal associations and mixed enterprises involving shareholding by the state, the Reich, municipalities and private individuals, such that by 1928 only 12% of electricity output emanated from purely private companies.[49] Denmark was distinct in that the central state had a minor role and the initiative came from below, from urban municipal electricity undertakings and rural electricity co-operatives, the 'andersalg', financed by local savings banks.[50] Both municipalities and co-operatives had shareholdings in large power and distribution companies, securing economies of scale from this joint ownership.

The reluctance of some municipalities to give up their control of operations is well attested and often linked to slow processes of system integration.[51] From very early on, large private generating companies emerged in all these countries, as they had in France, Italy and Spain. The Danish Gas Company built a large coal-fired plant in Copenhagen, and this came to supply most of the thermal power of eastern Denmark (Zealand). In Germany, the Allgemeine Elektrizitäts-Gesellschaft, Siemen, Lahmeyer and Stinnes companies were all erecting large thermal plants. The latter two made contracts with towns in the Ruhr and joined in 1899 to form RWE (Rheinisch-Westfalisches Elektrizitätswerke) a famous German enterprise that grew explosively in the 1920s, engaging in extensive share purchases in other companies. Public ownership was, however, not far away. RWE was part state owned while Sydcraft, supplying HEP in southern Sweden and Denmark, was created by the municipalities of Skåne in southern Sweden.[52] In Britain, in addition to the Newcastle-upon-Tyne Electricity Supply Company, established in north-east England from the late nineteenth century, other undertakings like the Clyde Valley Company and the Lancashire Power Company flourished in the first decades of the twentieth century.[53] They were, however, often overshadowed by the municipalities, such as the electricity undertakings of Manchester and Glasgow corporations. Similarly, in Sweden the Vattenfall not only had a very large plant at the Trollhattan Falls (cf. chapter 5) but a large thermal plant in eastern Sweden at Vasten.

It is when one turns to long-distance transmission that governmental agencies are particularly visible in these countries: that is, in promoting and participating in mixed enterprises and securing the agreement of small companies and municipalities to limit their activities to retailing electricity. In 1921 the Vattenfall constructed a 130 kV line connecting its plants at Trollhattan and Vasten and thereby created a vast interconnected network across eastern and western Sweden. By the early 1930s, all regional systems in the south of the country were interconnected and most of the HEP resources in the south had been harnessed. The Vattenhall was keen to expand into the north, and from the 1920s had been collaborating to this end with the leading Swedish manufacturer of high-voltage equipment, Allmäna Svenska Elektriska. One of the long-term fruits of this was the completion of the world's first 400 kV line in 1952, which stretched from a new power station in Harsprager to southern Sweden.[54] In Denmark, it was the municipalities and co-operatives who, through their share holdings, facilitated the development of two large regional networks. Nordsjællands Elektriciteit Selskab, a mixed electricity enterprise, based in the north-east of the country, developed a submarine cable that allowed HEP from the Sydkraft Company, in Sweden, to pass from Halsingburg across the Sound to Helsinger in Denmark. From 1915, HEP flowed from Sweden and thermal power flowed in the other direction from Denmark. It triggered off the interconnection of the whole of Zealand, with power emanating mainly from the Copenhagen thermal plant (cf. above) and the submarine cable. Another big regional network emerged in western Denmark (Jutland) following the construction of an HEP plant in the River Gudernia in 1920.[55]

In Germany, private, Reich, state and municipal shareholders participated in the regional networks that were emerging. They were complex organisations as the following examples illustrate. The Großkraftwerk power station started operations in 1923 in Mannheim with 37.5 MW capacity. It was owned by a joint stock company established in 1921, whose shares were held by Mannheim town council (26%), Badenwerke (26%, a state-owned energy utility needing customers for its HEP station on the River Murg), the Pfalzwerke (26%, a regional network on the left bank of the Rhine) and Neckar AG (22%, a mixed company itself needing a distribution facility for its planned HEP barrage on the River Neckar). The Großkraftwerk distributed electricity into a regional network near Mannheim and into the Pfalzwerke and Badenwerke networks. Part of the deal obliged the company to absorb any excess electricity from the HEP plants of the Badenwerke and Neckar.[56] Another example is the RWE, half of whose shares in 1914 were owned by municipalities and half by private companies. It had supply contracts with inter-municipal associations like the United Electricity Works. By 1924 it had 475 MW of capacity and claimed to have the largest coal plant in Europe, the Goldenbergwerk.[57] In the 1920s, RWE began a concentrated move to the south-east and in 1929 established a high-voltage line to its HEP plant at Vorarlberg in the Alps. It was also in conflict with the (mainly state-owned) Preussische Elektrizitäts AG with whom it finally came to an 'electricity peace' in 1927, settling territorial boundaries. A final example is the Elektrowerke undertaking owned jointly by the Reich and local governments and which, as early as 1918, had constructed a 100 km line to supply war industries in Berlin. The source was the huge plant at Zschornewitz near Bergkemnitz.

Thus in Germany, in the first three decades of the century, mixed enterprises, inter-municipal groups, state and Reich initiatives were all used in the establishment of regional networks. Purely private companies accounted for only 26% of capacity in 1913. In that year there were twenty-five regional companies, but in all but one the municipalities had a controlling interest.[58] The position by 1928 is shown in Table 8.5. The municipalities produced 3757 gigawatt hours or about one quarter of the total of 14479 gigawatt hours and it is likely that they sold most of that to final consumers. In addition, they distributed a further 20% of German total production purchased from other

Table 8.5 *Electricity supply in Germany, 1928 (gigawatt hours)*

	Production	Re-sale of other supplies
Reich and States	3819	552
Municipalities	3757	2780
Other public authorities	620	285
Mixed undertakings	4171	2193
Private	2112	1078
Total	14479	

Source: O. Mulert, 'The Economic Activities of German Municipalities', *Annals of Collective Economy* 5 (1929), 222–3, drawing on data from the Federation of Electricity Works, which accounted for 95% of all output.

sources – private companies, mixed enterprises, state and Reich undertakings. Purely private companies accounted for only 14% of total output.

In none of these countries, except Britain, did a truly unified nationally managed network emerge before the Second World War. The process of integration in Britain was initially slow, but, as the most industrially advanced country in Europe, the benefits from system integration were potentially huge. In 1900 there were already 65 separate private companies and 164 municipally owned undertakings. There were some joint ventures – such as the Stalybridge, Hyde, Mossley and Dukinfield Tramways and Electricity Board established in 1901 by Parliamentary Bill – but generally they struggled to get off the ground.[59] By 1926 there were 233 separate private companies and 360 municipal undertakings.[60]

A demand for government intervention had arisen early on. Calls for greater co-ordination between urban areas were being made in the early 1900s, and, immediately after the First World War, there was much agitation for administrative co-ordination through the establishment of district electricity boards. Following a report to Parliament by the Williamson Committee Report in 1918, the only gain was the establishment of a body, the Electricity Commissioners, to promote technical development. Another government committee was established in 1925 and reported in strong terms on the relatively high cost and low consumption of electricity, the proliferation of small plants and the need for interconnection.[61] The solution, ingenious said Hannah in the light of fears of nationalisation, was to set up the Central Electricity Board (CEB).[62] Its basic functions were to construct a national grid, close down small stations and standardise electricity frequencies. But it was the institutional arrangement that was truly innovative. Certain stations were to be 'selected'. The CEB would buy electricity from them, transmit and then resell, leaving the job of retailing to the companies and local authority undertakings. It bestowed the honour of being selected rather generously in order to oil the process of transition, and the work of Foreman-Peck and Waterson suggests that the best-practice local authority and private generating plants were equally efficient (though with a longish 'tail' of unselected municipal plants), which also would have facilitated a smooth transition.[63] The managers of the CEB were not appointed by the Treasury, and all capital was raised on the stock market without a Treasury guarantee. It was this that allayed the fears, even though the reality was that it was a publicly owned enterprise since none of the stock was equity.

On the face of it the Board was a success. The grid networks were set up first on a regional basis with the Board's first chairman, Duncan, experimenting in his home territory in Scotland and the national grid completed in 1933. Capital formation each year averaged £20 million, and in the inter-war period as a whole, the number of consumers increased tenfold and consumption per head of population increased proportionately more than in any of the other European countries shown in Figure 8.2. Production in the non-selected stations fell dramatically, the thermal efficiency gap with the USA was eliminated and the system load factor raised from 25% in 1926 to 37% by 1939. This part of the British story seemed a success. However, by the end of the 1930s there were still 600 small electricity undertakings in existence, mainly involved in retail distribution and with only a small turnover. In 1934, over 400 undertakings accounted for less than 10% of sales, distribution costs were high and the multiplicity of boundaries prevented efficient development of networks. The trouble was that local authorities accounted for 60% of the undertakings, and they were particularly stubborn. Not for them to give up empires and profits. Joint electricity authorities had emerged, but the experience was not encouraging and Herbert Morrison (a leading Labour Party figure who instigated the formation of the London Passenger Transport Board) did not see them as the way forward. Civic pride and political rivalries permeated the system. The Member of Parliament for Ashton-under-Lyne observed in 1937 that the local council would rather its electricity undertaking be taken over by a new public board than see it fall into the hands of Oldham borough, the neighbouring authority. Later, when nationalisation loomed, many municipalities were appalled at the prospect that the loss of their undertakings was to be treated simply as a bookkeeping entry within the public sector accounts and hence they would receive as compensation simply the amount of their *net* outstanding debt. This local parochialism explains in part the push to nationalisation in the 1940s, but there were wider issues involved.[64]

The problem of the distribution outlets had prompted the government to set up an investigatory body, the McGowan Committee, which in a report of 1936 identified economies that could be realised in marketing and finance from grouping into larger units and from the standardisation of voltages.[65] In so far as the economies of scale were at a regional (or sub-national level), the question was how regional business organisations would emerge. The Committee proposed that they should be developed from existing undertakings but recognised that legislation and compulsory powers would be necessary. Precisely how this would work out was not clear. Herbert Morrison had seen the solution in regional boards publicly owned on the lines of the Central Electricity Board, and in both electricity and gas the 'public board' element arose in part from the problems associated with a 'natural' or 'voluntary' emergence of larger units of business organisation.

It is important to note that support for public boards did not just come from the Labour Party. In the depressed economic conditions of the inter-war period, the Conservative Party could not reject public ownership out of hand, especially since it was in power during the creation of the CEB and the London Passenger Transport Board. The 'etatist' wing of the party was barely distinguishable on many issues from the Morrisonian wing of the Labour Party, and in 1938 Harold Macmillan described Labour's programme for the nationalisation of the Bank of England, coal mining, power, land and transport as mild compared with his own plan.[66] The public board received support from some civil servants, from the Conservative Minister of Fuel in 1942 and by Liberal Gwillam Lloyd George as Minister in 1943. The Conservatives' Industrial Charter of 1947 opposed nationalisation and direct planning in principle but fudged privatisation outside one or two small sectors in road and air transport, claiming that privatising the large public corporations would be too disruptive. Moreover, a large body of professional opinion was, by the late 1930s and 1940s, canvassing a more interventionist government stance in industrial matters. Even E. H. E. Woodward, General Engineer and Manager of the North Eastern Electricity Supply Company, who wanted larger business units, saw ownership as irrelevant and advocated public boards.[67] In the event, the legislation of 1947 created twelve such regional distribution boards for England and Wales and two for south Scotland to set alongside the North of Scotland Hydro-Electric Board, which had been established in 1943. Finally the CEB was replaced by the Central Electricity Generating Board, which took ownership of all the generating plants and all the national grid and became responsible for all generation and transmission to the area boards in England and Wales.

Thus in Britain, the clear division between private and public sector, identified in Part II, had some important consequences in the inter-war period. Faced with potentially large economic gains from system integration, the central government intervened to set up a semi-autonomous agency to construct and manage a national grid. In those continental European countries where municipal ownership had developed strongly by the First World War, mixed enterprises, inter-municipal associations and state power boards exercised the leverage for institutional adaptation to the new technology. But managed unified national systems did not emerge until after the Second World War. Sweden was more advanced than others because the drive to the north had started in the 1930s and a national network established with consumption at levels exceeded in Europe only by Norway (Figure 8.2). It was not a managed system, and the question of whether the state power board (the Vattenfall) or the private companies or some mixture should take the lead was the subject of extensive debates in the 1930s and 1940s.[68] In 1945, a compromise was agreed, but then the Social Democratic Party was elected in 1946 and ruled that the Vattenfall should be responsible – which effectively meant that all new lines of 200 kV or higher were to be built by the Vattenfall.

The Danish experience looked very similar to Britain's early on. In 1929 the central government set up an electricity council (Energiradet) as a force for national integration, but it quickly subsided into a purely advisory body like the Electricity Commissioners in Britain. Integration was left to the municipalities, co-operatives and companies. There was no mechanism for ensuring that the least-cost source of power would be used in every location and in every period. The residents of Zealand had to wait until 1954, when Kraftimport (later renamed ELKRAFT) was established to co-ordinate operations and the construction programme of the three large power groups that had come to predominate. In western Denmark (Jutland) in 1956, the regional groups merged into a body called ELSAM, which proceeded to build a new high tension grid. Some writers have argued that joining the eastern and western parts of Denmark was not so economically attractive given the dominance of thermal plants in both groupings.[69] Britain stands as counterevidence to this argument, and in any case there was the prospect, from the 1920s, of drawing on HEP from Sweden via the submarine cable at Helsingor (cf. above). Paradoxically, Jutland was eventually connected in the 1960s to Sweden via the Konti-Scan cable through Germany. At the end of the 1930s, the price of electricity was still relatively high in Denmark, whose consumption levels were still below the European average, though it continued to enjoy good access to British coal and its gas output per head of population was still higher than in all other countries (Table 8.2).

In Germany, a unified national network did not emerge under Weimar, despite the passage in 1919 of a bill in the National Assembly that presaged the development of a co-ordinated national high tension grid. There already existed a nationally owned electricity undertaking – the Elektrowerke – but it did not dominate the national scene and participated in German electricity supply in a manner similar to the regional undertakings. Plans for integration were conceived in terms of developing a system with some of the characteristics of the Bayernwerk, the Bavarian state system. This had a transmission grid taking and delivering supplies to and from municipal undertakings and private companies, as well as sending HEP to Munich and other big urban centres. Nothing emerged from these schemes for a national grid, but three regional groups were formed for the west, east and centre. Then in 1935, a law (Gesetz zur Förderung der Energiewirtschaft) was passed promulgating that all investment in generating power and in networks had to be approved by the Minister of Economics.[70] Control had effectively been established at the national level, even though the industry was never nationalised. The Reich, and later the Federal Government of West Germany after 1946, had extensive holdings in the industry, including Elektrowerke AG Berlin, Preussische Elektrizitäts AG, Bayernwerk AG, Energie-Versogung, Rhein-Main-Donau, Neckar AG, Braunschweigische Kohlenbergewerke AG. A unified organisation for the German power grid was finally established in 1948. Nine undertakings were involved, but the state owned four of them outright, it held 50% or more in a further five and the ninth was RWE, where the state had 30% ownership.[71]

In summary, the antagonism of the public to the growth of private regional monopolies was mitigated in part by the activities of the Reich, state and municipalities in both direct management and in their shareholdings in mixed enterprises, a striking feature of the German electricity industry. Any unwillingness of the private companies to get in bed with government institutions was reduced by the leverage that states and Reich exercised over the municipalities and by the ease with which the private companies were thereby able to raise capital. The net result was that, although the rise in electricity consumption levels in the inter-war period in Germany was less, proportionately, than in Britain and it did not have the same gas supplies as Britain, it was consuming 843 kWh per head of population by 1938, a level exceeded only in Sweden and Norway with vastly richer HEP resources (Figure 8.2). The presence of a large mixed-enterprise sector reflected an institutional response (not unlike Denmark) to the new technology, which in other countries had provoked a rather different institutional mix. The high tension networks were wholly publicly owned in Britain by the Second World War and largely private in France, but with the state totally committed by the late 1930s to directing future investment and planning. Belgium seems to have been in roughly the same position as France.[72] At the other extremes were Spain, where the expansion of generating capacity was more important than system integration, and Norway where the leverage of the state power board had ensured that regional harnessing of the HEP riches had, for the moment, obviated the need for national integration. In contrast, in Germany and Sweden, where system integration looked to be economically more desirable, state power by the mid-1930s was directed very actively to promoting national networks. In Denmark and Italy, the central government exercised little direct influence, and their relatively low consumption levels reflected this. Decisive action by the organs of central government seem, in sum, to have been influential in successful developments of the electricity system in the inter-war period.

Notes

1 G. Brondel, 'The Sources of Energy', in C. Cipolla (ed.), *Fontana Economic History of Europe: The Twentieth Century* (Glasgow: Fontana/Collins, 1973), 224.

2 Cf. H. Morsel, 'Etude comparée des nationalisations de l'électricité en Europe occidentale après la deuxième guerre mondiale', in M. Trédé (ed.), *Electricité et électrification dans le monde 1880–1980* (Paris: Association pour l'Histoire de l'Electricité en France, Presses Universitaires de France, 1990), 443–57.

3 F. Antolin, 'Public Policy in the Development of the Spanish Electric Utility Industry', Paper presented at European Historical Economics Society Conference on *A Century of Industrial Policy in Europe*, Oxford, Worcester College, 1992; M. Levy-Leboyer, 'The French Electrical Power System: An Inter-Country Comparison', in R. Maintz and T. P. Hughes (eds.), *The Development of Large Technical Systems* (Boulder, Colo.: Frankfurt and Westview Press, 1978), 245–62; A. Kaijser, 'From Local Networks to National Systems: A Comparison of the Emergence of Electricity and Telephony in Sweden', in F. Cardot (ed.), *1880–1980 une siècle de l' électricité dans le monde* (Paris: Presses Universitaires de France, 1987), 7–22.

4 L. Hannah, *Electricity before Nationalisation* (London: Macmillan, 1979), 78.

5 T. P. Hughes, 'Technology as a Force for Change in History: The Effort to Form a Unified Electric Power System in Weimar Germany', in H. Mommsen (ed.), *Industrielles System und politische Entwicklung in der Weimarer Republik* (Düsseldorf: Droste, 1977), 161; T. P. Hughes, *Networks of Power: Electrification in Western Society 1880–1930* (Baltimore: Johns Hopkins Press, 1983), 408–9; Hannah, *Electricity before Nationalisation*, 132–3; M. Levy-Leboyer, 'Panorama de l'électrification: De la grande guerre à la nationalisation', in M. Levy-Leboyer

and H. Morsel (eds.), *Histoire de l'électricité en France. II. L'Interconnection et le marché, 1919–46* (Paris: L'Association pour l'Histoire de l' Electricité en France, Fayard, 1994), 49–50.

6 A. Kaijser, 'Controlling the Grid: The Development of High Tension Power Lines in the Nordic Countries', in A. Kaijser and M. Hedin (eds.), *Nordic Energy Systems: Historical Perspectives and Current Issues* (Canton, Mass.: Science History Publications, 1995), 50; Levy-Leboyer, 'Panorama de l'électrification', 39.

7 Hughes, 'Technology as a Force' and Kaijser, 'Controlling the Grid', 38.

8 Hannah, *Electricity before Nationalisation*, 32.

9 Cf. M. Boiteux and P. Stasi, 'The Determination of the Costs of Expansion of an Inter-connected System of Production and Distribution of Electricity', originally 1952, and reproduced in J. R. Nelson (ed.), *Marginal Cost Pricing in Practice* (Englewood Cliffs, N. J.: Prentice-Hall, 1964), 91–126.

10 Morsel, 'Etude comparée des nationalisations', 468–9.

11 Cf. Levy-Leboyer, 'Panorama de l'électrification', 53.

12 G. Kurgen-van Hentenryk, 'La Régime économique de l'industrie électrique belge depuis la fin du XIX siècle', in F. Cardot (ed.), *1880–1980: Une siècle de l'électricité dans le monde* (Paris: Presses Universitaires de France, 1978), 119–34; in the same volume, U. Wengenroth, 'The Electrification of the Workshop', 357–66.

13 A. Fernandez, 'Production and Distribution of Electricity in Bordeaux, 1887–1956: Private and Public Operation', *Contemporary European History* 5(2) (1996), 162 and *Economie et politique de l'électricité à Bordeaux (1887–1956)* (Talence: Sciences PO Bordeaux, Presses Universitaires de Bordeaux, 1998), ch. 4.

14 Cf. Morsel, 'Etude comparée des nationalisations', 448.

15 Kaijser, 'Controlling the Grid', 48.

16 A. Carreras, X. Tafunell and E. Torres, 'The Rise and Decline of Spanish State-Owned Firms', in P. A. Toninelli (ed.), *The Rise and Fall of State Owned Enterprise in the Western World* (Cambridge University Press, 2000), 208–36. See also Antolin, 'Public Policy in the Development of the Spanish Electric Utility Industry' and R. Myro Sanchez, 'Public Enterprise in the Spanish Economy 1940–1985', in V. Zamagni, *Origins and Development of Publicly Owned Enterprises* (University of Florence, Ninth International Economic History Conference, Section B111, 1986), 54–9.

17 M. de Motes, 'L'Electricité, facteur de développement économique en Espagne: 1930–36' in Cardot (ed.), *Une siècle de l'électricité*, 57–68 and, in the same volume, C. Sudria, 'Les restrictions de la consummation de l'électricité en Espagne pendant l'après guerre 1944–54', 425–36; G. Nunez, 'Développement et intégration régionale de l'industrie électrique en Andalousie jusqu'en 1935', in Trédé (ed.), *Eléctricité et électrification*, 192.

18 Antolin, 'Public Policy in the Development of the Spanish Electric Utility Industry', 20 and elsewhere.

19 G. Tortella, *The Development of Modern Spain* (Cambridge, Mass.: Harvard University Press, 2000), 853.

20 Sudria, 'Les Restrictions de la consummation de l'électricité', 428.

21 P. F. Balbin, 'Spain: Industrial Policy under Authoritarian Politics', in J. Foreman-Peck and G. Federico (eds.), *European Industrial Policy: The Twentieth Century Experience* (Oxford University Press, 1999), 247.

22 L. Thue, 'The State and the Dual Structure of the Power Supply Industry in Norway, 1890–1940', in Trédé (ed.), *Electricité et électrification*, 227–34.

23 Kaijser, 'Controlling the Grid'.

24 Thue, 'Power Supply Industry in Norway', 223.

25 P. Schwob, 'Relations between the State and the Electric Power Industry in France', *Harvard Business Review* 13(1) (1934), 92.

26 Levy-Leboyer, 'Panorama de l'électrification', Table 11 and 'The French Electrical Power System', 254–7; Morsel, 'Etude comparée des nationalisations'; H. Morsel, 'L'Hydro-électricité en France: Du patronal dispersé a la direction nationale (1902–46)', in P. Fridensen and A. Strauss (eds.) *Le Capitalisme française* (Paris: Librairie Arthème, Fayard, 1987), 381–97; G. Ramunni, 'L'Elaboration du réseau électrique française: Un débat technique de l'entre-deux-guerres', in Cardot, *Une siècle de l'électricité*, 269–82; Schwob, 'Relations between the State and the Electric Power Industry', 92; R. L. Frost, *Alternating Currents: Nationalised Power in France 1946–70* (Ithaca, N. Y.: Cornell University Press, 1991), 15; Morsel, 'Etude comparée des nationalisations'.

27 V. Zamagni, *The Economic History of Italy 1860–1990* (Oxford: Clarendon Press, 1993), 280–1.

28 R. Giannetti, 'Resources, Firms and Public Policy in the Growth of the Italian Electrical Industry from the Beginnings to the 1930s', in Cardot (ed.), *Une siècle de l'électricité*, 41–50.

29 Ibid., 49.

30 Ramunni, 'L'Elaboration du réseau électrique française', 274. See also Morsel, 'Etude comparée des nationalisations'; Morsel, 'L'Hydro-électricité en France'; Levy-Leboyer, 'Panorama de l'Electrification'.

31 Giannetti, 'Resources, Firms and Public Policy in the Growth of the Italian Electrical Industry'.

32 Levy-Leboyer, 'Panorama de l'Electrification', Tables 1 and 2, 29 and 40. Note that the consumption levels here and in Table 8.4 for both France and Italy are less than those recorded in B. R. Mitchell, *International Historical Statistics: Europe 1750–1993* (London: Macmillan, 3rd edn, 1998), which is the source for Table 8.2.

33 Morsel, 'L'Hydro-électricité en France', 285.

34 F. Conti, 'The Creation of a Regional Electrical System: Selt Valdarno Group and the Electrification of Tuscany', in Trédé (ed.), *Electricité et électrification dans le monde*, 155–68. The same point was made about France by Frost, *Alternating Currents*, 10.

35 Giannetti, 'Resources, Firms and Public Policy in the Growth of the Italian Electrical Industry', 26.

36 G. Federico and R. Giannetti, 'Italy: Stalling and Surpassing', in Foreman-Peck and Federico (eds.), *European Industrial Policy*, 131.

37 Giannetti, 'Resources, Firms and Public Policy in the Growth of the Italian Electrical Industry', 48.

38 F. Amatori, 'Beyond State and Market: Italy's Futile Search for a Third Way', in Toninelli (ed.), *Rise and Fall*, Table 6.1, 131. See also R. Ciocca and G. Toniolo, 'Industry and Finance in Italy 1918–40', *Journal of European Economic History* 13 (1984), 113–36; F. Amatori, 'IRI: From Industrial Saviour to Industrial Group', in Zamagni (ed.), *Origins and Development of Publicly Owned Enterprises*, 8–13 and, in the same volume, F. Bonelli, 'The Origins of Public Corporations in Italy', 20–7.

39 V. Castronovo (ed.), *Storia dell'industria elettrica in Italia. IV. Daldopoguerra alla nazionalizzazione 1945–62* (Roma-Bari: Laterza & Figli, 1994), 856. See also Morsel, 'Etude comparée des nationalisations', 450.

40 K. Doukas, 'Ownership, Management and Regulation of Electric Undertakings in France', *The George Washington Law Review* 6(2) (January 1938), 152; P. Lanthier, 'The Relationship between State and Private Electric Industry, France 1880–1920', in N. Horn and J. Kocha (eds.), *Recht und Entwicklung der Grossunternehmen im 19. und frühen 20. Jahrhundert* (Göttingen: Vandenhoek and Ruprecht, 1979), 596–9; Schwob, 'Relations between the State and the Electric Power Industry in France', 82.

41 Schwob, 'Relations between the State and the Electric Power Industry in France', 92–4.

42 Ramunni, 'L'Elaboration du réseau électrique française', 274.

43 Frost, *Alternating Currents*, 15; N. Lucas, *Western European Energy Policies* (Oxford: Clarendon Press, 1985), 5.

44 Frost, *Alternating Currents*, 29 and Morsel, 'Etude comparée des nationalisations'.

45 Morsel, 'L'Hydro-électricité en France', 404.

46 D. H. Pinkney, 'Nationalisation of Key Industries and Credit in France after the Liberation', *Political Science Quarterly* 62 (1947), 371.

47 J. Moch, 'Nationalisation in France', *Annals of Collective Economy* 24 (1953), 103.

48 Morsel, 'Etude comparée des nationalisations'. See also M. Einaudi, 'Nationalisation in France and Italy', *Social Research* 15(1) (1948), 31.

49 O. Mulert, 'The Economic Activities of German Municipalities', *Annals of Collective Economy* 5 (1929), 209–76.

50 Thue, 'The State and the Dual Structure of the Power Supply Industry in Norway', 19, n.16.

51 Kaijser, 'Controlling the Grid', 34; Hannah, *Electricity before Nationalisation*, chs.2 and 3; Hughes, 'Technology as a Force'.

52 Hughes, *Networks of Power*, ch. 14; Hughes, 'Technology as a Force'; Lucas, *Western European Energy Policies*, 109.

53 Hannah, *Electricity before Nationalisation*, 40.

54 A. Kaijser, 'The Helping Hand: In Search of a Swedish Institutional Regime for Infrastructure Systems', in L. Andersson-Skog and O. Krantz (eds.), *Institutions and the Transport and Communications Industries* (Canton, Mass.: Science History Publications, Watson, 1999), 235; Kaijser, 'Controlling the Grid' and A. Kaijser, 'From Local Networks to National Systems: A Comparison of the Emergence of Electricity and Telephony in Sweden', in F. Cardot (ed.), *1880–1980: Une siècle de l'Electricité*, 7–22. See also,

E. Jakobsson, 'Industrialised Rivers: The Development of Swedish Hydropower', in Kaijser and Hedin, *Nordic Energy Systems*, 647.

55 Kaijser, 'Controlling the Grid'.
56 D. Schott, 'Power for Industry: Electrification and its Strategic Use for Industrial Promotion. The case of Mannheim', in D. Schott (ed.), *Energy and the City in Europe: From Preindustrial Wood-Shortages to the Oil Crisis of the 1970s* (Stuttgart: Franz Steiner Verlag, 1997), 169–193.
57 Hughes, *Networks of Power*, 409.
58 R. Messager, 'Municipalities and Managers: Heat Networks in Germany', in J. A. Tarr and G. Dupuy (eds.), *Technology and the Rise of the Networked City in Europe* (Philadelphia: Temple University Press, 1988), 286; W. Falk and H. Pittack, 'Publicly Owned Enterprises and Forms of Participation of the State in Private Enterprise in Germany before 1933', in Zamagni (ed.), *Origins and Development of Publicly Owned Enterprises*, 34–9; Wengenroth, 'Rise and Fall', 108.
59 Hannah, *Electricity before Nationalisation*, ch. 2.
60 R. Millward, 'The Political Economy of Urban Utilities in Britain 1840–1950', in M. Daunton (ed.), *Cambridge Urban History of Britain, III* (Cambridge University Press, 2001), Table 11.2.
61 Williamson Committee, *Report of a Committee Appointed by the Board of Trade to Consider the Question of Electric Power Supply*, Command 9062, Parliamentary Papers 1918, vi (London: HMSO, 1918); Weir Committee, *Report of a Committee Appointed by the Board of Trade to Review the National Problem of the Supply of Electricity Energy* (London: Board of Trade, 1926).
62 L. Hannah, 'A Pioneer of Public Enterprise: The Central Electricity Generating Board and the National Grid', in B. Supple (ed.), *Essays in British Business History* (Oxford: Clarendon Press, 1977), 207–26.
63 J. M. Foreman-Peck and M. Waterson, 'The Comparative Efficiency of Public and Private Enterprise in Britain: Electricity Generation between the World Wars', *Economic Journal* 95 (Supplement) (1985), 83–95.
64 Hannah, *Electricity before Nationalisation*, 331–2.
65 McGowan Report, *Report of the Committee on Electricity Distribution* (London: Ministry of Transport, 1936).
66 R. Millward and J. Singleton (eds.), *The Political Economy of Nationalisation in Britain 1920–50* (Cambridge University Press, 1995), ch. 2.
67 Hannah, *Electricity before Nationalisation*.
68 Kaijser, 'Controlling the Grid' and 'From Local Networks to National Systems'.
69 Kaijser, 'Controlling the Grid', 47; Lucas, *Western European Energy Policies*, 66–7.
70 H. K. Schneider and W. Schultz, 'Market Structure and Market Organisation in the Electricity and Gas Public Utilities of the Federal Republic of Germany', in W. J. Baumol (ed.), *Public and Private Enterprise in the Mixed Economy* (New York: International Economic Association, Macmillan, 1980), 75; Wengenroth, 'Rise and Fall', 112–13; H. Oeftering, 'The Participation of the German Federal State in Economic Enterprises', *Annals of Collective Economy*, 24 (1953), 271–88.
71 Wengenroth, 'Rise and Fall', 121.
72 Kurgen-van Hentenryk, 'La Régime économique'.

9   Railway finances and road–rail competition

By the 1930s, railway systems everywhere in Europe were in desperate financial straits. German rail revenues in 1933, for example, could not even cover operating costs. In Britain, the margin was inadequate to meet interest charges, and this was true for the trunk lines in Sweden run by the state railways (Statens Järnvägar, SJ), whose gross annual profits on average over the period 1931–5 were 33 million kroner, not enough to cover interest and related capital charges of 40 million kroner; the local and provincial lines run by private companies were in even worse financial condition. In France in 1933, the balance over all networks after meeting all capital charges was a deficit of 3860 million francs. Of course, general economic conditions in these depression years were bad, and some recovery took place in the second half of the 1930s. The financial problems did not, however, disappear. The deficits in French railways rose to 5934 million francs in 1937 and, as Dormois says, as an 'outcome of decades of subsidisation and regulations', was an ingredient in the nationalisation of the networks in the same year, to be followed by Sweden in 1939, Spain in 1944 and Britain in 1947.[1] Although the slogans under which this occurred were sometimes 'socialism' or 'autarky', the takeovers commanded wide support and reflected the inherent problems of economic organisation that were to bedevil inland surface transport for the rest of the century.

At the heart of the railway problem was the complex mixture of social and economic objectives that had accumulated during the nineteenth century. Reconciling them with financial probity, the railways' monopoly power and parliamentary willingness to provide subsidies was a constant problem, and in the inter-war period the emergence of a new vibrant rival in road transport was the final blow. In all countries, railways were used as an arm of military strategy, especially in France and Germany, and as an engine of economic growth in Spain and Italy. In chapter 4 it was argued that, for routes that fell into these categories, but which were unprofitable, governments leaned on the companies and, if that failed, provided subsidies or brought them into state ownership. The evidence of these practices is pervasive, and they continued into the inter-war period.

Sweden is a good case. The rail track doubled from 1900 to 1930, and government policy shifted from the nineteenth-century idea of linking up 'the economically most developed regions' to that of creating 'opportunities for regional economic growth over the entire country'.[2] Regional pressure groups bombarded Parliament (the Riksdag) with special pleading. To quote one typical incident, Lapland ore was carried by SJ from Norrbotten (the northern part of Sweden) to the south at a rate that was actually negotiated between the mining company LKAB and the government. SJ protested that the rates were uneconomic and objected to being used as a tool of government regional policy. It was not until 1929 that the government agreed to write off some of SJ's capital stock, shifting the burden thereby to taxpayers. The German National Railway (Deutsche Reichsbahn, DR) may have taken on more than any of the other systems if we accept the view of a recent scholar that it 'perceived its mission as assisting various … groups to achieve their goals. It sought to shield groups from technological and locational disadvantages, to allow all groups to participate especially in national life and to reduce disparities in standards of living among them'.[3]

The railway companies had, in any case, alienated many customers by their charging policies. Because each company usually had a monopoly of rail services for particular routes and regions and because they were providing a service (rather than commodities), they could discriminate between customer groups. The variable cost of a particular consignment was often low, and the companies charged 'what the traffic would bear' with freight grouped into classes according to the value of the goods being carried. This was often bitterly resented. Chapter 4 showed, for example, how competition from coastal steamers and waterway traffic prompted the companies to offer low rates to importers of American and Russian wheat and meat, which were not offered to domestic farmers. Complaints like this prompted two reactions. Firstly, central governments grew very sensitive about the monopoly position of railway companies and forced public interest obligations on them. They had to publish all their fares and freight rates, to provide services on demand (the common carrier obligation) and to provide a minimum number of services per day, and they were also required to avoid 'undue preference' between customers. The outcome was a fairly rigid system of standard charges with uniform passenger fares per kilometre and freight rates per kilometre across whole networks and territories. The companies increasingly pressed governments to allow tapering charges and special rates for individual consignments. Secondly, the companies reacted to their unpopularity by offering services in kind, like carrying government and postal traffic at below cost rates, offering special rates for journeys to work, providing generous insurance cover and generous space in marshalling yards. They could ill afford to do this.

By 1913, most railways systems, with the possible exception of that in Prussia, were on a knife edge. The range of unprofitable activities was widening, and to remain viable the companies increasingly needed government support. The delicate balance between financial and sociopolitical objectives would have tested the metal of any government. The requirement to both regulate and subsidise private monopolies was a formidable task. Much of the network in Italy and Germany was in public ownership before the First World War as were the trunk lines in Scandinavia and the western network in France. In the forty years up to 1913, railway finances were in clear decline. In Britain, the most private of all systems, net profits available to shareholders or for new investment were 4.4% of paid-up capital in 1870, falling to 4.1% in 1890, 3.6% in 1910 and 3.5% in 1912. The aggregate deficits over all the French networks by 1913 were such that the cumulative debt to the state was 617 million francs.[4]

Matters came to a head in the 1920s and 1930s. During the First World War, investment dried up, equipment and rolling stock were either destroyed or run down and the public utility role of the railways ensured that prices were never able to catch up to rising wage and fuel bills. So railways emerged from the war with even bigger deficits. Operating costs (mainly fuel, wages and maintenance) as a percentage of revenue (the 'operating ratio') were of the order of 65% in France, Germany and Britain in 1913. By the end of the war, operating ratios had climbed over 100%, and profits after interest charges were negative, as Table 9.1 shows. Thereafter the fortunes of each railway system were determined by how their own country's economy was affected by changes in world trading conditions and how protected they were from the onslaught of competition from road transport.

The days of large extensions of the rail track were over. Abstracting from boundary changes, track kilometres open in the United Kingdom actually fell, and in France, after allowing for the inclusion of Alsace-Lorraine, rose only slightly. The rest saw increases in the period 1919–38 ranging from 900 km in Norway to 2700 km in Italy.[5] Relative to population movements, there were no track extensions of any size. The depression of the 1930s hit all countries as industrial production fell. Rail revenues declined in France from 16 billion francs in 1929 to 12.5 billion in 1932, and over the same period in Germany from 5.4 billion Reichsmarks to 2.9 billion. Freight traffic fell by large amounts in Belgium, Denmark, the Netherlands and Norway in the first half of the 1930s.[6] Even the trunk network in Sweden run by SJ showed big financial losses. The passenger and freight receipts of the Spanish railway companies had been buoyant in the 1920s but collapsed in the 1930s.[7] The UK was different in that its manufacturing industry lost out in many overseas markets in the 1920s with immediate effects on railway coal traffic, which fell from 222 million tons in 1923 to 207 million in 1929. Traffic in other minerals and general merchandise also fell so that, after sharing the depressed conditions of all Europe in the 1930s, rail traffic in coal in the UK finished up in 1933 some 22% lower than in 1923, other minerals 23% lower and general merchandise 25% lower.[8] Total railway revenues fell from £218 million in 1921 to £150 million in 1933.

The broad stance of most governments was to shore up the railway undertakings financially, but in the light of the growing concentration of ownership, to continue to impose public interest obligations, including those inherent in the rate and fare structure inherited from the nineteenth century. Financial compensation for the effects of the First World War together with a rationalisation of organisational structure would allow, so it was argued, the complex set of socioeconomic objectives to be maintained. The adverse world trading conditions put a big dent in that approach, but even more important for the long run was that the true significance of road competition was largely ignored until the 1930s, and then the response was to impose restrictions on the road sector, rather than address the fundamental problems of the outdated railway price structure.

The initial reactions of central governments in the immediate postwar years were very similar. The year 1921 saw a basic agreement between the French government and the five major private companies plus the old Etat undertaking (the state-owned western network) and the Alsace-Lorraine railway (which had been taken back from Germany and placed into state ownership in 1918). An executive committee (Comité de Direction), containing representatives of all the undertakings, was set up to provide co-ordination, while a new Conseil Supérieure des Chemins de Fer was to act as an advisory body on all financial and technical issues. The price book (*cahier des charges*) allowed general and special freight rates. Within the former there had been four categories based on the value of the commodities transported, and this was raised to six classes in 1921.[9] In Germany, the Federal Constitution of 1919 had ruled in article 92 that a separate Reichsbahn, 'an autonomous economic enterprise', be formed from all the existing state networks.[10] The old nineteenth-century tariff structures typically had uniform rates per kilometre for both freight and passengers. From 1920, tapering rates were allowed, but it was still a system based on the 'value' of traffic rather than its cost. In 1923, the aim, if not the reality, of economic independence

Table 9.1 *Railway finances, 1913–1938*

	Britain			France			Germany				Sweden (Swedish State Railways)	
	Oper. Ratio (%)	Revenue	Gross Profits	Oper. Ratio (%)	Revenue	Net Profits	Oper. Ratio (%)	Revenue	Gross Profits	Interest etc.	Gross Profits	Interest Charges
		(£million)			(Million francs)			(Million Reichsmarks)			(Million kroner)	
1913	65.2	119.8	44.1	63.5	2058	77	66.0			852		
1921	104.1	217.8	−9.0	113.9	6453	−1206	123.6	34	−8.0		50	52
1925	82.7	199.7	34.6	84.2	10295	−586	85.1	6670	694	544	(1921–5 average)	
1926	89.6	171.9	17.9	75.8	13412	542	81.1	4540	861	846	60	55
1929	78.1	188.2	41.3	78.7	16174	304	83.9	5350	861	855	(1926–30 average)	
1930	80.6	177.7	34.4	88.4	16098	−1302	89.5	4570	480	792		
1932	83.7	149.6	24.4	102.9	12488	−3602	102.3	2930	−67		33	40
1933	82.3	149.6	26.5	103.8	11790	−3860	100.6	2920	−136		(1931–5 average)	
1937	79.4	171.4	35.3	116.2	12674	−5934	90.6	4420	416		75	38
1938	83.5	164.7	27.1				92.0	5130	468		(1936–40 average)	

Note:

Operating ratio is operating costs, including taxes, as a percentage of revenue. In Germany 1924–31, the allocations for reparation payments are included in operating costs. Gross profits are revenue less operating costs so defined. Net profits are gross profits less interest and related charges.

Sources: L. Andersson-Skog, 'From State Railway Housekeeping to Railway Economics: Swedish Railway Policy and Economic Transformation after 1920 in an Institutional Perspective', *Scandinavian Economic History Review* 49 (1996), Figure 1; P. S. Bagwell, *The Transport Revolution from 1770* (London: Batsford, 1974), 252, Table 6; K. Doukas, *The French Railroads and the State* (New York: Columbia Press, 1945), 185; W. M. W. Splawn, *Government Ownership and Operation of Railways* (New York: Macmillan, 1928), 68, 72; A. C. Mierzejewski, *The Most Valuable Asset of the Reich: A History of the German National Railway Company*, 2 vols. (Chapel Hill: University of North Carolina Press, 1999), I, Tables 2.3, 5.17, and II, Table 2.1; A. C. Mierzejewski, 'Payment and Profits: The German National Railway Company and Reparations 1924–1932', *German Studies Review* 18 (1995), 65–85, for data on interest charges for German railways 1913–30; A. W. MacMahon and R. Dittmar, 'Autonomous Public Enterprise – The German Railways', *Political Science Quarterly* 54 (1939), 488–9 for operating ratio.

was reinforced by calling the railway an undertaking, Unternehmen Deutsche Reichsbahn. The hope, as with the 1921 French agreement, was that the conversion of the seven state networks into one Reich system would yield economies of scale and that overall the undertaking would break even by the profitable lines subsidising the unprofitable. In Britain, the 1921 Railway Act reorganised the motley collection of railway companies into four large regional private monopolies, with the hope of facilitating economies of scale and national co-ordination. A Railway Rates Tribunal was established, and the value basis of freight charges confirmed in twenty-one new classes.

So far as increases in costs were concerned, the intention in many cases was to provide automatic adjustment in the average level of fares and rates in such a way as to shift the onus away from reliance on government subsidies and loans. In the case of France and Britain, specific financial benchmarks were to guide price changes. Thus in France, the 1921 agreement set up the 'Fonds Commun' into which the profits of each of the seven networks (net of all bonuses, taxes, interest payments and other capital charges) were to be pooled. It was anticipated that, after a recuperation period 1921–25, the more profitable networks of the Nord, Est and Paris–Lyons–Méditerranée would subsidise the less profitable Midi and Paris–Orleans as well as the two state undertakings.[11] Any overall surplus would go to the Treasury, while deficits would occasion price increases. It was a 'users' guarantee' which would effectively underwrite the state's contractual guarantee of interest to shareholders.[12] In Britain, the form was different but not the substance. A 'standard revenue' figure was agreed for each of the four companies. This related to annual gross profits and for the system as a whole was set at £44.1 million, the actual gross profits in 1913 (cf. Table 9.1) and equivalent to a 4.5% return on capital. It was later raised to £51.4 million. Cross-subsidisation would occur within each region so there was a standard revenue for each of the four new companies: £7.1 m. for the Southern, £8.5 m. for the Great Western, £26.1 m. for the London, Midland and Scottish and £15.2 m. for the London North Eastern.[13] In the light of the gloomy trading conditions of 1921, these targets were optimistic. They were realisable only by substantial savings from economies of scale, the likely source of which was never spelled out, and in any case all four companies were brand new, so that it took several years for them to find their feet.[14] In Sweden the state railway (SJ), though superficially a separate entity, was very much a part of the state's housekeeping, as Andersson-Skog puts it, since the central government set its aims, tariffs, construction programmes and finances.[15] Even though SJ was responsible for only the trunk network, its profits were concentrated on a very few lines: the

Stockholm–Gothenburg, Stockholm–Malmö and the line in the north from Lulea on the Norway border to Narvik on the Norwegian coast. Again, cross-subsidisation within overall financial balance was the aim.

It is possible that, in the absence of road competition, the systems put in place in the early 1920s might have survived, but it was a knife edge. In all countries, the number of strikes and wage costs were rising as the growing trade union movement pressed for higher wages and shorter working hours – the introduction of the eight-hour day from 1918 on the French railways was especially expensive.[16] Coal prices and therefore railway fuel costs had been on a long-term upward trend from the late nineteenth century, important for those reliant on the British coal industry, which was working more and more marginal seams. The period 1918–21 saw increases everywhere in passenger fares and freight rates, but the new systems do not seem to have been able to withstand much adversity. This was clear for the British railway companies, who, quite apart from the secular rise in costs, were faced in the 1920s with a decline in demand, as documented earlier. Aggregate gross profits never achieved the standard revenues. In other countries, the more favourable conditions of the 1920s allowed some return to financial stability. In Sweden, SJ was earning enough to cover all interest and related capital charges in the years 1926–30. In France, by 1926 when normality was supposed to have returned, gross profits were enough to cover all fixed charges and earn a net surplus of 542 million francs (Table 9.1). Operating ratios were paired back to the 80% mark by the end of the 1920s and surpluses were earned in 1928 and 1929.[17]

Most remarkable, and obscured in Table 9.1, was the performance of the Deutsche Reichsbahn – the largest enterprise in the capitalist world in the 1920s. In the nineteenth century, many public utilities in Germany had been used as cash cows, but now that the balance of electoral power had shifted, voters pushed for direct taxes and were less in favour of indirect taxes and high railway fares and rates. The 1924 Dawes Report on reparations nevertheless saw railway earnings as a useful means of securing payments to the victorious nations of the First World War. Egged on by a report from two railway specialists, Ackworth and Leverv, who disliked the German state-owned system, though providing no statistical proof of its inferiority, the Dawes Report led to the establishment of a separate *company*, the Deutsche Reichsbahngesellschaft.[18] It was to operate as a business but with a board of management containing representatives from the federal government and the reparation trustees. German apprehensions were raised further by the Dawes proposal that there should be a foreign railway commissioner, who could, if necessary, actually sell the company to generate repayment revenues. In the event, this was dropped in the 1924 Federal Railway Act. Many of the board members were German, and the injunction to behave as a private business had to be reconciled with a public purpose clause, which said that DR had to have regard for German economic interests. Nonetheless, the capital structure and financial targets were very tight:

40-year mortgage bonds	→	11.0 billion RM	→ Reparations
Ordinary shares	→	13.0 billion RM	→ Reich owned
40-year preference shares	→	1.5 billion RM	→ Reich owned
40-year preference shares	→	1.5 billion RM	→ DR (never placed)

Each year DR was expected to pay the reparations trustees 940 million Reichsmarks, comprising 1% redemption of mortgage bonds (100 million RM), 5% interest on mortgage bonds (550 million RM) and to divert 390 million RM of the transport tax payments. Thus the gross profits in Table 9.1 are recorded after deducting substantial taxes, and the railways accounted for 38% of the reparation payments under the Dawes plan.[19] Gross profits of 694 million RM were earned in 1925, 861 million RM in 1926 and indeed were positive for the rest of the decade, after which, as Table 9.1 shows, the effects of the depression started to dominate, so that 1933 saw a deficit of 126 million RM. By that stage, following the Lausanne Conference, the reparations regime was replaced by a flat once-and-for-all payment of 3000 million RM of German government bonds. The 'Gesellschaft' was dropped in 1936, and by an edict of 1937 the Minister of Transport became the Director-General of the Deutsche Reichsbahn.[20]

Road–rail competition

Some of the financial success of the German railways in the 1920s was due to the limited nature of competition it faced from road transport – in contrast to France and Britain. It is true that the German railways faced much more competition from inland waterways, especially in low-value, high-bulk traffic. DR also felt able to plead strongly to the Reich about competition from the road sector. Nonetheless, the statistics on water and road competition tell a different story. In 1913 some 17 billion ton km of goods were carried on Germany's inland waterways, an amount that exceeded all of the rest of western Europe put together. However, this figure fell in the 1920s, and the 1913 level was not regained until 1936, even if one allows for boundary and population changes.[21] The production of cars grew enormously in Germany in the years 1931–8, from 70000 per annum to 340000, overtaking Canada, France and the UK.[22] But this increase relates to the production of new vehicles and to the 1930s. All the attention given to the debate about the role of public works and highway development in the economic recovery of Germany should not lead us to lose sight of the fact that this was a phenomenon of the 1930s and Nazi rule, rather than the 1920s. At the start of the inter-war period, the number of motor vehicles in Germany was tiny relative to Britain and France, and its road system, no doubt reflecting the past hotchpotch of separate states, was one of the worst in Europe.[23] Indeed, more generally it was the extent of competition from road transport that was to have decisive long-term implications for all railway systems from the 1920s onwards.

The key economic characteristics of road transport were that it used relatively less capital per unit of labour than the railways, and its activities were economically detached from the road track infrastructure. In the 1920s, in some cases road transport did not make an economic contribution to the maintenance of roads, which were financed from general taxation. This was not the main source of road transport's competitiveness, since by the 1930s higher vehicle and fuel taxes were being levied, as in the UK, whilst in countries like Germany the road system was expected to be self-financing.[24] Rather, it was the fact that economies of scale were limited, and the industry developed in the form of thousands of small firms offering door-to-door services and levying tailor-made charges varying with weight, bulk, length of journey and risk of damage. In contrast to railways, there was no obligation to publish tariffs and no obligation to supply a minimum number of services. Nor were the wages of truck drivers subject to the same agreements approved for the 'cheminots' in France and railway workers in Britain. Like a plague of locusts, the lorries and coaches gnawed at the rigid giant sleeping next to them.

It was likely that road transport would be more attractive for short-distance, light freight and passenger traffic, whilst railways would have a cost advantage in long-distance, bulky heavy traffic. The railways could therefore be expected to lose some business. There was a large swathe of traffic in general merchandise and medium distance where the railways ought to have been able to out-compete road transport but where the outcome depended on the prices charged by railways. Here the railways were vulnerable. Road transport charges were closely linked to the coach and lorry firms' costs because it was a highly competitive industry. The origins of the railways' charging structure lay in the nineteenth-century practice of charging what the traffic would bear, and its elements were structured around the value of the traffic consignment. Rates and fares varied across the freight and passenger classes, which were not determined by cost but by the value to the customer. A lorry or coach firm might then be able to undercut the railway, even though its own costs were higher than railway costs.

To appreciate the impact of road transport it is therefore important to understand why railway rates and fares had taken this form. Two features of railway technology and economics provide the clues. Firstly, the integration of track and operating activities within a single company together with the rights of way they had acquired generated an industry with strong monopoly elements. This had prompted governments to promote public competition for contracts and to introduce legislation controlling fares and rates. The track infrastructure involved considerable economies of scale, and railways generally had a high ratio of capital to running costs. Also many costs, like signalling, were joint to different traffics. The variable costs of a particular journey and freight consignment were often very low, but in any case cost accounting techniques in the nineteenth century were inadequate for identifying the true cost of particular journeys or train loads or traffic groups. Secondly, railways provide services rather than commodities, and because they are non-storable, it was possible to charge different prices to different customers, even when they received similar services with similar costs to the railways. The extent to which such discriminatory prices could profitably be charged depended on whether customers had access to alternative modes. In the nineteenth century, there was severe competition on some routes from coastal steamships, waterways and canals, especially for bulky loads like coal and minerals, but in many areas of business the railway companies virtually had a transport monopoly.

The profit motive then ensured that fares and rates were never set below the identified variable costs of a particular journey or consignment, while the margin above that was determined by what the traffic would bear. The surplus over variable costs when aggregated over all traffics would have to be sufficient to cover all joint costs and capital charges. What the freight traffic would bear could often be proxied, in the absence of an alternative mode, by the value of the commodities being carried. Diamonds and furs would bear heavier charges per ton than coal and minerals. The outcome in all countries was that freight traffic was arranged into commodity groups. As we noted earlier, by the late nineteenth century there were seven classes in Britain and four in France, changed to twenty-one and six respectively in 1921. Passengers were often grouped into two or three classes, with differential seating facilities to add some credibility to the different prices. Such price structures could be found in both private and state undertakings.[25]

The net result was that by the 1920s, in some parts of their business, railway prices were less than costs, while in others they were above costs.

Unless charges were adjusted to reflect the costs of each piece of business, the railway undertakings were in danger of losing some of the high-value traffic to road transport operators, who might shy away from some low-value traffic where railway fares and rates were less than costs.[26] The railway did not lose out to road traffic in the inter-war period in coal and other really heavy and bulky loads. It did, however, lose out in a lot of general merchandise traffic, on distances up to 100 km, and lost shorter-distance passengers to the greater convenience of buses, coaches and private cars. As road transport technology improved, the railway stood to lose much more. It has been estimated that, in the years 1935–9 in Britain, road transport was carrying about 100 million tons of freight per annum in competition with railways, and of this, 50 million tons had been diverted from the railways and the other half had been generated by lowering prices.[27]

Some indication of the strength of the competition is given in Table 9.2. During the war many servicemen learnt to drive, and the 1920s saw many 'tramp hauliers' plying their trade throughout Britain completely unlicensed and unregulated. By 1924, there were 771 000 motor vehicles in Britain equivalent to nearly 20 per 1000 population. Large numbers could also be found in Denmark and France. In all three countries, railway freight traffic per head of population fell. In contrast, the bad state of the roads in Germany and the destruction of the First World War, together with the entrenched position of the railways in civil administration (cf. chapter 4) ensured that there were only 3 motor vehicles per 1000 population in 1924. The British total of 771 000 was not reached in Germany until ten years later, despite its greater population, and the argument applies equally to road freight vehicles as to cars and coaches. In the meantime, Germany saw a large rise in railway freight traffic. Even though the number of motor vehicles rose by 1.5 million in the period 1924–38 and there was a big expansion of the autobahns in the 1930s, motor usage by 1938 was still significantly less than in Britain and France in each of which the number of motor vehicles had risen by slightly more than 1.5 million. It is not surprising then to find French railway financial losses reaching astronomic proportions – operating costs exceeded revenues by some 2000 million francs by 1937, and the balance after fixed charges was nearly (−) 6000 million (cf. Table 9.1). Fierce competition from road transport saw private rail companies in Denmark seeking financial help from the state, which was taking on more shareholdings in such companies.[28] Road transport 'snatched' the general goods traffic in Sweden and a large proportion of freight traffic up to 100 km. The main sufferers were the local and provincial railways run by private companies with rising amounts of government subsidy. By 1928, a report

Table 9.2 *Transport patterns, 1910–1938*

	UK	Denmark	France	Germany	Sweden	Italy	Norway	Spain[a]	USA
(1) Rail track kilometres open per million population									
1910	803[b]	1214	1014	947	2555	510	1249	737	4178
1938	678[b]	1317	1014	913	2692	523	1380	687	4720
(2) Rail freight ton kilometres per head of population									
1913	841[b]	207	633	906	571	196	167	158	4537
1938	576[b]	184	631[c]	1357	825	264	276	196	3276
(3) State share (%) of railway activity in 1924									
Track kilometres	0	48.6	27.0	100	38.5	100	87.7	0	0
Freight ton kilometres carried	0	89.3	20.1	100	65.5	100	89.2	0	0
(4) Number of road motor vehicles per 1000 population									
1924	19[b]	14	14	3	10	2	8	5	154
1938	53[b]	40	54	25	35	8	31	10	229
(5) Merchant ships in 1938 in '000 tons per mill. pop.	225	316[d]	40	38	190	45	621[e]	37	94

Note:

[a] The entries for Spain for 1938 are affected by the Civil War. The rail track entry is interpolated from the entries in Mitchell, *International Historical Statistics: Europe 1750–1993* of 17000 km open in 1930 and 17500 in 1940. The freight and shipping volume figures relate to 1935. The road vehicle entries are based on the statement by Gomez-Mendoza that there were 101,000 vehicles in 1925 and 232,300 in 1930, a figure which then grew at 0.56% per annum in the 1930s (A. Gomez-Mendoza, 'Motor Cars and Railways in Inter-War Spain: Regulation vis à vis De-regulation', in L. Andersson-Skog and O. Krantz (eds.), *Institutions and the Transport and Communication Industries* (Canton, Mass.: Science History Publications, Watson, 1999), 207). This puts the total for 1938 at 234000. It is much less than Italy or Germany despite the fact that Gomez-Mendoza states that the Spanish total was similar to Germany and 60% higher than Italy. It is also difficult to reconcile this with the figure of 157000 for 1947 in Mitchell, *International Historical Statistics: Europe 1750–1993*.

[b] Britain only, i.e. excludes all Ireland. The decline in freight is overestimated to the extent that there was a recorded fall of over 2000 million ton km in 1928 due to a revision in the method of estimation. This amounts to a fall of about 50 km per head. Note also that the only data for 1913 are

in freight kilometres and so the estimate here was obtained by applying to the ton kilometre entry for 1920, the ratio between freight kilometres for 1913 and 1920. The populations for 1913 (41.2 million) and 1924 (43.4 million) were interpolated from the census data in Mitchell, *International Historical Studies: Europe 1750–1993* and for 1938 the population was taken to be 46.3 million, that is, the UK total of 47.5 million less the 1.22 million recorded in the census of 1938 for Northern Ireland.

c Excludes the freight carried on lines still in private ownership in 1938.

d Excludes ships less than 20 gross tons.

e Excludes sailing ships less than 50 gross tons and steamships less than 25 tons.

Sources: B. R. Mitchell, *International Historical Statistics: Europe 1750–1993* (London: Macmillan, 3rd edn, 1998) and B. R. Mitchell, *International Historical Statistics: The Americas: 1750–1993* (London: Macmillan, 4th edn, 1998), for rail track, shipping and road vehicles data. Railway ownership data from W. M. W. Splawn, *Government Ownership and Operation of Railways* (New York: Macmillan, 1928), 9, 12, 13, 15, 48. Population data from A. Maddison, *Dynamic Forces in Capitalist Development* (Oxford University Press, 1991), Table B-3 with population for Spain and Britain (1910 and 1913) interpolated from census data in Mitchell, *International Historical Statistics: Europe 1750–1993*. Northern Ireland census population for 1938 from Whitaker and Sons, *Whitaker's Almanack* (London: Whitaker and Sons, 1938).

suggested that half the networks were unprofitable, and by the 1930s a dual system had emerged comprising a financially self-sufficient trunk network operated by SJ and a network of sparsely used branch lines.[29]

Some of the differences across Europe reflected the various ways in which railways were shielded by their governments from road competition. In Germany it took some time for the road lobby to get its act together. The 1906 Reich Stamp law had already endorsed the taxation of motor vehicles for revenue purposes. By the 1920s, this excise tax was supplemented by an annual car tax, whilst income tax relief was available for those who used public transport to work. At the same time, DR itself increasingly engaged in the trucking business, giving it a lever to protect its railway business. The Fiscal Equalisation Law of 1927 prohibited the use of car tax revenues for road construction.[30] Over time, however, the road transport employers' association, Reichsverband der Automobilindustrie, started to argue that motorisation would stimulate the economy, and in the 1930s the excise tax on new cars was removed, tariffs on imported cars raised, road fees and licences lowered. The military authorities pushed for production of trucks, motor engines and tanks, and as transport planning came to be centralised in state and party agencies under the Nazis, road transport came to the fore. The German railways had been able to resist this pressure for so long because of their generally good technical and economic performance and because of their entrenched position in the civil administration of Prussia and then the Reich.[31] In Spain also the railways were protected. The number of motor vehicles remained low throughout the inter-war period, and rail freight traffic rose significantly (Table 9.2). The two major railway companies, Norte and MZA, had a strong influence on the government through their Asociación General de Transportes par Vía Férnea (AGTVF). It complained that road hauliers did not have the obligation to carry or publish rates and fares and did not pay the true cost of roads.[32] The Spanish government was not unreceptive, since it shared in rail company profits, quite apart from free carriage for government mail. Splawn estimated that the economic benefits to the government were equivalent to a 10% return to shareholders.[33] AGTVF complained that road legislation was weak. An act of 1924 had introduced licensing for routes and safety, and a 1929 act forced transporters to comply with fixed timetables and itinerary and with some obligation to carry passengers. AGTVF, however, wanted all road services in competition with railways to be banned! There appears to have been more rhetoric than substance in the rail companies' case in that the conditions and topography of the roads in Spain were not attractive for motor vehicles, so that carts and pack animals competed with the railways and in non-bulky textiles and hardware where journey time was not important. Despite the protestations of the companies, the length of the average rail freight haul did not decline in the inter-war period.[34]

Much tougher legislation was introduced in France and Britain, but not until the 1930s, and the emphasis was on constraining road transport rather than liberating the railways. The 1930 and 1933 Road Traffic Acts in Britain specified different kinds of licences for different kinds of business (local, national, passenger, freight, owner not in other businesses etc). Permissible routes were laid down, and vehicle safety and driver competence enforced. In France, a similar system was introduced by a decree of April 1934, which established regulations for road services, rates and schedules. Regional agreements were to be developed between road and rail transport and supervised by departmental committees within the Ministry of Public Works with co-ordination by a Directeur Générale de Chemins de Fer et la Voirie Routière.[35] Whilst this legislation had some impact on road traffic levels – passenger road journeys in Britain, for example[36]– it had little impact on railway finances. There was now a recognition that any given route might not need both road and rail services, and indeed the 1934 decree in France laid down that traffic could be diverted to the least-cost mode.[37] By the late 1930s, in all countries 'transport co-ordination' became the buzz phrase. In France, a Conseil Supérieure de Transport replaced the Conseil Supérieure de Chemins de Fer, which had been established in 1921. In Britain, the Boscowen Transport report of 1931 had preceded the Road Traffic Acts, and the Labour Party by the 1930s had stopped talking about bringing just railways into public ownership. It was now transport nationalisation.[38]

Rail freight and passenger volumes picked up in the late 1930s, but practically all systems were in financial difficulties. In Sweden, SJ was in surplus, but it had responsibility only for trunk lines. The local and provincial lines run by private companies had been badly hit by road competition, as noted earlier, and were in deep financial trouble, as were the French and British networks. The crunch had come. It was no longer credible on the one hand to allow private railway companies a monopoly of their service whilst bailing them out with subsidies. The Swedish Parliament (the Riksdag), under strong pressure from regional groups, decided in 1939 to bring the private networks under the ownership of SJ. The latter was most reluctant because it had a financially viable trunk system, which had now to cross-subsidise the other networks.[39] In France, there were few complaints when the state took over all the railways in 1937. It was coloured by the antagonism of the Popular Front and other left-wing elements towards the French *rentier* class who, especially in the form of the great French families, had been very generously treated by government guarantees of railway dividends. The *rentiers* suffered little from the takeover, which was more of a centralisation than a nationalisation. The shareholders, through the existing companies, had legal rights to the concessions and to interest payments. The market value of stock was therefore negotiated rather than settled in court. All franchises and assets were transferred to a new body, the Société Nationale des Chemins de Fer Français (SNCF), whose capital stock was made up as follows:[40] 2.84 million shares of 500 francs (1.42 million francs) split into 1.39 million class A shares (held by Nord, Est, P–L–M, P–O and Midi) and 1.45 million class B shares (held by the state).

The 1.45 million class B shares held by the state were deemed to represent the assets of the old Etat network and of Alsace-Lorraine, plus past subsidies and Treasury advances. The five private companies formally held the Class A shares, which attracted 6% interest payable to 1982, when the shares would be amortised. SNCF did not have to pay these charges until 1955 – a device to sustain the credibility of the new company – but stockholders who had been in receipt of government guarantees in the past could receive interest payments under the terms of the old franchises and up to their expiry date. For the moment all were satisfied.[41] In Spain, investment by the private companies had dried up and, as part of its naturalisation and nationalisation programme, the government took over the railways from 1941 and formed them into a new legally independent entity RENFE (Red Nacional de los Ferrocarriles Españoles).[42] In Britain, nationalisation was delayed by the war, but when it came in 1947, the new 'Railway Executive' was but one of several undertakings that formed the British Transport Commission. The parallel organisation in France was the Conseil Supérieure de Transport. Uniform practices, economies of scale, co-ordination between road and rail, elimination of rate wars, reduction of rail deficits were all hopes for the future.

Conclusion to Part III: the road to state enterprise

During the 1914–50 period, the infrastructure industries experienced three significant changes: the moves to system integration in electricity supply and telephones, the increased state involvement in the railway problem, and state ownership and control over key natural resources like coal and oil. The problems of coal and oil are discussed in detail in chapter 11. The first two changes shared a central problem, that of regulating large monopolies in tandem with providing them with subsidies. With respect to institutional change, France and Britain were somewhat behind the others but, as a result of the 1946–8 nationalisations, they caught up, so that by the late 1940s a substantial state presence in the ownership of energy, telecommunications and transport was common throughout western Europe.

Part III has sought to demonstrate that much of the institutional structure observable at the end of the 1940s could be seen at the end of the 1930s, by which time central governments had taken a strongly interventionist stance on the infrastructure industries. Telephone technology involved low marginal running costs with significant spillovers from increasing the number of connections. National networks were therefore favoured and required the absorption of local, sometimes municipally owned, enterprises. Such monopoly networks would need regulating, but there were further complications arising from the aim of many governments, Sweden and Norway being perhaps the best examples, to spread the networks comprehensively to promote social and political unification. The state also wanted close control over telephone networks because of their strategic properties with respect to the flow of information. From the late nineteenth century, throughout western Europe, the number of telephone connections to businesses and households rose and the success here seems to have depended more on how effectively the state overcame local resistance to network development than to whether or not the systems were state owned. In fact, however, the latter was pervasive by the inter-war period. State subsidies had been granted for inherently unprofitable telecommunications sectors – whether as infant industries or because of geographical remoteness. The emergence of national networks run by large private monopolies meant that central governments were faced with the prospect of regulating monopoly prices and profits, while at the same time providing subsidies. That uneasy mixture prompted many countries to shift to state ownership. The fact that the state-owned enterprises were not autonomous entities but were administered as sections of a ministry of post and telecommunications, or some such body, reflected the strong state desire to exercise close supervision of the flow of information.

Some of these selfsame forces were at work in electricity supply and railways. In the inter-war period, system integration in electricity supply promised economic benefits arising from a concentration of generation on large plants and from the inter-connection of different consumption and supply conditions, especially important as between hydroelectricity sectors and the thermal zones. Integration with private firms involved the agreement of source suppliers, agreement on joint use of transmission lines and the willingness of retailers to accept supply from the grid. Integration may not have carried great economic benefits in Norway (because of its abundance of HEP sites) nor Spain (where there was often no surplus to export). In France and Italy, the private electricity networks continued to dominate, much transmission capacity was built in the inter-war period, and indeed Italy finished up with one of the most extensive transmission networks, if that is measured in kilometres per head of population or per square kilometre of area. In both countries, supply to large business customers was raised considerably and average consumption levels rose in the period 1919–39 at about the European average. However, the residential and other domestic sectors remained with low consumption levels, and the French and Italian governments were criticised for not pushing system integration further. By 1938, a plan had been developed in France, though the war frustrated its implementation. In Italy, little was done and, after emerging from the war as a defeated nation, the state was in an ambivalent position in trying to force system integration on the private sector. Complaints about the lack of a capillary system continued into the 1950s, and it was not until after ENEL was formed in 1962 that a national system emerged.

Rather more decisive activity by the central governments of the UK, Germany and Sweden saw above-average growth rates in electricity supply, while consumption levels continued to lie above the European average. In the UK, the Central Electricity Board was established in 1926 to build a national grid, which was complete by the early 1930s and was thereafter managed as an integrated unit. In Sweden, the state power board (the Vattenfall) did not have a monopoly but was instrumental in developing a large network in the south and in the drive to the north from the 1930s. A national network emerged by the late 1930s, but a truly managed system had to await the outcome of a debate finally settled in 1948 when the Vattenfall was given the responsibility for the system management. In Germany, there was no dominant state enterprise, but the reach of Reich, state and municipal enterprise was such that only 12% of electricity was supplied by purely private enterprises for most of the 1930s. A 1935 law placed responsibility for national investment planning in the hands of central government, though it was 1948 before a true national grid emerged. Denmark witnessed only a minor role for its central government in the inter-war period, when two large regional groupings emerged (and involved extensive participation of municipal undertakings). Not until the 1950s was system integration achieved even with these two groups.

Finally, the railways had inherited from the nineteenth century a culture of customer complaints (especially from the business sector), which reflected a tension between the railway's monopoly in some sectors and competition from shipping in others, while the state was torn between the need for regulation and the railways' needs, in some areas, for state subsidy. The systems were becoming unprofitable by the early 1920s. At that point, central governments in general were willing to shore up railway finances temporarily, in the hope that reorganisation, rationalisation and streamlining of the institutional structures would allow the unprofitable business to be financed by the profitable sectors, whilst fare and rate increases would shift financial support from governments to customers. This policy was under threat from the beginning in the face of wage rises, an increase in coal prices and resistance to fare and rate increases. The advent of competition from the new marauding hordes of petrol-driven coaches, trucks and cars on the developing road tracks was the final blow. The road transport industry was, structurally, the complete opposite of the railways – small-scale firms, no public interest obligations. The railways could survive successfully only by changing the pricing structures inherited from the monopoly days of the nineteenth century, but it was to be decades before that happened.

Notes

1 J.-P. Dormois, 'France: The Idiosyncrasies of *Voluntarisme*', in J. Foreman-Peck and G. Federico (eds.), *European Industrial Policy: The Twentieth Century Experience* (Oxford University Press, 1999), 71.

2 L. Andersson-Skog, 'From State Railway Housekeeping to Railway Economics: Swedish Railway Policy and Economic Transformation after 1920 in an Institutional Perspective', *Scandinavian Economic History Review* 49 (1996), 36; J. Bohlin, 'Sweden: The Rise and Fall of the Swedish Model', in Foreman-Peck and Federico (eds.), *European Industrial Policy*, 153–4.

3 A. C. Mierzejewski, *The Most Valuable Asset of the Reich: A History of the German National Railway*, 2 vols. (Chapel Hill: University of North Carolina Press, 1999), I, xv. See also A. C. Mierzejewski, 'The German National Railway Company, 1924–32: Between Private and Public Enterprise', *Business History Review* 67 (1993), 406–38 and 'The German National Railway Company Confronts its Competitors, 1920–39', *Business and Economic History* 25 (1996), 89–102.

4 T. S. Barker and C. I. Savage, *An Economic History of Transport* (London: Heinemann, 1974), 83; H. J. Bressler, 'The French Railway Problem', *Political Science Quarterly* 37 (1922), 212.

5 B. R. Mitchell, *International Historical Statistics: Europe 1750–1993* (London: Macmillan, 3rd edn, 1998).

6 Ibid.

7 A. Gomez-Mendoza, 'Motor Cars and Railways in Inter-War Spain: Regulation vis à vis De-regulation', in L. Andersson-Skog and O. Krantz (eds.), *Institutions and the Transport and Communications Industries* (Canton, Mass.: Science History Publications, Watson, 1999), 199.

8 Barker and Savage, *Economic History of Transport*, 157.

9 K. Doukas, *The French Railroads and the State* (New York: Columbia Press, 1945), 165 and 295.

10 A. C. Mierzejewski, 'The German National Railway Company between the World Wars: Modernisation or Preparation for War?', *Journal of Transport History* 11 (1990), 40–60 and *Most Valuable Asset*, I, ch. 1; A. W. MacMahon and W. R. Dittmar, 'Autonomous Public Enterprise – The German Railways: Part III', *Political Science Quarterly* 55 March (1940), 179; A. von der Leyen, 'The German Federal Railway Company', *Annals of Collective Economy* 2 (1926), 322–3.

11 F. Caron, 'The Evolution of the Technical System of Railways in France 1832–1939', in R. Maintz and T. P. Hughes (eds.), *The Development of Large Technical Systems* (Boulder, Colo.: Frankfurt and Westview Press, 1978), 99.

12 H. H. Dougall, 'Railway Rates and Rate Making in France since 1921', *Journal of Political Economy* 35 (1933), 298.

13 Barker and Savage, *Economic History of Transport*, 158.

14 G. W. Crompton, ' "Efficient and Economical Working?": The Performance of the Railway Companies 1923–33', *Business History* 27 (1985), 222–37; 'Squeezing the Pulpless Orange: Labour and Capital on the Railways in the Inter-War Period', *Business History* 31 (1989), 66–83.

15 Andersson-Skog, 'State Railway Housekeeping'.

16 Dougall, 'Railway Rates in France', 300.

17 Doukas, *French Railroads*, 103.

18 A. C. Mierzejewski, 'Payment and Profits: The German National Railway Company and Reparations 1924–32', *German Studies Review* 18 (1995), 65–85 and *Most Valuable Asset*, I, ch. 4; von der Leyen, 'The German Federal Railway Company', 2, 323–4; A. W. McMahon and W. R. Dittmar, 'Autonomous Public Enterprise – The German Railways: Part I', *Political Science Quarterly* 54 (December 1939), 491–4.

19 Mierzejewski, 'Payment and Profits' and *Most Valuable Asset*, I, 265; A. W. McMahon and W. R. Dittmar, 'Autonomous Public Enterprise – The German Railways: Part II', *Political Science Quarterly* 55 (March 1940), 35; von der Leyen, 'The German Federal Railway Company', 2, 328–34.

20 *Most Valuable Asset*, II, ch. 2; McMahon and Dittmar, 'Autonomous Public Enterprise – The German Railway: Part I', 499.

21 Mitchell, *International Historical Statistics: Europe* 1750–1993, Table F5. Note that A. C. Mierzejewski makes much of the threat from road vehicles yet can record only that 'in 1925 … trucks had 2% of the market. By 1930, trucks had doubled their modal share and by 1937 had tripled it.' This is still only 6%. See 'The German National Railway Company Confronts its Competitors 1920–39', 89–90.

22 R. Overy, *War and Economy in the Third Reich* (Oxford: Clarendon Press, 1994), 70–1; McMahon and Dittmar, 'Autonomous Public Enterprise – The German Railway: Part II', 503.

23 Overy, *War and Economy*, 69.

24 McMahon and Dittmar, 'Autonomous Public Enterprise – The German Railway: Part III', 186; P. S. Bagwell, *The Transport Revolution from 1770* (London: Batsford, 1974), ch. 8.

25 P. Levy, 'The Railroads in France', *Annals of the American Academy of Politics and Social Science* 187 (1936), 188; Dougall, 'Railway Rates in France'; L. Andersson-Skog, 'Political Economy and Institutional Diffusion. The

Case of the Swedish Railways and Telecommunications up to 1950', in Andersson-Skog and Krantz (eds.), *Institutions and the Transport and Communications Industries*, 248–9; P. J. Cain, 'Private Enterprise or Public Utility?: Output, Pricing and Investment in English Railways', *Journal of Transport History* 1 (1973), 9–28; G. R. Hawke, 'Pricing Policy of Railways in England and Wales before 1881', in M. C. Reed (ed.), *Railways in the Victorian Economy: Studies in Finance and Economic Growth* (Newton Abbott: David and Charles, 1969), 76–110; Mierzejewski, 'The German National Railway Company Confronts its Competitors'; McMahon and Dittmar, 'Autonomous Public Enterprise – The German Railway Part III', 191.

26 G. Walker, 'Transport Policy before and after 1953', *Oxford Economic Paper* 5 (1953), 90–116.

27 G. Walker, *Road and Rail* (London: Allen and Unwin, 1947), 128.

28 L. Andersson-Skog, 'National Patterns in the Regulation of Railways and Telephony in the Nordic Countries to 1950', *Scandinavian Economic History Review* 47(2) (2000), 30–46.

29 Andersson-Skog, 'State Railway Housekeeping', 35–6.

30 G. Yago, *The Decline of Transit: Urban Transportation in German and US Cities 1900–70* (Cambridge University Press, 1984), 33–4. For the activities of the Reichsbahn in protecting its markets against road competition, see Mierzejewski, *Most Valuable Asset*, I, 355–7 and II, 29–56.

31 Mierzejewski, *Most Valuable Asset*, I, 355–7 and II, 29–56.

32 Gomez-Mendoza, 'Motor Cars and Railways', 200–3.

33 W. M. Splawn, *Government Ownership and Operation of Railways* (New York: Macmillan, 1928), 57.

34 Gomez-Mendoza, 'Motor Cars and Railways', 206.

35 H. H. Dougall, 'Railway Nationalisation and Transport Co-ordination in France', *Journal of Political Economy* 40 (1938), 225; H. H. Dougall, 'Public and Private Operation of Railways in France', *Annals of the American Academy of Politics and Social Science* 201 (1939), 211–16; Walker, 'Transport Policy'.

36 D. Aldcroft, *Studies in British Transport History* (Newton Abbott: David and Charles, 1974), ch. 8.

37 Doukas, *French Railroads*, 234.

38 Dougall, 'Railway Nationalisation', 227–8; J. Singleton, 'Labour, the Conservatives and Nationalisation', in R. Millward and J. Singleton (eds.), *The Political Economy of Nationalisation in Britain 1920–50* (Cambridge University Press, 1995), 16; for Sweden, see B. Fullerton, 'Deregulation in a European context – the case of Sweden', in P. Bell and P. Clarke (eds.), *Deregulation and Transport: Market Forces in the Modern World* (London: David Fulton Publishers, 1990), 125–40.

39 Andersson-Skog, 'State Railway Housekeeping', 33; Andersson-Skog, 'Political Economy', 251; Bohlin, 'Swedish Model', 160; J. Ottosson, 'Path Dependence and Institutional Evolution – The Case of the Nationalisation of Private Railways in Inter-War Sweden', in L. Magnusson and J. Ottosson, *Evolutionary Economics and Path Dependence* (Cheltenham: Edward Elgar 1997), 191–5.

40 Doukas, *French Railroads*, 239; E. Chadeau, 'The Rise and Decline of State-Owned Industry in Twentieth Century France', in P. A. Toninelli (ed.), *The*

Rise and Fall of State Owned Enterprise in the Western World (Cambridge University Press, 2000), 187. For discussion of the early moves to nationalisation, see H. H. Dougall, 'The French Solution for the Railway Problem', *Journal of Political Economy* 36 (1934), 385–92.

41 G. Harcovi, 'Nationalisation of the French Railways', *Annals of the American Academy of Political and Social Science* 190 (1939), 217–26; Le Besnerois, 'The National Railroad Company and the Financial Amendement of the French Railroads', *Annals of Collective Economy* 18 (1947), 29–33; Dougall, 'Railway Nationalisation'; Dougall, 'Public and Private Operation'; Doukas, *French Railroads*, part 6.

42 A. Carreras, X. Tafunell and E. Torres, 'The Rise and Decline of Spanish State-Owned Firms', in Toninelli (ed.), *Rise and Fall*, 210–11.

Part IV

State Enterprise c. 1945–1990

10 The new state, economic organisation and planning

As 1945 drew to a close, Europeans looked to the future rather than the past. There was to be no return to pre-war conditions. They were not glorified as the nineteenth-century world had been in the immediate aftermath of the First World War. By 1945, France was determined to avoid any repeat of the three German invasions since 1870. The defeated nations, Germany and Italy, rejected the past. Elsewhere in parts of Scandinavia, the UK and the Low Countries, there was more pride in the outcome of the war, but what they shared with France, Germany and Italy was the memory of the economic conditions of the inter-war period and a need to repair the physical damage from the war.

The credibility of capitalism was in question. The high unemployment levels of the 1930s, the collapse of banking systems, crises on stock exchanges and exchange rate instability meant that management of the macro-economy became a prime responsibility of government. The plight of the poor in the 1930s and the social intermingling during the war put pressures on government to adopt explicit policies for raising the living standards of lower-income groups. The war was a collective effort, and a 'one nation' philosophy pervaded many postwar governments. It was unlikely, moreover, that reconstruction would be left to the market. Shifting resources from military to civilian use would mean wild movements in prices and the prospect for some of juicy profits and rents for resources in inelastic supply. Leaving it to the market had been rejected during wartime and was likely to be avoided in the immediate years of reconstruction. All of which made conditions ripe for the electoral success of social democrats and socialists. For them there was another item on the agenda. If the market had defects, why not plan the economy more systematically, remove the uncertainties about investment and avoid the bottlenecks that created excess rents and profits?

Whatever its political hue, the new state in the late 1940s was expected to manage the macro-economy, ensure a fair allocation of resources for reconstruction and target the living standards of the poor. The infrastructure industries would have a central role for two reasons. Firstly, all

171

countries were keen to switch their manufacturing capacity away from armaments to consumer and capital goods to raise living standards. Manufactured goods (as opposed to services) were especially important because of the pressure to increase exports in the face of the dollar shortage. The USA had suffered little physical damage during the war and its merchant shipping fleet had actually increased in size. The USA had also been a prime source of credit, via lend-lease, during the war. It therefore emerged as Europe's main creditor but also as the main foreign source of raw materials, capital goods and intermediate manufactured goods. At the going exchange rates, there was excess demand for dollars. Hence the pressure of European countries to raise their export levels, and the main source in the short run was manufactured exports. Manufacturing could only do this with access to key intermediate inputs like steel, coal, oil, electricity and freight transport. These infrastructure sectors did not suffer more physical war damage than manufacturing plants, but the export targets could not be reached without prior development, domestically, of these intermediate inputs.

Secondly, many of the services produced by the infrastructure industries were either important items of working-class budgets or were essential ingredients of current residential patterns. Water supply and transport were 'essentials' in that demand was inelastic with respect to income and price. Fuel as a sector had a low price elasticity – there were no short-term substitutes – even though that was not necessarily true of any one fuel like electricity. In the circumstances of the 1940s and the 1950s, governments could not escape the political pressures to stop rail fares, gas, water and electricity tariffs rising faster than wages. Nor could access to services, in the context of a one-nation state, be markedly different in different parts of the country. The idea of the 'universal service' became common. There would be uniform fares per kilometre, freight rates per ton kilometre for similar goods, gas rates per cubic metre and electricity tariffs per kilowatt hour in different parts of the country irrespective of the varying costs of supply. The history of monopoly in some of the infrastructure industries meant that some of this was not new. But the standardisation and proliferation of this type of price structure across whole countries and its continuation in the face of rising demand, new technologies and new cost structures was to lead to problems. Even the call charges for telephones, hardly an essential, came to be standardised for distance zones (local, long distance, international), which was especially ironic since costs were much less sensitive to distance than in many of the other services of the infrastructure.

All of this enhanced the role of the state in economic life and extended the range of functions that these industries were expected to fulfil. As we saw in Part III, many of them had been brought into public ownership in

Table 10.1 *Public enterprise shares of economic activity, 1971 (% of national totals)*

	Employment	Fixed Capital Formation	Net Output
UK	7.2	18.7	10.2
France	9.6	22.7[a]	11.6[b]
Germany	7.9	18.2[c]	12.7
Italy	7.2	53.0[d]	17.1
Sweden	6.5	9.5	6.5

Notes:
[a] Excludes investment in financial institutions.
[b] Excludes agriculture and finance.
[c] Excludes housing.
[d] Not comparable with other data since it includes all the investment by joint stock subsidiaries of IRI, ENI etc. See source.

Source: G. Corti, 'Perspectives on Public Corporations and Public Enterprises in Five Nations', *Annals of Collective Economy* 47 (1976), 47–86.

the nineteenth and early twentieth centuries, with several organised as state monopolies. This was true especially for railways, post and telecommunications. In the energy industries of Germany and Scandinavia, private firms could also be found, though they were often outnumbered or outgunned by mixed enterprise, municipal undertakings and state power boards. By the 1940s, public enterprise accounted for about 10% of GDP in most countries and, since they were in very capital-intensive sectors, accounted for about 20% of annual capital formation and less than 10% of employment. Its scope did not change much over the next thirty years, and the slightly smaller shares recorded in Table 10.1 for 1971 reflect the slightly smaller share of all transport, energy and communications in national output rather than any diminution of state and municipal enterprise.

The early 1970s in fact proved a key turning point in the second half of the twentieth century. It saw the quadrupling of oil prices and the collapse of the Bretton Woods fixed exchange rate regime. As Table 10.2 shows, the golden age 1950–73 witnessed very high growth rates of real income with all countries catching up on the USA, whose lead had been achieved, in part, because of its limited damage during two World Wars. In the UK, the growth rate of living standards was only slightly better than the USA, so that by 1973 its GDP per head lay behind all except Italy, Norway and Spain. From the mid 1970s, exchange rates were liberalised and government budget expansion halted, to be followed in the 1980s by

Table 10.2 *Income per head 1950–1992 (levels of GDP per head in 1990 dollars and annual average growth rates of GDP per head in %)*

	UK	Denmark	France	Germany (West)	Sweden	Italy	Norway	Spain	USA
1950 level	6847	6683	5221	4281	6738	3425	4969	2397	9513
1950–73 growth rate	2.5	3.1	4.0	5.0	3.1	5.0	3.2	5.8	2.4
1973 level	11992	13416	12940	13152	13494	10409	10229	8739	16607
1973–92 growth rate	1.4	1.6	1.7	2.1	1.2	2.4	2.9	1.9	1.4
1992 level	15738	19293	17959	19351	16927	16329	17543	12498	21558

Note:
Data relate to 1990 boundaries, except for West Germany which relates to 1989.

Source: A. Maddison, *Monitoring the World Economy 1820–1992* (Paris: OECD, 1995).

privatisation and a general liberalisation of all markets. Convergence on USA income levels continued, and UK growth was not so far behind the others. Nonetheless, by 1992 it had been overtaken by Italy and Norway, leaving only Spain with a lower GDP per head, a remarkable turnaround from the mid-nineteenth century when our story began.

The 1914–45 heritage and the technological changes 1945–90: An overview

It is a theme of Part III that the scale of government intervention in the energy, telecommunications and transport sectors of western European countries by the late 1930s was a potent indicator of what was to emerge by 1950. To be specific, by 1950 in France and Britain, railways, airlines, telecommunications, gas supply, electricity supply and coal mines were all nationalised. The state had exercised a strong grip on the central banks for a long time, and this was reinforced by their nationalisation in France, Britain and the Netherlands in 1946. More than 90% of the business in telecommunications and railways was in state ownership in Spain, Sweden and Norway. The Reichspost and the Reichsbahn were in the hands of the new Federal Republic of West Germany, which, in addition to Lufthansa, had extensive interests in coal, gas, electricity and manufacturing through its major holding companies. The state holding undertakings in Spain, Instituto Nacional de Industria (INI), and Italy, Istituto per la Ricostruzione Industriale (IRI), had less-dominant but still-significant shareholdings in electricity, airlines and manufacturing, and the Italian state had direct control over trunk telephone lines and the railway system. Finally, central governments had extensive holdings in oil companies: British Petroleum, Azienda Generale Italia Petroli, Compañía Arrendetaria del Monopolio de Petróleos in Spain, the Compagnies Françaises de Raffinage et des Pétroles. In Denmark, the state's role was less direct, often taking the form of shareholdings jointly with municipalities, co-operatives and private companies; by 1946 this included joint ownership of the airline SAS with the governments of Finland, Norway and Sweden.

Most of this increased activity of the state had emerged, as we saw in Part III, by the end of the 1930s, by which time the central governments had taken a strong grip on all the infrastructure industries. Many of the above institutions (except in Spain) had been established before the Second World War. Chadeau records that nationalisations in France in the twentieth century were often ushered in by socialist governments, but he recognises that the shift to public ownership in France was a consistent long-term tendency from the start of the century onwards.

Pontusson argues that public ownership was less important in Sweden than in other parts of western Europe, reflecting the more pragmatic attitude of the Social Democrats from the 1930s onwards. However, if we note that there was no coal industry to nationalise and only a small gas industry (some of which was in municipal hands), that telecommunications and trunk railways had been in state ownership from the mid-nineteenth century, large parts of electricity from the early 1900s and non-trunk railways from 1939, Sweden does not look much different from the rest.[1]

What is, however, indisputable is that in the immediate postwar period the role of these state institutions and the grip of central government was confirmed and reinforced. There were no privatisations of any significance. Control of the electric power transmission grid was effectively placed in the hands of state-controlled enterprises in Sweden and Germany. The state-owned airlines British European Airways and SAS were set up in 1946. In 1948, the Norwegian Parliament (the Storting) approved the takeover by the Telegrafslyret of the remaining private telephone companies. In France and Britain in 1939, large parts of coal, electricity and gas supplies were still in the hands of private companies or municipalities. The immediate postwar years then saw an unambiguous shift of ownership to the state. Electricité de France, Charbonnages de France and Gaz du France were established in 1946, the National Coal Board in 1947, the British Electricity Authority (controlling the Central Electricity Generating Board and the Area Boards) in 1948, the Gas Council (controlling the Area Boards) in 1949.

This confirmation and in some cases extension of the role of the state was not just a technocratic matter, but the role of ideologies and political parties seems to have been strongest in the final institutional form of state enterprise, rather than as a central causative force in the shift to state ownership. The 1930s had seen the emergence of social democratic and other left-wing parties – elected to office in Sweden in the mid 1930s and in France in the form of the Popular Front. The year 1937 saw the formation of an important democratic coalition in Denmark, and in 1945 the British Labour Party was voted into office. Fascist autarkic policies rapidly dominated the scene in Germany and Spain, less so in Italy. In trying to isolate the impact of the programmes put forward after 1945 by these countries, we should distinguish those who were to be the victors of the Second World War from the vanquished. Ideological factors affected the policies of the victors towards the infrastructure in two ways. Firstly, planning, that is, a conscious national direction of the economy, was the policy chosen for the short-run reconstruction of economies devastated by war and, in some cases as in France, as a clear long-term solution. The market was no longer to be trusted. Secondly, the infrastructure industries produced services that were a key part of the planning process, because they were either strategically important (transport, coal, oil) or, like gas, electricity and coal, were important items in the budget of low-income families – important in the sense that price and income demand elasticities were small.[2] The result was strong state control of the infrastructure. Arm's-length regulation had not proved very effective in the interwar period. Public ownership then came to be the way the state exercised its control. So the centre-left alignment in many western European countries tipped the balance towards public ownership. But a large part of that had occurred by 1939, and by the late 1940s a consensus had emerged in many countries.[3] The distrust of capitalism was an especially strong ingredient in the nationalisation of coal mines, whose labour force had been in the vanguard of the trade union movement and socialist parties and in the advocacy of nationalisation.[4] This is discussed in more detail in chapter 11 in the context of a wider treatment of the exploitation of natural resources like coal, oil and natural gas. That same distrust also lay behind the large-scale intervention in the financial sector in France. Evidence of the influence of 'the great economic and financial hierarchies' was but the latest in a continuing obsession in some quarters with the French financial aristocracy.[5] In addition to the central bank, four commercial banks were nationalised along with thirty-six insurance companies. Huge areas of economic activity were, however, left in the private sector in all countries: land, commerce and much of manufacturing. Despite the neo-Marxist rhetoric, the 'means of production' had not been taken into public ownership. Nearer to the mark was the appeal of the 'return of the great monopolies to the nation'.[6]

Many of the new state enterprises established after the war in France and Britain were national monopolies, that is, public ownership took the form of nationalisation. The British Electricity Authority, British Transport Commission, Electricité de France, Charbonnages de France, Gaz du France and the National Coal Board were national entities, not regional or municipal bodies, and they had no national competitors. They were part of the national reconstruction after the war and were expected to promote the national interest. The Second World War also had a more general effect in that it softened attitudes to a strong state presence in the economy.[7] Drawing on the experience of the First World War, administrative planning during the Second World War appears to have been successful, especially in terms of the role in Vichy France of the 'Comité d'Organisation' and, in Britain, the control of prices and the high performance of the railways.[8] The war also contributed in some very specific ways to the spread of public ownership. In particular, the Conseil National de Résistance in France was at the forefront of accusations of collaboration with the enemy aimed at firms in banking, insurance, power, coal and manufacturing, most specifically by the Renault motor company and the Gnome et Rhône engine company, both of which were taken into state ownership in 1946.[9]

The economic policies of Germany, Italy and Spain in the 1930s and 1940s also involved a conscious national direction of the economy. These were clearly not outcomes of social democratic programmes, neither can they be readily attributed to a weighty ideological commitment. Whether there was any depth to fascist economic policy has been a matter of some debate.[10] Most commentators now argue that there was no strong commitment of principle for or against private ownership. Rather it was a matter of establishing control. At one level the emphasis was on autarky, with firms naturalised in Spain (that is, passed to indigenous owners) and pressures everywhere to use domestic resources. The reluctance of German steel barons to use German iron ore led to the establishment of the Herman Goering works (BERG) in 1936. The reluctance of car manufacturers to produce the Beetle led to the state-owned Volkswagen factory. The development of import substitutes and other autarkic policies were implemented in Germany by state holding companies like VIAG and VEBA (established in 1923 and 1929) and which had extensive interests in electricity, coal, tin, lead and oil, as well as by big private firms like the chemical giant IG Farben.[11] Arm's-length regulation was sufficient to secure state influence in the fascist states because it was backed by violence. In the other states, regulation required legislation and in some cases public ownership.

Although Franco's government, in the period 1941–8, acquired a wide range of financial holdings in the infrastructure and manufacturing, its direct ownership and administration was limited to the railways, the telephone system and tobacco (Tabacalera). The rest consisted in part of shareholdings by INI in enterprises that accounted for relatively modest shares of total activity in their respective industries: ENDESA and ENHER in electricity supply, En Elcano in maritime transport, En Bazan in shipbuilding, ENASA in engineering and ENDASA in aluminium. In other cases, INI held shares jointly with other companies in engineering enterprises like HispanoAviac, CASA, BYNSA and Marconi, chemical firms like FEFASA and in the fledgling Iberia airline.[12] In Italy also railways and trunk line telephones were under direct state ownership, whilst the holdings of IRI amounted by the late 1930s to 27% of electricity supply, 52% of telephone subscribers, 90% of merchant shipping tonnage, 80% of shipbuilding, 45% of steel and 11% of cars. During the Second World War, Italy's military spending was a smaller proportion of national income than that of most of the other major belligerents, though it was badly affected by the invasions, losing one quarter of the capital stock of the railways, 85% of merchant shipping and one half of the stock of road vehicles.[13]

The former fascist countries therefore emerged from the Second World War with a set of infrastructure industries that, in Germany and Italy, had been badly damaged, but whose ownership, and this includes Spain, bore a close resemblance to the pattern in other western European countries. The late 1940s saw few changes in this respect, as the painful reconstruction proceeded. There were no plans to expand the state sector in Italy nor in the new Federal Republic of Germany, where state action was now under deep suspicion. The state holdings in the German infrastructure industries and manufacturing amounted to no more than what had been transferred to it from the Third Reich and the Prussian state. They were simply an inheritance rather than a conscious drive to public ownership as in Britain and France, who had now effectively 'caught up' with the rest of western Europe. A conscious national direction of the economy, facilitated in part by a large public sector, was now a common feature of all.

The new functions, which the infrastructure industries were expected to take on, were in fact additions to the various non-commercial functions inherited from the pre-1939 period – as tools of national unification and regional development, owners and managers of strategic resources and disseminators of politically sensitive information. Moreover, in these sectors, governments still had to address the economic problems inherent in their technologies, in particular those of natural monopoly and network externalities that generated price controls, subsidies, franchising and rate of return regulation. From the 1950s, technological changes presented new challenges. In surface transport, it was mainly a result of the very rapid development of the motor vehicle. As the cost of vehicle manufacture fell as a result of innovations in factory layout and from new metals, and as oil prices fell, the road-rail problem we discussed in Part III now took on monumental proportions. The old nineteenth-century rate structure still bedevilled the railways, and the period from the late 1940s up to the 1970s saw railway passenger traffic stagnate in many countries as the railway undertakings shifted only slowly to a more competitive rate structure. A new issue arose, road congestion, that is, the availability of an infrastructure (the road) with no access charges – fine with low traffic volumes but chaotic otherwise. The introduction of access charges had to wait for the new century so that in the meantime everyone queued.

The transformations in airline technology also caused problems for the railways, though, in Europe, with its heterogeneous political groupings, small states and dense populations, railways were less vulnerable than in the USA, where the airlines devastated rail passenger traffic – by the early 1990s it was down to only 10% of the 1950 level. In both Europe and America, the technical transformation of the narrow-bodied propeller aircraft of the 1930s to the wide-bodied jets of the 1960s offered the prospect of new leisure and business services and challenged the monopolies of national carriers and the strict control of fare levels and structures. All forms of transport were, of course, major consumers of oil. The part dependence on supplies from the politically turbulent Middle East, together with the discovery of large oil and natural gas supplies in European waters, changed the profile of strategic issues facing Western governments who were deeply involved in the regulation and ownership of the oil and gas sectors. Clemenceau's remark during the First World War that a 'drop of oil is worth a drop of blood' seems to have been taken on board by all twentieth-century governments. Finally, there is the telecommunications industry, which, for three decades after the Second World War, blissfully flourished on a relatively simple technology and institutional setting. The main technological developments were in the telephone exchanges, where calls were routed, and various options arose for replacing manual switching by automatic gear. The main service on offer was telephone voice communication provided over an integrated national network. The only piece of terminal equipment was the telephone. Technical standards for switching equipment and telephone sets were regulated by the same PTT who operated the network. The development of information technology from the 1970s changed everything. It greatly facilitated, in all sectors of the economy, the splintering and outsourcing of services from manufacturing firms to new service firms in accounting, R & D, computers, consultancy, maintenance, plumbing and painting. It encouraged the break-up of vertically integrated operations in transport and energy – divorcing rail track from train services, separating generation, transmission, distribution and retailing in electricity. But IT had probably its biggest impact in telecommunications in facilitating, through the microprocessor, a new vast range of services at the end of the network – telex, fax, personal computers, email and private networks. Natural monopolies were no longer a dominant feature, raising the possibility of competitive solutions. The security issues were now very different from those that had made government officials worry about the telegraph and telephone. Telecommunications, per se, were not the main security problem and need no longer be anchored to a government department.

Economic Organisation

Although many historians and commentators have wanted to see the origins and ideology behind state enterprise in their country as rather distinctive, there was, by 1950, a common pattern. It was argued in the early part of this chapter that the problems inherent to network industries and the technological developments in the supply of infrastructure services had forced public authorities to intervene quite strongly, and by the late 1940s a common pattern had emerged, at least in the energy, telecommunications and transport sectors. Some countries, it is true, saw very little change in ownership after the Second World War. Swedish historians often emphasise this, invoking the pragmatic approach of their Social Democratic Party and their loss of electoral power.[14] But the Swedish trunk network in rail and telegraph, together with the major part of the electricity and gas industries, were already in the hands of state or municipal bodies and there was no coal industry to nationalise. Historians of Germany often argue that the Federal Republic shied away from extending public ownership in the late 1940s and early 1950s in part because of the sullied reputation of the central state and in part because of the opposition of the occupying American administration to 'socialisation'. But public ownership by the late 1930s was as widespread in Germany as in many other European countries. It accounted, as late as 1963 for example, for 81% of investment in the West German energy sector and 72% in transport and communications, which may be compared with 91% and 74% for France.[15] The same applies to Italy.

The socialist case was advanced most strongly in France and Britain, whose nationalisations in the years 1945–8 effectively brought them up to the level of the others. In France, the neo-Marxist cry for commandeering the means of production had less weight than the idea of wresting control of the great monopolies from the hands of the old financial families and, as the Conseil National de Résistance argued, to 'free the directed economy from its association with Vichy, Fascism and Stalinism'.[16] By the end of the 1940s, it was clear that the outcome was not fundamental socialism. Some of the rhetoric did mean that public ownership extended beyond the purely infrastructure industries – into coal and iron and steel, as in Britain, to the Gnome and Renault companies, accused in France of collaboration with the enemy during the war. But public ownership was also extensive in manufacturing in Germany and Italy. For the sectors in which we are interested, energy, telecommunications and transport, the public authorities in all countries had taken a strong grip by the end of the 1930s. Similarly, socialist views on the way state enterprises should be organised and administered were not widely accepted. There was a drive in France and Britain for trade union representation on the supervising boards. In the 1940s, this was not so much a neo-Marxist idea as a democratic syndicalist view of parliament, workers and managers running the industry outside the control of the state. In France, 'Nationaliser n'est pas étatiser' was the slogan – to be nationalised does not mean to be controlled by the state. In the event, union representatives on the supervising boards in France created havoc in the late 1940s because of divided loyalties, and their role was later relegated. In Britain, despite strong lobbying from the Union of Postal Workers, none of the boards had union representatives. They were staffed by scientists, financiers, administrators and other specialists.

State enterprise after 1945 and in the years up to the market liberalisation and privatisations of the 1980s was organised, broadly, in one of three ways. The first way was as a section or agency in a government department. A second form was a legal entity separate from government but called a public establishment or corporation. Thirdly, there were the joint stock companies with the state owning, in practice, anything from 25% to 100% of the shares. Of course, there was still a large number of municipal undertakings, especially in transport, electricity, water and gas supply. In France, they fell into a particular legal category, the 'régie', a territorial administration directly responsible for the service in question, and the undertaking itself had no separate legal status. Such enterprises had become common in France in water, gas and in electricity distribution, though paradoxically, and just to show how labels could be misused, the Parisian Transport authority, the Régie Autonome de Transport Parisienne, was not really a 'régie' since it was an independent entity![17] Municipal enterprise was still widespread in local transport and water supply in the UK, and in Germany and Scandinavia more generally. As late as 1991, over 50% of electricity distribution in Sweden was in municipal hands.[18] In Germany, both the municipal and regional governments (the Länder) had significant holdings in energy and transport, whilst in Denmark, the municipalities continued to be involved extensively in joint ventures with private companies, co-operatives and the central government.

For the large part, we concentrate here on enterprises operating at the level of the nation state. Why the three forms of enterprise? To a large extent it reflected the broad aims under which they had been established, though there was some inertia when the aims changed, so that their historical origins played a strong role. The first category is the enterprise located in a government department – classically the post and telecommunications undertakings: the Telegrafslyret in Norway, the Televerket in Sweden, the Deutsche Bundespost in Germany, the General Post

Office in Britain, the Azienda di Stato per i Servizi Telefonici for Italian trunk telephone lines, the Post-og Telegrafvaesenet similarly in Denmark and the PTT in Belgium, France and the Netherlands. They were not legally separate from the government, the staff were civil servants and, although they increasingly had a separately identified set of accounts, their budget was part of the budget of their supervising ministry. All their expenditures were approved by parliament and all revenues were explicitly treated as payments to the government. The Deutsche Bundespost was governed by special legislation – an act of 1953 that made the Federal Government responsible for the property of the DBP, but it was public law not company law.[19] In all these cases, as we argued in Part III, the advantage of a single national network and the growing unwillingness to achieve this by arm's-length regulation of private monopolies, prompted public ownership, and the fact that the state wanted directly to control the flow of information explains why they finished up as part of a government department. So also for the Italian state railways, the Azienda Autonoma delle Ferrovie dello Stato, and in Germany the Deutsche Bundesbahn, where similar motives were present. In the case of the latter, there was a special act of 1951, similar to that for post and telecommunications. Over time, the importance of railways, telegraph and telephone as channels of communication, which the governments felt they needed to control, diminished as a result of the liberalisation of the printed press and of new electronic and airborne methods of communication. The institutional setting then came under threat, as we shall see in later chapters.

The second form of state enterprise is typified by the 'établissement public' in France and the public corporation in Britain. These were legally separate entities, governed neither by public law nor company law. There were precedents in Britain, the London Passenger Transport Board and the Central Electricity Board, but for France, after 1945, their legal identity was seen as innovatory, a public establishment of an industrial and commercial character, provided with a civil personality and financial autonomy.[20] The staff were not civil servants and were governed by special legislation, which established the enterprises as commercially independent, and was headed by a supervisory board separate from government. They reflected recognition by the 1940s that state enterprise was an important distinctive element in the economy. They had certain public duties – as we shall see – but their management was expected to be 'businesslike' in their dealings and behaviour. It was the form taken in electricity supply by Electricité de France, the British Electricity Authority and the Ente Nazionale de l'Energia Elettrica in Italy. Gaz du France and Charbonnages de France had a similar independence, as did the Gas Council and the National Coal Board in Britain as well as the British Transport Commission. The newly nationalised railway enterprise in Spain in 1941, Red Nacional de Ferrocarriles Españoles, was a public corporation (*sociedad estatad*) answerable to the Ministry of Public Works but with its own legal identity, autonomy and business orientation.[21]

The third form of organisation was the joint stock company, the 'société anonyme' in France, with state ownership of shares. For the large part, the aim here was to allow government access to, or leverage on, resources and services, but where the enterprise was essentially a profit-making business, operating often in a competitive environment, domestically or internationally. Government involvement in airlines and oil companies characteristically took this form. In the inter-war period, governments acquired shares in companies dealing in foreign oil supplies: Azienda Generale Itali Petroli, British Petroleum, Compagnie Française Pétrole. These companies flourished after the war, sometimes merged with others. Similarly, government shares in airlines, whose commercial importance really dates from the 1950s, had their origins before 1939. Air France, Alitalia and Lufthansa all date from the inter-war period, but the latter two, as organs of the defeated combatants, were wound up after the war. They re-emerged in the mid 1950s with the Federal Government owning 74% of Lufthansa and the Italian government 60% of Alitalia, rising in both cases to nearly 90% by the 1980s.[22] When the state took shares in manufacturing firms, it was usually competing with private firms. The Federal Government of West Germany had substantial holdings in the big conglomerates VIAG, VEBA and BERG, which were involved in chemicals, engineering and other German manufacturing sectors as well as electricity and coal. The Instituto Nacional de Industria (INI) in Spain was 100% state owned but gave financial and other general support to its subsidiaries in electricity, oil distribution and the airline Iberia in competition with private firms, as did INI's subsidiaries in manufacturing. In Italy, the analogous institutions provided a multi-layered support and access to finance. The Istituto per la Ricostruzione Industriale (IRI) and Ente Nazionale Idrocaruri (ENI, the state-owned oil and gas company established in 1953) were 100% state owned, and they held majority shares in subsidiaries like STET (telephones) and Azienda Generale Italia Petroli (AGIP). Even that layer was not directly involved in operations but was effectively 'società finanziarie' exercising part ownership of telephone companies and others in methane gas products and piping.[23]

These three categories do not capture all the nuances of state enterprise organisation. Electricity was generated and distributed by various companies and groupings like RWE, VIAG, VEBA in Germany, and ELKRAFT and ELSAM in Denmark (cf. Chapter 8), but the state and the municipalities had dominant shareholdings, and when it came to transmission, they all came together as joint participators in the national grid. Similarly, the desire for controlling monopoly profits and exercising close scrutiny over communications was manifest in Denmark by the Post-og Telegrafvaesenet providing postal and telegram services and inter-regional and international telephone lines, while the rest of the telephone network was provided by regulated concessionary companies (Kjøbenhavns, Fyns Kimmunale, Jydsk).[24] Trunk railway lines were the business of the Deutsche Bundesbahn and the Danske Statsbaner, but the provincial lines in both countries were left to the company sector, in which, however, state and municipalities had important stakes. Sweden provided another variant. Televerket, as we noted earlier, was part of the public law sector – it was an *affärsverk*, commonly translated as a 'trading agency'. But so also were the state railways, Statens Järnvägar, and the state power board, the Vattenfall. They were integral parts of government, not actually answerable to a minister but rather to the cabinet (King-in-Council). They were distinct from the 'state companies' in road haulage, provincial railways, tobacco and so on. The idea that the trading agencies' format reflected their dependency on state finance for investment may reflect their early nineteenth-century history, but does not square readily with the fact that, by the 1950s, many state enterprises elsewhere in Europe relied heavily on state finance (railways in France, Britain and Germany, for example). Moreover, although Coombe has argued that the trading agencies were similar to British public corporations, like the National Coal Board, they were constitutionally different. There was no comparable legal entity in Sweden, and symptomatic of the awkward position of the trading agencies within the government machine is that by the 1960s moves were afoot to establish new kinds of state enterprises within the aegis of an umbrella body. A state enterprise commission was established in 1970 (Statsforetag, renamed later as Procordia) as a holding company for the state companies with the intention that some of the trading agencies would be included later. Full 'corporatisation' did not come until the 1980s. Finally, we should note that, although the British Overseas Airways Corporation and British European Airways were set up as public corporations, the role of the state, in what was a highly competitive international setting, was more like a major shareholder. In contrast, when Société Nationale des Chemins de Fer Français was established in 1937, it was not really a nationalisation of the French railways but more a rearrangement of share ownership with the state taking a dominant position. The private shares were not due to be amortised until 1982, and in the intervening period the structure of SNCF was, as we saw in Chapter 9, a product of a particular historical moment when a more radical reorganisation was not possible. In Spain, Telefonica was nationalised in the 1940s, but the dictatorial regime was content to leave it with company status; the government became the primary shareholder with three board members and a 'state delegate' with wide powers. Again that position became less anomalous over time as these methods of communication became less a security matter and more an economic one.[25]

Whatever the form of organisation, state enterprises were distinguished from other forms of enterprise by what was expected of their behaviour and role in the economy. They had two objectives that, when taken together, crystallised their distinctiveness. On the one hand, they were expected to operate in 'the public interest', which, vague though that was, meant that, at a minimum, they could be required to undertake activities outside a conventional business brief, and ultimately linked to government policy in economic, social and political affairs. On the other hand, they were expected to operate in a businesslike fashion, which, again at a minimum, meant that they were expected to break even financially. There was, therefore, from the beginning a tension between the two objectives, and this was at the heart of many of the difficulties of state enterprise in the 1945–90 period. How this occurred is one of the themes of Part IV. The importance of non-commercial obligations was most likely in the state enterprises integrated with government departments. On the other hand, the public corporations and especially those enterprises established under company law were often in a more competitive environment so that the break-even requirement had more demanding implications. This tension is characteristic of all public-sector activities – like policing and education – since all operate under some kind of budget constraint. For state enterprises, there was, however, a ready form of comparison in financial terms, namely private-sector firms. Moreover, procedures to deal with the tension between commercial and non-commercial objectives were not well articulated in the early postwar period, so that state enterprise went through a severe learning process.

The more precise was the 'public interest' obligation the more readily could it be quantified and addressed. The guiding statements were, however, notoriously imprecise. In the defeated nations, there was some understandable hesitancy in the early postwar years about formalising the role of state agencies. In Italy, the IRI received little guidance other than to 'run the shareholdings it possesses' and do that 'in the public interest'.[26] The Deutsche Bundesbahn and the Deutsche Bundespost were required by their acts to take into account the main lines of the policy of the Federal Government. The Basic Constitutional Law (the Grundgesetz, 1949) allowed the government of the Federal Republic to intervene in issues where major interests of the state were at stake, provided that, in the case of action by state enterprises, there was no other mechanism by which the objectives could be achieved. The qualification looks significant, but the potential area of interest was large.[27] Elsewhere, the aims were no more precisely specified. State enterprises in France were expected to operate in 'the public interest', and although enterprises like Air France operated under company law, government representatives on the supervisory board ensured that it had to take the public interest into account.[28] The 1946 legislation for the National Coal Board in Britain required the Board 'to develop coal mining in ways which, as may seem . . . [to the Board] . . . best calculated to serve the public interest'.[29] In Italy, ENI, from its inception in 1953, was expected to 'carry out initiatives of national interest in the fields of hydrocarbons and natural gas'.[30] Electricity was nationalised in 1962 in Italy within the terms of Article 43 of the constitution that made provision for state enterprise, where there was a 'pre-eminent general interest'.[31] Despite its drive for competition, the European Economic Community reinforced the vague nature of state enterprise objectives by recognising the special problems of providing 'services of general economic interest'.[32] One solution of all these problems of defining public interest was to go for 'universal service' – standardising prices and service quality throughout the country, as noted earlier.

In some cases, there were certain quite specific duties, such as those falling on electricity companies in Germany and Denmark to co-ordinate energy supplies through the national grids, a duty also explicitly laid on the state power board in Sweden. But when it came to specifying what national considerations had to be taken into account, the legislation and directives were often silent or vague. The British Transport Commission was required to provide 'an adequate and efficient system of inland transport' and the British Electricity Authority to provide 'cheap electricity, especially in rural areas'.[33] The Televerket was expected to ensure efficient Swedish telephone services at the lowest cost.[34] INI was seen to be a key agent, in Franco Spain, in promoting self-sufficiency, while ENEL was expected to promote 'balanced economic development' by giving priority to southern Italy.[35]

How these requirements, even when specific, were to be reconciled with the second broad aim – to break even – was never spelled out in the legislation nor in the early guidelines. The aim that revenue (albeit including government grants and subsidies) should cover expenditure, including all capital charges, was clear, and although there are many ways of estimating cost and depreciation, the intention was unambiguous in all countries. It was also more easily monitored than the vague public purposes. The Swedish trading agencies operated within the framework of public administration and were to return all surpluses to the Treasury, but revenues were expected to cover expenditures, including interest charges and the amortisation of loans. Similarly for the Deutsche Bundesbahn, though part of public administration, 'income had to cover expenditure including an acceptable return on capital'. The Deutsche Bundespost was expected to offer special rates and services to cities like Berlin and to groups like students, while breaking even and handing over a certain proportion of revenue to the Federal Government.[36] Kuisel emphasised the 'financial equilibrium' expected of all French state enterprises, a message reinforced by the terms of Marshall Aid, which tied modernisation to balanced accounts.[37] The British Nationalisation Acts of the 1940s hardly mentioned profits, but if any were realised, they had to be reinvested in the industry; in general the requirement was that revenues should cover all outgoings, taking one year with another or on an average of good and bad years.[38] Putting the matter a different way, for Italy, IRI and ENI were to make neither profits nor losses.[39]

Economic planning c. 1945–75

Notwithstanding the vague public purposes and the tension with breaking even, state enterprises were a potentially vital tool in the reconstruction of the European economies in the years 1945–51 and in the arrangements for long-term planning that were characteristic of the period up to the 1980s. Did the state enterprise sector actually play a distinctive role or was it no more, in the planning process, than the sum of its parts?

I use the term 'planning' in this chapter to refer to something quite restricted and distinctive, specifically the attempts by central governments to guide the economy at an aggregate (all sector) level, with the prime aim of raising the long-term growth of productive potential. The focus is therefore not the Keynesian inspired manipulation of aggregate demand or the Friedman-like control over the money supply for purposes of controlling prices. Nor is it concerned with state control of resources and prices during war and reconstruction, though, as we shall see, it did merge with that in the period 1945–51. Nor does it refer to any form of state intervention. The Italian government's explicit provisions for encouraging investment in the south, the Mezzigiorno, could have been undertaken without any formal national plan. So also the French desire to invest heavily in nuclear power and the British government's support in the 1960s for the Beeching proposals to cut back the Victorian railway network. Rather, the emphasis in planning is on the productive potential of the whole economy, its long-term growth rate and the co-ordinating activity of the state at a national level.

In the first decade or so after 1945, some Western governments (but certainly not all) became persuaded that 'the market' needed some support if it were to deliver high long-term growth rates of national output. Soviet plans had been publicised since the 1920s and were introduced in a command economy with a small private sector and controlled prices. Western European governments were not amenable to imposing rules and orders, Soviet style, but some states were sympathetic to the idea of engaging in what came to be known as 'indicative planning'.[40] Practice varied, but the methodology and ingredients of a 'Plan' may be summarised as follows. It would start with an analysis of the recent performance of the economy and would identify the main obstacles to growth – whether these were bottlenecks in skilled labour, poor transport, limited energy sources and so on. A target growth rate of GDP would then be established, say 3% per annum for a five-year period; this was a conditional target not a forecast. An estimate would then be made of what fixed capital formation would be necessary in the private and public sectors to generate the physical capacity for that growth rate. The public sector's plans would be made explicit, and the private sector invited to state what it thought feasible, given the proposals for public investment. The growth rate and investment outlays would imply certain levels of imports of raw materials and capital goods and hence the target export growth rate. What is left in the 3% growth of GDP is the annual growth in private consumption and government current expenditure on health, policing and so on. Several iterations and alternative scenarios would be floated by the planning staff. Moreover, and very importantly, there would be implications for government policy in certain key areas – such as inflation, the exchange rate, regional growth – and decisions would be required if the plan were to stand any chance of success.

The origins of planning in the above sense can be traced to the perceived under-investment by the private sector in the 1930s and to the idea that investment in different sectors was interdependent. Motor car production is partly contingent on how much steel is likely to be available, domestically, and at what cost. Export propensities will depend on how much railway and autobahn development occurs. The Plan would reveal bottlenecks, identify inconsistencies and in general highlight the obstacles to growth. A key element was investment. Public investment could be directed, and clearly the large presence of government in the infrastructure industries by the late 1940s meant that state enterprises would be a key element in the plan. It was not generally the aim to order and direct the private sector. Here the theory was that business investment was sensitive to expectations about the future (as Keynes had emphasised, though he cannot be seen as the driving force in France). If private firms could be induced to give some indication of what might possibly happen, this itself would overcome uncertainties by establishing expectations about the future. As we shall see, two issues proved central to the success or otherwise of planning. One was whether governments proved willing to make decisions about explicit policy choices identified in the planning process. The other was the willingness of private firms, and indeed in some countries, state enterprises, to execute the promised investment programmes.

Neither Sweden nor Germany subscribed to the notion of planning as described above. There were five plans in Sweden in the years up to 1970: the Myrdal Plan of 1947–52, the second (1950–55) plan, the Svennilson Plan of 1955–60, followed by those for 1960–4 and 1965–70.[41] They were little more than Keynesian-style demand management programmes. The Social Democratic Party, which governed Sweden during the war (as a neutral), certainly had aspirations to planning in the full sense. The Myrdal Planning Commission envisaged the nationalisation of insurance credit and of other sectors, and in 1948 the SDP was instrumental in securing arrangements for an integrated national electricity grid (cf. chapter 8) by declaring that all new power lines above 200 kV should be cleared through the state power board, the Vattenfall.[42] There was much opposition to long-term planning from the business sector and from other political parties, and the SDP lost its majority in the Lower House in 1948. It had tried to sell the idea of planning as a way of reducing unemployment – a major fear from the interwar period, which did not, however, materialise after the war.[43] The main impetus for the Myrdal Plan of 1947–52 came from the 'plan' that had to be drawn up for obtaining Marshall Aid from the USA. As with all the other western European countries, the documents prepared for Marshall Aid had to show how the economy was to be developed in a world of freer trade and what part aid would play in that. The Myrdal plan emphasised 'balanced development' in industry, health and education. In fact the 'Swedish model', as it came to be called, comprised a government commitment to macroeconomic demand management, a large welfare state and a highly organised central wage bargaining system.

In Germany, the state had to be kept in the background in the aftermath of twelve years of dictatorship, although, as we have seen, a large part of the infrastructure was still in state hands and remained there. If anything, the emphasis was on liberalising markets, and the 'Social

Market Economy' paradigm originated in a neo-liberalist school of economics. The money supply was to be controlled and competition in industry promoted by the state, in recognition of a past history of cartels and hyperinflation. It also looked to a just economy, where social services and a less unequal distribution of income would get their due weight, a gloss that Arndt claimed was added by Müller-Armack, the Secretary of State for the Ministry of Economic Affairs. The Social Market Economy was essentially a theme for promoting the reconstruction of Germany and the move to a liberalised economy. There was no need for a Plan, said Müller-Armack.[44]

Of course Germany, like everybody else, had to cope with shortages of raw materials and dollars in the late 1940s. It invested heavily and controlled prices in housing, electricity, coal and steel. Free markets were not allowed to operate initially, so that rationing, import quotas, licences and government allocation of key resources was the order of the day.[45] So also, in different ways, in Britain, France and Italy. The labour force and other resources had to be switched from military to civilian use. Loss of life had been greatest in Russia (17 million) and least, proportionately, in the UK and USA (each about 350000).[46] The physical damage to transport, electricity stations and manufacturing plants had to be addressed, and we find in all countries the main emphasis for state action in investment and recovery was, apart from housing, in so-called 'basic industries' – coal, steel, transport, electricity and engineering. Of all the combatants, the USA had suffered least, in economic terms, during the war. It was both the main creditor, in financial terms, and the main source of raw materials and new capital goods. Hence the dollar shortage and the pressure on all countries to develop exports, which had fallen away to only small proportions of their 1938 levels. To devote resources to exports meant either cutting consumption expenditure (private and/or government) or cutting investment (public and/or private). In the event, the main weight fell on private consumption levels so that, in Britain, the population 'starved with Strachey' (the Minister of Food) and 'shivered with Shinwell' (the Minister of Fuel). Leaving the market to solve these problems by movements of relative prices would open the door to excess profits and other major injustices in a setting of meagre living standards. Governments became heavily involved in allocating consumption goods by rationing and allocating capital and intermediate goods across firms by quotas.

Reconstruction policies therefore largely avoided market solutions, but the horizon was short term and, despite state direction of resources, the emphasis was not on achieving target long-term growth rates of GDP. There were some in Britain who did hope the one would lead to the other, and in France it did. The institutions that were set up in Britain to cope with shortages of the reconstruction period had the potential of being used for long-term planning. In the late 1940s, one-third of all consumer expenditure was subject to rationing, two-thirds of imports required licences, steel, timber, coal and other scarce intermediate inputs were allocated by quotas, licences were required for most new buildings, and price controls operated on 40% of goods. 'Britain was heading... [especially in the cold winter of 1947] ... not for a New Jerusalem but for starvation corner.'[47] Signs of economic planning may be seen in the Labour Party election manifesto of 1945, which looked to the setting up of a National Investment Board.[48] During the next three years coal, electricity, gas and railways were nationalised and steel was on the cards. A National Investment Advisory Council was established in 1948 to advise about finance for investment. However, finance was not the issue. There was no shortage of finance. The shortages were in resources, and the main scarcities were raw materials, steel, coal and so on, and the centrepiece of the government's resource allocation scheme was the Investment Programming Committee, its main instruments being steel allocations, building and import licences, all with an eye to export performance.[49] Neither the motor car manufacturers nor the textile mill owners needed to fear nationalisation as long as they met their export targets. Two of Labour's Chancellors of the Exchequer, Dalton and Cripps, saw these institutions as a real start for 'central planning'. The Supplies and Services Acts introduced laws that underpinned the licensing and rationing, and the 1947 act included the objective of ensuring resources were available and used to benefit all groups in Britain. Herbert Morrison (hardly a left-winger) thought this was the essential basis for economic planning. Labour lost power in 1951, by which time there had been considerable relaxation of controls, but, in any case, most economists and civil servants saw the controls and institutions as temporary measures, and the advisers influenced by Keynes thought of planning only in terms of manipulating the government budget and developing national income accounts.[50]

By the late 1940s, France had three features that epitomised – more than in later years, and more than ever in any other country – the link between planning and state enterprise. There was investment in the basic infrastructure industries to reduce bottlenecks, which was organised and executed in the context of a long-term plan (the Monnet Plan 1946–52), and since state enterprise dominated the infrastructure sector and could be readily directed to meeting plan targets, it was a dominant element in the process. Sixty percent of capital formation in 1946–52 was in the public sector and 30% in 1949–53 was in public enterprise. The Monnet

Plan gave priority to six basic sectors: coal, steel, electricity, transport, cement and farm machinery. Coal-mining equipment was outdated (rather than damaged by the war), hydroelectricity was thought by some to have been neglected by the ten electricity oligopolies in the interwar period. Public aid was needed, and for many it was unthinkable without public ownership.[51] Improvement in energy supplies, especially hydroelectricity, was seen to be the first step to reviving manufacturing industry, and targeting electricity (and indeed the electrification of nearly 50% of the railways) would help heal France's traditional Achilles heel: its meagre coal supplies. The plan was constructed by first assembling information on the availability of labour and raw materials, estimating the maximum output that could be achieved in each sector with these resources, and then deriving the investment requirements for ensuring adequate capacity. In broad terms, the target was that output levels in the basic sectors should by 1952 be 25% above the 1929 (pre-depression) levels. The requirement to produce a plan for Marshall Aid in 1947/8 underlined the need, according to Monnet, for a plan for renovating the French economy and where the sums added up correctly.[52] Private firms were leaned on to meet the target and could be refused access to resources; for state enterprise the targets were imperatives.

Why was there in France so much apparent commitment to strategic thinking, to looking further ahead than the next year and to forming an explicit plan? The answer seems most likely to lie in how France perceived itself after a war that represented the third invasion since 1870.[53] Symptomatic of motives was the fact that the first brief for a five-year plan asked for a strategy for securing that the coal and iron resources of the Ruhr, as well as those in eastern France, could be harnessed for the reconstruction and modernisation of the French economy. To this end the Commissariat du Plan was attached to the Prime Minister's office. The Monnet Plan reflected French fears that Germany would be allowed, by the allies, to recover as quickly as France in a way that threatened French security. If France was not to be allowed to expropriate the Ruhr, at least it should be under international control. The USA demurred, and France was able only to demand that Germany be required to raise its coal exports to France.

Most observers have judged that this first French plan was effective. Heavy industry showed impressive increases in output, even though the targets were met by the early 1950s only in two subsectors, oil refining and tractors, and demand had been overestimated in railways, cement and coal.[54] The more intriguing question is whether France, with its planning and its commitment of state enterprises to the plan, did any better in reconstruction than the other western European countries.

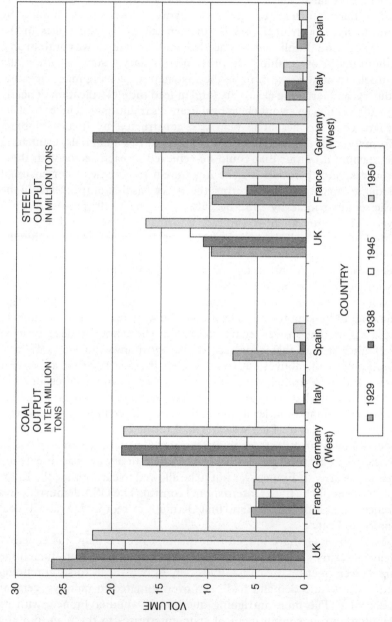

Figure 10.1 Coal and steel production during depression, war and reconstruction, 1929–1950.

Source: B. R. Mitchell, *International Historical Statistics: Europe 1750–1993* (London: Macmillan, 3rd edn., 1998).

Notes:
The French data on coal relate to hard coal and lignite, the German and Spanish to hard and brown coal. The 1929, 1938 and 1945 entries for Italy relate to 1924 boundaries and the 1950 entry to 1954 boundaries. The West German figures for coal for 1929 and 1938 were derived by assuming they accounted for one half of the all-German total; in the case of steel, the assumption was that 0.5 million tons were produced in the east. The 1945 entry for steel in Germany is 1946.

Those countries not directly involved in the war showed a fairly continuous increase in activity in the infrastructure industries. As Figures 10.1, 10.2 and 10.3 demonstrate, electricity and rail freight in Sweden rose uninterruptedly over the sample years 1929, 1938, 1945 and 1950. The entire rail track remained open. Spain had just over 17000 km open in 1930. This was probably badly damaged during the Civil War, data on which are not available. By 1950, some 18000 km are recorded to be open.[55] Likewise, after the Civil War, electricity supply, rail freight, coal and steel showed continuous increases. The fortunes of the coal industry over this period are difficult to gauge, since the decline in French and British output during the war was more to do with outdated equipment

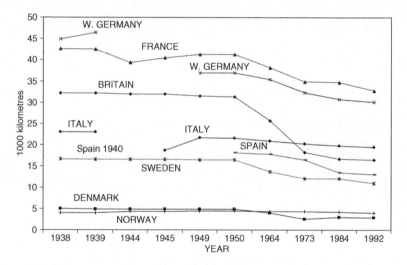

Figure 10.2 Rail track open, 1938–1992.

Source: B. R. Mitchell, *International Historical Statistics: Europe 1750–1993* (London: Macmillan, 3rd edn., 1998).

Notes:
The entries for West Germany for 1938 and 1939 were derived by assuming that 75% of the all-German track was located in West Germany. The 1945–50 entries exclude Saarland. France lost Alsace-Lorraine 1940–4. Tenda and Briga were transferred from Italy to France in 1947. In addition Italy ceded Fiume, Istria and part of Venezia-Giulia to Yugoslavia in 1945, and Trieste was under international occupation 1945–54. The entries for Spain for 1973 and 1984 are estimates and the 1984 and 1992 data exclude narrow-gauge lines. The entry for West Germany for 1992 refers to 1988.

and old seams than physical destruction. The big German recovery after the war was more a matter of relaxing price controls than of investment in the industry. Indeed the German entries for coal in Figure 10.1 have to be taken with a pinch of salt in that they purport to relate to West Germany in the period 1929–50 and involve some rough estimates of the pre-war split between east and west.

Outside coal, however, a clearer pattern emerges. At one extreme was Germany, which emerged from the war with very low levels of steel production, electricity supply and rail freight and much damage to the railway track. By 1950, there had been a large recovery, though for steel and rail freight this amounted to only some 50–70% of pre-war levels. At the other extreme was the UK, which, of those involved in the war, was least affected in terms of physical damage. Electricity and steel showed continuous rises from 1929. The entire rail track remained open, and rail freight traffic increased. In this light, the French recovery by 1950 does look quite impressive. While the absolute size of damage by the end of the war was not as large as in Germany, the proportional decline in electricity, steel, rail track open and rail freight was about the same. All had recovered by 1950, if not to the levels of 1929. So the Monnet Plan may indeed have given France an edge in the immediate postwar period, though there were obviously many other factors involved. Italy lost only 8% of its industrial assets during the war, but its rail track and bridges suffered badly.[56] Without a plan, it managed to return to 1929 levels in steel and electricity by 1950, if not in rail freight.

The experience of planning in France in 1945–52 was not typical of what was to follow, if only because the levers on private firms had to be replaced by more indirect coaxing. Nor is it the case, and this is the important point for the theme of this chapter, that state enterprises played an especially crucial part in the success or otherwise of the long-term plans that emerged in France, Britain and Italy over the next twenty-five years. It was probably in Italy more than anywhere else that state enterprise became an important instrument of economic policy, but this occurred invariably outside the planning framework. The 1950s saw extensive investment in telecommunications and motorways by IRI. In 1950, the development fund for the south, Casmez (Cassa per il Mezzigiorno), was set up and, by a law of 1957, 60% of the new industrial plant of state enterprises had to be in the south and 40% of all their new investments (raised to 80% and 60% in 1971).[57] In the years 1953–7, the Italian government formed the oil and natural gas state enterprise ENI, the airline Alitalia and the Ministry of State Share Holdings to oversee all companies with significant government shareholdings, whilst the electricity industry was restructured in 1962 with most of generation and

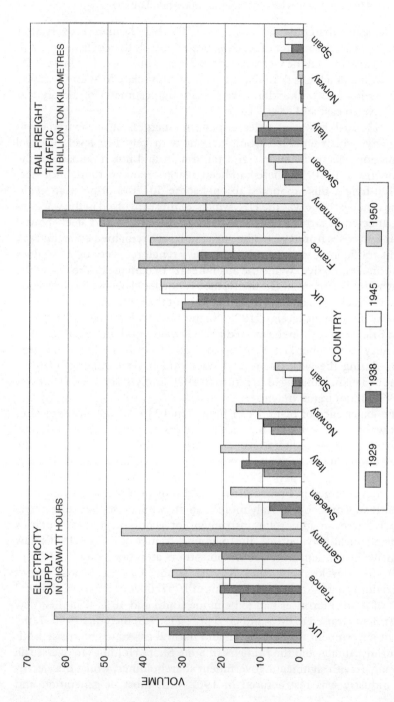

Figure 10.3 Electricity supply and rail freight during depression, war and reconstruction, 1929–1950.

Source: B. R. Mitchell, *International Historical Statistics: Europe 1750–1993* (London: Macmillan, 3rd edn., 1998).

Notes:

The 1929 and 1938 entries for West Germany for electricity were derived by assuming that one third of the all-German total was produced in the East; for rail freight it was one quarter. The 1945 entries for Germany relate to 1946, as does the Norway entry for electricity. The 1929, 1938 and 1945 entries for Italy relate to 1924 boundaries and the 1950 entry to 1954 boundaries. The rail data for the UK cover Britain only. The rail data for France covers state-owned lines only from 1938. The 1950 rail figure for Germany excludes Saarland, and the Norway entry includes, for the first time, freight carried free of charge.

transmission in the hands of the new nationalised enterprise ENEL. Some observers have seen these measures as partial efforts at planning involving increasing use of state enterprise, but there was no explicit plan.[58] Similar developments could be seen, albeit with different origins, in Spain, whose low level of industrialisation was attributed to bottlenecks in energy and transport and to a lack of entrepreneurial talent. Franco believed economic autarky was the only solution once foreign capital had dried up after the Civil War. In any case, military strategy, for the dictator, required that the energy shortage and low industrialisation be overcome. Electricity, coal and steel came to be the central 'trilogy' of industrialisation from the 1940s. INI led the way by investing in oil, electricity, steel and transport, accounting for 61% of infrastructure investment in the 1950s, and as late as the 1980s INI accounted for over a half of the national output of electricity, coal and steel. Throughout the 1940s, 1950s and early 1960s, the economy was directed and state enterprise was the tool, but there was no long-term indicative plan until 1965, when a development plan, prompted by the World Bank, was introduced. The development of a strong nucleus of basic industries remained an unchanged goal of the Franco regime, with or without a formal plan, right up to its end.[59]

In Italy, early attempts at planning failed to secure parliamentary agreement until 1967, when the first official plan, for 1966–70, was approved. It was geared to the correction of regional imbalances and the improvement of the social and economic infrastructure. It also gave state enterprise some very specific operational tasks, and all state investment was to be approved by CIPE, the Inter-Ministerial Committee for Economic Planning, established in 1967 with the brief to guide the planning process. The private sector, especially in the guise of the employers' federation, Confindustria, was suspicious of planning though happy to go along with state investment in basic industry, leaving manufacturing to private firms.[60] The left and the unions were suspicious of IRI as a vestige of fascism, but were attracted to the emphasis on investment in the south. Many observers have judged that little of any effect emerged from planning that would not have occurred anyway. Romano Prodi thought that CIPE affected economic choices 'infrequently and marginally'.[61] Development of the infrastructure only materialised in sectors governed by the state, and state enterprises like IRI and ENI often paid only lip service and did not necessarily implement the plan. A later plan document for 1971–5 reflected a new concern for growth but it was never approved by Parliament.

Many European countries, like Italy, had been watching developments in France, where GDP growth was very strong in the 1950s and where the Monnet Plan was followed by a series of Five-year indicative plans right through to the 1970s and beyond. Planning techniques changed over time as public investment increased its share of economic activity, input-output analyses were introduced and investment schemes evaluated by new techniques, including time-stream investment appraisal using discount rates set by the Commissariat du Plan. The focus of the plans changed over time reflecting the dominant worries about the economy. The second (Hirsch) 1954–8 plan shifted the emphasis away from the infrastructure to manufacturing and in the third plan (1957–61) the centrepiece was the drive to adapt French institutions to cope with international competition. The government budget was introduced for the first time in the fourth plan (1962–5), where investment in housing, transport and other social infrastructure came to form a central element of a medium-term set of objectives, reinforced in the fifth plan for 1966–70 by a regional focus, whilst in the 1970s international competition again featured strongly and especially in the sixth plan (1970–5).

While the French plans always aimed for transparency and rationality in economic issues, they came to be seen more and more as a reflection of the government's medium- and long-term economic policy and hence open to political debate.[62] The label of 'planning' was sustained but the content varied, and the plan became associated with 'dirigisme'. From the second plan onwards there were, strictly speaking, no obligations imposed on private or public firms, but it was only in the public sector that the programmes involved both a set of objectives and some surety about implementing them.[63] The supporters of indicative planning argued that it could only work when there was a core that did what the government wanted. State enterprise projects were reviewed by the Commissariat du Plan, even though their investment programmes and output targets were linked to target national growth rates of GDP in the same way as private industry. In the 1954–8 plan, some projects of Electricité de France (EDF) and Société Nationale des Chemins de Fer Français (SNCF) were rejected, but these state enterprises went elsewhere for finance.[64] The French plans may well, as some observers have argued, been fairly effective in illuminating the context of decision making in the 1950s and early 1960s, if not beyond.[65] They may also have been a necessary format, in France, for debate about economic policy. But they were open to the accusation of raising issues without solving them and indeed of abdicating responsibility. So far as the infrastructure industries were concerned, the main economic problems related to the conflict between road and rail, the search for alternatives to coal, the regulation of airline fares, competition and monopoly in telecommunications. These issues are considered in the next three chapters. They were not resolved in the planning process. That criticism applies even more to broader macro-economic issues like the exchange rate, the government deficit and wages policy, the resolution of which was often central to achieving the target growth rates.

This latter stricture is particularly apposite to the national plans of the UK in the 1960s. Towards the end of the 1950s, it had become apparent that several Continental countries were enjoying a faster growth of GDP than the UK and that, in particular, France was about to overtake the UK level of income per head. Perhaps the UK had not grown as quickly because it was not sufficiently well organised to do so, and perhaps there was a case, at a minimum, for government and industry to set out an assessment of expectations and intentions with respect to the near future?[66] This line of thought led to the establishment, by the Macmillan Conservative Government, of the National Economic Development Council in 1962, then to a first tentative plan in 1963 called the Conditions Favourable to Faster Growth, and finally in 1965 to the National Plan produced by the Department of Economic Affairs, a new ministry set up by the new Labour Government. A target annual growth rate of 3.8% per annum for GDP in 1964–70 was adopted, and the document had all the hallmarks of an indicative plan. Britain's major macroeconomic problem, in an era of fixed exchanges rates and commit-ments to the sterling area, was its balance of payments, and the success of the plan rested on an improved export performance. The latter was contingent on stopping the spiral of British export prices. The Labour government had refused to devalue the currency, and so export success depended on an 'incomes policy' for controlling wages and prices. This was relatively virgin territory and certainly did not solve the balance of payments problem, which led to a forced devaluation in 1967, followed by austerity measures that undermined all the public investment pro-grammes in the plan. The plan was 'murdered', and Conservative gov-ernments never again mentioned the word 'planning' except to vilify the Labour Party. A plan is not a policy, and some of the early warning signs can be found in speeches by Harold Wilson in the early 1960s, rashly heralding national economic plans as the means of solving Britain's balance of payments problems and halting Britain's relative economic decline.[67] In the infrastructure sector there were problems to face about Britain's huge railway network, the choice of generating plant for elec-tricity supply, the decline of the coal industry, the rising deficits of the nationalised industries and their falling level of self-finance. Neither of the 1960s plans provided solutions to these problems.

Notes

1 E. Chadeau, 'The Rise and Decline of State-Owned Industry in Twentieth Century France', in P. A. Toninelli (ed.), *The Rise and Fall of State Owned Enterprise in the Western World* (Cambridge University Press, 2000), 190–1; J. Pontusson, 'The Triumph of Pragmatism: Nationalisation and Privatisation in Sweden', *West European Politics* 11(4) (1988), 129–40; R. Millward, 'The 1940s Nationalisations in Britain: Means of Production or Means to an End?', *Economic History Review* 50(2) (1997), 209–34.

2 Chadeau, 'Rise and Decline', 198.

3 J. -P. Dormois, 'France: The Idiosyncrasies of *Voluntarisme*', in J. Foreman-Peck and G. Federico (eds.), *European Industrial Policy: The Twentieth Century Experience* (Oxford University Press, 1999), 77; M. Einaudi, 'Nationalisation in France and Italy', *Social Research* 15(1) (1948), 22–43; Millward, 'The 1940s Nationalisations in Britain'.

4 R. Millward and J. Singleton (eds.), *The Political Economy of Nationalisation in Britain 1920–50* (Cambridge University Press, 1995), chs. 3 and 14.

5 J. Moch, 'Nationalisation in France', *Annals of Collective Economy* 24 (1953), 97; Einaudi, 'Nationalisation'; M. R. Myers, 'The Nationalisation of Banks in France', *Political Science Quarterly* 64 (1949), 189–210.

6 Einaudi, 'Nationalisation', 29. J. Bohlin argues that socialism had given way to pragmatism in the Swedish social democratic party by the 1930s; see 'Sweden: The Rise and fall of the Swedish Model', in J. Foreman-Peck and G. Federico (eds.), *European Industrial Policy: The Twentieth Century Experience* (Oxford University Press, 1999), 160.

7 Cf. L. Jorberg, and O. Kranz, 'Scandinavia 1914–70', in C. Cipolla (ed.), *The Fontana Economic History of Europe: Contemporary Economies*, 2 parts (Glasgow: Fontana/Collins, 1976), part 2, 440; Bohlin, 'Swedish Model', 161–2.

8 D. Aldcroft, *British Railways in Transition* (London: Macmillan, 1968), Ch. 3; R. L. Frost, *Alternating Currents: Nationalised Power in France 1946–70* (Ithaca, N. Y.: Cornell University Press, 1991), 29–34; R. F. Kuisel, 'The Legend of the Vichy Synarchy', *French Historical Studies* 6 (1970), 385–98; R. F. Kuisel, 'Technocrats and Public Economic Policy: From the 3rd to the 4th Republic', *Journal of European Economic History* 2 (1973), 53–99; Dormois, 'The Idiosyncrasies of *Voluntarisme*', 74.

9 Einaudi, 'Nationalisation', 27. See also L. Jouhaux, 'Nationalisation in France', *Annals of Collective Economy* 20 (1949), 215–21; D. H. Pinkney, 'Nationalisation of Key Industries and Credit in France after the Liberation', *Political Science Quarterly* 62 (1947), 368–80; 'The French Experiment in Nationalisation, 1944–50', in E. M. Earle, *Modern France* (Princeton University Press, 1951), 354–67.

10 J. S. Cohen, 'Was Italian Fascism a Developmental Dictatorship?', *Economic History Review* 41 (1988), 97–113; W. Sauer, 'National Socialism: Totalitarianism or Fascism?', *American Historical Review* 73 (1967), 404–24; W. Feldenkirchen, 'Germany: The Invention of Interventionism', in Foreman-Peck and Federico (eds.), *European Industrial Policy*, 98–123; G. Federico and

R. Giannetti, 'Italy: Stalling and Surpassing', in Foreman-Peck and Federico (eds.), *European Industrial Policy*, 124–51; U. Wengenroth, 'The Rise and Fall of State Owned Enterprise in Germany', in Toninelli (ed.), *The Rise and Fall of State Owned Enterprise*, 103–27; R. Overy, *War and Economy in the Third Reich* (Oxford: Clarendon Press, 1994), ch. 1.

11 Wengenroth, 'Rise and Fall'; H. Oeftering, 'The Participation of the German Federal State in Economic Enterprises', *Annals of Collective Economy* 24 (1953), 271–88.

12 A. Carreras, X. Tafunell and E. Torres, 'The Rise and Decline of Spanish State-Owned Firms', in Toninelli (ed.), *The Rise and Fall of State Owned Enterprise*, Tables 9.2, 9.3 and 9.4.

13 V. Zamagni, 'Italy: How to Lose the War and Win the Peace', in M. Harrison (ed.), *The Economics of World War II: Six Great Powers in International Comparison* (Cambridge University Press, 1998), 212.

14 Bohlin, 'Swedish Model', 152–76; D. V. Verney, *Public Enterprise in Sweden* (Liverpool University Press, 1959), ch. 2; M. Fritz, 'Post-War Planning in Sweden', in E. Aerts and A. S. Milward (eds.), *Economic Planning in the Post-War Period* (Leuven University Press, 1990), 43–51.

15 J. van Hook, 'From Socialisation to Co-Determination: The US, Britain, Germany and Public Ownership in the Ruhr', *Historical Journal* 45 (2002), 179–93; Wengenroth, 'Rise and Fall', 103–27.

16 Kuisel, 'Technocrats and Public Economic Policy', 81; idem, *Capitalism and the State in Modern France* (Cambridge University Press, 1981), 202.

17 A. Hirschfield, 'The Role of Public Enterprise in the French Economy', *Annals of Public and Collective Economy* 44 (1973), 225–69.

18 J. Summerton, 'Coalitions and Conflicts: Swedish Municipal Energy Companies on the Eve of Deregulation', in A. Kaijser and M. Hedin (eds.), *Nordic Energy Systems: Historical Perspectives and Current Issues* (Canton, Mass.: Science History Publications, 1995), 172.

19 Centre Européen de l'Entreprise Publique (CEEP), *The Evolution of Public Enterprises in the Community of the Nine* (London: CEEP English Editions, 1973); CEEP, *Public Enterprises in the European Community* (London: CEEP English Editions, 1978).

20 W. C. Baum, *The French Economy and the State* (Princeton University Press, 1958), 180.

21 This interpretation of the position of RENFE was kindly supplied to me by Francisco Comin. For France and Britain, see Hirschfield, 'Public Enterprise in the French Economy'; G. N. Ostergaard, 'Labour and the Development of the Public Corporation', *Manchester School* 22 (1954), 192–226.

22 A. Mantegazza, 'Alitalia and Commercial Aviation in Italy', in H.-L. Dienel and P. Lyth (eds.), *Flying the Flag: European Commercial Air Transport since 1945* (Basingstoke, UK: Macmillan, 1998), 158–94; H.-L. Dienel, 'Lufthansa: Two German Airlines', in Dienel and Lyth (eds.), *Flying the Flag*, 87–125.

23 G. Stefani, 'Public Undertakings in Italy and the Prospects for Economic Programming', *Annals of Public and Collective Economy* 37 (1966), 41–63.

24 CEEP, *The Evolution of Public Enterprises in the Community of the Nine*, 37.

25 D. Coombe, 'State Enterprise in Sweden', in *State Enterprise: Business or Politics* (London: Allen and Unwin, 1972), 185; Verney, *Public Enterprise in Sweden*, 8; L. Jeding, 'Liberalisation and Control: Instruments and Strategy in the Regulation of Reform of Swedish Telecommunications', in L. Magnusson and J. Ottosson, *Evolutionary Economics and Path Dependence* (Cheltenham: Edward Elgar, 1997), 172–3; J.-P. Olivier, 'Public and Collective Economy in Sweden', *Annals of Public and Collective Economy* 40 (1969), 435–53. Information on the nationalised Telefonica was kindly supplied by Francisco Comin.

26 M. V. Posner and S. J. Woolf, *Italian Public Enterprise* (London: Duckworth, 1967), 172.

27 K. H. Neumann and B. Wieland, 'Competition and Social Objectives: The Case of West German Telecommunications', *Telecommunications Policy* 10 (1986), 123; M. Dieck. 'Collective Economy Undertakings in the Federal Republic of Germany', *Annals of Public and Collective Economy* 39 (1968), 229.

28 N. Niertz, 'Air France: An Elephant in an Evening Suit', in Dienel and Lyth (eds.), *Flying the Flag*, 8–49; E. G. Lewis, 'Parliamentary Control of Nationalised Industry in France', *American Political Science Review* 51 (1953), 171.

29 Millward, 'The 1940s Nationalisations in Britain', 229.

30 Posner and Woolf, *Italian Public Enterprise*, 121.

31 G. Zanetti (ed.), *Storia dell' industria elettrica in Italia. V. Gli sviluppi dell ENEL. 1963–1990* (Roma-Bari: Laterza & Figli, 1994), 962.

32 CEEP, *Public Enterprises in the European Community*.

33 Millward, 'The 1940s Nationalisations in Britain', 229.

34 Jeding, 'Liberalisation and control'.

35 A. Gomez-Mendoza, 'Competition between Private and Public Enterprise in Spain, 1939–59: An Alternative View', *Business and Economic History* 26(2) (1997), 696–708; Stefani, 'Public Undertakings in Italy', 55.

36 Pontusson, 'The Triumph of Pragmatism', 130; Verney, *Public Enterprise in Sweden*, 37; CEEP, *The Evolution of Public Enterprises in the Community of the Nine*.

37 Kuisel, *Capitalism and the State in Modern France*, 210. See also Baum, *The French Economy and the State*, 189.

38 Millward, 'The 1940s Nationalisations in Britain', 230.

39 Posner and Woolf, *Italian Public Enterprise*, 31.

40 A. Shonfield, *Modern Capitalism: The Changing Balance of Public and Private Power* (Oxford University Press, 1956). On the essentials of planning as a mechanism for drawing out the implications of sustained growth and illuminating decision making in the private sector, see J. J. Bonnard, 'Planning and Industry in France', in J. Hayward and M. Watson (eds.), *Planning, Politics and Public Policy* (Cambridge University Press, 1975), 93–110, and R. Opie, 'Economic Planning and Growth', in C. Feinstein (ed.), *The Managed Economy* (Oxford University Press, 1983), 147–68.

41 G. Ohlin, 'Sweden', in R. Vernon (ed.), *Big Business and the State* (Cambridge, Mass.: Harvard University Press, 1974), 126–41; Olivier, 'Public and Collective Economy in Sweden'; Bohlin, 'Swedish Model'.

42 A. Kaijser, 'From Local Networks to National Systems: A Comparison of the Emergence of Electricity and Telephony in Sweden', in F. Cardot (ed.), *1880–1980: Une siècle de l'électricité dans le monde* (Paris: Presses Universitaires de France, 1987), 7–22.

43 Fritz, 'Post-War Planning in Sweden'; Pontusson, 'The Triumph of Pragmatism', 46.

44 A. Müller-Armack, 'The Principles of the Social Market Economy', *German Economic Review* 3 (1965), 103; G. Behrendt, 'Ownership Policy in the Federal Republic of Germany', *German Economic Review* 3 (1965), 285; H. J. Arndt, *West Germany: Politics of Non-Planning* (New York: Syracuse University Press, 1966), 357.

45 C. Bucheim, 'Attempts at Controlling the Economy in Western Germany (1945–69)', in Aerts and Milward (eds.), *Economic Planning in the Post-War Period*, 2.

46 S. Broadberry, 'The Impact of the World Wars on the Long Run Economic Performance of the British Economy', *Oxford Review of Economic Policy* 7(3) (1988), 25–36.

47 C. Newton, 'The Sterling Crisis of 1947 and the British Response to the Marshall Plan', *Economic History Review* 37(3) (1984), 391–408.

48 Labour Party, *Let us Face the Future: A Declaration of Labour Policy for the Consideration of the Nation* (London: Labour Party, 1945).

49 M. Chick, *Industrial Policy in Britain 1945–51: Economic Planning, Nationalisation and the Labour Governments* (Cambridge University Press, 1998), chs. 2, 3 and 4.

50 N. Rollings, '"The Reichstag method of governing"?: The Attlee Governments and Permanent Economic Controls', in H. Mercer, N. Rollings and J. Tomlinson (eds.), *The 1945 Labour Government and Private Industry* (Edinburgh University Press, 1992), 15–36; Chick, *Industrial Policy in Britain 1945–51*; J. Tomlinson, 'Labour's Management of the National Economy 1945–51: Survey and Speculations', *Economy and Society* 18(1) (1989), 1–24; J. Tomlinson, *Public Policy and the Economy since 1900* (Oxford: Clarendon Press, 1990), ch. 8. Forums for tripartite bargaining and voluntary debates on long-term growth (in Development Councils) were also introduced in this period and seen by Shonfield, *Modern Capitalism*, as part of the institutional nuts and bolts of planning.

51 J. Hackett and A. Hackett, *Economic Planning in France* (Cambridge, Mass.: Harvard University Press, 1963); Kuisel, *Capitalism and the State in Modern France*, 233; P. Massé, '"Electricité de France" Faces Expansion Problems', *Annals of Public and Collective Economy* 26 (1955), 40–58; J. Chevrier, 'The French Electricity Supply Company: The First Ten Years', *Annals of Collective Economy* 28 (1957), 284–300.

52 Kuisel, *Capitalism and the State in Modern France*, 228.

53 F. Lynch, 'Resolving the Paradox in the Monnet Plan: National and International Planning in French Reconstruction', *Economic History Review* 37(2) (1984), 226.

54 Baum, *The French Economy and the State*, 24–5; P. Estrin and P. Holmes, *French Planning in Theory and Practice* (London: Allen and Unwin, 1983); S. Wickham, 'Development of French Railways under the French Four Year

Plans', *Bulletin of the Oxford University Institute of Statistics* 24(1) (1962), 167–84.

55 B. R. Mitchell, *International Historical Statistics: Europe 1750–1993* (London: Macmillan, 3rd edn, 1998).

56 V. Zamagni, *The Economic History of Italy 1860–1990* (Oxford: Clarendon Press, 1993), 321.

57 M. Kriele, 'Public Enterprise and the Pursuit of Strategic Management: Italy', in K. Dyson and S. Wilks (eds.), *Industrial Crisis: A Comparative Study of the State and Industry* (New York: St. Martin's Press, 1988), 192–219; Zamagni, *Economic History of Italy*, 370.

58 Posner and Woolf, *Italian Public Enterprise*, 30–40.

59 J. B. Donges, 'From an Autarchic towards a Cautious Outward looking Industrialisation Policy', *Weltwirtschaftliches Archiv* 107 (1971), 33–72; P. M. Acena and F. Comin, 'Industrial Planning in Spain under the Franco Regime (1940–75)', in Aerts and Milward (eds.), *Economic Planning in the Post-War Period*, 61–72: Gomez-Mendoza, 'Competition between Private and Public Enterprise in Spain, 1939–59'; P. F. Balbin, 'Spain: Industrial Policy under Authoritarian Politics', in Foreman-Peck and Federico (eds.), *European Industrial Policy*, 233–67.

60 F. Bianchi, 'The IRI in Italy: Strategic Role and Political Constraints', *West European Politics* 10(2) (1987), 269–90; G. Fraenkel, 'Italian Industrial Policy in the Framework of Economic Planning', in Hayward and Watson (eds.), *Planning, Politics and Public Policy*, 128–40.

61 R. Prodi, 'Italy', in R. Vernon (ed.), *Big Business and the State* (Cambridge, Mass.: Harvard University Press, 1974), 47; G. Pasquino and U. Pecchini, 'The National Context: Italy', in Hayward and Watson (eds.), *Planning, Politics and Public Policy*, 75; Kriele, 'Public Enterprise and the Pursuit of Strategic Management: Italy', 196.

62 Y. Ullmo, 'The National Context: France', in Hayward and Watson (eds.), *Planning, Politics and Public Policy*, 22–51.

63 Bonnard, 'Planning and Industry in France', 99; Shonfield, *Modern Capitalism*, 84.

64 C. A. Michalat, 'France', in R. Vernon (ed.), *Big Business and the State* (Cambridge, Mass.: Harvard University Press, 1974), 105 29.

65 P. Estrin and P. Holmes, *French Planning in Theory and Practice* (London, Allen and Unwin, 1983), 86.

66 Political and Economic Planning (PEP), 'Planning for Growth', *Growth in the British Economy* (London: Allen and Unwin, 1960), ch. 10, p. 220; Federation of British Industry, *The Next Five Years* (London: FBI, 1960), 18–19.

67 Opie, 'Economic Planning and Growth'; P. Meadows, 'Planning', in F. Blackaby (ed.), *British Economic Policy 1960–74* (Cambridge University Press, 1978), 402–17; S. A. Walkland, 'Economic Planning and Dysfunctional Politics in Britain 1945–83', in A. M. Gamble and S. A. Walkland (eds.) *The British Party System and Economic Policy: 1945–1983: Studies in Adversary Politics* (Oxford: Clarendon Press, 1984), 92–151.

11   Coal, oil and security

In the third quarter of the twentieth century, oil replaced coal as the major source of energy in western Europe. During the last quarter, the growing power of the nations with oil reserves and the price increases introduced from the early 1970s by their cartel, the Organisation of Petroleum Exporting Countries (OPEC), ensured that oil lost its predominance and mixed regimes of nuclear, HEP, oil, natural gas and coal emerged. Before the Second World War, coal was dominant, and the concentration of deposits in the UK, the Low Countries and Germany had vital effects on the energy policies of other European countries. I said little in earlier chapters about the structure of the coal industry and how it was regulated. As a natural resource, coal has certain similarities to oil, and in this chapter I attempt to explain how and why coal and oil were owned and regulated, to draw out the implications for the generation of electricity supply and to identify the key interests of the state.

The economic organisation of the coal and oil sectors was very different from the other infrastructure industries. In brief, private enterprise has been dominant in much of the period since 1850, albeit with governments not far away. The need to control monopoly elements by price regulation and profit constraints was not strong. In the case of coal, in the nineteenth and early twentieth century, large numbers of both small and large firms existed with the share of joint stock companies tending to rise. The state intervened mainly in the interests of safety standards in the mines, though some states also drew royalties from leases and concessions, but it was only in the Netherlands and Prussia that governments came to own coal deposits, and even these were small. Miners tended to be in the forefront of the socialist labour movements and pressed for nationalisation, which occurred after the Second World War, but only in France and Britain. By that stage the industry was in decline. It had been protected from foreign competition in the 1930s, and the decades after the war saw more protection and subsidies in all western European countries up to the 1970s. In the case of oil, there were no indigenous resources before the Second World War. Exploration for crude oil in the Middle East and North Africa and its transport to Europe was undertaken by large international joint stock companies and, as noted briefly in earlier chapters, France and Britain secured shareholdings in such companies. Oil usage was quite low, but its distribution within each European country was often controlled by licensing or by governments setting up companies like Azienda Generale Italia Petroli and the Compagnie Française de Pétroles with significant state shareholdings. The period 1950–73 was the boom time for oil in western Europe. The big international oil companies like Shell and Esso dominated exploration and distribution, with most governments achieving some leverage by continuing share ownership. From the 1960s, large deposits of oil and natural gas were discovered in the North Sea, and several state-owned companies like Statoil in Norway were established to develop these reserves. Each government was, of course, very keen to ensure that these reserves were recognised as being on its territory, and oil revenues came to form a significant source of income for some governments.

How is one to explain these structures and the behaviour of governments? Much stemmed from the basic technological and economic characteristics of natural resources. There are four central issues:

(1) Coal and oil are not natural monopoly industries, and with open markets there was every chance that private enterprise would generate a competitive environment.
(2) Working conditions were often dirty, uncongenial and dangerous, especially in the early years of each industry.
(3) Coal and oil became key intermediate inputs of modern economies for which there were few short-term substitutes. They had, therefore, a strategic and military significance in time of war and other crises.
(4) When the prices of coal and oil were settled in free markets, even when the structure was very competitive, the revenues generated gave a return not only in the form of wages and normal business profits, but also as rental income for access to the resource and as royalty for the user cost of depleting stocks and thereby foregoing future revenues.[1] These represented attractive sources of tax revenue, which were particularly important when hitherto unused parts of sovereign territory yielded reserves of oil and natural gas in the twentieth century.

These ideas will be used to explain firstly the pattern in coal, then later oil and natural gas. All had implications for the way electricity generation developed in the 1950–90 period.

The mining of coal does not appear to be subject to significant economies of scale. Early work methods were similar to putting-out systems, with the mine owner leasing out parts of the coal face for small teams to deliver coal to the surface. The nineteenth century saw the emergence of large joint stock companies, but they rarely dominated whole coalfields, and many of the benefits of scale came from transporting and cleaning coal underground and above. Rights of way were a problem when coal seams passed through the land of different owners, but these were minuscule issues compared to the railway rights of way. Both the coal and oil industries generated products rather than services, so that much of inland surface distribution could be handled by relatively divisible units in rail or road vehicle haulage. These are not natural monopoly conditions, and the coal industry of the nineteenth century had all the hallmarks of a classic competitive industry. By 1913, the UK reached its peak output of 292 million tons per annum, and the other major producers were Germany (277 million tons, of which 87 million tons was the low-calorific value lignite/brown coal), France (41 million tons) and Belgium (24 million tons).[2] Taxation was not a prime interest of government, and many deposits were privately owned. Taxing land rents was a contentious issue in the nineteenth century, though royalties accrued when governments operated concession systems as in France and the British government nationalised coal royalties in 1938. A stronger interest of governments lay in the strategic significance of coal as a key intermediate input. Short-run substitutes were absent – the short-run price elasticity of demand was low. This was less of a problem for UK and Belgium with their own large coal deposits than France, a major power with relatively meagre coal supplies, and this underlay the preoccupation with building up hydroelectricity, as we saw in chapter 8, and with planning for post-1945 links to the Ruhr coalfields. Through the Napoleonic Code and the mining code of 1811, the French government was able in the nineteenth and early twentieth century to exercise its rights over the subsoil and operate concession systems that at least gave the state some leverage in times of crisis.[3] Strategic and economic interests were at stake in the Netherlands, whose government in the early years of the twentieth century was concerned about the infusion of foreign (colonial) capital and labour into the industry. A 1901 law established the government's right to all unclaimed coal concessions, and in 1902 it set up its own mining enterprise, Staatsmijnen, which was producing about one third of all Dutch coal by the middle of the century.[4] Germany was very well endowed with coal, but the Prussian state's wide geographical spread in the middle of Europe meant security issues were always important. Moreover, the classic integration of coal, iron and steel enterprises led to strong interest groups in the large industrial firms, and in 1893 the Coal Syndicate of Westphalia and the Rhineland was established.[5] In 1903, the Prussian state took part share ownership in the Hibernia Company to provide some leverage against the coal cartel. Then 1905 saw a Prussian law ensuring that all unclaimed coal concessions were to become state property. By the 1950s, about one fifth of all the output of the Ruhr coalfield was in the hands of the Federal Government through its holding companies, and Hibernia accounted for one half.[6]

Otherwise, before 1939 there was little direct state operation of mining. Rather more important for the state was the regulation of working conditions and coping with the demands of the labour force. Working on oil rigs was often dangerous, but by the time North Sea oil had been discovered, labour legislation, sanitary conditions and wage levels ensured tolerable conditions. This was not the case in the nineteenth-century coal industry. The expansion in Germany, Britain, Belgium and France was effected by a huge increase in the labour force, with in some cases old mines very intensively worked. By the early years of the twentieth century, the miners had become a politically powerful section of the labour force in France and Britain – to add to their traditional role of being a highly disgruntled set of workers. The special characteristics of mining labour stemmed from three sources. One was that the work was dirty and dangerous, with a death rate in some coalfields in the mid-nineteenth century four times that for all occupied males.[7] Secondly, marginal costs rose rapidly with the scale of production because a large part of a colliery's costs were sunken (in the economic sense), geological conditions varied enormously and changing the volume of employment was the chief way of meeting demand fluctuations over significant periods. Since the demand for coal was sensitive to the economic cycle, the steeply rising marginal costs made for the well-documented violent fluctuations in coal prices and mining wages in the nineteenth century. Thirdly, the highly regionalised and non-urban disposition of coal deposits in Britain and France made for closed communities and, in conjunction with the above two issues, a disgruntled labour force. By the early twentieth century, the miners were pressing for nationalisation with a strength that was not to be found in any other industry.

A second problem was one of production and capacity. By 1939, the industries in Germany and France, but especially in Britain and Belgium, were old with all the best seams worked. The Second World War saw an absolute decline in coal output in Germany, Britain, Belgium and France (even after allowing for the loss of Alsace and Lorraine; see Figure 10.1). These problems were not to disappear after the war, since the severe balance of payments problem of the European economies in the late 1940s put a premium on exports and on the supply of key intermediate inputs, like coal, to exporting industries. It is not clear that any particular blame lies at the feet of the coal owners – at least for the economic rather than social problems of these industries. The resource-based nature of the industry means that output increases are likely to be accompanied by diminishing returns unless new coal deposits are found or investment made in cutting and hauling. There is plenty of evidence that such investment took place from the mid-nineteenth century onwards, and output per man-hour rose over significant periods.[8] Nonetheless, the sheer scale of the expansion in the latter part of the nineteenth century meant that it was a labour intensive expansion and, given the age of the coal workings, the limits were being approached by the 1940s. At best, improvement might be possible with a substantial reorganisation of the industry, not so much to exploit economies of scale, but rather to raise productivity by eliminating inefficient pits. Private ownership had appeared to fail to do this in the inter-war period. In both World Wars, the mining companies and their owners had emerged with a very poor public image. In France and Britain, the mining unions were especially vocal with a lot of political clout, and it is here that nationalisation occurred with the creation in 1946 of Charbonnages de France and the National Coal Board. Thus nationalisation came to these coal industries much more on the back of a capital versus labour confrontation than was the case in railways, gas, electricity and telecommunications, where government ownership sprang more clearly from regulatory issues. Over the nineteenth and twentieth centuries, the coal industry experienced, perhaps more than any other industry, the bleak winds of supply and demand, and the neo-Marxist picture of a class struggle makes more sense here than in the other twentieth-century examples of state ownership. The trade unions had less leverage in Belgium and the Netherlands, though the National Coal Commission in the former and the state-owned Staatsmijnen in the latter wielded considerable influence. An enhancement of the role of the discredited central state was unthinkable in Germany and Italy. The unions had little power in Spain, and Scandinavia did not have a coal industry, so nationalisation was restricted to Britain and France.

In 1950, the major coal producers were still providing Europe's main source of primary energy and had all but recovered the output levels of 1938 (Figure 10.1). In the next twenty years, oil started to out-compete coal such that oil rose from supplying 14% of Europe's total energy consumption in 1950 to 60% by 1970, and coal fell from 82% to 28%.[9] Oil was meeting the increased demand for fuel in transport and from electricity generating plants, while petroleum products mushroomed in manufacturing. Oil has a certain flexibility and mobility, which makes it attractive for industrial uses. But the major reason for its extensive usage from the early 1950s to the early 1970s was that its price fell absolutely, and therefore by large amounts relative to the prices of coal, gas and electricity. By the 1950s, most consumers had been connected to electricity supply, so that, as Figures 11.1a. and 11.1b illustrate for the UK, gas and electricity tariffs moved close to each other – in contrast to the pre-war period, when electricity was still being connected and its price had been falling relative to other prices for several decades (see Figure 8.1). The price of coal, however, was rising faster than other prices, as old seams were exhausted and diminishing returns set in. Oil therefore made many gains until the huge price increases of the OPEC cartel in the early 1970s.

Governments protected and subsidised their coal industries less because of the national security issues than because of the political consequences of running down the labour forces. The latter were huge in Germany and Britain, and their unions were politically strong in France and Britain, and often the coalfields were often highly concentrated geographically, making for the classic mid-century 'regional problem'. Some of France's strategic worries were mitigated by the establishment of the European Coal and Steel Community (ECSC) in 1951. This precursor of the European Economic Community had a supranational authority settling prices and quotas and also allocating subsidies. It included Belgium, the Netherlands, Luxembourg, Germany and Italy, but Britain, as was to become the common practice, feared the supranational body and opted out.

For France, however, the ECSC provided some element of guaranteed access to German coal and steel.[10] This was the only bright spot for coal after 1950, as it was outgunned by oil in the primary energy market throughout western Europe and by electricity in the secondary markets. The industry was then protected in two ways. Imports of coal from countries like Poland were subjected to tariffs and quotas. Contracts favourable to coal usage in electricity generating plants were enforced, by the respective governments, between the domestic electricity industry and the domestic coal industry. Contracts for the use of coal in generating plants carried prices that did not reflect coal costs and were below world coal prices, but they slowed down the rate of decline of coal. These were common practices in postwar West Germany, whose government also leaned on the oil companies to restrict imports. The year 1968 witnessed a new law to support the coal industry. The Ruhrkohle was formed from twenty-six companies whose equity holdings were surrendered in exchange for fixed-interest bonds guaranteed by the Federal Government. Contracts were made with electric power and steel firms on terms that subsidised the coal industry.[11] Germany's large output of lignite for industrial use and its success in developing coal products offset in part

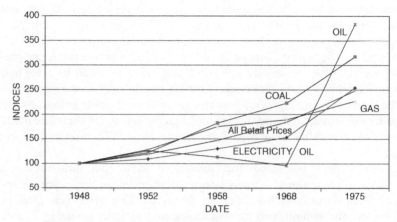

Figure 11.1a Fuel price indices, 1948–1975 (UK) (1948 = 100).

the decline in sales of hard coal, so that the industry's total output per head of population declined on average at only 0.3% per annum in the period 1950–73.[12] Spain also protected its coal industry at some cost to the development of its manufacturing. From the 1960s, however, tariff protection was reduced, and the Spanish coal companies collapsed. In 1967, the Asturia companies were bought out by the government, and Hunosa was set up as a subsidiary of INI, but one that proved to be a real financial burden.[13] The coal industry in Britain was protected by tariffs, and the Central Electricity Generating Board was obliged to make long-term contracts with the National Coal Board at prices below the world level.[14] This huge industry, with a work force approaching 1 million in 1946, nonetheless declined fairly consistently at about 2.6% per annum over the whole of the second half of the twentieth century, and not surprisingly it was the scene of bitter industrial disputes in the early 1970s and 1980s. In France, the decline was the most rapid and reflected that country's determination to widen its fuel base and avoid its past strategic weaknesses. A commitment to oil and the absence of excise duties on heavy fuel oil was favoured by the Treasury and industrialists because of the low oil price it generated. Together with the later commitment to an independent nuclear programme, this led to a decline of coal output per head of population of 4.1% per annum for 1950–73 and 5.9% for 1973–92.

The protection afforded to western Europe's coal industries was relaxed as oil supplies became available – especially noticeable in Belgium and Spain from the 1960s, whilst in France, Germany and Britain it was the general liberalisation of markets from the mid 1970s that prefaced an

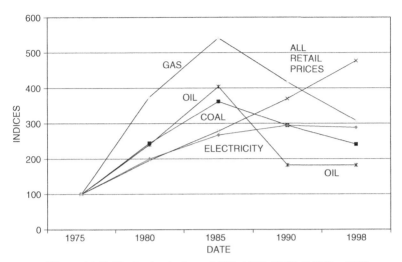

Figure 11.1b Fuel price indices, 1975–1998 (UK) (1975 = 100).

Notes:
Oil: for 1948–70, the entries are derived from the data on the price of
oil used by the gas industry (gas oil) in Table 92 of Department of
Trade and Industry, *UK Energy Statistics 1972* (London: HMSO,
1972). For 1970–98, the source is the index of heavy fuel oil used by
industry in DTI, *Digest of UK Energy Statistics 1999* (London: HMSO,
1999), Table 9.13.

For the other fuels and all retail prices for 1948–68 the source is
R. Pryke, *Public Enterprise in Practice* (London: Mckibbon and Kee,
1971). The electricity, coal and gas prices are based on revenue per
unit sold calculated from the nationalised industries' annual reports and
the Ministry of Power's annual Digest of Energy Statistics. Retail prices
are proxied by the GDP deflator. For 1968–75, the source is the
Ministry of Power, *Digest of Energy Statistics 1978* (London: HMSO,
1978). For 1975–98, the entries are weighted averages of retail coal
prices and of electricity and gas tariffs and, together with the retail
price index, are taken from DTI, *Digest of Energy Statistics 1999*
(London: HMSO, 1999), 240–4.

increase in coal imports. Figure 11.2 shows the position of the main
coal-producing countries. France and Spain were importing coal throughout the postwar period, though Spain's production of lignite flourished
in the 1980s. The Netherlands' coal industry had disappeared by the mid
1970s. Belgium became a net importer by the 1960s, and its industry
thereafter declined to oblivion by the 1990s. French production was

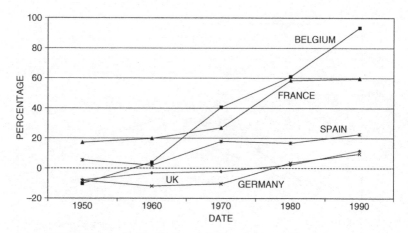

Figure 11.2 Coal imports (net) as % total coal consumption, 1950–1990.

Sources: United Nations, *World Energy Supplies* 1950–74 (New York: Statistical Office, Department of Economic and Social Affairs, Series J 19, 1976). OECD, *Energy Statistics of OECD Countries 2000–1* (Paris: International Energy Agency, 2003).

Notes:
The raw data are in metric tons and cover all types of coal and lignite, except for Germany 1980–90 where lignite has been excluded (390 million tons in 1980 and 357 million tons in 1990) and seem to have been excluded in the 1950–70 figures, if comparisons are made with B.R. Mitchell, *International Historical Statistics: Europe 1750–1993* (London: Macmillan, 3rd edn, 1998), Table E.2. The 1950–70 data are from *United Nations, World Energy Supplies 1950–74,* Table 3 and the 1980–90 data from OECD, *Energy Statistics,* II, 222–45, where net imports plus production are taken as total consumption.

down to 10 million tons by the 1990s, importing 60% of its coal require-ments. Even the UK and Germany were net importers by the 1980s. In part, this reflected a demand for particular types of coal, and they were importing only 10% of their consumption. Nonetheless, Britain's output had fallen to 85 million tons by the early 1990s. West Germany's coal industry was still being heavily protected into the late 1980s and beyond – coal subsidies accounted for two thirds of all energy subsidies – though the modest decline to 177 million tons by 1989 was also due to the more buoyant industrial market for its lignite (110 million tons).[15]

The crude oil and natural gas industries were, like the early coal industry, dominated by private enterprise. Exploration and operations certainly required large capital investment, and the pipeline distribution networks had natural monopoly elements. The distribution of oil and petroleum products within Europe could be handled effectively by fairly small units (road tankers and railways), and the fact that oil was sold, from the very beginning, extensively on world markets, meant that, whatever scale economies existed in exploration, operations and in the transit of crude oil, these were not inconsistent with competition between private sector firms, albeit approaching oligopolistic conditions. Thus the underlying technology and economics go some way to explain the basic structure of exploration, operation and distribution. How can we explain the role of the state, with its tendency to take part share ownership in international companies and set up state-owned enterprises when it came to domestic oil and gas reserves?

National security is the key here, and the foreign source of much of Europe's supplies explains many of the preoccupations of European governments in the twentieth century. Georges Brondel, an engineer who headed the Oil and Gas Directorate of the EEC for much of the 1970s, pointed out that, 'Of all the major industrial regions in the world, Western Europe is the only one, apart from Japan, to be so largely dependent upon imported sources for supplies of energy.'[16] By the early 1960s, oil had taken over from coal as the key primary energy input with limited possibilities of substitution in the short run. The inelasticity of demand with respect to price in the short run is exemplified, par excellence, by the effect of the quadrupling of crude oil prices by the OPEC cartel in 1973/4. The impact on relative fuel prices is shown in Figure 11.1a. The prices of the primary inputs coal and oil determined the main direction of fuel prices, with gas and electricity tariffs and other retail prices keeping close to each other. Coal is the leader up to the 1970s, when oil and natural gas took over. Users of oil were not able to switch easily to alternative products, so that much of the 1973/4 oil-price increases were passed on in the prices of final products and services, and it took decades for the use of oil in electricity generating plants to be replaced by other fuels. In 1973, France was producing 68000 gigawatt hours of electricity from oil-fired plants, or 40% of its total supply, a figure that had fallen to only 19% by 1980, and it was 1990 before the figure reached 2%, despite a huge nuclear programme. Germany's oil-based electricity accounted for 15% of its output in 1973, falling to 7% in 1980 and 2% by 1990. For the UK, the figures are 26%, 12% and 9%, reflecting the role of UK North Sea oil.[17]

To start the oil story from the beginning, the foreign source of supplies in the early part of the twentieth century explains the early pattern of government involvement. The European states wanted some control over the flow of oil from the Middle East and over distribution within the home country, as well as encouraging the development of domestic refinery capacity. Before the First World War, the British government had part ownership of the Anglo-Persian Oil Company, which itself had 50% of the shares of the Turkish Petroleum company in which the Deutsche Bank had a 25% share.[18] These British interests were consolidated in 1914 in a new company, British Petroleum, and by 1919 the British government was a majority shareholder 'to secure foreign oil supplies for military needs . . . and avoid reliance on foreign oil supplies in times of crisis'.[19] Likewise, a French law of 1925 restricted imports to companies authorised by the state, and such companies had to develop refinery capacity in France, whilst a 1928 law established quotas for oil imports. A year earlier, one such company had been set up by the government, Compagnie Française des Pétroles, vested with the government's financial holdings in oil companies, including some of the former German shares in the Turkish Petroleum Company forcibly redistributed after the war. CFP was expected to get involved in all stages of oil production and sale, and by 1929 the government held 35% of the shares.[20] These joint ventures were successful in securing foreign oil supplies for the domestic markets in Europe. The oil production of BP before the Second World War exceeded the total of all British oil requirements. Half of French oil imports and of French refinery capacity was controlled by CFP, and 88% of all French oil requirements were controlled by CFP or some company with government involvement.[21]

The other countries were not so lucky. In the inter-war period, neither Germany nor Italy had shareholdings like Britain and France in the big oil companies. In the 1920s, Germany developed programmes for deriving oil from coal, set up refineries on the coast, and from the 1930s looked to south-east Europe for oil. The Azienda Generale Italia Petroli was established in 1926 to explore for oil, and it built up a distribution network within Italy that catered for about one quarter of Italy's needs pre-1939 and 50% by the 1960s. In Spain, Compañía Arrendetaria del Monopolio de Petróleos (CAMPSA) was set up in 1927 as a mixed enterprise with Spanish banks as the main shareholder and with responsibility, assigned by the government, for oil distribution and storage. It had no financial interests in overseas oil reserves and neither did any other Spanish enterprise except one called CEPSA, which was formed in 1929 with a base in the free-market Canary Isles, and acquired rights to explore and operate in Venezuela. There was an unsuccessful attempt from 1942, through a subsidiary of the Instituto Nacional de Industria (INI), to distill oil from Spain's mineral resources. Otherwise, the main feature of the period up to the 1940s was the import of both crude and refined oil by the international oil companies, who were obliged to sell only to CAMPSA, which in its turn licensed dealers for retailing.[22]

The second half of the twentieth century saw the discovery of substantial deposits of oil and natural gas in western Europe. Algeria, Libya and other African countries proved to have significant reserves, but subject, like the Middle East, to continuing political uncertainties. The reserves in Europe were very unevenly spread, as is shown by the data on annual production per head of population in Figure 11.3. By that measure the only large outputs by 1973 were of oil in Norway, and they were double the national outputs of the next highest, the Netherlands and Germany, who were still meeting the bulk of their requirements from imports (Figure 11.4). Natural gas supplies were better developed by 1973, with some production in France and West Germany, relatively more in Italy and the UK, but even the latter's production levels were less than 10% of those of the Netherlands. The major change in the last quarter of the century was the exploitation of North Sea oil and gas by the UK and especially Norway, whose exports by 1990 were over ten times the volume of its domestic consumption (Figure 11.5).

The Netherlands, the UK and Norway were therefore lucky, since they were not the only ones to engage in exploration. The international oil companies like Shell and Esso were active throughout Europe, but each state ensured there were also exploration companies that had some government link. As early as 1945, the French had established the Bureau Recherches des Pétroles and the Régie Autonome des Pétroles (later merged into Elf-Erap) to explore and produce oil in French overseas territories and complement the work of CFP. Deposits of oil and gas were first found in Lacq in France (1948–51) and in the Sahara in 1956. In Italy, the state-owned Azienda Generale Italia Petroli (AGIP) had not been successful in developing overseas production and was expected to be wound up in 1946, but the energetic new head, Mattei, took advantage of the discovery of methane gas to secure a monopoly enterprise for the development of hydrocarbons in the Paduan Plain. The new enterprise, Ente Nazionale Idrocaruri (ENI), was established in 1953, with subsidiaries for methane products, petroleum, distribution (AGIP), overseas development (AGIP Minerana) and later nuclear (AGIP-nucleare).[23] In Germany, Deminex, an enterprise with mixed government and private interests, was set up to explore for oil.[24] It had limited success and was taken over by the part state-owned Vercinigten Elektrizitäts u. Bergwerk (VEBA) in the early 1970s. Indeed, the exploratory outcomes of the

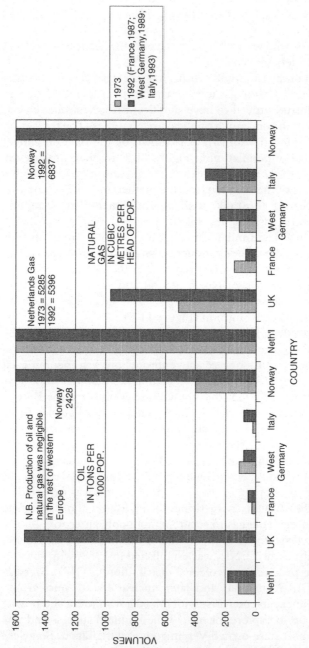

Figure 11.3 Production of oil and natural gas in 1973 and 1992.

Note:

The sources for oil and gas data are Mitchell, *International Historical Statistics: Europe 1750–1993*. Population data from A. Maddison, *Monitoring the World Economy 1820–1992* (Paris: OECD, 1995).

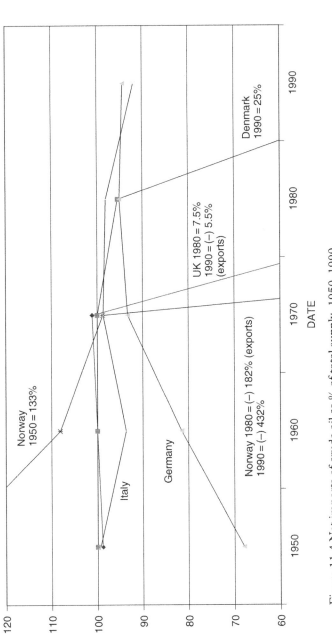

Figure 11.4 Net imports of crude oil as % of total supply, 1950–1990.

Notes:
For sources, see notes to Figure 11.2. The raw data for crude oil are in metric tons and cover crude petroleum, natural gas liquids and (for 1980–90) additives. For 1950–70 the source is UN, *World Energy Supplies*, Table 6 where the data on 'apparent supply' are used for total supply. For 1980–90 the source is OECD, *Energy Statistics*, II, 222–45, where net imports plus production are taken as total supply.

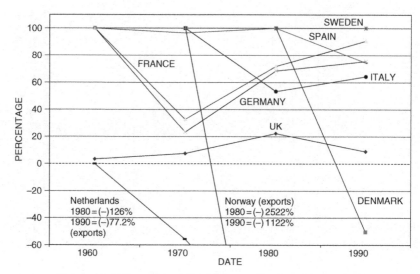

Figure 11.5 Natural gas net imports as % of total consumption, 1960–1990.

Note:
The source is OECD, *Energy Statistics* (see Figure 11.2), II, 222–45. Total consumption is taken to be net imports plus production. The raw data are in terajoules.

activities of Italy, France and Germany were fairly limited in comparison to what emerged in the North Sea. The year 1959 saw the discovery of a huge gas field in the northern part of the Netherlands, where a mixed enterprise – Nederlands Aardolie Maatschappij, joint owned by Shell, Esso and the state mining company Staatsmijnen – was set up to exploit the findings.[25] Then from the mid-1960s, the more northern part of the North Sea revealed huge deposits of oil and gas in the British and Norwegian sectors.

The rather uneven success in development meant that foreign supplies continued to be important for western Europe. How can we explain the behaviour of governments in this period? The two central elements were security of supplies and tax revenues. The importance of oil supplies did depend on how far each country had alternatives in the form of hydro-electricity and coal and how far it was able to overcome the environmental fears about nuclear power. Moreover, whilst France and the UK needed to plan for secure supplies because they were major political powers, that posture was not meaningful for small countries like Denmark nor, initially at least, was it an option for the defeated nations after the Second World War, Germany and Italy. The potential tax revenues were very important for all governments in the second half of the twentieth century, as all were committed to rising public expenditure programmes. On the other hand, they did not want to stifle the profitability of exploration and development. When therefore indigenous reserves of oil and gas were at stake, the general thrust of government policies was to secure national sovereignty and property rights over geographical areas with potentially significant reserves, and ensure that the desire for government income did not deter the exploration and development of the fields. Where, as in natural gas, natural monopoly elements occurred in the nationwide integrated distribution networks, prices were regulated by central government.

Thus Germany and Italy, with limited indigenous sources but unable, as defeated belligerents in the Second World War, to exercise an aggressive foreign policy, simply allowed the free market to operate. Italy was especially well placed to do that given its advantageous Mediterranean position with respect to the Middle East and to North Africa, acting as an entrepôt for the rest of Europe. Mattei sold ENI's gas at world market prices and used the profits to finance investment in developments at home and abroad, often independently of the foreign policies of the Italian government. Much of the initial supplies came from the Anglo-Iranian company, but later Russian sources were used.[26] Most of the increase in energy demand in Italy from the mid-1950s onwards was met by oil. Coal was feasible only on the coast from imports, and the state-owned electricity enterprise Ente Nazionale de l'Energia Elettrica (ENEL) favoured oil and gas over nuclear. Table 11.1 shows what energy source each country used for generating electricity in the period 1950–90. It is derived from data produced in international agencies, which has the virtue of providing some element of standardisation across countries at the cost of some gaps in the series. The table reflects how much oil-fired generating plant capacity was built in the 1950s and 1960s. Indeed, the increases were especially large, ironically, in the period 1969–73, just before the OPEC oil price hike. Thereafter, we see a major scaling down of oil usage in France, Germany and even the UK, despite its North Sea deposits. The major exception to this scramble was Italy, and by 1990 it was still producing 97000 gigawatt hours of electricity, 47% of its total, from oil, even though over 90% of its oil supplies were imported.

Germany initially also saw a vast increase in its use of oil, over half imported. Total consumption of oil rose from 4.5 million tons in 1955 to 83.6 million tons in 1965. It was an open market dominated by the international oil companies, and by 1964 the tariff on imported oil had been abandoned. In the 1960s, much came from North Africa (59% by

Table 11.1 *Electricity generation by source of fuel, 1950–1990 ('000 gigawatt hours, net)*

	Year	HEP	Nuclear	Coal[a]	Oil	Natural gas	Gas derivatives	Other[b]	Subtotal classic thermal (excluding HEP and nuclear)	TOTAL
UK	1950	2	0	–	–	–	–	–	65	67
	1960	3	2	–	–	–	–	–	124	129
	1969	4	26	159	33	0.3	1	0	193	222
	1973	5	24	161	69	3	2	0	229	263
	1990	7	59	202	26	3	2	1	234	299
Denmark	1950	0	0	–	–	–	–	–	2	2
	1960	0	0	–	–	–	–	–	5	5
	1969	0	0	6	10	0	0	0	16	16
	1973	0	0	6	12	0	0	0	18	18
	1990	1	0	22	1	0.2	0	0.1	23	24
France	1950	16	0	–	–	–	–	–	17	33
	1960	41	0.1	–	–	–	–	–	31	72
	1969	52	5	45	18	6	4	1	74	131
	1973	48	14	27	69	10	7	1	113	175
	1990	57	298	29	8	3	4	1	45	400
Germany (West)	1950	9	0	–	–	–	–	–	47	56
	1960	13	0	–	–	–	–	–	99	112
	1969	14	5	147	27	9	7	3	192	211
	1973	15	11	167	41	34	11	3	254	280
	1990	18	139	205	10	34	9	4	262	420
Sweden[c]	1950	17	0	–	–	–	–	–	1	18
	1960	31	0	–	–	–	–	–	4	35
	1969	42	.06	–	–	–	–	–	16	58
	1973	60	2	–	–	–	–	–	16	78

	Year									
	1990	72	65	1	1	0.4	0.5	2	5	142
Italy	1950	23	0	–	–	–	–	–	2	25
	1960	47	0	–	–	–	–	–	8	55
	1969	42	1	6	46	46	2	4[d]	63[d]	106
	1973	39	3	3	84	4	3	3[d]	97[d]	139
	1990	35	0	30	97	37	3	4[d]	170[d]	205
Norway[c]	1950	18	0	–	–	–	–	–	0.1	18
	1960	31	0	–	–	–	–	–	0.2	31
	1969	57	0	–	–	–	–	–	0.2	58
	1973	73	0	–	–	–	–	–	0.2	73
	1990	120	0	0.1	0.006	0	0.2	0.102	0.4	121
Spain[c]	1950	2	0	–	–	–	–	–	5	7
	1960	16	0	–	–	–	–	–	3	19
	1969	31	1	–	–	–	–	–	21	52
	1973	30	6	–	–	–	–	–	40	76
	1990	26	52	58	7	0.5	0.5	0.5	66	144

Notes:

[a] Hard coal, brown coal, lignite etc.

[b] Wood, peat etc.

[c] The 1960–73 figures for Sweden, Norway and Spain relate to gross production and therefore include the small amount of power used for pump storage etc. The relevant net figures for the components of classic thermal energy for Spain for 1990 involve an element of rounding up.

[d] Includes geothermal sources (wind, tide, solar etc).

Source: For 1950: United Nations, *World Energy Supplies 1950–74* (New York: Statistical Papers J19, Department of Economic and Social Affairs, 1976). It seems these figures relate to gross rather than net production.

For other years for the UK, Denmark, France, Germany and Italy: Statistical Office of the European Communities (Eurostat), *Energy Statistics: Yearbook 1969–73* (Brussels: Eurostat, 1974) and *Energy Yearly Statistics 1990* (Brussels: Eurostat, 1992).

For other years for Sweden, Norway and Spain: International Energy Agency, *Energy Statistics of OECD Countries 1960–75* (Paris: OECD, 1991) and *Energy Statistics of OECD Countries 2000–1* (Paris: OECD, 2003).

1970), but from the 1980s some 15% was coming from the new British sector in the North Sea.[27] Germany differed from Italy in its coal endowments, and coal-fired generating plants were producing some 200000 gigawatt hours of electricity per annum in the early 1990s, nearly one half of total supply. Denmark also was heavily reliant on imports from the 1950s to the 1970s, and indeed its switch from coal to oil was fairly smooth since both were imported. By 1972, 94% of its energy supply was oil. It had been attempting to develop its own gas and oil reserves, but was delayed by boundary problems in the North Sea.[28] In that year, Dansk Naturgas was established with the sole right to transmit gas long distance to retail distribution organisations. Initially it was Norwegian natural gas, but some of its own natural gas reserves had come on stream by the 1980s. The rise in oil prices led to a virtual abandonment of oil-fired generating plants by 1990, when Denmark was importing just one quarter its oil requirements and was a net exporter of gas. Better ways of using coal led to the dominance of coal-fired electricity generation, though electricity was still relatively expensive in Denmark.

As a major political power, France was perhaps in the most difficult position. It had fairly meagre coal supplies, as we have seen. In 1950, the government ruled that companies distributing oil within France should meet 90% of their requirements from French refineries, and the part state-owned Compagnie Française des Pétroles (CFP) effectively operated a cartel. After some financial scandals, Elf-Erap merged in 1976 with Société National d'Aquitaine to form Société National Elf-Aquitaine (70% owned by the French government).[29] The success of CFP and Elf-Erap in developing supplies of oil and gas in French territories was undermined by the fragile position of French North Africa. Several oil companies were taken over by the newly independent Algerian government such that by 1970 only CFP and Elf-Erap remained. Then 51% of oil reserves and 100% of gas reserves were nationalised, and France was left with only a promise that its supplies were secure. Attention then shifted to the Middle East, which accounted for 80% of France's supplies of oil by 1978.[30] The nuclear option was, in these circumstances, very attractive, and by 1990, when France was importing 90% of its oil and natural gas, three quarters of electricity supply came from nuclear generating plants (Table 11.1). Sweden was in a somewhat similar position. It did have relatively more HEP capacity, but imported 100% of its oil and gas. Oil-fired generating plants met the entire rise in demand for electricity in the period 1945–73, but the oil price hike forced it away. By 1990, hardly any electricity was produced from oil, coal or gas, with nuclear and HEP taking almost equal shares.[31] Spain also was heavily dependent on imports of oil and natural gas and was well located with respect to

North African supplies. The Spanish government moderated the rise in oil prices in the 1970s through CAMPSA and INI's holdings in various refineries (all were consolidated in the 1990s into the Instituto Nacional de Hidrocarbonas). Spain's relatively low oil prices and high energy consumption made it attractive for industrial investment in the 1970s, though the price controls were relaxed in 1979. Because of its good geographical position, Spain became a net exporter of refined oil products. Where it did fail was in the use of Algerian natural gas, since as late as 1990 there was no national distribution network – simply the carboys containers, distributed by Butano (a joint INI and CAMPSA venture).[32] The cost of imported oil eventually tipped the balance in favour of nuclear, but Spain also, like Denmark, was able to exploit better ways of using coal, here both imported and domestic, so that by 1990 one quarter of Spain's electricity supply came from HEP capacity with the rest split roughly equally between coal and nuclear (Table 11.1).

Even the major European oil and gas producers in the North Sea had vastly reduced their dependency on oil-fired generating plants by 1990. Norway had made little use of oil and gas anyway, so well blessed was it with HEP capacity. In the Netherlands, oil-fired plants accounted for 37% of total electricity generated in 1980, but by 1990 this had dropped to 4% – natural gas and coal here being the main energy sources.[33] Even in the UK, the oil plants accounted for only 9% of total electricity in 1990, with two thirds produced from coal (Table 11.1). Countries like Norway and the UK benefited economically from indigenous oil sources only in the sense that the relative cost of oil did not increase as much as it would otherwise have done.[34] For the UK government, there was also the security dimension and tax revenues. It is significant that the government used its licensing powers as a physical control over the developments (not unlike the rights of way of nineteenth-century railways), rather than to generate income, which it did by taxing profits. Licences were granted to the major international oil companies, including BP, in which, by 1970, the government still had a 48% share. The Heath government exerted control over production by redefining the UK, in 1973, to include the continental shelf. The state-owned National Coal Board and British Gas were also involved in exploration and operations, though the former's interests were taken over, following the 1975 Petroleum and Submarine Pipelines Act of 1975, by a new state enterprise, the British National Oil Corporation (BNOC), empowered to operate all stages of production including resale of oil purchased from other companies exploiting the British sector. The licences were sold off in 100 mile square blocks, and for each licence, a work programme was agreed with BNOC, which was to be a 51% co-licensee, and all gas had to be sold to the state-owned

British Gas. The licences were not auctioned off, since they were basically a tool of control over development. Hence, licences were at the Minister of Fuel's discretion and commanded a modest fee. There was a royalty of 12% of sales, but the whole basis of government income was revised by the introduction in 1975 of the Petroleum Revenue Tax (PRT).[35] The tax was 45% of profits net of licence fees and royalties, and the companies also paid the normal corporation (business) tax on profits net of licence fees, royalties and the PRT. In fact, in recognition of the heavy initial outgoings on production platforms and submarine pipelines in an uncertain environment, all capital expenditure each year could be treated as an outlay for the purpose of calculating assessed profits, and the capital expenditure could be 'uplifted' by a factor of 75% to provide an additional cushion. Thus control plus tax revenue were the driving forces, moderated by recognition of the uncertainties in this kind of venture. The significance of the tax revenue may be gauged by its being equivalent, in the 1980s, to about one half of the British government's budget deficit (the public sector borrowing requirement).[36] Later changes were made to the tax system, and the resort to a wider range of fuels in electricity generation and in industry in the last quarter of the century removed some of the security dimensions. At the least, in the drive to privatisation, the new Conservative governments of the 1980s must have been less concerned about the leverage and control afforded by their ownership of BP and BNOC. Even under the Labour government of 1974–9, the government's stake in BP fell to 26%, and in 1987 all BP shares were sold to the private sector. The exploration and production activities of BNOC were regrouped into a new private concern, Britoil, which was bought out by BP in 1988. In the meantime, British Gas's oil and gas interests were hived off in 1984 to Enterprise Oil, which was then sold to the private sector.[37]

The contrast is with Norway, where Statoil was established in 1972 to look after all the country's interests in Norwegian waters and to exercise public control over supplies. Initially it granted concessions to joint stock companies partly owned by the government, which also had a 52% interest (in 1981) in Norsk Hydro, Scandinavia's biggest chemical enterprise, which also had oil interests.[38] In the late 1970s and 1980s, the government extended its control over the distribution of oil products with the aim of establishing total control of all oil production and sale – with the fear in some quarters that a monster was being created, albeit under the aegis of the Minister of Oil and Energy. We shall return to some of these issues when we discuss the premises of privatisation in chapter 15.

Notes

1 That is, there is a general expectation that, other things being equal, the price of a depletable resource will be higher next year than this, simply because stocks will be lower. Supplies will be withheld from the market this year as long as the expected profits next year, suitably discounted, exceed the profits from selling this year. On the margin, the market-determined price this year will exceed all current opportunity costs and rents, by a mark-up (the user cost or royalty) just equal to the discounted value of next year's mark-up.

2 B. R. Mitchell, *International Historical Statistics: Europe 1750–1993* (London: Macmillan, 3rd edn, 1998).

3 E. Chadeau, 'The Rise and Decline of State-Owned Industry in Twentieth Century France', in P. A. Toninelli (ed.), *The Rise and Fall of State Owned Enterprise in the Western World* (Cambridge University Press, 2000), 193.

4 M. Davids and J. L. van Zandem, 'A Reluctant State and its Enterprises: State-Owned Enterprises in the Netherlands in the "Long Run" 20th Century', in Toninelli (ed.), *Rise and Fall of State Owned Enterprise*, 256.

5 N. Lucas, *Western European Energy Policies* (Oxford: Clarendon Press, 1985), 173.

6 F. Vinck and J. Boursin, 'The Development of the Public and Private Sectors of the Coal Mining Industry in Europe: A Comparative Study' *Annals of Public and Collective Economy* 33 (1962), 309–10.

7 N. K. Buxton, *The Economic Development of the British Coal Industry* (London: Batsford, 1978), 140; J. Benson, 'Coal Mining', in C. Wrigley (ed.), *A History of British Industrial Relations 1875–1913* (Hassocks, Sussex: Harvester Press, 1982), 187–208.

8 D. Greasley, 'Fifty Years of Coal Mining Productivity: The Record of the British Coal Industry before 1939', *Journal of Economic History* 50(4) (1990), 877–902; idem, 'The Coal Industry: Images and Realities on the Road to Nationalisation', in R. Millward. and J. Singleton (eds.), *The Political Economy of Nationalisation in Britain 1920–50* (Cambridge University Press, 1995), 37–64.

9 G. Brondel, 'The Sources of Energy', in C. Cipolla (ed.), *Fontana Economic History of Europe: The Twentieth Century* (Glasgow: Fontana/Collins, 1973), 224.

10 R. Lebois, 'Charbonnages de France', *Annals of Collective Economy* 28 (1957), 256–64.

11 G. H. Kuster, 'Germany', in R. Vernon (ed.), *Big Business and the State* (Cambridge, Mass.: Harvard University Press, 1974), 77; U. Wengenroth, 'The Rise and Fall of State Owned Enterprise in Germany', in Toninelli (ed.), *Rise and Fall of State Owned Enterprise*, 121–7.

12 The rate of decline here and for the other countries is measured in terms of coal output per head of population and derived from the coal data in Mitchell, *International Historical Statistics: Europe 1750–1993* and the population data in A. Maddison, *Monitoring the World Economy 1820–1992* (Paris: OECD, 1995).

13 G. Tortella, *The Development of Modern Spain* (Cambridge, Mass.: Harvard University Press, 2000), 341.

14 W. Ashworth, *The State in Business: 1945 to the mid 1980s* (London: Macmillan, 1991).

15 Mitchell, *International Historical Statistics: Europe 1750–1993*; W. Feldenkirchen, 'Germany: The Invention of Interventionism', in J. Foreman-Peck and G. Federico (eds.), *European Industrial Policy: The Twentieth Century Experience* (Oxford University Press, 1999), 109.

16 Brondel, 'The Sources of Energy', 239.

17 Statistical Office of the European Communities (Eurostat), *Energy Yearly Statistics 1990* (Brussels: Eurostat, 1992), 114. See also Table 11.1 below.

18 Lucas, *Western European Energy Policies*, 186.

19 Ø. Noreng, 'State-Owned Oil Companies: Western Europe', in R. Vernon and Y. Aharoni (eds.), *State-Owned Enterprise in Western Economies* (London: Croom Helm, 1981), 133.

20 Noreng, 'State-Owned Oil Companies', 133.

21 Lucas, *Western European Energy Policies*, 9.

22 A. Carreras, X. Tafunell and E. Torres, 'The Rise and Decline of Spanish State-Owned Firms', in Toninelli (ed.), *The Rise and Fall of State Owned Enterprise*, 227–9; Tortella, *The Development of Modern Spain*, 349.

23 P. H. Frankel, *Mattei: Oil and Politics* (London: Faber and Faber, 1966); M. V. Posner and S. J. Woolf, *Italian Public Enterprise* (London: Duckworth, 1967); G. Stefani, 'Public Undertakings in Italy and the Prospects for Economic Programming', *Annals of Public and Collective Economy* 37 (1966), 41–63; J. M. Sheahan, 'Experience with Public Enterprise in France and Italy', in W. G. Shepherd (ed.), *Public Enterprise: Economic Analysis in Theory and Practice* (London: Heath & Co., 1976), 128–83. See also R. Mazzolini, 'European Government-Controlled Enterprises: Explaining International Strategic and Policy Decisions', *Journal of International Business Studies* 10(3) (1979), 16–27.

24 Lucas, *Western European Energy Policies*, 191.

25 Davids and van Zandem, 'State-Owned Enterprises in the Netherlands', 260.

26 Lucas, *Western European Energy Policies*, ch. 4; Frankel, *Mattei: Oil and Politics*.

27 Lucas, *Western European Energy Policies*, 187–94.

28 Ibid, ch. 2.

29 Noreng, 'State-Owned Oil Companies', 135, 139.

30 Lucas, *Western European Energy Policies*, 39; Sheahan, 'Experience with Public Enterprise in France and Italy'.

31 Lucas, *Western European Energy Policies*, ch. 3.

32 Carreras, Tafunell and Torres, 'The Rise and Decline of Spanish State-Owned Firms', 230–1.

33 Eurostat, *Energy Yearly Statistics 1990*, 115.

34 T. Whiteman, 'North Sea Oil', in D. Morris (ed.), *The Economic System in the UK* (Oxford University Press, 1985), 229–50.

35 M. G. Webb and M. J. Ricketts, *The Economics of Energy* (London: Macmillan, 1980), ch. 6; T. Weyman-Jones, *The Economics of Energy Policy* (Aldershot: Gower, 1986), ch. 7; Ashworth, *The State in Business*.

36 Webb and Ricketts, *The Economics of Energy*, 173–9.

37 Ashworth, *The State in Business*, 12, 36, 39.

38 Noreng, 'State-Owned Oil Companies', 137–8.

12   Airline regulation and the transport revolution

By 1950, the trunk networks in railways, telegraph and telephone were owned and operated throughout western Europe by state monopoly enterprises, which, in some countries, also operated the secondary lines. Much of their economic environment was determined not by arm's-length regulation of fares, rates and supply conditions, but by policies established with their supervising ministries (of transport, communications etc.) and ultimately determined by parliaments. How these policies affected profitability and productivity is evaluated in chapter 14. Here I am more concerned with examining how technological change affected the institutional setting. In the case of telecommunications, it was the advent of microprocessors and the development of information technology that transformed a simple industry (telephone at the end of a network) into one with complex facilities for transmitting information via computers, mobiles, fax, videotex and email. This was to come in the last quarter of the century.

Before that came the revolutions in road and air transport. Airline business was small beer in the late 1940s, but by the 1970s had become a major industry, especially on the passenger side. The wide-bodied, large-capacity aircraft that emerged in the late 1950s had, eventually, a big effect on shipping in Europe and some effect on railways, though nothing like the impact on rail in the USA. The competition from road transport had started in the inter-war period and, especially on the passenger side, developed fiercely after 1950 as cheaper and more reliable vehicles entered the market. Figure 12.1 shows the growth in the sheer numbers of road passenger vehicles. At the heart of continental Europe's overland tourist and freight routes, France, Germany and Italy took the lead, and, even when allowing for population size, Italy and Germany stand out from the rest (Table 12.1). To some extent, the relative roles of rail, road, air and shipping are a matter of geography. France is an interesting benchmark, since by the early 1990s its passenger transport business was equivalent to each of its inhabitants travelling some 1000 km per annum by rail and 1000 km by air, whilst on average each family had

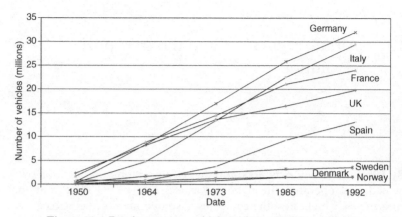

Figure 12.1 Road passenger vehicles, 1950–1992 (in millions).

Source: B. R. Mitchell, *International Historical Statistics: Europe 1750–1993* (London: Macmillan, 3rd Edition, 1998). The 1950 data for France relate to 1951, for Germany exclude West Berlin and Saarland, and for Spain include Spanish Morocco.

one car. Germany and Denmark were similar, at the centre of mainland western Europe, albeit at lower levels of air, road and rail business, except for cars in Germany, which developed very strongly. In contrast, the more geographically peripheral countries like the UK and Norway, with more difficult access by surface across Europe, were much stronger in airlines and relatively less active in rail and motor car. Sweden and Spain were roughly in between these two, and in both cases air travel was strong relative to the other modes. This leaves Italy, for which air was the weakest transport mode for passengers, while rail and road passenger traffic was among the highest in Europe.

The patterns in freight are less straightforward to characterise. The losses of merchant shipping in passenger traffic were offset in part by the rise in oil tankers in the first few decades after 1945, but then the period 1975–82 saw an absolute decline (except for Denmark) in the tonnage of the shipping fleets. Road-freight transport increased fourfold or more in the second half of the twentieth century, and rail freight eventually fell in the last quarter of the century (except in Italy). At the heart of the rail problem was its rate structure, which had been inherited from the days of the nineteenth century when it had a virtual monopoly of most inland transport. As we saw in chapter 9, in the twentieth century the railway faced a huge number of small-scale road transport firms able to offer door-to-door tailor-made service at tailor-made competitive prices. The decades after 1945 were then taken up by a slow adaptation of the rail pricing structure to these more competitive conditions. Since railways still had a strategic value and increasingly looked a desirable alternative in congested areas where road traffic was undercharged, they benefited from rising subsidy levels. Those receiving the least subsidy, and/or least able to adapt to increased competition from road and air transport, went into decline. The extreme case was Britain's railways, which suffered one of the lowest subsidy levels in Europe (in the 1980s[1]) and whose rail track had been cut back more savagely than others in Europe (cf. Figure 10.2). It was the only country whose rail freight business declined in the period 1950–73, and by 1992 its freight and passenger business, relative to population, was the lowest in the sample shown in Table 12.1 (apart from Spain and Norwegian rail passengers). The implications of these trends for the accountability, profitability and productivity of railways will be considered later in chapter 14.

The major regulatory change followed the rise of aviation. Here there is an institutional puzzle. The costs of using air space are small – like road space, when it is not congested. Since the technology and economics of road transport involve few economies of scale, a highly competitive industry emerged in all countries, with open access to road space at zero user charges (setting aside the late growth in motorway toll charges and congestion charges). There are probably more economies of scale in the airline business, but it is possible to imagine that open access to the skies would have allowed several airlines to emerge in Europe carrying passengers and freight within and across countries in a fairly competitive environment, not unlike that which emerged in the USA in the 1930s. Instead, by the late 1940s the picture of European air travel was of each country having one monopoly carrier and with airspace tightly controlled by each nation state. Indeed, as late as 1991 one minister of transport characterised air travel as a business that combined equipment at 'the most modern state of art, with rules out of Byzantine'.[2]

How and why had this occurred? There were three factors:

(1) Airspace has significant military value, so that each nation state wanted to ensure it held exclusive property rights of the airspace above ground.

(2) The marginal cost of airlines using air space is zero (in the absence of congestion), but airspace, like road space, does have an economic value, which governments would want to exploit for tax purposes. The owners of airspace were large operators (France, Italy etc.), such that within Europe there was not enough space and/or nations to provide the competition between air routes that would drive down

Table 12.1 *Surface transport, 1950, 1973 and 1992*

		UK	Denmark	France	Germany (West)	Sweden	Italy	Norway	Spain	USA
(1) Rail freight ton kilometres per head of pop.	1950	737[a]	279	931[b]	862[c]	1228	221	424	262	5673
	1973	466[a]	400	1418[b]	1118	2259	321	700	345[d]	5913
	1992	274[a]	365	873[b]	977[e]	2138	376[b]	535	243[d]	6261
(2) Rail passenger kilometres per head of pop.	1950	662[a]	790	631[b]	606[c]	943	501	454	254	336
	1973	545[a]	720	858[b]	642	593	708	400	448	71
	1992	562[a]	885[f]	1092[bg]	648[e]	644	836[b]	512	417	39[h]
(3) Road passenger motor vehicles per 1000 pop.	1950	46	23	41[i]	10[j]	43	6	18	32[k]	
	1973	242	240	278	274	309	244	200	109	
	1992	344	308	415	494	414	509	372	335	
(4) Road commercial motor vehicles per 1000 pop.	1950	20	14	17[i]	8[j]	13	4	18	29[k]	
	1973	34	40	63	18	25	18[l]	50	26	
	1992	47	58	64	23	34	47[l]	70	64	
(5) Merchant shipping in 1000 tons per million pop.	1950	220	326	77[m]	16[n]	328	62	2030	43	186
	1973	518	840	157[m]	126[n]	716	168	5900	135	70
	1992	83[o]	1134[p]	66[m]	66[en]	345	140[q]	465	74[r]	78[p]

Notes:

[a] Britain, state railways only.

[b] State-operated lines only.

[c] Excludes Saarland.

[d] Includes narrow gauge lines and incorporates a new method of estimating traffic volumes.

[e] 1989.

[f] Excludes ferry crossings.

[g] There was a slight change from 1975 in the treatment of Paris suburban tickets.

[h] Amtrak only.

[i] 1951.

[j] Excludes West Berlin and Saarland.

[k] Includes Spanish Morocco in number of vehicles (but not population).

[l] Excludes buses.

[m] Excludes ships less than 100 gross tons. The pre-1950 data in the other tables are in net tons.

[n] Excludes ships less than 60 gross tons.

[o] Excludes ships less than 500 gross tons.

[p] 1991.

[q] Excludes certain recreation vessels and also that part of the sailing fleet that is not fishing.

[r] Excludes fishing vessels.

Sources: B. R. Mitchell, *International Historical Statistics: Europe 1750–1993* (London: Macmillan, 3rd edn, 1998).
B. R. Mitchell, *International Historical Statistics: The Americas: 1750–1993* (London, Macmillan, 4th edn, 1998).
A. Maddison, *Monitoring the World Economy 1820–1992* (Paris: Organisation for Economic Cooperation and Development, 1995), Appendix, relating to 1989 population boundaries.

the charges for access. Thus each nation was able to exact a significant rental income for its airspace.

(3) Like nineteenth-century railways and telegraph, airlines were a means of communication with potential military and social significance. At a minimum that might lead to government subsidies and at the limit to state ownership of airlines.

Thus what we see in the early years of aviation, before 1940, is first of all the abandonment of open skies. The 1919 Paris Air Convention endorsed each country's sovereignty over its airspace – an upward extension of the national prerogative over airspace (similar to oil and mineral rights below ground). Significantly, the Netherlands, a small country with everything to be gained from open skies, was not a party to the agreement.[3] It heralded the restriction of cabotage rights (for example, the American airline Trans World Airlines (TWA) carrying passengers within France from Paris to Lyons), of fifth freedom rights (TWA carrying passengers from London to Paris) and a general horse trading over air rights.

The Italians, for example, refused to let the British airline Imperial Airways over-fly their territory en route to Egypt unless revenues were shared with an Italian airline which never carried a single passenger while the Greeks insisted that the British pay duty on fuel, wherever it was loaded, if it was used on flights over Greek territory.[4]

Secondly, as a new industry, the airline business saw many fledgling firms. Because of the limited opportunity to expand at will on international routes, many stuck to their domestic market, which became overcrowded, and many firms became unprofitable, especially in the early 1920s, and went bankrupt. At one stage, there were twenty companies operating the British domestic market.[5] The gate was open for governments to subsidise an industry, particular routes (to the colonies) and services (airmail) that were unprofitable but whose development they wished to support for political and military reasons. Merger activity was common, and from this invariably emerged a single company as the nation's 'chosen instrument' with state subsidy. Each was based in the capital city at the centre of a spoke network with extensions to the colonies. KLM was established in 1919, and by 1929 the majority of shares were held by the Dutch government. Sabena began in 1923 as the Belgian national carrier. The Italian government held all the shares in Alitalia when it started in 1924. In the same year AB Aerotransport was set up with a Swedish government subsidy and a monopoly concession. It was owned by Junkers until 1935 when, with the subsidy growing alarmingly, the state took a 50% shareholding. In 1926, Lufthansa was established with part ownership by the Reich. Air France was set up in

1933 with 25% of shares state owned and enjoying a 78% subsidy on turnover.[6] Foreign companies were outlawed in the British domestic market, and in 1935 British Airways was established with government subsidy to avoid the humiliating bankruptcy of several unprofitable companies. Its main area of operations was continental Europe to distinguish it from Imperial Airways set up in 1924 to service the British Empire – especially India, South Africa and Australia.[7] This was the chosen instrument to fly the flag using aircraft manufactured in Britain – like the flying boat, perhaps good in the tropics but not likely to lead in European and American commercial markets. The other countries with colonies also used their airlines to service countries like West Africa, Indonesia (Air France) and the Dutch East Indies (KLM), whilst Belgians living in the Congo put up some of the initial funds for Sabena. Meanwhile, Germany, under restrictions as a result of the First World War, concentrated on commercial activity in a European-centred network. The USA had few flag-waving ambitions, and airline development mushroomed in the large homogenous domestic market such that, by the end of the 1930s, the US airlines had more passengers than the rest of the world combined.

After 1945, the trends discernible before the war became fixed institutional features. Each country had a national carrier more than 50% state owned and dominating domestic routes. It is useful to see the full list:[8]

> Air France: Reconstructed in 1947 as a company with 70% state ownership, 28% other public authorities and 2% private.
>
> Alitalia: Forcibly delayed reformation (as a defeated belligerent) until 1957. A subsidiary of Istituto per la Ricostruzione Industriale (IRI), part owned by Trans World Airlines (TWA) but more than 50% state owned.
>
> BOAC and BEA: Imperial Airways and British Airways merged in 1940 to form the (100% state owned) British Overseas Airways Corporation, part of which was hived off to form British European Airways in 1946. The two firms merged into British Airways in 1975.
>
> Iberia: Established in 1943 as a subsidiary of the Spanish state holding company Instituto Nacional de Industria (INI).
>
> KLM: Reconstructed in The Hague in 1946. The state owned 94% of the shares, but this declined later (to 55% by 1985).
>
> Lufthansa: Delayed reconstruction (again because of the war) until 1954 at which point 74% of shares were held by the government of the West German Federal Republic.
>
> Sabena: Emerged after the war with a subtitle – Belgian World Airlines.

> SAS: Scandinavian Airlines System. A mixed enterprise estab-
> lished in 1946, 50% owned (in 1973) by the governments of
> Denmark, Norway and Sweden.

Governments advanced their control over airspace and perceived their airlines as the chosen instruments for pursuing strategic objectives and, in the case of France and the UK, for fostering local aircraft manufacture. These aims often conflicted with financial imperatives, but did not stop the Chairman of Air France declaring in 1966 that the airline had to 'link France to the numerous places where it had political or economic interests ... to pay continuous attention to costs, but as the national airline ... to preserve the public service, from which it received the constraints and the greatness'.[9] Alitalia, to take another example, was directed to develop routes to southern Italy and the islands.[10] The main problem, which all the European countries faced at the start of the postwar period, was the competitive threat from the American airlines, coupled with technological change that was making for bigger and better aircraft. The USA accounted for 60% of all civil aviation traffic, and its domestic market was ideal for developing big airlines like TWA, United Airlines and American Airlines. The Second World War was important in improving navigational aids and airports, and the twin-engined mono-plane of the 1930s had, by the 1950s, been replaced by the DC-4s and Lockheed Constellation, which had better pressurisation, bigger pay-loads and could travel longer distances.[11]

The outcome of this tension between the aims of the European governments and the economic threats from the USA was firstly a price cartel, which effectively protected European airlines from American competition. The International Air Transport Association (IATA) was formed in 1945 and became the central body for setting international air fares. Unanimity was required for all changes, so that the small and/or high-cost countries were in a strong position. Fares were set sufficiently high to protect the high-cost airlines such as Air France with its Caravelle and BOAC and BEA with their expensive Comet, Britannia, Trident and VC10 aircraft. Horse trading on air rights continued. In 1946, the famous Bermuda agreement was signed between the USA and the UK, confirming routes and frequencies in a model followed in other bilateral agreements. The USA had to agree to the IATA regime but did get generous rights to flights within Europe, and in any case, carriers like TWA and Pan American were content to make easy profits on the transatlantic routes.[12] The potentiality of tourist traffic was largely frustrated up to the 1960s. Charter airlines taking tourists on inclusive tours (hotel and flight) were being offered, but the number of independent airlines and their routes

were severely circumscribed by the regulators. In the meantime, scheduled carriers introduced tourist class in 1952–3 and economy class in
1958–9. Neither of these deals achieved the significant cost savings that
would arise from the charter airlines' practice of matching hotel beds with
aircraft seats. The tourist and economy flight schemes were only offering
off-peak capacity.

The period from the late 1950s to the mid 1970s then saw major
technological and institutional changes, which threatened but did not
break the IATA system. Piston-engined aircraft reached their apotheosis
with the DC-7C and the Lockheed Super Constellation. These were
aircraft capable of travelling long distances, but they were soon to be
overtaken by the jets. In 1958 Pan American operated its first Boeing 707,
heralding the start of the jet age and completing American dominance of
aerospace. At the same time, Europe was losing its colonies, which in any
case were not the growth markets for the scheduled airlines, who were
looking to intra-European and transatlantic routes. In 1958, for example,
Air France faced international competition on 38% of its routes; by 1967
this had risen to 93%.[13]

Rising living standards and better aircraft boosted the demand for
tourist travel, and the scheduled airlines continued their limited response.
Advanced booking became the key to fuller utilisation of scheduled
services. The Advanced Booking Charter was introduced in 1971 for
groups, and the APEX fares for individuals from 1975. One further
twist on the flight-only deals sanctioned by IATA was the introduction
in the 1960s of charter flights offered to groups of people associated with
clubs. Someone wanting a cheap flight to East Africa would therefore join
the East African Cultural Association (did it ever hold any meetings!) and
thereby become eligible for a cheap fare. All of these responses were
overtaken during the 1960s and 1970s by the growth of the charter
inclusive tour combining flights with hotel accommodation. They were
initially able to exploit the glut of secondhand piston-engined aircraft
when jets took over the scheduled services – though by the end of the
1960s the jets had also come to dominate the charter markets.[14] The
charter business developed earlier and more quickly in Britain, and this is
reflected in the airline passenger flows recorded in Figure 12.2. The
British did have to travel for the sun and were perhaps more prone than
others to welcome the inclusive tour package as a 'means of travel direct
to a beachside hotel, in what amounted to a hermetically sealed tube,
without having to risk any encounter with foreigners'.[15] The French did
not need aircraft to go on holiday. Britain also had a long tradition of
entrepreneurial pilots, and independent airlines had flourished on colonial routes under cabotage rights – the 'colonial coach'. The pressure on

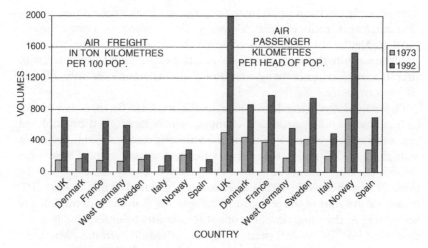

Figure 12.2 Airline traffic in 1973 and 1992

Note: The 1992 entries for Germany relate to 1989 and for air freight for other countries to 1991.

Sources: B. R. Mitchell, *International Historical Statistics: Europe 1750–1993* (London: Macmillan, 3rd edn, 1998) and population data from A. Maddison, *Monitoring the World Economy 1820–1992* (Paris: Organisation for Economic Cooperation and Development, 1995).

domestic civil aviation boards and IATA to approve new airlines and charter routes proved too much, and in the UK the dam broke in 1965 when the government approved forty-six new licences for independent airlines and abolished the monopoly of BOAC and BEA on scheduled services. By 1969, there were 5.7 million Britons on foreign holidays and half were on package tours. There were new independent airlines like Dan-Air, and several were linked to shipping companies wanting to spread their risks: Silver City with P&O, Cunard Eagle with the Cunard Steamship Company. Eventually, as the business spread to other European countries, non-scheduled services boomed (rising at 40% per annum in the late 1960s), and the scheduled carriers relented and set up their own charter companies: Condor (Lufthansa), Martins (KLM), Balair (Swissair), Air Charter International (Air France), British Air Tours (BEA). Also new scheduled services, such as Laker's Sky Train (low fares, no frills), came on the scene in the 1970s triggering great transatlantic price wars.[16]

The IATA-regulated scheduled services remained intact, however, and resistance continued well into the 1980s. There were two underlying threats to the existing system. One was the continuous downward pressure on costs and prices as the jets became bigger and more sophisticated.[17] The IATA regime supported the highest-cost airlines, so that the more innovatory were not able to fully reap the advantages of technological advances. Financial problems were exacerbated by the 1970s depression and oil-price hike, when airlines like Alitalia, having built up a capacity on the trans-Atlantic routes, now had to cut back.[18] The second threat came from the USA, which was unencumbered with subcontinental nation state airlines and airspace rights and throughout took the lead in pressuring for deregulation. Self-sufficient airlines were able to develop within the USA, and it is perhaps surprising that domestic liberalisation did not arrive until the 1978 Airline Deregulation Act. Labour productivity was often more than double European levels. There were 1125 passengers per employee in Delta airline in 1978 and 1099 in Eastern, as compared to 333 in Air France, 374 in Alitalia, 308 in British Airways and 460 in Lufthansa. Of course, there were some American airlines not far away – TWA at 665 and Pan Am at 358, but they were to go to the wall eventually – and the pattern of US/European relative productivity was not unique to airlines, as we shall see later. Nonetheless, the continuing evidence of European air fares well above American (200% in 1983) was a constant reminder of what deregulation might achieve.[19]

In fact, the attempts at deregulation in the 1970s were resisted. The year 1977 saw a Bermuda 2 agreement between the UK and the USA, but the UK got its way and, rather breathtakingly, had the nerve to complain about the USA's generous fifth freedom rights under the Bermuda 1 agreement. Then in 1978, the US Civil Aviation Board withdrew its anti-trust immunity from IATA, which it asked to show 'just cause'. Led by France, the bulk of IATA's members joined to oppose change.[20] The Dutch supported the USA, and indeed within Europe it was the Anglo-Dutch Treaty of 1984 that sparked off freedom of routes and carriers in Europe, and the trend to deregulation was reinforced by the moves to enforce the Treaty of Rome's provisions on free competition such that, by the late 1990s, full cabotage rights were available to all EU members.

Notes

1 C. Nash, 'European Railway Comparisons – What Can we Learn?', in K. J. Button and D. C. Pitfield (eds.), *International Railway Economics* (Aldershot: Gower, 1985), 266.
2 Malcolm Rifkind, British Minister of Transport quoted in P. J. Lyth, 'Experiencing Turbulence: Regulation and De-Regulation in the International Air

Transport Industry 1930–90', in J. McConville (ed.) *Transport Regulation Matters* (London: Pinter, 1997), 156.

3 M. Dierikx, 'KLM: An Airline Outgrowing its Flag', in H.-L. Dienel and P. Lyth, *Flying the Flag: European Commercial Air Transport since 1945* (Basingstoke, UK: Macmillan, 1998), 127; P. J. Lyth, 'Institutional Change and European Air Transport 1910–85', in L. Magnusson and J. Ottoson (eds.), *Evolutionary Economics and Path Dependence* (Cheltenham: Edward Elgar, 1996), 171.

4 Lyth, 'Experiencing Turbulence', 155.

5 P. W. Brooks, 'The Development of Air Transport', *Journal of Transport History* 1(2) (1967), 164–83.

6 J. Ottosson, 'The State and Regulatory Orders in Early European Civil Aviation', in L. Magnusson and J. Ottosson, *The State, Regulation and the Economy: An Historical Perspective* (Cheltenham: Edward Elgar, 2001), 148–65; J. Ottosson, 'The Making of a Scandinavian Airline Company: Private Actors and Public Interests', in L. Andersson-Skog and O. Krantz (eds.), *Institutions and the Transport and Communications Industries* (Canton, Mass.: Science History Publications, Watson, 1999), 267–80; Dierikx, 'KLM: An Airline Outgrowing its Flag'. See also the following in Dienel and Lyth (eds.), *Flying the Flag*: N. Niertz, 'Air France: An Elephant in an Evening Suit' (pp. 18–49); H.-L. Dienel, 'Lufthansa: Two German Airlines' (pp. 87–125); A. Mantegazza, 'Alitalia and Commercial Aviation in Italy' (pp. 158–94).

7 P. J. Lyth, 'The Changing Role of Government in British Civil Aviation', in R. Millward and J. Singleton (eds.), *The Political Economy of Nationalisation in Britain 1920–1950* (Cambridge University Press, 1995), 65–87; B. K. Humphreys, 'Nationalisation and the Independent Airlines in the United Kingdom 1945–1951', *Journal of Transport History* 3 (1976), 265–81; P. J. Lyth, 'A Multiplicity of Instruments: The 1946 Decision to Create a Separate British European Airline and its Effects on Airline Productivity', *Journal of Transport History* 11(2) (1990), 1–17; P. J. Lyth, 'Chosen Instruments: The Evolution of British Airways', in Dienel and Lyth (eds.), *Flying the Flag*, 50–86.

8 See references in previous two footnotes and also Centre Européen de l'Enterprise Publique, *The Evolution of Public Enterprises in the Community of the Nine* (London: CEEP English Editions, 1973).

9 Niertz, 'Air France: An Elephant in an Evening Suit', 21.

10 Mantegazza, 'Alitalia and Commercial Aviation in Italy', 165.

11 Brooks, 'The Development of Air Transport', 72–3.

12 Lyth, 'Experiencing Turbulence', 157–8.

13 Niertz, 'Air France: An Elephant in an Evening Suit', 20; see also P. J. Lyth, 'The History of Commercial Air Transport: A Progress Report', *Journal of Transport History* 14(2) (1993), 166–80.

14 Brooks, 'The Development of Air Transport'.

15 P. J. Lyth and M. L. Dierikx, 'From Privilege to Popularity: The Growth of Leisure Air Travel', *Journal of Transport History* 15(2) (1994), 103.

16 Lyth, 'Experiencing Turbulence', 163; Lyth and Dierikx, 'From Privilege to Popularity'.
17 Though the downward pressure stopped in the 1980s (cf. Dienel and Lyth (eds.), *Flying the Flag*, 11).
18 Mantegazza, 'Alitalia and Commercial Aviation in Italy', 183.
19 Lyth, 'Experiencing Turbulence', 166 and Table 8.1. For the general issue of US/European productivity, see S. N. Broadberry, 'Manufacturing and the Convergence Hypothesis: What the Long-Run Data Show', *Journal of Economic History* 53(4) (1993), 772–95.
20 A. Dobson, 'Regulation or Competition?: Negotiating the Anglo-American Air Services Agreement of 1977', *Journal of Transport History* 15(2) (1994), 144–64; Dierikx, 'KLM: An Airline Outgrowing its Flag', 131; Lyth, 'Institutional Change and European Air Transport 1910–1985', 182–3.

13 Telecommunications 1950–1990: from calm to storm

The break-up of the monolithic state-owned post and telecommunications enterprises from the 1980s was a central feature of the first phase of the privatisation process. Although much has been made of the ideological lead offered by the USA and by the privatisation of British Telecom, much of the institutional change can be better understood as a product of technological and economic developments, which undermined the case for publicly owned monopolies. With this in mind, it is useful to highlight four features of telecommunications that affect the institutional setting. The central activity is the transmission, at low running costs, of voice or visual images across a network of lines with the information routed by switching exchanges. Such public switching telephone networks have all the characteristics of natural monopolies – qualified to some extent when satellite and cable facilities are also available. This information is then received and processed at terminals (telephones, computers, fax machines etc.). Thirdly, given the complex nature of the equipment, some economic gains could accrue from having national or international specification standards. Fourthly, telecommunication networks have the property that, if a new connection is set up (a new telephone subscriber for example), there are benefits accruing not only to the new subscriber but to the rest of the existing subscribers, each of whom now has a potentially new contact. In economic terms, the social cost of a new connection is less than its private cost. These characteristics suggest that we might expect an industry with the following features. Firstly, a single transmission company – that is, a single public telecom operator (PTO) – whose monopoly power is regulated by the state. Terminal equipment might be supplied, installed and manufactured by a competitive industry – as for electricity fires, gas stoves, central heating systems in other utilities. The switching equipment used by the PTOs could also be supplied by a competitive electrical equipment manufacturing industry similar to that making electricity generating plant and other electrical goods. Technical standards for equipment would be established and monitored by a government department or agency. Finally, the spillovers from expanding the number of connections could be met by some element of state subsidy to the PTO.

What had emerged by the late 1940s was something very different, but this was less a product of ideology than a reflection of the simplicity of the early telecommunications systems and of certain specific aims of governments. What had emerged were national networks operated by state-owned enterprises, that is, in each country, a single state-owned PTO (like the Deutsche Bundespost), usually an integral part of a ministry of posts and telecommunications. The switching equipment was invariably supplied by private electrical equipment manufacturers. Terminal equipment was often supplied instead by the PTO, who also often set technical standards for all equipment. The monopoly position of the PTO was de facto regulated by ministerial and parliamentary monitoring of tariffs and supply conditions. Finally, the range of services supplied and structure of tariffs reflected a commitment to universal service – providing open access to the network to everybody at prices that were in some sense 'affordable'.

Let us consider each of these features in turn. Firstly, public ownership by a single enterprise of a national network was the rule by 1950 and reflected, in part, the unwillingness of governments, in the inter-war period when the national networks crystallised, to use arm's-length regulation of private monopolies, especially when these monopolies might have to be subsidised to facilitate social objectives. This I argued and illustrated in Part III, and there is no need to repeat the point here. Hence, by 1950 there was the Deutsche Bundespost, the PTT in France, Belgium and the Netherlands, Televerket in Sweden, Telefonica in Spain, the Telegrafslyret in Norway (where all private telephone companies had disappeared by 1960) and the General Post Office in the UK.[1] In the 1950s, and indeed earlier, there were demands for smaller separate networks for large organisations, so that we find railway systems, electricity enterprises, the police, taxi services, ministries of defence, royal palaces, all with their own facility. For the main networks, one PTO was the rule, except in Denmark and Italy, where trunk lines were operated by state enterprises (Post-og Telegrafvaesenet and Azienda di Stato per Servizi Telfonici) and non-trunk lines by various regional telephone companies. However, these were not major departures from the general picture in that the companies were under indirect state control. In Denmark, there were the three regulated concession companies (Kjøbenhavns, Fyns Kimmunale, Jydsk) with shares owned by the state, municipalities and co-operatives, whilst in Italy, five telephone companies were, in the 1950s merged into Società Italiana per l'Esercizio Telefonico (SIP), a subsidiary of Società Finanziana Telefonico (STET), part state-owned, and itself a subsidiary of Istituto per la Ricostruzione Industriale (IRI),

100% state owned.[2] In both Italy and Denmark there was one single national network operated by enterprises with a strong state element, albeit with different parts of the systems operated by different enterprises. Why, however, were the trunk operators, and indeed the state enterprises in all the other countries, invariably integral parts of government departments? This I attributed in chapter 7 to the importance of communications for national defence – a demand to have quick access and control, access in crises, as the Swedish authorities put it as late as the 1980s.[3] These reasons for public ownership and integration with government would come under threat with the growth of new means of communications – airlines, internet, satellites, mobile phones.

There are two factors that explain what had emerged in the equipment market. For the first few decades after 1945, the telecommunications systems were fairly simple: voice transmission to a terminal with the one telephone handset. Given the need for technical standardisation and compatibility with the national network, not much was lost by the state enterprises installing and maintaining the telephone handset. Indeed, in some countries like Spain the telephones were owned by Telefonica and rented out to users. Once terminal equipment became something more than a single handset, there were likely to be pressures to open up the market, as for appliances in the other utilities. In the case of switching equipment, there was a wide range of potential suppliers, including Siemens, Italtel, Philips and Ericsson,and the PTOs were often pressured in the first few postwar decades into using whichever of the above had manufacturing plants in the home country. The Italian, British and German equipment markets were protected in that overt preference was given to domestic firms. Telefonica bought its equipment from a Spanish firm that was a subsidiary of the state owned Instituto Nacional de Industria (INI). In France, a company that was a subsidiary of the Directorate of Telecommunications supplied equipment to the Directorate, though it faced competition from others. As for technical specifications, so long as the state enterprises had monopolies, no great conflict of interest was involved in these same state enterprises setting technical standards for telephone handsets and switching equipment. The PTOs in collaboration with the ministries of telecommunications set the technical standards, a practice that became less defensible once the customer premises equipment market boomed and the PTOs were in competition with private firms manufacturing fax machines, mobile-phones, telex facilities and so on.

Finally, there is the question of subsidies and the spread of telephone usage. Figure 13.1 shows telephones per 1000 inhabitants in the key expansion period from 1950 up to the early 1980s, after which the

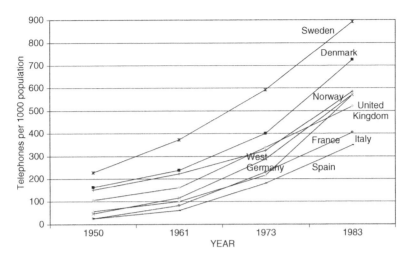

Figure 13.1 Telephone penetration levels, 1950–1983 (number of telephones per 1000 population).

Note:
The 1950 entry for Germany excludes Saarland. The 1973 and 1983 entries for Italy included San Marino.

Sources: B. R. Mitchell, *International Historical Statistics: Europe 1750–1993* (London: Macmillan, 3rd edn, 1998) and population data from A. Maddison, *Monitoring the World Economy 1820–1992* (Paris: Organisation for Economic Cooperation and Development, 1995).

telephone was no longer the dominant piece of equipment at the end of the national network, and indeed statistics on telephone penetration then died out of the standard sources. Spain and Italy had the lowest levels, but even there, in the early 1980s, the number of telephones was roughly equivalent to one telephone handset per family. European governments had been committed to expanding connections since waiting lists were common – in Norway they lasted to the 1980s. The recovery in quality and quantity in Germany after the war was astonishing as telecommunications changed from a mainly business tool to an item of mass consumption.[4] Government pressure for an expansion of connections was consistent with the economic argument about spillovers, but it was achieved within the more general umbrella of 'universal service', which was designed to accommodate additional aims and constraints, which can now be examined.

Table 13.1 *Net profits★ in posts and telecommunications, 1966–1980*

	UK (£ million)		Denmark (1000 kroner)		Germany (DM 1000 million)	Italy (billion lira)	Netherlands (million guilders)		
	General Post Office		Post-og Telegrafvaesenet	Regional non-trunk telephone companies	Deutsche Bundespost	Società Finanziaria Telefonica (non-trunk STET companies)	PTT		
	Post	Telecom.					Telephone	Telegraph	Post
1950							35	0	−3
1955							16	3	−14
1960							64	3	3
1964	7	38							
1965	1	39					35	1	−56
1966	7	38			0.3				
1967	4	35	154		0.4				
1968	−6	50	121	61	0.5	15.0			
1969	−25	61	190	80	0.3	16.2			
1970	−73	93	141	164	−0.5	18.4			
1971	−13	58		170	−1.5	18.4			
1972	−43	10			−0.5				
1973	−58	−61			−0.5				
1974	−109	−194			−0.8				
1975	−9	155			0.6		175	38	−152
1976	24	365			1.2				
1977	40	326							
1978	33	336							
1979	34	129							
1980							204	64	−166

*Net profits comprise all receipts and grants less all operating expenses, depreciation, taxes, interest and all other capital charges.

Sources: United Kingdom: W. Ashworth, *The State in Business: 1945 to the mid 1980s* (London: Macmillan, 1991), Table 5.10.

Denmark: Centre Européen de l'Entreprise Publique, *The Evolution of Public Enterprises in the Community of the Nine* (London: CEEP English Editions, 1973), 49 and 52. The data for Post-og Tel. relate to financial years starting in the year quoted. Regional telephone companies are part state owned and the entries are aggregates of Telefon-Aktieselkab, Jydsk Telefon-Aktieselkab and Fyns Kommunale Telefonselkab.

Germany: CEEP, *Evolution of Public Enterprises* 85; CEEP, *The Financing of Public Enterprises in the Countries of the European Community* (London: CEEP English Editions, 1978), 173.

Italy: CEEP, *Evolution of Public Enterprises*, 249. Società Finanziaria Telefonica (STET) owns only non-trunk lines and exchanges and is a financial subsidiary of the state holding enterprise IRI.

Netherlands: M. Davids, 'The Dutch Way: Privatisation and Liberalisation of PTT', *Business History* 47 (April 2005), Table 1.

The marginal cost of a telephone call is quite small. User charges set equal to such costs would likely generate financial deficits since joint costs and other overheads would not be covered. The classic way round that is to have a two-part tariff, with a low running charge plus a connection charge, which would absorb some of the consumer surplus into industry revenue. To promote expansion, most PTOs set connection charges below cost. If they were also to set a low running charge, they would likely need a subsidy. There was, however, a further problem. The connection costs and marginal user costs vary with the remoteness of the subscriber, the geographical distance over which the call is made, the time of day and year (peak or otherwise) and the length of the call in minutes. A tariff system closely related to such a cost structure would likely mean lower prices in densely populated areas and for business users with many calls to make. This would not be consistent with the one-nation approach that characterised the immediate postwar period. Instead, the tariff structures that emerged had much less differentiation between different groups, with fairly uniform charges for connection irrespective of location and a running rate closely based on the geographical distance of the call. Charges were low for local calls relative to trunk calls, residential relative to business calls, rural areas relative to urban.[5] The local, residential and rural sectors were financially unremunerative. The deficits might be met by government subsidies but more commonly were cross-subsidised by high charges for the trunk, business and urban sectors, so that the PTOs could meet their statutory requirement to break even in financial terms. The somewhat patchy data in Table 13.1 suggest that telecommunication services in the 1950–80 period generated revenues that covered their costs and that it was the postal services that made losses.[6] The non-trunk lines in Denmark and Italy together with the whole of the telephone network in the UK and the Netherlands clearly managed to earn enough revenue to cover all their outgoings including interest and related capital charges. It was the postal services that generated losses.

The typical structure of telephone tariffs was seen to provide a universal service. It comprised connection charges varying according to whether the customer was business or not, a charge for local calls that varied little with length of call in minutes, and charges for trunk calls differentiated between domestic and international. Foreman-Peck and Mueller have estimated that, by the mid-1980s, the real resource cost of a local call, measured in the then European unit of account, was 0.1 ECUs for 3 minutes, and trunk calls averaged somewhere between 0.3 and 0.4 ECUs for 3 minutes.[7] Tariffs displayed a different picture. Table 13.2 indicates that charges for local calls of 3 minutes in 1986 in the Netherlands and Spain were less than costs, and for the other countries

Table 13.2 *Telephone tariffs, 1986 (charges for 3 minute calls in ECUs*)*

	UK	Denmark	France	Germany (West)	Italy	Belgium	Netherlands	Spain
Local	0.21	0.10	0.11	0.11	0.20	0.14	0.06	0.03
Trunk up to 100 km	0.56	0.36	0.15	1.0	1.62	0.69	0.26	0.60
Other trunk (domestic)	0.56	n.a.	1.59	1.66	1.72	0.69	n.a.	1.07
International (peak charge to another EC member)	1.94	1.37	1.85	1.67	2.92	2.22	1.75	3.17

*European Currency Units, including VAT.

Source: J. Foreman-Peck and J. Mueller (eds.), *European Telecommunications Organisation* (Baden-Baden: Nomosverlagsgesellschaft, 1988), Table 1.6.

we should remember that there was often no restriction on the duration of the calls. In the 1960s, you could make a telephone call from a remote village to a nearby town for a matter of pence and stay on the phone all day long. Trunk calls, on the other hand – and these would often be business calls – carried tariffs well above running costs. The result, in 1987 in France for example, was that local calls generated 67% of the traffic of the entire system, 56% of the costs, but only 15% of revenues.[8] Telecommunications had not been a priority in the first four French plans, and the sector was starved of investment for a long period. In 1986, 87% of its investment was self-financed – a high figure for state enterprises. The telephone system had a bad reputation for a long time, and as late as the 1960s the French network was no bigger than that in New York or Chicago.[9] It is difficult to see this solely as a product of public ownership. All the countries in Figure 13.1 had state-owned systems yet with very different networks. Littlechild's finding, that state systems were less sensitive to income and population levels than private systems, might hold for his worldwide sample but makes little sense within Europe.[10] The very high penetration levels in the Swedish system served by the state trading agency Televerket may be contrasted with the low levels in Italy (albeit with a large number of public call boxes) with its more decentralised semi-private set of companies. Nor is population density much of a guide. The low figure for Spain is sometimes attributed to its 60000 villages, each with less than 100 inhabitants, but what then of Norway?

By the 1980s, three factors were making for institutional change. First and foremost was technological change from new information technology and microprocessors.[11] Second was the pressure from the business sector for changes in the tariff structure, which it saw as prejudicial to its interests. Third was the widening in the range of modern communications, which undermined the importance of state ownership of the telephone network for national defence and security. The technological change that more than any other threatened the current institutional regime was the emergence of new customer premises equipment and value added services. New customer premises equipment included computers, modems, multiple telephone handsets, fax and telex terminals. New value added services included audio and visual conferences, mobile networks (with phones), email, fax and telex plus a proliferation of private automatic branch exchanges. The supply and installation of this equipment and services was a big industry with no significant natural monopoly elements. By analogy with much of the manufacturing sector in Europe, there were strong pressures on governments to reduce the dominance of the PTOs in the markets for customer premises equipment and value added services. By extension, if the PTOs were to face competition in these markets, there was no case for their continuing to set technical standards and license other firms. By the end of the 1980s, it was clear that changes were underway and were being reinforced by pressure from the European Union, aiming for an internal market by 1992.[12] Paradoxically, ten years earlier the UK, the first to privatise their network, was actually the most 'closed' in the 'attachments' market. It had made for good trunk services but limited development of customer premises equipment and value added services whose markets were opened up in the UK from 1982.[13] There was a longer tradition of more open customer premises equipment markets in the Netherlands and Italy, but also in the two countries where the classic state-owned PTO was to hang on the longest – France and Germany. The customer premises equipment market became fully liberalised in France from the mid-1980s, though the Directorate General of Telecommunications and its subsidiaries were still major players.[14] The German market was characterised by very high technical standards set by the Deutsche Bundespost, which was a major player in all markets but the Ministry of Posts and Telcommunications had started, by the mid 1980s, to license competitors. In Spain by the mid 1980s, Telefonica still had big shareholdings in equipment suppliers like Sintel and held the monopoly of the supply and installation of all telephone handsets, modems and mobiles, but the market was opened by a law of 1987.[15]

The makers of switching gear and other equipment for the PTOs had been dominated by large equipment manufacturers, and what we see from the 1980s is a liberalisation of these markets through the reduction in protection and preference for domestic firms. The case had been put in Germany in 1981 by a Monopoly Commission report. There were similar moves in Sweden and Britain. In both, the switching equipment and CPE/VAS markets, the part involvement of PTOs meant they had a conflict of interest of growing severity in their role as regulator for technical standards. Hence, new independent agencies were established by the General Directorate of Telecommunications in Denmark in the early 1980s, and in Britain took the form from 1984 of the British Approvals Board for Telecommunications. A new licensing office, ZZF, was set up in Germany in the 1980s, and the Commission Nationale de la Communautés et des Libertés in France in 1987 (within the Ministry of Post and Telecommunications).[16]

The expansion of the equipment and services markets generated a huge increase in demands on the transmission networks, very much business led, and gave added momentum to the business sector's demand for more favourable tariff structures. In the face of high business tariffs, some illegal networks developed as well as prompting large companies (like International Business Machines (IBM) in France) to sell or lease off spare capacity to others. By the end of the 1980s, tariff changes were underway and they were unfavourable for local, residential and rural sectors and favoured trunk, business and urban sectors. The tariffs became more cost based – for example, in France distance steps were retained, but the tariffs were linked more to time of day and duration of call.[17] The main problem for the PTOs and their governments was that the beneficiaries were likely to be high-income and business groups who made long-distance calls, while the bulk of the (voting) population would suffer.[18] Hence, the speed with which these price changes were introduced varied considerably, reflecting the strength of the different groups.

There was a similar hesitancy about the position of the PTOs themselves. Private automatic branch exchanges developed readily, and there were instances where the PTO devised separate network facilities – like Transpac (a subsidiary of the French Directorate of Telecommunications). For the main networks, despite the advent of satellite and cable, there were still in the 1980s substantial natural monopoly elements. Telecommunications in Britain were taken out of the Ministry of Posts and Telecommunications in 1969 and became part of a new public corporation, the Post Office. In 1981, the telecom section became a public corporation in its own right as British Telecom, which was then privatised in 1984. From 1982, it had to co-exist with a new network company Mercury, which operated initially with leased lines. It was focused on business users and had 1000 large clients by 1986, with high access charges and low running tariffs. BT was, however, to dominate the network for the foreseeable future. The abandonment of public ownership in the UK in 1984 was the only major privatisation of PTOs in the 1980s. In Germany, it was difficult politically, since it required a change in the basic law of the constitution of the Federal Republic, which was possible only with a two-thirds majority in Parliament. Similarly, the need for independent regulation of the PTOs was recognised, but progress was slow. Oftel was established in 1982 in the UK and Commission Nationale de la Communautés et des Libertés in France in 1987. Elsewhere, such new independent bodies came later – not till 1993 in Sweden when the regulatory function passed from the PTO to the National Posts and Telecommunications Agency.

Another process that was continuing, again at a slow pace, was the disentanglement of the PTO from the supervising ministries, obviously a prerequisite for privatisation. The fact that the process had started in the 1980s suggests that the importance of having PTOs under close state control for reasons of national defence and security was diminishing. Telecommunications was separate from the post, as a business unit, early in the century in Norway (the Telegrafslyret), Sweden (Televerket) and Spain (Telefonica), and was clearly separately supervised in Italy. The separation in the UK occurred in 1981, as already noted. In France, the Directorate General of Telecommunications had been established as a separate entity within the French Ministry of Post and Telecommunications in 1945, but it was not until 1967 that it was allowed to borrow on the capital market, and it was the 1970s before it had separate accounts.[19] From 1987, Telecom Denmark (Statens Teletjeneste) was the agency responsible for operating the trunk routes in Denmark independent of postal services. These separations of post and telecommunications were all signs of a growing commercialisation and independence from government, but it was taking even longer for the telecommunications enterprise to be an entity outside the ministry. Clearly this had occurred early in Norway, Sweden and Spain, and in the UK in 1969, albeit then still part of the Post Office. The other countries had to await the 1990s – when French Telecom and the Swedish Telia AB were established. Germany was the most resistant, and by 1990, even though telecommunications had its separate budget, it was still part of Deutsche Bundespost operating under public law and under the direction of the Ministry of Post and Telecommunications and the Ministry of Defence, continuing the long historical tradition that continued also in the railways.[20]

Notes

1 For Norway, see H. Espeli, 'From Dual Structure to State Monopoly in Norwegian Telephones, 1880–1924', Working Paper, Norwegian School of Management, Scandvika, Norway, January 2002; J. Foreman-Peck and D. Manning, 'Telecommunications in Norway', in J. Foreman-Peck and J. Muller (eds.), *European Telecommunications Organisation* (Baden-Baden: Nomosverlagsgesellschaft, 1988), 221–36.

2 S. E. Jeppson, K. G. Paulsen and F. Schneider, 'Telecommunications Services in Denmark', in Foreman-Peck and Muller (eds.), *European Telecommunications Organisation*, 109–29, and in the same volume, J. Foreman-Peck and D. Manning, 'Telecommunications in Italy', 181–201. See also Centre Européen de l'Entreprise Publique, *The Evolution of Public Enterprises in the Community of the Nine* (London: CEEP English Editions, 1973).

3 L. Jeding, 'Liberalisation and Control: Instruments and Strategy in the Regulation of Reform of Swedish Telecommunications', in L. Magnusson and J. Ottosson, *Evolutionary Economics and Path Dependence* (Cheltenham: Edward Elgar, 1997), 166–82.

4 On Germany, see F. Thomas, 'The Politics of Growth: The German Telephone System', in R. Maintz and T. P. Hughes (eds.), *The Development of Large Technical Systems* (Boulder, Colo.: Frankfurt and Westview Press, 1978), 179–213.

5 K. H. Neumann and B. Wieland, 'Competition and Social Objectives: The Case of West German Telecommunications', *Telecommunications Policy* 10 (1986), 125.

6 The wider questions about the role of profits are discussed in chapter 14.

7 Foreman-Peck and Mueller (eds.), *European Telecommunications Organisation*, 39.

8 G. D. Nguyen, 'Telecommunications in France', in Foreman-Peck and Mueller (eds.), *European Telecommunications Organisation*, 146. For more discussion of telephone tariffs and universal service, see G. Knieps, 'De-Regulation in Europe: Telecommunications and Transportation', in G. Majone (ed.), *De-Regulation or Re-Regulation?: Regulation in Europe and the United States* (London: Pinter, 1990), 72–100.

9 C. Bertho-Lavenir, 'The Telephone in France 1879–1979: National Characteristics and International Influences', in Maintz and Hughes (eds.), *The Development of Large Technical Systems*, 155–73.

10 S. Littlechild, 'The Effect of Ownership on Telephone Concentration', *Telecommunications Policy* 7 (1983), 246–7.

11 For the view that technological change was a prime mover in de-regulation of telecommunications, see P. Koebel, 'De-Regulation in the Telecommunications Sector: A Movement in Line with Recent Technological Advances', in Majone (ed.), *De-Regulation or Re-Regulation?*, 110–23. For background, see G. D. Nguyen, 'Telecommunications: A Challenge to the Old Order', in M. Sharp (ed.), *Europe and the New Technologies: Six Case Studies in Innovation and Adjustment* (London: Pinter, 1985), 87–133; K. Dyson, 'West European States and the Communications Revolution', in K. Dyson and P. Humphries

(eds.), *The Politics of the Communications Revolution in Europe* (London: Cass, 1986), 10–55; Koebel, 'De-Regulation in the Telecommunications Sector'.
12 Knieps, 'De-Regulation in Europe: Telecommunications and Transportation'.
13 J. H. Solomon, 'Telecommunications Evolution in the UK', *Telecommunications Policy* 10 (1986), 186–92.
14 Nguyen, 'Telecommunications in France'.
15 D. Manning, 'Telecommunications in Spain', in Foreman-Peck and Mueller (eds.), *European Telecommunications Organisation*, 237–55.
16 A. Haid and J. Muller, 'Telecommunications in the Federal Republic of Germany', in Foreman-Peck and Mueller (eds.), *European Telecommunications Organisation*, 169; in the same volume, see also Nguyen, 'Telecommunications in France' (pp. 131–54), J. Foreman-Peck and D. Manning, 'Telecommunications Policy in the United Kingdom' (pp. 257–78) and Jeppson, Paulsen and Schneider, 'Telecommunications Services in Denmark' (pp. 109–29).
17 Nguyen, 'Telecommunications in France'.
18 J.-.P. Coustel, 'Telecommunications Services in France: The Regulatory Movement and the Challenge of Competition', *Telecommunications Policy* 10 (1986), 229–43. For the UK, see M. Florio, 'The Privatisation of British Telecom', *Economia Pubblica* 33 (2) (2003), 187–220 and *The Great Divestiture: The Welfare Effects of British Privatisation* (Cambridge, Mass.: MIT Press, 2004). For more on the role of interest groups, see K. Morgan and D. Webber, 'Divergent Paths: Political Strategies for Telecommunications in Britain, France and West Germany', in Dyson and Humphries (eds.), *The Politics of the Communications Revolution in Europe*, 56–79; also in the same volume, P. Humphries, 'Legitimising the Communications Revolution: Government, Parties and Trade Unions in Britain, France and West Germany', 163–94.
19 Bertho-Lavenir, 'The Telephone in France 1879–1979'; Jeding, 'Liberalisation and control'.
20 J. Richardson, 'Policy, Politics and the Communications Revolution in Sweden', in Dyson and Humphreys, *The Politics of the Communications Revolution in Europe*, 80–97; C. B. Blankart, 'Strategies of Regulatory Reform: An Economic Analysis with Some Remarks on Germany', in Majone (ed.), *De-Regulation or Re-Regulation*, 211–22; Haid and Muller, 'Telecommunications in the Federal Republic of Germany'.

14 Economic policy, financial accountability and productivity growth

State enterprises were formed as a result of government disinclination to leave the infrastructure industries to arm's-length regulation of private firms. As we have seen in earlier chapters, a whole raft of non-commercial obligations were laid on them: promoting regional development and network integration, aiding working-class living standards, curbing monopoly profits, controlling strategically important resources like coal, oil and airspace. After 1945 these obligations came to be formalised under the title of the 'public interest'. This still left many policy areas unspecified – in particular, how far should public sector prices reflect costs in different sectors, how should investment projects be evaluated? Left to their own devices, state industry managers would tend to look for a 'business approach'. This then raises the issue of how pricing and investment policy could reflect the public interest. Such conundrums generated a whole new industry of professional economists designing price and investment policies for public-sector firms. In this chapter I first provide a brief outline of the economists' theory about state enterprise. Put crudely, it amounted to advocating cost-based tariffs, fares and rates. There was considerable resistance to widespread adoption of such policies because they conflicted violently with the policy objectives under which state enterprise had been established. I then ask how far the actual and the recommended policies were consistent with the key financial requirement laid on state enterprise, that of ensuring that revenues covered costs. Finally, we examine how the productivity record of state enterprises compares with privatised regimes.

Much of the normative economic theory of state enterprise can be summed up as requiring the following:

(1) Output should be expanded in each sector as long as the additional economic benefits exceed the resource costs – but no further.
(2) Policies for altering the distribution of income in an economy should employ the tax-transfer system as its chief instrument, rather than bending the rule in (1).

Setting aside the problem of economies of scale (generating natural monopoly conditions) and external effects (from congested roads, education and communications spillovers etc.), the rule in (1) has a very simple interpretation. It is a plea for cost-based prices subject to the requirement that any monopoly power is not exploited. Since the economic benefits of extra output to consumers can be interpreted as being reflected in the price they pay, the rule is that output should be expanded, for each product and service, in each sector and region, as long as the associated marginal cost is less than price. If price is greater or less than marginal cost, resource savings can be made by reallocating resources across sectors until prices are equal to marginal costs. This led scholars to object that a price equal to short-run marginal costs would not cover overheads.[1] The answer lay in rule (1), which implied a criterion for investment decisions: undertake all investments where the present value of the stream of revenues exceeds the present value of the stream of costs. Put in terms of annual costs, this was equivalent, as the French economists ably demonstrated, to requiring an expansion of capacity when long-run marginal cost was less than price.[2] With these rules, prices would be equal to both long- and short-run marginal costs – at least when all such investments had been undertaken. Moreover, our assumption that there are no significant economies of scale guarantees that long-run marginal costs would equal long-run average costs. Average cost would equal average revenue, total cost would equal total revenue and the enterprise would be breaking even, just earning a normal return on its capital.

External effects and natural monopoly conditions raise significant theoretical and practical problems, but even without those complications, the advocates of marginal-cost pricing faced much opposition. Under the regimes that emerged in the late 1940s, a shift to cost-based tariffs, rates and fares would have had wide implications. It would have meant much higher charges for peak-period services, in electricity supply and railways for example, than for off-peak periods. It would have involved a shift away from the traditional railway practice of levying rates for freight traffic that reflected the value of the consignment to a system based on costs. It would have required capital projects to be evaluated by discounted cash-flow techniques. It would have required that prices clear markets – since otherwise, with rationing and queuing, they would not equal marginal costs. The most celebrated example of the early implementation of marginal-cost pricing linked to investment planning was the *tarif vert* of Electricité de France, though it should be noted that initially it only applied to industrial customers, and the residential sector was much smaller than in Britain and Germany and would in those countries have required the costly installation of time-of-day meters.[3] Elements of marginal-cost pricing could be found in several other state enterprises. For example, the Central Electricity Generating Board imposed time-of-day differentials on its charges to its bulk retailers, the area electricity boards in England and Wales. But for much of the period 1945–80, there is little evidence of its being adopted as a general practice, notwithstanding the entreaties of economists and civil servants.

There were very good reasons for this opposition, because marginal cost pricing flew in the face of the objectives and guidelines that governments set for their state enterprises. So far as the general level of public-sector prices is concerned, governments were loathe, in times of shortages, to let prices clear markets. This was evidently so in the reconstruction period of the late 1940s and was especially important for commodities like coal. Nor were governments willing to expose their coal industries to the full blast of market forces after the reconstruction years, when oil and electricity ate into their consumer markets. A true marginal-cost pricing regime would have allowed coal prices to be determined at the world level, but competition from Poland and other coal-rich countries would have raised the unemployment of coal miners in Britain, France, Belgium and Germany to even higher levels. Again, when inflation took off in the late 1960s in all European countries and then accelerated with the 1973/4 oil price hike, governments generally were reluctant to let public sector prices follow the market, hoping instead, by restricting their increase, to set examples for the rest of the economy. Moreover, the impact on particular customer groups of the introduction of marginal-cost pricing would have conflicted strongly with universal service provision. For example, this was a long-standing problem in the railways. In the 1920s, German politicians, civil servants and railway personnel alike saw 'the overall solvency of the [German railway system] ... as desirable ... [but] ... rejected economic measures of the viability of individual services ... [since the aim was] ... to shield groups from ... locational disadvantages'. The railway was 'actively engaged in subsidising disadvantaged groups such as the poor, peasants, veterans, and the aged... It was also an agent in the government's efforts to support infant industries and to promote exports'.[4] This philosophy persisted into the post-1945 period. Cost-based tariffs proved to be a difficulty even in French electricity. With the *tarif vert*, the full logic of cost-based pricing was finessed when it came to supplying scantily populated regions where distribution costs were high. Such regions were given a fictitious population for purposes of calculating the tariff.

In fact, all state enterprises from the 1950s onwards saw the gradual introduction of cost-based tariffs, rates and fares, but the process was slow and was much more the result of growing financial pressure on managers from the 1960s onwards and of growing competition from other firms, rather than from following the advice of economists. Competition increased in part as a product of technological changes and, from the mid-1970s, as a result of liberalisation of markets. The western European coal industry had declined so much by the 1970s that the coal enterprises lacked the power to resist freer competition from other fuels and in particular the growing international trade in coal, as described in chapter 11. It was also increasing competition from road transport that forced the railways to offer cheap rates when their costs were low (off-peak passengers, bulky long-distance freight loads) and raise charges where costs were high (peak passenger travel, small consignments of short-distance freight traffic).[5] Air travel, as indicated earlier, was initially dominated by scheduled services with fares fixed by IATA and implicitly linked to the costs of the least efficient carriers. A growing competition for the European state airlines followed the introduction of faster, bigger and more comfortable aircraft and came from the American airlines and from the emergence of non-scheduled charter services, both of which eventually undermined the IATA system, though it was over a very long period, and not until the 1990s were some of the main features of pricing and air rights overthrown. The introduction of cost-based pricing structures invariably made some groups worse off and some better off. This was the case in telecommunications where, again as we saw earlier, the shift to a more cost-based tariff system was ushered in by the great technological changes in customer premises equipment and proved economically beneficial for businesses, urban areas and long-distance callers at the expense of the residential, rural and short-distance customer groups.

In summary, each European government exerted pressure, formally or informally, on state enterprises to undertake non-commercial activities, and initially the universal service provision with uniform prices was consistent with that stance. The impact of advice from professional economists seems to have been small, with marginal-cost pricing more a matter for the economics journals than for state-enterprise managers. The push to a more cost-based pricing structure came from rising financial pressures, from changes in technology and from market liberalisation. Much of this occurred slowly but did materialise even before the privatisation and deregulation of the 1980s and 1990s. In the 1960s, European governments had become more concerned about the finances of state enterprises as the continuing list of non-commercial obligations clashed with the explicit directive of these enterprises to break even in financial terms. The problem manifested itself in two ways. One was the extent to which state enterprises could self-finance their capital investment programmes. The second and related phenomenon was the level of annual profits or losses.

Although the treatment of state enterprises varied across countries, their financial relationship to the state may be characterised simply as follows. Capital investment by state enterprises was, alongside road building, current expenditure on police and so on, part of public expenditure programmes, whilst their operating surpluses were, along with taxes, social security payments and so on, part of government income. State enterprise investment was financed by ploughed-back profits and by loans or fixed interest stock issued or guaranteed by the state or the capital market. The operating surpluses were allocated to paying interest, redemptions and related capital charges and meeting any specific capital taxes or charges required by the state. Any balance left over was available, in some countries, for financing investment. This self-financing element came increasingly to be a concern of governments. On a priori grounds there was nothing wrong in resorting to external finance. Indeed, when it involved the capital market (whether for public or private enterprise), there was likely to be a more stringent test of the economic viability of the project than when internal funds were used. This, however, is not the issue here. Rather, I am concerned to evaluate how far state enterprises were able to meet the financial obligations laid on them by governments. As public expenditure rose in the 1950s and 1960s, Treasury departments of state came to be more and more wedded to the idea that state enterprises should raise the level of self-financing. The worry was that prices were not being set sufficiently high enough to generate funds that could be invested back in the business. Instead, these enterprises were absorbing funds from the state and the private capital market, and thereby overexpanding relative to the private industrial sector, which traditionally financed much of its investment from profits.

The scale of the problem and the reaction of governments varied across Europe. Some indication of the extent to which prices were allowed to fall below costs is given in the data for state railways in Table 14.1. For each country it shows the proportion of costs not covered by revenue. Costs are proxied by outgoings on current and capital expenditure. Revenues exclude government subsidies and grants and hence relate simply to traffic receipts. On that basis, the state railways in Italy set the lowest rates and fares (relative to costs) and therefore, implicitly, received the largest government support. Belgium, Denmark, Germany, France and the Netherlands were covering only about 50–60% of their costs, while railways in Sweden and the UK had least support from their governments. In France and the UK, worries about finance emerged in important government papers: the Nora Report of 1967 in France and two white papers in the UK in 1961 and 1967.[6] In the latter, target rates of return were set, and during the 1960s at least the financial position of the nationalised industries did improve. The Nora Committee report well

Table 14.1 *Subsidies to state railways, 1977*
(percentage of current and capital expenditure
not covered by traffic receipts)

Italy	69
Belgium	50
Germany	46
France	44
Netherlands	43
Norway	40
Denmark	37
Britain	28
Sweden	16

Source: Interpolated from the chart in Table 10.4 of
C. Nash, 'European Railway Comparisons – What Can
we Learn?', in K. J. Button and D. C. Pitfield (eds.),
International Railway Economics (Aldershot: Gower,
1985), 267.

expressed the difficulties of running state enterprises. It felt that it was important to define the three roles of the state: to ensure a good return on the nation's capital, to provide subsidies and grants for supporting public services, and to manage the macro-economy. It posed three questions:

Question I: Quelle est la mission du secteur?
Question II: Comment financier les grandes entreprises publiques?
Question III: Comment diriger les entreprises publiques?[7]

In other words, what are the aims of the public sector and how are state enterprises to be financed and managed? The view of the Nora Committee was that explicit contracts be introduced to govern the relationship between the state and the enterprises, setting out targets, non-commercial obligations and financial accountability. Some contracts were drawn up with electricity, railways and radio/TV enterprises, and there were some cuts in subsidies and increases in self-financing as a result of the recommendations. However, in both France and Britain these developments were overtaken, as we shall see, by the crushing effects of the late 1960s and 1970s inflation of the general price level and the associated squeeze on public-sector prices. This lowered annual profits and the degree of self-financing of investment in Britain and in several other European countries. In France, the main effect was on annual profits.

An indication of the scale of the self-financing problem is given in Table 14.2, where every attempt has been made to assemble data that are comparable across countries. The entries relate to the percentage of annual capital investment financed from net operating surpluses – defined here as revenues less all operating expenses, taxes and interest charges but without deducting depreciation provisions. Three features emerge. Firstly, it seems that about 30–40% of investment was being self-financed by the early 1960s, notwithstanding some variability across sectors and countries. The major source of finance was external – in many cases the state. The self-financing ratios were well below what was happening in the private sector, where new equity issues and debentures traditionally accounted for only a small proportion of investment finance. Secondly, it is clear from the German data and we know it is true of several other countries that the railways were unable to meet much of their vast investment programmes from internal sources. Thirdly, there is some tendency to secular decline over the 1960s and 1970s in the self-financing ratio. To some extent this was a product of inflationary trends in the late 1960s and 1970s. The general price level was rising in all European countries at some 6% or more in the late 1960s, rising to 20% or more in some countries by the mid-1970s, fuelled by the oil price hike of 1973/4. This had a major impact on the costs of the infrastructure industries, and the increases in costs were not completely passed on in their own prices so that the finance available for investment often fell. This is evident in Table 14.2 for electricity supply and state-owned industry in Italy, for the aggregate of all public corporations in Britain and the railways in Germany. This was less the case in France, where the 1970s squeeze took the form of reduced finance from the state and increasing resort to the capital market.[8]

The picture from annual profits is even clearer. If it is desired to compare the profitability of public and private enterprise, the most appropriate measure would be gross operating profits before interest and other capital charges, as a percentage of the capital stock. Since state enterprises finance a large part of their investment from fixed-interest borrowing, it would be inappropriate to compare profits after interest charges, since private firms rely much less on fixed-interest debt. However, my real concern is to evaluate how far state enterprises met the financial objectives set by their governments. The requirement to break even implies that revenue, including all government grants and subsidies, should be just enough to cover all outgoings including taxes, depreciation, interest and other capital charges. The test is how far such net profits approached zero. Note that grants and subsidies should be included as part of revenues because the question is how far state enter-prises met their financial targets, and these targets included some explicit financial allowances for non-commercial activities.

Table 14.2 *Financing of investment in European public enterprises 1963–1976 (% of annual fixed capital formation which was self-financed)* [a]

| | Italy | | France | | Germany | | | UK |
	Electricity	Industry[b]	Electricity	All Public Enterprises	Railways & posts	Telecom	All Public Undertakings[c]	All Public Corporations
1961	–	–	–	30	–	–	–	–
1962	–	–	–	23	–	–	42	–
1963	34	27.4	–	20	–	–	49	40
1964	38	27.4	–	23	0	43	49	37
1965	33	39.4	36	25	4	28	57	38
1966	30	39.4	36	–	0	43	71	29
1967	27	39.4	39	40	9	46	75	25
1968	19	39.4	40	44	-0.5	41	76	35
1969	27	39.4	49	47	22	37	72	44
1970	23	27.5	55	48	18	11	70	36
1971	16	27.5	53	–	26	15	66	34
1972	6	27.5	64	52	-46	32	–	25
1973	4	27.5	66	53	-7	36	–	23
1974	0	27.5	35	36	-31	34	–	2
1975	0	–	44	37	-46	58	–	11
1976	0	–	40	35	-36	72	–	33

Notes:

[a] Operating surplus, before depreciation but after taxes and interest charges, as a percentage of gross fixed capital formation and addition to stocks.

[b] Annual averages for 1960–4, 1965–9 and 1970–74.

[c] Enterprises where public authorities own 50% or more of shares.

Sources:

Italy: Electricity data for Ente Nazionale de l'Energia Elettrica (ENEL) from A. Sembenelli, 'Investimenti, strategie e vincoli fininziari', in G. Zanetti (ed.), *Storia dell' industria elettrica in Italia. V. Glisviluppi dell ENEL. 1963–1990* (Roma-Bari: Laterza & Figli, 1994), 740, 741, 747, 748. Industry data refers to Istituto per la Ricostruzione Industriale (IRI) and taken from Centre Européen de l'Entreprise Publique, *The Financing of Public Enterprises in the Countries of the European Community* (London: CEEP English Editions, 1978), 148.

France: Data for Electricité de France from CEEP, *The Financing of Public Enterprises*, 115. Entries for all public enterprises for 1972–6 from CEEP, *The Financing of Public Enterprises*, 97; 1967–70 data from Centre Européen de l'Entreprise Publique, *The Evolution of Public Enterprises in the Community of the Nine* (London: CEEP English Editions, 1973), 143; data for 1961–5 from the Nora Report (Groupe de Travail du Comité Interministeriel des Entreprises Publiques, *Rapport sur les entreprises publiques* (Paris: La Documentation Française, Editions de Secrétariat Général de Gouvernment, Direction de la Documentation, April 1967), 54).

Germany: For Bundesbahn and Bundespost, see CEEP, *The Financing of Public Enterprises*, 167, 174. Data on all public undertakings from CEEP, *The Evolution of Public Enterprises*, 63.

Britain: Central Statistical Office, *National Income and Expenditure* (London: HMSO, various issues, 1957–90).

Table 14.3 *Net profits[a] of state railways (selected years 1949–1975)*

	UK British Rail (£ million)	Germany Deutsche Bundesbahn (billion DM)	Sweden Statens Järnväger (million kroner)	Italy Ferrovie della Stato (billion lira)	Spain Red Nacional de Ferrocarriles Españoles (billion pesetas)
1949	−16.3	—	−1.2 (1948)[b]	—	−0.7
1953	−2.1	—	−8.0[b]	—	−0.8
1958	−94.3	—	−14.0[b]	—	−1.8
1960	−122.4	—	−19.0[b]	—	−2.4
1963	−159.2	—	−19.0[b]	−60.5[c]	−4.9
1965	−159.0	−1.3	−19.0[b]	−60.5[c]	−3.5
1966	−160.2	−1.1	−34.0[b]	−290.5[c]	−3.8
1967	−186.6	−1.5	−34.0[b]	−290.5[c]	−3.8
1968	−184.6	−1.2	−34.0[b]	−290.5[c]	−5.9
1969	−94.5	−1.0	−34.0[b]	−290.5[c]	−4.6
1970	−92.7	−1.25	−34.0[b]	−290.5[c]	−3.7
1971	−109.9	−2.5	−26.0[b]	−290.5[c]	−3.8
1972	−147.8	−2.5	−26.0[b]	−476.9[c]	−3.1
1973	−153.1	−2.5	−26.0[b]	−476.9[c]	−2.4
1974	−158	−2.8	−26.0[b]	−476.9[c]	−4.4
1975	−61	−4.4	−26.0[b]	−476.9[c]	−13.7

Notes:

[a] Net profits comprise all receipts and grants less all operating expenses, depreciation, taxes, interest and all other capital charges.

[b] Annual averages over five-year periods.

[c] Annual average 'operating deficits' for 1963–5, 1966–71 and 1972–75.

Sources: United Kingdom: T. Gourvish, *British Railways 1948–73: A Business History* (Cambridge University Press, 1986), 585; T. Gourvish, *British Rail 1974–97: From Integration to Privatisation* (Oxford University Press, 2002), 21–2. Passenger grants are included from 1969. After 1973, profits reflect, in part, the writing-down of assets and new funding for public service obligations.

Germany: CEEP, *Evolution of Public Enterprises,* 85; CEEP, *The Financing of Public Enterprise,* 166.

Sweden: Entries are five-year annual averages derived from five-year totals of 'net income' less interest charges interpolated from Figure 1 of L. Andersson-Skog, 'From State Railway Housekeeping to Railway Economics: Swedish Railway Policy and Economic Transformation after 1920 in an Institutional Perspective', *Scandinavian Economic History Review* 49 (1) (1996).

Italy: CEEP, *The Financing of Public Enterprise,* 128–9.

Spain: Data kindly supplied by Francisco Comin from the Archivo Historico Ferrorario, Fundacion de los Ferrocarriles Españoles.

Table 14.4 Net profits[a] in state energy enterprises (selected years 1949–1981)

	UK (£ million)			Denmark (thousand kroner)	France (million francs)			Germany (million DM)			Italy (million lira)
	Electr.	Gas	Coal	Electr.	Electr.	Gas	Coal	Electr.	Gas	Coal	Electr.
1949	7	–	9.5	–	–	–5.5	1.2	–	–	–	–
1951	3	–	–8.2	–	4.4	–	0.9	–	–	–	–
1952	7	–	0.5	–	–	–	–4.7	–	–	–	–
1954	19	–	–19.6	–	3.1	–	–9.4	–	–	–	–
1956	12	3.8	12.8	–	–	–	–	–	–	–	–
1960	16	2.1	–21.3	–	–	–	–120	–	–	–	–
1965	85	11.1	–24.8	–	2	–	–	–	–	–	0
1966	21	3.9	0.3	–	25	–	–	130	–	–	0
1967	55	–12.9	–	–	–12	–	–	109	–	–	0
1968	101	17.5	–8.9	116	–157	–272	–166	112	–	–	0
1969	65	13.7	–26.1	138	–16	–190	–54	117	1.6	–161	0
1970	–56	2.0	0.5	–	–56	–180	–4	135	–2.3	–59	0
1971	–23	15.1	–157	115	–179	–115	–29	–	–8.6	–41	0
1972	2	5.6	–83.7	–	51	–	–	–	–	–	–268
1973	–	–	–	–	2	–107	–124	–	–	–	–520
1974	–	–	–	–	–1420	–282	–12	–	–	–	–
1975	–	–	–	–	–341	91	–566	–	–	–	–
1980	–	–	–	–	–655	17	–	–	–	–	–
1981	–	–	–	–	–	–	–	–	–	–	–2000

Notes:

[a] Net profits comprise all receipts and grants less all operating expenses, depreciation, taxes, interest and all other capital charges.

Sources:

United Kingdom: For 1949–54 the sources for coal and electricity are the *Annual Accounts* of the National Coal Board and of the electricity boards in England, Wales and Southern Scotland. Thereafter, the electricity entries exclude Southern Scotland and, together with coal, are taken from G. and P. Polanyi, *Failing the Nation: The Record of the Nationalised Industries* (London: Fraser Ansbacher, 1974), 20. This is also the source for the Gas Council and area boards.

Denmark: Aggregate of all the seven major electricity distribution companies (except IFV) reported in CEEP, *The Evolution of Public Enterprises*, 53.

France: Entries relate to Charbonnages de France, Electricité de France and Gaz du France (combined with EDF for 1949). Note that the 1949–54 data are in billion old francs. Sources are W. C. Baum, *The French Economy and the State* (Princeton University Press, 1958), Table 26; CEEP, *Evolution of Public Enterprises*, 139 and 148–51; CEEP, *Public Enterprises in the European Community* (London: CEEP English Editions, 1978), 84–93; F. Vinck and J. Boursin, 'The Development of the Public and Private Sectors of the Coal Mining Industry in Europe: A Comparative Study', *Annals of Public and Collective Economy* 33 (1962), 385–491. The 1968–71 entries for coal are aggregates of the data in CEEP, *Evolution of Public Enterprises* for CDF and the Houillères du Bassins for Centre du Midi, Lorraine and Nord et Pas de Calais.

Germany: The electricity entries relate to Vereinigte Industrieunternehmen AG (VIAG), which accounted for 7.6% of electricity generated in West Germany in 1970. See Tables III and XIV of R. Keutgen, 'The Vereingte Industrie-Unternehmen AG: A German Public Enterprise', *Annals of Public and Collective Economy* 42 (1971), 305–46. The entry for gas covers the ten publicly owned gas enterprises, and the entry for coal covers the four mining enterprises with large state holdings, CEEP, *Evolution of Public Enterprises*, 10.

Italy: Source is the data on ENEL compiled by A. Giuntini in the statistical appendix of Zanetti (ed.), *Gli sviluppi dell ENEL*, 869–70. See also N. Lucas, *Western European Energy Policies* (Oxford: Clarendon Press, 1985), 161.

Table 14.5 Net profits[a] of national airlines (selected years 1951–1977)

	UK BOAC/BEA (£ million)	Netherlands KLM (million guilders)	France Air France (million francs)	Germany Lufthansa (million DM)	Italy Alitalia (million lira)
1951	-4.1	10.5	-1930 (1950)	-	-260 (1950)
1955	1.3	-	-3260	-20.5	-
1956	-	23.0	-	-20.1	49
1957	2.3	-	-	-27.1	5
1961	5.8	-76.7	-61(1960)	-109.1	-
1962	-	-	-	-46.4	1055
1965	20.9	-	34	43.0	-
1971	17.3	-96.3	12(1970)	-34.0	-
1972	-	-	-	56.8	-6266
1973	22.4	-	-	-45.7	-
1975	-1.8	-	-354	33.5	-
1976	2.7	77.5	-	112.3	-
1977	95.8	-	-	39.7	11,122

Note:

[a] Net profits comprise all receipts and grants less all operating expenses, depreciation, taxes, interest and all other capital charges.

Sources: The main source is H.-L. Dienel and P. Lyth (eds.), *Flying the Flag: European Commercial Air Transport since 1945* (Basingstoke: Macmillan, 1998).

United Kingdom: Up to 1973 the entries are an aggregate of the profits of BOAC and BEA. Thereafter they relate to British Airways. The source is P. Lyth, 'Chosen Instruments: The Evolution of British Airways', in Dienel and Lyth (eds.), *Flying the Flag*, Tables 3.2, 3.3, 3.4, 3.5.

The Netherlands: Data on Royal Dutch Airline (KLM) from Table 5.3 of M. Dierikx, 'KLM: An Airline Outgrowing its Flag', in Dienel and Lyth (eds.), *Flying the Flag*.

France: Table 2.2 of N. Niertz, 'Air France: An Elephant in an Evening Suit', in Dienel and Lyth (eds.), *Flying the Flag*.

Germany: Table 4.3 of H.-L. Dienel, 'Lufthansa: Two German Airlines' in Dienel and Lyth (eds.), *Flying the Flag*.

Obtaining comparable data across enterprises and countries is, again, fraught with problems, and Tables 14.3, 14.4 and 14.5 rely in part on data collected by the Centre Européen de l'Entreprise Publique (CEEP) and although there are several gaps and omissions, they provide a good guide for our test. One message is clear: taken as a whole, state enterprises failed to break even over the period 1948–80. The reason could be that the complex of non-commercial objectives were insufficiently supported by governments or that the industries were inefficiently managed. The latter issue is addressed in the next section of this chapter, but it is well to note in advance that there is no clear evidence that state enterprises in Europe had an inferior productivity record to the private sector. Rather, for much of the period, governments and public enterprises were learning to reconcile the non-commercial objectives with break-even require-ments and they largely failed. This conclusion is reinforced once it is recognised that state-enterprise managers were able in some sectors to generate normal profits, and these were invariably industries that were young, growth sectors less saddled with a past accumulation of non-commercial obligations.

Thus the railways, one of the oldest and largest utilities, expected since the mid-nineteenth century to promote national unification and to pro-vide equal access to all, were already in deficit in the late 1940s. By the mid-1970s, the annual losses of French railways (SNCF) were 1.1 billion francs.[9] The time series data in Table 14.3 show continuing large finan-cial deficits from the late 1940s through to the mid-1970s, in Spain, Germany and Britain, whilst the five-year average profit data for Sweden and Italy paint the same picture. Europe's old coal industries were in the process of rapid decline and the entries in Table 14.4 for France, the UK and Germany again tell a similar story. On the other hand, the huge expansion in telecommunications (cf. Table 13.1) and electricity supply was profitable at least until the early 1970s. The profit-ability of airlines, as a brand new industry, varied considerably across countries and periods, as Table 14.5 shows. Up to the 1970s, KLM, BOAC, BEA and Alitalia managed to hold their own financially. Air France started off disastrously but was breaking even by the late 1960s. Lufthansa took even longer. Most state enterprises suffered in the early 1970s from the restriction on public-sector price changes as general inflation took off and governments tried to use public-sector price restraints to set examples for others. Governments seemed unwilling to immediately subsidise the price restrictions so that recorded deficits increased. Electricity supply in 1971 witnessed losses of 179 million francs in France, £23 million in the UK and 268 million lira in Italy in 1972.[10] Railway deficits approached record levels in 1973. The postal service in the UK recorded a loss of £109 million in 1974, whilst in the Netherlands the loss in 1975 was 152 million guilders (Table 13.1). When, later on, an attempt was made to recover the financial position, huge increases in public-sector prices were necessary so that this whole episode from the late 1960s to the late 1970s, became an indelible blot on the record of public enterprises and an important ingredient of the drive to privatisation.

Productivity growth under nationalised and privatised regimes 1950–90

Whatever level and type of service provided by state enterprises, an important question is whether the service is produced more or less cheaply than in other institutional settings. Was productivity higher and did it grow faster in state enterprises than in private enterprises? Such questions about what came to be known as 'X efficiency' formed an important element in the debate on privatisation from the 1970s onwards. In the early postwar period, they were little discussed. Professional economists and other commentators focused instead on the issue of 'allocative efficiency' – how price levels and investment criteria would affect the allocation of resources between different parts of the economy (cf. previous section). Indeed, the rationale for the boundary between public and private was rarely examined in the 1950s and 1960s. Europe had mixed economies and, so the argument went, the main issue was to look at how the behaviour of public firms would best promote allocative efficiency in such economies.

Two forces made for a changed perspective. One was the problem of running state enterprises that were unprofitable. The huge financial losses that arose in the 1970s led many to think that these enterprises were badly managed. Another element was the long-standing distrust of public enterprise in the USA. American economists came to dominate much of the post-1950s' academic economics literature, and some of them were articulating persuasive critical theorems about the state sector. Alchian, de Alessi and many others were arguing that what characterised state enterprise was the inability of taxpayers, as ultimate owners, to exert pressure on management. In private firms, each shareholder, it was argued, had a unilateral ability to sell shares and change managerial behaviour.[11]

In this light, how did European state enterprises perform in the period c. 1948–80? The issue is not whether state enterprises were profitable – since their monopoly position and supervision by governments removed the significance of profits. Nor is X efficiency concerned with the levels of production and the range of products and services. Rather, the focus is the volume of resources used to produce the various constellations of services and products. Common measures are output per employee hour (labour productivity) or, better still, one that brings in capital as well as labour, total factor productivity (TFP). The latter is output per unit of combined labour, capital and land, with these factors of production often combined by weights related to their share of costs. Raw material inputs are usually ignored in so far as output is measured as value added, that is net output. The main problem in evaluating state enterprise in these productivity terms is to find appropriate comparators. There have been many studies of public and private enterprises where they co-exist, as in the different municipalities of post-1945 USA, in nineteenth-century and early twentieth-century Britain, in Australian airlines and Canadian railways. The results are mixed, but an important message from many of the studies is that, for infrastructure enterprises, productivity performance was enhanced when they faced competition. For X efficiency, market structure was more important than ownership.[12]

Evaluating European state infrastructure enterprises over the post-1945 period is difficult because their monopoly position meant there were few private firms with which comparisons could be made. The alternative is to look at how these state enterprises performed relative to similar sectors in other countries like the USA, where private enterprise was more common. To make any sense of such comparisons, it is important to place the experience of state enterprises within the wider setting of the fortunes of whole economies and in a long-term perspective. For example, labour productivity in the USA in the infrastructure industries was often double that in Europe, as we shall see. However, that was true in the nineteenth century when such firms were often privately owned in Europe. It was also true of US and European (private) manufacturing in the nineteenth and twentieth century. What is at issue is the impact on the infrastructure industries of the shift to state ownership in the more recent past.

Productivity trends through the second half of the twentieth century were affected by the problems of reconstruction after the Second World War and by the increasing accessibility of modern technology, allowing modern economies to catch up and converge on each other's income levels. In order to assess the place of the infrastructure industries in this picture, it is important to recognise that they are part of the service sector, which has come to account for over two-thirds of the labour force of the advanced economies in the last quarter of the twentieth century. Developments in the service sector have proved central to an understanding of the pattern of economic growth across different countries. In what follows attention has to be restricted to countries on whom comparative studies have been performed, and this means Germany, France and the UK. By the middle of the nineteenth century, Britain was economically dominant, with the highest level of income per head in the Western world and still enjoying a very high growth rate of industrial output. Towards the end of the century, national income per head was growing faster in the USA, who overtook Britain's level around the turn of the century. America became the technology leader in the twentieth century and suffered nowhere like the same devastation as Europe in the two World Wars. Since 1945, Europe has narrowed the gap, though, by the 1990s, American national output per hour worked was still 20% higher than in many European countries. The process of overtaking and convergence over the very long term varied across sectors. There was no catch up or convergence in manufacturing. In the nineteenth century, USA labour productivity in manufacturing was roughly double that in the UK and, setting aside short-term oscillations, that gap persisted to the end of the twentieth century. The availability and choice of different quantities of natural resources as well as product mix account for the stability in comparative productivity levels: mule spinning machines, skilled labour and fine cotton cloth in Britain; ring spinning machines, unskilled labour and coarser cloth in America. Germany showed labour productivity levels in manufacturing some 20% above the UK level in the late nineteenth century, a gap that was still present at the end of the twentieth century.[13]

This stability in comparative productivity levels in manufacturing suggests that, since British economic growth was less than the USA in the late nineteenth century, and indeed less than Germany and France, the proximate causes cannot lie in manufacturing. There are two main candidates. One is agriculture, which had shrunk to tiny proportions in Britain by the start of the twentieth century – about 5% of the labour force. Agriculture's share of output was much bigger but was declining in America and the continental European countries and, given its low productivity level, agriculture's decline played an important role in the catch up with Britain. The other part of the story is services. The available evidence suggests that the level of labour productivity in services in the USA and Germany in the late nineteenth century was less than in Britain. Table 14.6 shows that since the 1870s the levels in the USA and Germany grew and overtook the UK in the twentieth century. This was a major cause of the faster economic growth. Broadberry's thesis is that services were affected very much by changes in office technology (telephone, telegraph, typewriters, copiers etc.) in which the USA and Germany performed better than Britain, whose comparative advantage lay in networked services such as finance, whose productivity level remained higher in Britain into the interwar period, and with respect to Germany,

Table 14.6 *Labour productivity in the UK, the USA and Germany,*
1869–1990 (Output per employee: selected years: UK =100)

	Agriculture		Industry		Services		Total Economy	
	USA	Germany	USA	Germany	USA	Germany	USA	Germany
1871[a]	87	56	154	86	86	66	90	60
1911[a]	103	67	193	122	107	81	117	76
1935[a]	103	57	191	99	120	86	133	76
1950	126	41	244	96	141	83	163	74
1973	131	51	215	129	137	111	152	114
1990	151	75	163	117	129	130	133	125

[a] The USA data relate to annual averages of 1869/71, 1909/11 and 1937.

Source: S. N. Broadberry and S. Ghosal, 'From the Counting House to the Modern Office:
Explaining Comparative Productivity Performance in Services since 1870', *Journal of
Economic History* 62(4) (2002), Table 1.

up to the 1970s.[14] The shift to mechanised techniques in other services
had parallels in manufacturing where, however, competition across countries ensured that comparative productivity levels remained stable.
Services, in contrast, were traditionally not traded so freely, so that
British productivity in services fell further and further below the levels
in the USA and Germany, but without any major impact on the output of
British services.

That story does not carry over so readily to the second half of the
twentieth century. Europe started to reduce some of America's lead in
services as well as in industry. In addition, there was the complication that
the period from the 1940s to the 1970s is usually viewed as one where
nationalisation and heavy regulation characterised many service activities
in Europe, giving way to more competition as deregulation and privatisation took the stage from the late 1970s. Yet Germany's gains in services as
a group continued through both these periods, while output per employee
in British services rose relative to the USA in the first phase as well as the
second (Table 14.6). The post-1945 picture is in fact quite complex.
Economic losses during the war were much bigger in Europe than in
America, so an element of catch up with America was involved, at least for
the first few decades. We also have to allow for particular resource
endowments, such as the discovery of North Sea oil and gas, to set against
America's generally rich endowment of oil, coal and other minerals and
France's strengths in hydroelectricity. As the second half of the century
unfolded, competition and trade increased, not only in commodities,

but also in services, so that technological imitation and catch up became common.

The Second World War widened the gap in productivity levels between the USA and Europe, whose capital stock was severely run down, especially that in the infrastructure industries. Hence, the period since 1945 has in part been one of retrieving the pre-war relative productivity levels. The top half of Table 14.7 covers the period 1950–73 and confirms earlier studies, which have demonstrated a superior productivity performance in the British nationalised industries (railways excepted), relative to the USA.[15] The element of catch up is suggested by the fact that total factor productivity in manufacturing was also growing faster than in US manufacturing and that France and Germany, more devastated by the war than Britain, were doing even better in all sectors for which comparable data are available.

The dividing point in Table 14.7 is taken as the early 1970s – following the oil shock and the subsequent retreat from Bretton Woods and marking the shift to more deregulated economies. What can we deduce about productivity growth as between the two periods? The first period is one where the European infrastructure industries were in public ownership, the second, one of deregulation and privatisation from 1979, albeit at different speeds in different industries and countries. Some writers have argued that British performance in the infrastructure industries improved relative to other countries as it moved to more deregulated and privatised institutions.[16] Table 14.7 is derived from recent work by O'Mahony and involves new data on hours worked and capital services, which represent a considerable improvement on earlier studies.[17] The data suggest a much better performance of the UK nationalised electricity industry in the period 1950–73 than the same industry in the USA, while for 1979–97, which covers most of the privatised period, the total factor productivity (TFP) growth is less than in the USA, is less than growth in the more mixed regime in Germany, and all are less than the state-owned Electricité de France. O'Mahony and Vecchi indeed conclude 'that the productivity record ... [of the UK electricity industry] ... after privatisation can be summarised as being unremarkable ... Relative to its own past experience, or that in other countries, productivity in the UK privatised industry does not appear to have shown any pronounced improvement.'[18] In the case of air transport and communications (as well as manufacturing), it seems that the total factor productivity growth rates in the UK exceeded those in the USA in both periods. The American rates are of the order of 60–80% of the British growth rates. At the most, one might argue that Britain does slightly better, relative to America, in the second period, though of course all the growth rates (except

Table 14.7 *Productivity growth: international comparisons, 1950–1995 (annual average % growth in total factor productivity)*

	UK	USA	France	Germany
		1950–73		
Electricity	5.51	3.93	n.a.	n.a.
Gas	4.71	3.02	n.a.	n.a.
Coal mining	1.34	0.82	6.86	2.47
Railways	1.60	4.45	n.a.	n.a.
Air transport	11.53	9.55	n.a.	n.a.
Communications	2.13	1.73	n.a.	4.18
Manufacturing	3.28	1.95	4.22	4.12
		1973–95		
Electricity	1.53[a]	2.57[a]	3.69[a]	2.17[a]
Gas	4.16	−4.09	n.a.	0.79
Coal mining	7.89	3.09	2.21	0.37
Railways	1.17	5.90	n.a.	1.69
Air transport	4.48	2.81	n.a.	n.a
Communications	4.08	2.84	5.55	4.23
Manufacturing	1.85	1.21	2.47	1.89

Notes:
[a] 1979–97.

Total factor productivity growth is calculated as the growth rate of net output per hour weighted by labour's share of value added, plus the growth rate of net output per unit of capital services weighted by the remaining share of value added. In several cases, shares in value added had to be approximated by the data for wider industry grouping.

Sources: Derived from tables in chapter 4 of M. O'Mahony, *Britain's Productivity Performance: An International Perspective* (London: National Institute of Economic and Social Research, 1999). The 1979–97 data for electricity are from M. O'Mahony and M. Vecchi, 'The Electricity Supply Industry: A Study of an Industry in Transition', *National Institute Economic Review* 177 (2001), Table 4.

Table 14.8 *International comparisons of levels of capital intensity and productivity, 1950/1973/1995 (indexes based on UK = 100: selected sectors)*

	USA			France			Germany		
	K/L	TFP	Q/L	K/L	TFP	Q/L	K/L	TFP	Q/L
Electricity, gas and water									
1950	345	214	425	319	37	64	112	120	109
1973	228	219	370	220	88	143	121	119	134
1995	158	115	163	168	87	120	104	79	84
Transport and Communications									
1950	338	141	189	157	66	68	223	56	65
1973	223	139	174	130	107	113	166	81	92
1995	121	111	113	135	110	117	156	85	100
Distributive Trades									
1950	405	113	162	208	93	126	178	71	76
1973	188	119	146	172	116	139	182	90	106
1995	151	135	155	165	126	143	141	106	111
Finance and Business services									
1950	245	136	194	77	104	92	57	73	55
1973	106	182	187	57	215	169	79	150	134
1995	87	122	115	75	134	112	119	141	169
Manufacturing									
1950	273	216	290	104	72	77	92	84	74
1973	173	159	186	142	89	101	152	102	115
1995	161	142	171	171	103	130	156	108	126

Total economy

1950	339	146	195	133	74	79	135	65	63
1973	193	138	168	120	109	116	168	104	119
1995	128	112	121	149	118	132	172	109	129

Note:

K/L measures capital intensity as capital services (K) per employee hour (L). Q/L is labour productivity measured as net output (Q) per employee hour. TFP is total factor productivity measured as output per unit of labour and capital weighted by their base year shares of value added. All the 1950 entries for levels (except for Q/L) were derived from the growth rate data for the different countries and the 1973 level data.

Source: Derived from tables in chapter 4 of O'Mahony, *Britain's Productivity Performance.*

telecommunications) are less. Turning to the other sectors, the improved performance in UK gas for 1973–95 is largely a product of the newly discovered North Sea natural gas coming on stream in the 1970s, whereas US gas sales were declining faster than labour and capital could be shed. The output of coal was declining in Britain throughout the second half of the twentieth century and, together with the railways, remained in public ownership for all but the last few years. Employment also declined throughout, but whereas railway equipment was kept more or less intact, the decline in coal output was so severe that eventually it led to closure of mines, disposal of assets and hence a rise in capital productivity, which did not emerge until the last quarter of the century. In France and Germany, the whole process started later, since coal output was rising in the first period. The railway industry collapsed in the USA in the face, as noted earlier, of competition from airlines. These huge retrenchments of coal in Britain and railways in the USA were accompanied by higher TFP growth rates than in the railway industry in Britain and the coal industry in the USA. These trends seem unrelated to the pattern of ownership.

In order to extend the comparisons with France and Germany, it is necessary, because of data limitations, to use broader industry groupings, as in Table 14.8, where the nationalised sectors are not so easily identifiable. This table includes one group for transport and communications as a whole and one for the utilities: gas, electricity and water combined. Such group data have prompted Broadberry and Hannah to argue that the British performance in the infrastructure industries improved in the second period.[19] The table records index levels of total factor productivity (with UK = 100) in 1950, 1973 and 1995. It also includes index measures of capital per unit of labour (K/L) and labour productivity (Q/L). It does appear from the table that, in comparison to the USA, the British utilities show a deterioration in total factor productivity (TFP) in the first period whilst in the second period they show a large gain. But the 1970s saw, as we have seen, the start of returns from North Sea oil and gas. Moreover, the trends were similar in financial services, which were not nationalised. The distributive trades, which were not strongly regulated, declined relative to the USA in both periods. The transport and communications group includes many private-sector road transport firms in both the first and the second period, as well as the railways in the European countries that were in public ownership for both periods. TFP and labour productivity improved relative to the USA in the first period and even more so in the second. Whilst it is possible to point to the healthy investment record of the privatised British utilities in electricity and the like and in the transport sector in the 1973–95 period, the same could be said about the 1950–73 period, as is clear from Table 14.8.

The picture of public ownership is also muddied once it is recognised that the German and French infrastructures were heavily regulated and also largely publicly owned in the 1973–95 period. If the big gains in productivity in the British electricity and gas sectors relative to Germany in the period 1973–95 are attributed to privatisation (as opposed to North Sea gas), how is one to account for transport and communications, where German growth was greater in both periods, perhaps because, in terms of productivity levels, Germany was still behind Britain in the 1990s? Similarly, whilst capital intensity in French utilities (electricity in particular) was two or three times higher than in Britain, the overall TFP level was still lower than in Britain in the 1990s. The sheer size of the investment programme in French electricity was reflected in big gains in labour productivity relative to Britain, but one should recognise that Electricité de France was a nationalised enterprise and it dominated the energy sector for much of the second half of the twentieth century.

In summary, there is no evidence of a poor productivity growth record for state enterprises in Europe in the second half of the twentieth century. Total factor productivity growth in the European state-owned infrastructure industries in the period 1950–73 was, if anything, slightly better than that of similar industries in the more private-sector orientated USA. Nor does it appear that the early shift to privatisation and deregulation in Britain during the last quarter of the twentieth century was associated with a superior productivity record to that in other countries or to Britain under the nationalised regime of the 1945–73 period.

Notes

1 For a review of the early debates, see N. Ruggles, 'The Welfare Basis of the Marginal Cost Pricing Principle', *Review of Economic Studies* 17(1) (1949/50), 29–46.

2 See M. Boiteux, 'La Vente au coût marginal', *Revue Française de l'Energie* 81 (1956), 113–117, reproduced in English as ch. 3 of J. R. Nelson (ed.), *Marginal Cost Pricing in Practice* (Englewood Cliffs, N. J.: Prentice-Hall, 1964). Also M. Boiteux, 'La Tarification des demandes en pointe: Application de la théorie de la vente au coût marginal', *Revue Générale de l'Electricité* 58(8) (1949), 321–40, reprinted in English in *Journal of Business* 33 (1960), 157–29 and as ch. 4 of Nelson (ed.), *Marginal Cost Pricing*.

3 M. Chick, 'Le Tarif vert retrouvé: The Marginal Cost Concept and the Pricing of Electricity in Britain and France 1945–73', *Energy Journal* 23(1) (2002), 97–116; M. Boiteux, 'Le Tarif vert d'Electricité de France', *Revue Française de l'Energie* 82 (1957), 137–151, reprinted as ch. 6 of Nelson (ed.), *Marginal Cost Pricing*.

4 A. C. Mierzejewski, *The Most Valuable Asset of the Reich: A History of the German National Railway Company* (Chapel Hill: University of North Carolina Press,

1999), I, xv, and 'The German National Railway Company Confronts its Competitors 1920–39', *Business and Economic History* 25 (1996), 90. For French electricity, see Boiteux, 'Le Tarif vert', 143. For price restrictions in the 1970s, see *The Economist*, 'Public Sector Enterprise: The State in the Market' (30 December 1978), 37–58.

5 For the process in Sweden, see B. Fullerton, 'Deregulation in a European Context – The Case of Sweden', in P. Bell and P. Cloke, *Deregulation and Transport: Market Forces in the Modern World* (London: David Fulton Publishers, 1990), 125–40.

6 Groupe de Travail du Comité Interministériel des Entreprises Publiques (Nora Report), *Rapport sur les entreprises publiques* (Paris: La Documentation Française, Editions de Secrétariat Général de Gouvernment, Direction de la Documentation, April 1967); H. M. Treasury, *The Financial and Economic Objectives of the Nationalised Industries*, Command 1337 (London: HMSO, 1961); H. M. Treasury, *Nationalised Industries: A Review of Financial and Economic Objectives*, Command 3437 (London: HMSO, 1967). See also National Economic Development Office, *A Study of UK Nationalised Industries* (London: HMSO, 1976).

7 Nora Report, *Rapport sur les entreprises publiques*, 12. See also J. J. Bonnard, 'Planning and Industry in France', in J. Hayward and M. Watson (eds.), *Planning, Politics and Public Policy* (Cambridge University Press, 1975), 93–110; J. M. Sheahan, 'Experience with Public Enterprise in France and Italy', in W. G. Shepherd (ed.), *Public Enterprise: Economic Analysis in Theory and Practice* (London: Heath & Co., 1976), 123–83.

8 See J.-F. Picard, A. Beltran and M. Bungener, *Histoire de l'EDF* (Paris: Dunod, 1985), 111.

9 Centre Européen de l'Entreprise Publique, *Public Enterprises in the European Community* (London: CEEP English Editions, 1978), 84–93.

10 Some explanation is needed for the curious entries for Italian electricity in Table 14.4. ENEL started off in the early 1960s without the traditional 'development fund' provided for investment in public sector industries. Accounting conventions in the early period ensured that any deficits were matched by implicit or explicit government subsidy so that recorded net profits were zero as in Table 14.4. See A. Sembenelli, 'Investimenti, strategie e vincoli fininziari', in G. Zanetti (ed.), *Storia dell'industria elettrica in Italia. V. Glisviluppi dell ENEL. 1963–1990* (Roma-Bari: Laterza & Figli 1994), 733–74.

11 A. A. Alchian, 'Some Economics of Property Rights', *Il Politico* 30 (1965), 816–29, reproduced in A. A. Alchian, *Economic Forces at Work* (Indianapolis: Liberty Press, 1977); L. de Alessi, 'An Economic Analysis of Government Ownership and Regulation: Theory and Evidence from the Electric Power Industry', *Public Choice* 19 (1974), 1–42; W. A. Niskanen, *Bureaucracy and Representative Government* (New York: Aldine-Atherton, 1971).

12 For some recent surveys, see W. N. Megginson and J. M. Netter, 'From State to Market: A Survey of Empirical Studies on Privatisation', *Journal of Economic Literature* 39 (2001), 321–89; D. Newbery, *Privatisation, Restructuring and Regulation of Network Industries* (Cambridge, Mass.: MIT Press, 1999); M. Florio, *The Great Divestiture: The Welfare Effects of British Privatisation*

(Cambridge, Mass.; MIT Press, 2004), ch. 4; M. Sawyer and K. O'Donnell, *A Future for Public Ownership* (London: Lawrence Wishart, 1999); Y. Aharoni, 'The Performance of State Owned Enterprise', in P. A. Toninelli (ed.), *The Rise and Fall of State Owned Enterprise in the Western World* (Cambridge University Press, 2000), 49–76. For earlier surveys, see G. Yarrow, 'Privatisation in Theory and Practice', *Economic Policy* 2 (1980), 232–64 and R. Millward, 'The Comparative Performance of Public and Private Ownership', in J. Kay, C. Mayer and D. Thompson (eds.), *Privatisation and Regulation: The UK Experience* (Oxford: Clarendon Press, 1986).

13 S. N. Broadberry, 'Manufacturing and the Convergence Hypothesis: What the Long-Run Data Show', *Journal of Economic History* 53(4) (1993), 772–95. This underlines the dangers of simply comparing labour productivity levels unless one can be sure that the other factors of production – capital, land, natural resources – are the same. One recent example in the infrastructure sector is the study by M. Baily, 'Competition, Regulation and Efficiency in Service Industries', *Brookings Papers in Microeconomics* 2 (1993), 71–159. Baily found that, in the late 1980s and early 1990s, labour productivity levels were significantly higher in the USA for airlines, banking, telecommunications and retailing and he attributed this to the more competitive environment in the USA. He identified various attributes to be measured (for example for airlines, hours flown, passenger kilometres, number of cockpit, cabin, ramp and maintenance personnel, tickets issued, ticket staff etc.). How these varied with factors beyond the control of the airline companies was quite crucial in judging performance. In a blistering 'Comment' (ibid., 131–44) R. Gordon said Baily had no controls: no control for proportion of flights that were international (compare Belgium to the USA); no control for language problems, such that Lufthansa needed more ticket staff in Florence than did USA airlines, many of whose passengers would accept English. The development of the 'hub' system of airports, which Baily saw as important for American success was very much 'conditioned by lack of land, gates and runways . . .' and this, said Gordon, was the 'basic reason why London Heathrow . . . and Frankfurt have spread-unit flight patterns' instead of the bunched patterns conducive to the effective development of hub airports (p. 140).

14 S. N. Broadberry and S. Ghosal, 'From the Counting House to the Modern Office: Explaining Comparative Productivity Performance in Services since 1870', *Journal of Economic History* 62(4) (2002), 967–98. See also M. Ambramovitz, 'Catching-up, Forging Ahead and Falling Behind', *Journal of Economic History* 46 (1986), 385–406; B. von Ark, 'Sectoral Growth Accounting and Structural Change in Post-War Europe', in B. von Ark and N. Crafts (eds.), *Quantitative Aspects of Post-War European Growth* (Cambridge University Press, 1996), 84–164; S. N Broadberry, 'How Did the US and Germany Overtake Britain: A Sectoral Analysis of Comparative Productivity Levels', *Journal of Economic History* 58 (1998), 275–407; S. N Broadberry, 'Britain's Productivity Performance in International Perspective 1870–1990', in R. Barrell, G. Mason and M. O'Mahony (eds.), *Productivity, Innovation and Economic Performance* (Cambridge University Press, 2000), 38–57.

15 In a detailed investigation of thirty British industries, Iordanoglou concluded that productivity growth in the publicly owned firms (in transport, communications

and energy) was higher than that in the private firms (in manufacturing) and than in comparable infrastructure industries in the USA. See C. F. Iordanoglou, *Public Enterprise Revisited: A Closer Look at the 1954–79 UK Labour Productivity Record* (Cheltenham: Edward Elgar, 2001). Similar conclusions are in R. Millward, 'Productivity in the UK Services Sector: Historical Trends 1856–1985 and Comparisons with USA 1950–85', *Oxford Bulletin of Economics and Statistics* 52 (1990), 423–36.

16 S. N. Broadberry, 'Anglo-German Productivity Differences 1870–1990: A Sectoral Analysis', *European Review of Economic History* 1(2) (1997), 258; Broadberry and Ghosal, 'From the Counting House to the Modern Office', 980; L. Hannah, 'A Failed Experiment: The State Ownership of Industry', in R. Floud and P. Johnson (eds.), *The Cambridge Economic History of Modern Britain: Structural Change and Growth 1939–2000* (Cambridge University Press, 2004), 103–4.

17 M. O'Mahony, *Britain's Productivity Performance: An International Perspective* (London: National Institute of Economic and Social Research, 1999).

18 M. O'Mahony and M. Vecchi, 'The Electricity Supply Industry: A Study of an Industry in Transition', *National Institute Economic Review* 177 (2001), 95.

19 Broadberry, 'Anglo-German Productivity Differences 1870–1990', 258; Hannah, 'A Failed Experiment', 103–4.

Part V

Conclusions

15   The road to deregulation and privatisation?

The end of the twentieth century witnessed a major institutional change in Europe, that of deregulation and privatisation. It is a huge topic with a vast literature and the analysis of its history has yet to be written.[1] The aim in this conclusion is to draw on the research findings of this book to answer two questions. How far was the move to deregulation and privatisation prompted by economic and technological change? How far were the premises of deregulation and privatisation, as that process started in the 1980s, supported by the prior economic history of the infrastructure industries?

Although we await a comprehensive history of the incidence and timing of deregulation and privatisation, much has been written in support of the changes. Some has come from economic theory and has usually characterised regulatory bodies and especially public enterprises as inferior institutions, better replaced by competition and private enterprise. The analysis of property rights in public and private firms suggests weak incentive mechanisms in the former for monitoring managerial performance. Regulation of industry has been characterised by some economists as a process whereby the regulated firms come to dominate the scene and capture the regulator. Principal-agent theory sees asymmetries in the information between managers and owners, though this argument and the property rights argument leaves to empirical verification whether the problem is worse in large private joint stock companies than in public enterprises. Theories of public choice characterise politicians and civil servants as maximising their own utility rather than acting as disinterested officials. And finally, since, according to the 'Austrians', economic costs are opportunity costs and hence essentially subjective, public officials cannot meaningfully engage in devising cost-based pricing schemes and investment rules for the public sector.[2] Much broader in scope are the claims that deregulation and privatisation enhance consumer sovereignty and wider share ownership and thereby promote economic freedom, reduced power for trade unions and less political interference.[3] Finally, there are the more bread-and-butter issues, which are effectively explicit manifestations of the above factors. Thus deregulation and privatisation are expected to raise managerial efficiency, reduce the financial drain of public enterprises on the public purse, offer a better solution to market failure problems (such as natural monopoly) and introduce competition to sectors that do not need monopoly.

This last set of factors, with specific expectations about efficiency, competition and the public finances will dominate our focus here. Most of them seem to have figured quite prominently in the declared objectives of deregulation and privatisation programmes in western Europe.[4] However, there is much misunderstanding about why the infrastructure industries were regulated in the past and why, in some instances, they were brought under public ownership, whether at state or municipal level. Firstly then, by looking at the conclusions of the previous chapters, we may review that past history. Then we can examine the specific factors that, from about the 1970s, were making for change in the institutional structures.

It is not an exaggeration to say that the regulation and public ownership of the infrastructure industries has been perceived in ways that conflict with the historical record. A populist conception is that they were established as state-owned monopolies in the 1940s in the wake of the economic depression of the 1930s and of the success of administrative planning in the Second World War. The fact that they were ushered in by social democratic parties was, for some observers, less crucial, since the public/private divide and the regulatory form were not seriously challenged for the next thirty years as a political consensus reigned. A more polar view, from the right, was that state enterprises were instruments of socialism, part of the means of production, the takeover of which was central to the Marxist story of a class struggle. At the other pole, the hard left-winger would certainly see state enterprises as having that potential but would argue that, since they existed in a predominantly capitalist economy, that potential was never realised; it was state capitalism.[5] In the early postwar decades, mainstream economists said little about the public/private divide. They concentrated on devising pricing and investment rules for public enterprises that would optimise the allocation of resources across different sectors of the economy, and on designing regulatory devices appropriate for natural monopoly conditions, in the form of controls on prices and rates of profit and formulae like the (rpi−x) rule, which restricted price increases to the rise in the cost of living (rpi) less amounts equal to some assumed productivity growth (x). Finally, the large financial losses and state support associated with the railways, postal services and other public enterprises led many to view these enterprises as managerially inefficient, a view that gained ground in the 1970s with the acceleration in the size of financial deficits.

There are several problems with that story. The origins of both regulation and government ownership date back well into the nineteenth
century and reflected a wide range of economic, social and political
objectives. Moreover, these objectives, in conjunction with economic
and technological factors, are just as important, and probably more
important, than ideological surges, in accounting for the institutional
mix that emerged in the 1950s. It is indeed amazing how much time
politicians have spent arguing about regulation and public ownership in
terms of capitalism versus socialism when the behaviour, performance
and organisation of these industries had little to do with that debate. The
mixed economy has dominated the modern economies of western
Europe, but one group of politicians distrusted the public sector and
another group distrusted the private sector. As for the role of economists,
the kind of pricing and investment policies they advocated often flew in
the face of the basic aims of government and the industry managers in the
post-1945 period. Finally, in so far as managerial efficiency is concerned,
there is no general evidence that public enterprises in western Europe had
an inferior productivity growth performance than comparable infrastructure industries in the predominantly private enterprise economy of
the USA.

What then were the central factors that had brought government to
regulate and in some cases own these particular sectors? What problems
were dominant by the 1970s and what economic and technological
factors were making for institutional change? How far did these problems
and forces match up to the arguments advanced by the growing number
of advocates of liberalisation and privatisation? The origins of government involvement in the infrastructure industries can be traced back to
the need for rights of way for railway track, telegraph lines and gas and
water mains. In the 1830s and 1840s when the story begins, entrepreneurs in these sectors were seeking powers from local and central government for compulsory acquisition of land or of rights to use land. These
tracks and distribution systems had all the characteristics of natural
monopolies, and governments followed up the easing of rights of way
by controlling prices and profits and by monitoring the engineering and
financial soundness of the companies. None of this required direct government ownership, and many of the new infrastructures in France,
Germany, the UK, Spain and Italy were built and operated by private
enterprises. The same was true, at the end of the century, for electricity
supply and tramway systems. Of course, the interest of the state extended
beyond monopoly controls, but here again arm's-length regulation or
subsidies could be the limit of government involvement. The railway
system developed rapidly in Britain in the 1830s and 1840s providing

cheaper transport for a country that was ahead of the rest of Europe in industrialisation and urbanisation. Conscious of Britain's lead, the governments of France, Italy, Spain and of the German states sought to encourage development by guaranteeing rates of return for investors in railways and providing subsidies for particular sections of track. In Scandinavia, the railway and telegraph offered great opportunities for securing social, political and cultural unification of their scattered regions. A similar factor was at work in Belgium, a newly independent state established in 1830, and Italy in the 1860s. Subsidies were feasible instruments for developing and sustaining sectors that would otherwise be unprofitable. Some sectors had significant strategic value for the military – the railway systems in France and Germany especially – but here again subsidies could be used.

Public ownership, when it did occur, was therefore not operating in a vacuum – several instruments of policy such as interest guarantees and subsidies were available. However, in some cases speed in the introduction of a new infrastructure was deemed vital, and this seems to have been the case in Belgium in the 1830s, Sweden in the 1850s and Italy in the 1860s, and here the state stepped in to build and/or operate at least the trunk lines. In some other cases, the sectors proved so unprofitable that no subsidy scheme was credible – a classic instance was the western part of the French railway network at the end of the nineteenth century. Finally, central governments were very sensitive to communication channels, which had military potential, and the desire to exercise close control seems to explain why everywhere telegraphs came into state ownership and why the Prussian state took over its railways in the 1870s, faced as it was by large hostile neighbours on both its western and eastern borders. State enterprise in the nineteenth century was not therefore a product of some great ideological surge.

The same can be said for local government. It was not municipal socialism that heralded the rise of municipal enterprise, since the initial surge can be dated in Germany, Scandinavia and Britain to the period 1850–80, well before the debates and propagation of municipal socialism in the 1890s and 1900s. In fact, explaining the pattern of municipal ownership is not a straightforward matter, since many towns 'stayed private'. Public ownership at the local level in the nineteenth century meant gas, water, electricity and tramways. Clearly this was not feasible when the units of local government were either too small (as in Belgium), were not empowered to undertake economic activity (as in France), were undeveloped (as in Spain and Italy) or were simply a fragmented mess (as in nineteenth-century London). Municipal enterprise in gas, electricity and tramways seems to have been more common in the growing industrial towns of western Europe, whose councils, faced with mounting programmes for public health and other services, were desperate for new revenue sources. The tax-paying leaders of the councils looked to control the profits of these local monopolies not by arm's-length regulation, but by expropriation of their trading profits, effectively taxing local customers – many of whom would not be paying the official local taxes. Municipal enterprise was not therefore found where the tax base was good nor in towns without pressing public health problems. It is significant that in France, Italy and Spain, all slow to urbanise and with small or weak local government units, it was the concession system rather than municipalisation that dominated the nineteenth century. Water supply cannot be explained in that way. It generally made losses, financially, and the explanation for the widespread municipal ownership throughout western Europe seems to lie in the significant health dimensions of supplies and the fact that the real cost of water supply rose in the nineteenth century as reservoirs and long-distance systems had to be constructed. The technical standards being set by central and local governments for good quality water in conjunction with control of water charges seems, at least if the British evidence is any guide, to have made widespread expansion of high-quality supplies unprofitable, so the municipalities stepped in.

In the early twentieth century, national networks emerged in electricity supply, river basins came to be recognised as the optimal focus of development for water supply, and economies of scale were envisaged in some quarters for gas supply. In these circumstances, the role of central government came to dominate over local government. At the same time, the significance of information flows, social unification and military strategy in the services provided by railways and telecommunications continued into the twentieth century. Two further issues now came on the scene. At the end of the nineteenth century and turn of the new century, the technical possibilities and economic gains from the development of national networks in telecommunications and electricity supply became apparent. This was by no means easy to achieve. The development of long-distance transmission lines and the concentration of production (in electricity) in large generating plants created problems when private companies had to merge or join forces with other companies. The problem was exacerbated in Scandinavia, the UK and Germany, where many municipalities were firmly entrenched. Most telephone systems had been nationalised by 1913, but in the case of electricity it took much of the inter-war period for the central governments of these countries to subdue local interests, so that in Britain the Central Electricity Board emerged with a national grid by the early 1930s, national investment planning was centralised in Germany by the 1935 energy law, and a national network was in place in Sweden in the late 1930s, though it was not until the late 1940s that truly centrally managed systems emerged in Sweden and Germany with heavy involvement of state and municipal enterprise.

A second issue in the inter-war period was the growing uneasiness of many states in dealing with private-sector regional or national monopolies – and the potential was certainly there in railways, telecommunications and electricity. On the one hand, governments wanted the economies of scale from big networks to be fully exploited, accepting that this would require regulation of prices and profits. On the other hand, they had certain aims with respect to parts of these systems – related to military and strategic issues and to questions of national unification – and in some circumstances this would mean government subsidies. The two were difficult to combine, and the growing distrust of this kind of arm's-length regulation and subsidy was providing an additional argument for public ownership. The classic cases were the railway networks, whose financial position had been weakened by mounting non-commercial obligations and, in the 1920s, by wage costs rising faster than fares and freight rates. The advent of a new competitor in the form of road transport proved the turning point, and the railways were nationalised in France, Sweden, Spain and the UK in the period 1937–47, so that by the end of the 1940s, all major railways in western Europe were run by state enterprises.

In the 1950s, central governments were also deeply involved in the affairs of Europe's coal, oil and aviation industries. These are not public utilities; they are not networks, not natural monopolies. All share three common features. Airspace together with deposits of coal and oil are key inputs for other sectors, with few short-run substitutes, and are geographically fixed. They are therefore strategically significant in times of war or other crises. Secondly, access generates income in the form of economic rent, while deposits of coal, oil and natural gas generate royalties reflecting the user cost of depleting stocks and foregoing future revenue. Governments wanted to secure some leverage on the development of these resources to ensure their availability as a tax source and because of their strategic value. On the other hand, the business of producing and distributing coal and oil and operating airlines does not involve natural monopoly conditions, so that it might be expected to generate competitive conditions with lots of suppliers. And this is what emerged for coal and oil in the nineteenth century and in the first half of the twentieth, albeit with some large joint stock companies emerging in the coal industries of Belgium, Britain, France and Germany and in the international oil industry. The particular strategic significance of coal and oil deposits depends on where they are located. With large indigenous supplies, there was little need for state ownership of the coal industries in Germany and Britain. Italy, Spain and the Scandinavian countries had limited or poor quality supplies and, from the late nineteenth century, sought to reduce their dependence on coal imports by developing hydroelectricity. France had a bigger coal industry, but one that was relatively modest, given its energy needs, and had to import large amounts of coal. It operated a concession system for exploitation of its coal fields, which could therefore be quickly brought under state control, but they were located in the strategically vulnerable north-eastern part of France and were lost early on in the three German invasions of 1870, 1914 and 1940. France's main strategy therefore was to diversify its energy sources to HEP, and to nuclear in the second half of the twentieth century. The nationalisations of the coal industries of France and Britain in 1946 had little to do with their strategic significance, but rather with poor working conditions and the emergence of a politically active labour force who demanded nationalisation. Indeed, the coal industries of France, Germany and Britain all declined in the latter part of the twentieth century and all were protected in various ways, France less so as it widened its energy sources. By the end of the century, while some element of protection remained, state ownership had virtually disappeared.

When it came to oil supplies, before the Second World War, the known exploitable deposits were located outside Europe, and this explains why governments took shareholdings in companies like Compagnie Française des Pétroles and British Petroleum. For the indigenous deposits of oil and natural gas exploited from the 1960s in the North Sea, the important issue was to secure clear property rights, and this was achieved by various forms of a concession system. The Norwegian publicly owned Statoil enterprise and the British National Oil Corporation were established to exploit and distribute some of the supplies, and state-owned or mixed enterprises like Elf-Aquitaine, ENI and Deminex emerged in other European countries who were, however, not as successful as Norway and the UK in finding indigenous supplies. In the long term, state ownership was not needed to secure tax revenues and property rights, and the privatisation of these companies from the 1980s is perhaps not surprising.

The aviation industry might also have developed as a mainly privately owned competitive industry but for one key difference. Airspace, like coal and oil deposits, is a natural resource with economic value and perhaps even bigger military significance. Shortly after the First World War, each European country was quick to assert sovereignty over its own airspace, so an open-skies regime for Europe was blighted from the beginning. Nonetheless, this would not have been inconsistent with the emergence of a set of private competitive airlines operating throughout

Europe and overseas, paying appropriate fees for landing rights. The complicating factor was that airlines, as well as airspace, were deemed to have strategic significance. It would not be enough for a country to rely on services from any old company. Each country wanted at least one national carrier, and the normal military reasons for such a transport facility were greatly enhanced by the desire of countries like Belgium, France, Italy and Britain to secure good links and supplies with their colonies in Africa and Asia. These considerations might have caused governments to take out some shares in the airline companies – and this was the case in Air France and Alitalia in the early inter-war period. However, the finances of these airlines were rather shaky in the early embryonic days of air transport, and there was an even greater threat posed by the economic superiority of American airlines, who had flourished in their huge land mass, uncluttered as it was by national frontiers. The result was, firstly, that some of the national carriers like Air France and BOAC were 100% state owned, while in others like Lufthansa, Alitalia, SAS and Iberia, central governments had a clear majority holding. Secondly, the IATA system established in 1945 ensured that fares were set at such a level as to protect even the highest-cost European carriers against American competition.

In summary, concern about natural monopoly, preserving national carriers, ensuring sovereignty over natural resources and airspace could be achieved by arm's-length concessions and regulation of prices and profits. The variety of strategic and political considerations associated with network spread and the expansion of services in railways, airlines and the telephone system could potentially have been secured by subsidies. By the end of the 1930s, the combination of regulation and subsidies was proving politically unpalatable. When this was added to the inability to support some services even with subsidy and with the desire in the case of telecommunications to control the flow of information, the balance was tipped towards state enterprise.

Thus the set of economic and non-economic obligations laid on the infrastructure industries by 1950 reflected some very specific aims of governments. They had little connection with the conception of state enterprise as a socialist-inspired element of the means of production. Coal, it is true, was a battleground between capital and labour, and especially in France and Britain. The ventures of public enterprise into manufacturing, which are outside the boundaries of this book, perhaps also might be characterised in these terms, though they were, at least in part, concerned with bailing out firms in financial difficulties in some key sectors like motor cars, shipbuilding and steel. For much of energy, telecommunications and transport, the ideological brickbats of capitalism versus socialism played little part in accounting for the accumulation of objectives and constraints that the infrastructure industries faced. Even the new dimensions of state activity that emerged after the Second World War, and on the back of memories of the 1930s depression, had little impact. The infrastructure industries were a key element in European reconstruction after the war, but that was a very special period with rationing and licensing the order of the day, giving way to freer market transactions in the early 1950s. Planning was on the agenda and taken seriously in some quarters as a role for the state in promoting the long-term growth of productive potential. It had some success in France, but neither there nor elsewhere did it address the substantive economic and institutional problems of energy, telecommunications and transport.

What then were the problems of regulation and public enterprise that paved the way for privatisation and deregulation? They did not, despite much theorising to the contrary, lie in any obvious deficiencies in X efficiency, that is, in managerial competence. All the evidence suggests that, in terms of conventional total factor productivity growth figures, the state enterprise sector in western Europe performed as well as the private sector of the European economies and as well as the counterpart infra-structure industries in the USA in the period from the late 1940s to the mid 1970s. Thereafter, in the last quarter of the century, the privatised regimes performed no better, and also performed no better than those parts of the infrastructure industries that remained public. This is not to deny that many observers thought that public-sector industries were inefficient in that sense and extrapolated that judgment from the poor financial record of the industries, which we will consider shortly. However, the evidence on productivity does not support that inference.

What is more central is the range and complexity of the non-commercial obligations laid on state enterprises. What was the rationale for state enterprise? That was a valid question to ask in the second half of the twentieth century, and neither the opponents nor the supporters of state enterprise acknowledged the long list of obligations that had accumulated. There were two major problems facing state enterprise and its regulation by the 1970s. The first was that the industries had come to their current position as a product of a wide-ranging set of objectives, for which the current institutional format was no longer necessarily optimal. Why, for example, should telecommunications be run by a section of a government department? The origins were in questions of national security. Was the telecoms sector still the dominant instrument for security? The second central problem was that the procedures and institutions for meeting these obligations were not sufficiently planned and costed. All state enter-prises were expected to break even and, for the large part, they rarely did.

Thereby they failed to meet one of their few quantifiable management targets.

These two issues, when allied to the technological changes of the last thirty years, provide the key to understanding the shift to deregulation and privatisation. They led to financial failure, a move to cost-based prices, less monopolistic markets and a revision of the instruments used for promoting social unity, for ensuring strategic capacity in times of war and other crises and for controlling the flow of information. Arm's-length regulation had lost some of its bad odour inherited from the inter-war period. As Lebaron said, 'talk of the state "pulling out" was simplistic. The state was, rather, breaking the link between control and ownership, replacing the most visible mode of intervention by less visible ones.'[6]

The inability of state enterprises to reconcile the break-even target with the non-commercial obligations of state enterprises manifested itself in a consistently large shortfall of earnings below operating costs and capital charges. It was also, in some countries, reflected in the relatively low portion of capital investment programmes financed from internal sources. These financial results deteriorated even further in the aftermath of the 1973/4 oil price hike and the downturn of economic activity, exacerbated by the fact that public-sector price increases were held below cost increases. Governments were wrestling with rising public expenditure programmes, and the deficits of public sector industries were one target. It is significant that many observers of the shift to deregulation, but especially privatisation, place much emphasis on the impetus given by rising budget deficits, that is, rising public sector borrowing requirements. The timing of the privatisations varied across Europe but closely followed financial crises.[7] During the period when they were still in the public sector, the increasing pressure to produce a better financial performance was a key element in the gradual shift to cost-based tariffs, fares, rates and energy prices. The tradition of universal service provision with uniform prices per kilometre travelled, or per cubic foot of gas, distance of telephone call and so on had been sustained under the hope that the unprofitable sectors would be sustained by the more profitable ones. Ever since the 1920s, with the advent of road competition, that hope was misplaced for railways, which, slowly and creakily, shifted to pricing structures that rewarded off-peak long-distance traffic when booked in advance, and penalised short-distance, short-term bookings of peak traffic. The railway was one of the oldest examples of this phenomenon, but from the 1960s a shift to cost-based prices was occurring. The technological revolution in telecommunications was creating great opportunities for the development of terminal equipment for business users, yet this customer group, along with other urban-based and long-distance callers, had been subsidising local, rural, residential users. The pressure from business customers and their access to alternative networks could not be resisted.

The technological changes in telecommunications and airlines were also undermining the case for dominant national carriers. It was no longer sensible to have customer premises equipment proliferating in the form of computers, email, mobile phones and fax and yet have a market solely supplied by the main network provider and regulated by the selfsame body. Hence, the customer premises markets were being opened up by the sort of competition that had long characterised the switching gear market. In airlines, the onward march of bigger and faster planes lowering costs in the face of fixed IATA fares led to a flourishing of charter airlines and a relaxation of entry conditions in scheduled services, though the IATA system lasted to the end of the century.

One of the driving forces behind state ownership was the desire to secure social and political unification, but much had been achieved by the second half of the twentieth century, and it was no longer clear that the old institutions were the best. There were new means of communication (roads, airlines and telecommunications) other than railways for securing links to remote communities, the colonies had now become independent, and universal provision had been closely associated with financial failure. The strategic significance of certain resources and services remained. But there was no need for each country to give one airline a monopoly of all air travel. The financial returns to government for indigenous oil and natural gas deposits together with the necessary affirmation of sovereignty could be achieved by asserting property rights, granting concessions and levying taxes. Neither is it clear that control of information flows required that telecommunication networks be operated from within a government department.

This still leaves many sectors where natural monopoly conditions apply and where there would be advantages for a single supplier, supported for non-commercial obligations by explicit subsidy schemes. Electricity transmission grids, natural gas distribution networks, water supply systems, trunk telecommunications networks, railway systems, all were still dominated by the single supplier. Despite all the claims during the privatisation debates about the importance of competition, little had emerged by the 1990s. The reservations that grew in the inter-war period about arm's-length regulation of private-sector monopolies had disappeared by the 1990s. On the other hand, the evidence does not suggest that privately owned networks in Europe are more efficient than publicly owned networks. Nor, moreover, is the claim that privatisation is essential to pave the way for deregulation all that convincing, even though it did work that way in Britain. Deregulation preceded privatisation in many parts of continental Europe. The classic case for deregulation seems stronger than that for privatisation.

Notes

1 For recent reviews of the various paths to deregulation and privatisation, see J. Clifton, F. Comin and D. D. Fuentes, *Privatisation in the European Union: Public Enterprises and Integration* (London: Kluwer, 2003); V. Wright, *Privatisation in Western Europe* (London: Pinter, 1994); D. Bös, 'Privatisation in Europe: A Comparison of Approaches', *Oxford Review of Economic Policy* 9(1) (1993), 95–111.

2 Recent surveys of these theories may be found in W. N. Megginson and J. M. Netter, 'From State to Market: A Survey of Empirical Studies on Privatisation', *Journal of Economic Literature* 39 (2001), 321–89, and in M. Florio, *The Great Divestiture: The Welfare Effects of British Privatisation* (Cambridge, Mass.: MIT Press, 2004).

3 Y. Aharoni, 'The United Kingdom: Transforming Attitudes', in R. Vernon (ed.), *The Promise of Privatisation* (Washington: US Council of Foreign Relations, 1988), 23–56. M. Beesley and S. Littlechild, 'Privatisation: Principles, Problems and Priorities', *Lloyds Bank Review* 149 (1983), 1–20, reproduced in J. Kay, C. Mayer and D. Thompson (eds.), *Privatisation and Regulation: The UK Experience* (Oxford: Clarendon Press, 1986).

4 R. Stephens, 'The Evolution of Privatisation as an Electoral Policy, c.1970–1990', *Contemporary British History* 18(2) (2004), 47–75; M. Chick, 'Nationalisation, Privatisation and Regulation', in M. W. Kirby and M. B. Rose (eds.), *Business Enterprise in Modern Britain* (London: Routledge, 1994), 315–38; M. Davids and J. L. van Zandem, 'A Reluctant State and its Enterprises: State-Owned Enterprises in the Netherlands in the "Long Run" 20th Century', in P. A. Toninelli (ed.), *The Rise and Fall of State Owned Enterprise in the Western World* (Cambridge University Press, 2000), 177–93; G. Federico and R. Giannetti, 'Italy: Stalling and Surpassing', in J. Foreman-Peck and G. Federico (eds.), *European Industrial Policy: The Twentieth Century Experience* (Oxford University Press, 1999), 124–51; P. Fridensen, 'Atouts et limites de la modernisation par en haut: Les Entreprises publiques facé à leurs critiques (1944–1986)', in P. Fridensen and A. Strauss (eds.), *Le Capitalisme française* (Paris: Librairie Arthème, Fayard, 1987), 169–88; J. Pontusson, 'The Triumph of Pragmatism: Nationalisation and Privatisation in Sweden', *West European Politics* 11(4) (1988), 129–40; U. Wengenroth, 'The Rise and Fall of State Owned Enterprise in Germany', in Toninelli (ed.), *The Rise and Fall of State Owned Enterprise*, 103–27.

5 For a view of both sides, see J. R. Shackleton, 'Privatisation: The Case Examined', *National Westminster Bank Review* (May 1984), 59–71. For a classic statement from the left see R. Miliband, *The State in Capitalist Society* (London: Quartet Books, 1973).

6 F. Lebaron, 'The State and the Market: The Rise of the Economic Rationale', *Contemporary European History* 9(3) (2000), 470.

7 A. Carreras, X. Tafunell and E. Torres, 'The Rise and Decline of Spanish State-Owned Firms', in Toninelli (ed.), *The Rise and Fall of State Owned Enterprise*, 15–16; Pontusson, 'The Triumph of Pragmatism: Nationalisation and Privatisation in Sweden', 134; Federico and Giannetti, 'Italy: Stalling and Surpassing', 144; Wengenroth, 'The Rise and Fall of State Owned Enterprise in Germany', 122–3; Chick, 'Nationalisation, Privatisation and Regulation', 323.

Appendix: Infrastructure service levels and public ownership c. 1910: a statistical analysis

The first issue considered here is the extent to which a detailed statistical analysis supports the proposition in chapter 6 that the pattern of regulation and ownership had little effect on the level of infrastructure development. The second issue is what factors determined the pattern of regulation and ownership. I analyse the cases of three sectors, railways, telephones and gas, as they had developed by the early 1900s. The data are good for these services and a cross-section comparison is made of eight European countries: Britain, Denmark, France, Germany, Sweden, Italy, Norway and Spain. The main sources are given in Tables 2.1, 2.2, 3.1, 4.1 and 7.1.

The level of infrastructure development, such as rail track per head of population, may be affected by the level of GDP per head (GDPPH in Table A.1 below) and by energy sources (COALPH, coal output per head), as well as the proportion of mileage in public ownership (OWN). Countries with high population density (POPDEN) may need well-developed infrastructures. Finally, when military matters loom large in a nation's thinking, a well-developed infrastructure may be seen as an important strategic weapon. Here I measure the defensive element by military expenditures as a percentage of all central government expenditures (MILB). The measures of the dependent variable, infrastructure development, are gas supplies, rail track and telephone numbers all expressed per head of population. These are shown as PENLEV in column 2 of Table A.1. Observation numbers 1–8 (NOBS in column 1) correspond to gas supplies per head for the UK, Denmark, France, Germany, Sweden, Italy, Norway and Spain in that order; observations 9–16 relate to railways and 17–24 to telephones. However, these penetration levels are not directly comparable, since they are each measured in different units (cubic metres, mileage, telephone numbers). It would appear then that any regression analysis would have to treat each sector separately, which would reduce the statistical significance of the results, since with only eight countries there would be only eight observations. A way round that is to express each sector's penetration level as a percentage

Table A.1 *Infrastructure levels and economic data, 1910*

NOBS	PENLEV	INDPEN	POPDEN	MERTPH	COALPH	GDPPH	OWN	MILB
1	96	370	370	265	581	4024	28.8	27.7
2	34	124	187	179	0.1	3037	78.6	14
3	16	62	191	40	103	2734	2.4	40.7
4	20	77	312	49	386	2606	30.8	47.4
5	9	35	31	161	1	2450	94.5	12
6	6	17	320	33	2	2087	2.5	15.9
7	15	58	19	708	1	2079	50	12
8	6	23	101	45	21	1504	2.5	25.3
9	499	19	370	265	581	4024	0.1	27.7
10	754	29	187	179	0.1	3037	56.2	14
11	630	24	191	40	103	2734	5.9	40.7
12	588	23	312	49	386	2606	92.8	47.4
13	1587	61	31	161	1	2450	32.3	12
14	317	12	320	33	2	2087	77.1	15.9
15	776	30	19	708	1	2079	85.4	12
16	458	18	101	45	21	1504	0.1	25.3
17	16	18	370	265	581	4024	100	27.7
18	42	446	187	179	0.1	3037	1.2	14
19	7	8	191	40	103	2734	100	40.7
20	19	21	312	49	386	2606	100	47.4
21	39	43	31	161	1	2450	68	12
22	2	2	320	33	2	2087	64.7	15.9
23	31	34	19	708	1	2079	50.7	12
24	2	2	101	45	21	1504	5	25.3

Notes and Definitions:
Each observation (NOBS) corresponds to a particular economic sector in a particular country.
Observations 1–8 relate to the gas sector in the UK, Denmark, France, Germany, Sweden, Italy,
Norway and Spain in that order. Observations 9–16 relate to railways and 17–24 to telephones.
PENLEV: for observations 1–8, gas supplied in 1900 in cubic metres per head of population;
for 9–16, rail track mileage in 1910 per million population; for 17–24, number of telephones
in 1913 per 1000 population.
INDPEN: Penetration levels, as in PENLEV, expressed as percentages of the levels in the
USA, where the gas figure was 26, rail 2595 and telephones 91.
POPDEN: Population in 1910 divided by area in 1911.
GDPPH: This is 1913 GDP per head of population in 1985 dollars.
MERTPH: Merchant shipping in 1913 in tons per thousand population.
COALPH: Coal output in 1912 in tons per 100 population.
OWN: For observations 1–8, the percentage of gas undertakings c.1890–1908 in public
ownership; for 9–16, the percentage of rail track mileage in public ownership in 1906; and
for 17–24 the percentage of telephone exchanges in public ownership in 1913.
MILB: Military expenditures as a percentage of all central government expenditure, 1891–5.

Sources: Tables 2.1, 2.2, 3.1, 4.1 and 7.1 of the text, except for military expenditure. Swedish coal output is taken to be negligible. The data on military expenditures for Britain, France and Germany are taken from D. E. Schremmer, 'Taxation and Public Finance: Britain, France and Germany', in P. Mathias and S. Pollard (eds.), *Cambridge Economic History of Europe. VIII. The Industrial Economies: The Development of Economic and Social Policy* (Cambridge University Press, 1989), 358 (for UK 1893), 403 (for France 1890) and 462 (for Germany 1891–5). The entry for Spain is an annual average for 1850–90 and the source is G. Tortella, *The Development of Modern Spain* (Cambridge, Mass.: Harvard University Press, 2000), 417. For Italy, the entry is for 1890 and the source is V. Zamagni, *The Economic History of Italy 1860–1990* (Oxford: Clarendon Press, 1993), 160. The entries for Denmark (14%), Sweden (12%) and Norway (10%) are guesses based on their non-belligerent status in the First World War and their cultural and political links.

of US levels for gas, railways and telephones respectively. This index of penetration levels is recorded in column 3 as INDPEN, which is the dependent variable for our first set of regressions. The other data outlined above appear in the other columns of the table.

The regression results recorded in columns A and B of Table A.2 confirm the proposition that public ownership had little effect on penetration levels. Only the coefficients marked with an 'a' are statistically significant, and the only one of any size was that on GDP per head with a coefficient of 3.6. Since the variables are measured in logs, this implies a very high elasticity of penetration levels with respect to income levels. Population density and coal output have inverse links with penetration levels, probably reflecting their low levels in Scandinavia, relative to Germany, but only population density was significant, and the quantitative effect was small. Military expenditures had a positive but again not significant effect. There may be differences within each sector, which are obscured in the aggregates. To explore this, a dummy was created for the gas sector. This had a strong positive coefficient, suggesting that, after controlling for the economic variables, the level of penetration (relative to the USA, that is) was higher in gas than railways and telephones, as we might expect. It had little effect, however, on the size of the other coefficients so that my general conclusions remain unaltered.

Columns C, D and E of Table A.2 report the regressions where public ownership is the dependent variable. Here again a dominant influence was GDP per head. The coefficient on population density was negative, large and significant, so that the urbanisation pressures highlighted in the text are not reflected. More likely this result is picking up the pressures to unification and the strength of local government in Scandinavia. The scale of merchant shipping was introduced as another dimension of industrialisation, and it is capable of exerting a significant inverse effect as shown in column C, probably reflecting the small amount of shipping

Table A.2 *Regression analysis of penetration levels*

| | Dependent variables | | | | |
| | Index of penetration levels (INDPEN) | | Ownership (OWN) | | |
	A	B	C	D	E
Independent variables					
Constant	-22.9^a	-25.0^a	-30.4	-27.2	-30.1
GDP per head	3.7^a	3.6^a	6.5^a	4.1	6.6^a
Population density	-0.5	-0.6^a	-2.0^a	-1.0	-2.1^a
Coal output per head	-0.1	-0.3	-0.1	-0.3	-0.1
Public ownership	-0.1	-0.1	–	–	–
Index of Penetration levels	–	–	-0.3	-0.6	-0.3
Merchant shipping tonnage per head	–	–	-1.4^a	–	-1.4
Military expenditures	–	1.3	–	1.6	-0.2
Number of observations	24	24	24	24	24
R^2	0.57	0.62	0.18	0.19	0.20
R^2 (adj)	0.45	0.48	-0.04	0.03	0.09
DW	1.98	2.16	2.29	2.10	2.30

Notes:
[a] Significant at the 5% level.
All variables are measured in logarithms. A correction for first order auto-correlation was tried for all regressions and improved all the regressions except that in column B.

in Germany, relative to Scandinavia. The scale of military expenditures may reflect the determination of some countries to control their economic systems and hence to spread public ownership. Columns D and E indicate a strong positive effect but with no general statistical significance and at the same time reducing the significance of merchant shipping. The dummy for gas was not significant and had little effect on the other variables, so that there is nothing in the statistics to suggest that gas was different from the other two sectors, even though public ownership there was more municipal than state.

In summary, the factors I have been able to quantify are unable to explain the pattern of public ownership across these European countries in the early 1900s. The conclusions of chapter 6, in this context, are neither rejected nor confirmed by regression analysis. The other general message is that there are no obvious deleterious effects on penetration rates of state ownership of railways and telephones or municipal ownership of gasworks. Since GDP, area, population, shipping and coal supplies were included in these regressions, it is also likely that more sophisticated models are needed. In particular, the observed penetration rates are reflecting both demand and supply factors, which need to be unscrambled.[1]

Note

1 Wallsten's conclusion that private ownership of telephone exchanges raised penetration rates in the period c. 1880–1914 may have to be qualified by the fact that his data for Scandinavia (where penetration rates were high) seem to understate the scale of state and municipal ownership. See S. Wallsten, 'Ringing in the 20th Century: The Effects of State Monopolies, Private Ownership and Operating Licences on Telecommunications in Europe 1892–1913', Paper presented at Annual Conference of the Economic History Society, University of Birmingham, April 2002.

Bibliography

Abelshauser, W., 'Germany: Guns, Butter and Economic Miracles', in M. Harrison (ed.), *The Economics of World War II* (Cambridge University Press, 1998), 122–76.

Acena, P. M. and Comin, F., 'Industrial Planning in Spain under the Franco Regime (1940–75)', in E. Aerts and A. S. Milward (eds.), *Economic Planning in the Post-War Period* (Leuven University Press, 1990), 61–72.

Aharoni, Y., 'The United Kingdom: Transforming Attitudes', in R. Vernon (ed.), *The Promise of Privatisation* (Washington, DC: US Council of Foreign Relations, 1988), 23–56.

'The Performance of State Owned Enterprise', in P. A. Toninelli (ed.), *The Rise and Fall of State Owned Enterprise in the Western World* (Cambridge University Press, 2000), 49–76.

Alchian, A. A., 'Some Economics of Property Rights', *Il Politico* **30** (1965), 816–29.

Aldcroft, D., *British Railways in Transition* (London: Macmillan, 1968).

'British Shipping and Foreign Competition: The Anglo-German Rivalry, 1880–1914', in D. Aldcroft, *Studies in British Transport History* (Newton Abbott: David and Charles, 1974), 53–99.

British Transport since 1914 (Newton Abbott: David and Charles, 1975).

Alessi, L. de, 'An Economic Analysis of Government Ownership and Regulation: Theory and Evidence from the Electric Power Industry', *Public Choice* **19** (1974), 1–42.

Amatori, F., 'IRI: From Industrial Saviour to Industrial Group', in V. Zamagni (ed.), *Origins and Development of Publicly Owned Enterprises* (University of Florence, Ninth International Economic History Conference, Section B111, 1986), 8–13.

'Beyond State and Market: Italy's Futile Search for a Third Way', in P. A. Toninelli (ed.), *The Rise and Fall of State Owned Enterprise in the Western World* (Cambridge University Press, 2000), 128–56.

Ambramovitz, M., 'Catching-up, Forging Ahead and Falling Behind', *Journal of Economic History* **46** (1986), 385–406.

Ambrosius, G., 'Changes in the Function and Organisation of Public Enterprises in Germany since the Nineteenth Century', in V. Zamagni (ed.), *Origins and Development of Publicly Owned Enterprises* (University of Florence, Ninth International Economic History Conference, Section B111, 1986), 14–19.

American Telegraph and Telephone, *Telephone and Telegraph Statistics of the World* (1913).

Anastassopoulos, J.-P. C., 'The French Experience: Conflicts with Government',
in R. Vernon and Y. Aharoni (eds.), *State-Owned Enterprise in Western
Economies* (London: Croom Helm, 1981), 99–116.

Anderson, L., 'Hard Choices: Supplying Water to New England Towns', *Journal
of Interdisciplinary History* **15**(2) (1984), 211–34.

Andersson-Skog, L., 'From State Railway Housekeeping to Railway Economics:
Swedish Railway Policy and Economic Transformation after 1920 in an
Institutional Perspective', *Scandinavian Economic History Review* **49** (1996),
23–42.

'The Making of the National Telephone Networks in Scandinavia: The State
and the Emergence of National Regulatory Patterns 1880–1920', in
L. Magnusson and J. Ottosson (eds.), *Evolutionary Economics and Path
Dependence* (Cheltenham: Edward Elgar, 1996), 138–54.

'Political Economy and Institutional Diffusion. The Case of the Swedish
Railways and Telecommunications up to 1950', in L. Andersson-Skog and
O. Krantz (eds.), *Institutions and the Transport and Communications Industries*
(Canton, Mass.: Science History Publications, Watson, 1999), 245–66.

'National Patterns in the Regulation of Railways and Telephony in the Nordic
Countries to 1950', *Scandinavian Economic History Review* **47**(2) (2000), 30–46.

'Compensating the Periphery. Railway Policy and Regional Interest in
Northern Sweden', in L. Magnusson and J. Ottosson (eds.), *The State,
Regulation and the Economy: An Historical Perspective* (Cheltenham: Edward
Elgar, 2001), 127–47.

Andersson-Skog, L. and Krantz, O. (eds.), *Institutions and the Transport and
Communications Industries* (Canton, Mass.: Science History Publications,
Watson, 1999).

Andic, A. and Veverka, J., 'The Growth of Government Expenditures in
Germany since Unification', *Finanzarchiv* N.F. **23**(2) (1963/4), 169–278.

Antolin, F., 'Las empresas de servicos publicos municipales', in F. Comin and
P. M. Acena (eds.), *Historia de la empresa publica en España* (Madrid: Espasa
Calpe, 1991), 283–330.

'Public Policy in the Development of the Spanish Electric Utility Industry',
Paper presented at European Historical Economics Society Conference on
A Century of Industrial Policy in Europe, Oxford, Worcester College, 1992.

'Iniciativa privada y politica en el desarrollo de la industria electrica en Espana:
La hegemonia de la gestion privada, 1875–1950', *Revista de Historia
Economica* **17**(2) (1999), 411–45.

Ark, B. von, 'Sectoral Growth Accounting and Structural Change in Post-War
Europe', in B. von Ark and N. Crafts (eds.), *Quantitative Aspects of Post-War
European Growth* (Cambridge University Press, 1996), 84–164.

Armand, L., 'The French National Railways: A National Service', *Annals of Public
and Collective Economy* **28** (1957), 301–9.

Armstrong, J., 'Government Regulation in the British Shipping Industry, 1830–1913:
The Role of the Coastal Sector', in L. Andersson-Skog and O. Krantz (eds.),
Institutions and the Transport and Communications Industries (Canton, Mass.:
Science History Publications, Watson, 1999), 153–73.

Arndt, H. J., *West Germany: Politics of Non-Planning* (New York: Syracuse University Press, 1966).

Ashley, P., *Local and Central Government* (London: John Murray, 1906).

Ashley, P. C., 'Municipal Trading in Great Britain', *Quarterly Journal of Economics* **15** (1901), 458–64.

Ashworth, W., *The History of the British Coal Industry. V. 1946–82: The Nationalised Industry* (Oxford University Press, 1986).

The State in Business: 1945 to the mid 1980s (London: Macmillan, 1991).

Aspinall, B., 'Glasgow Trams and American Politics, 1894–1914', *Scottish Historical Review* **56** (1976), 64–86.

Association d'Histoire de l'Electricité en France (ed.), *L'Electricité dans l'histoire: Problèmes et méthodes* (Paris: Presses Universitaires de France, 1995).

Attali, J. and Stowdze, Y., 'The Birth of the Telephone and Economic Crisis: The Slow Development of Monologue in French Society', in I. de Sola Pool (ed.), *The Social Impact of the Telephone* (Cambridge, Mass.: MIT Press, 1977), 97–111.

Avebury, Lord, 'Municipal Trading', *Contemporary Review* **78** (1900), 28–37.

Bagwell, P. S., *The Transport Revolution from 1770* (London: Batsford, 1974).

Baily, M., 'Competition, Regulation and Efficiency in Service Industries', *Brookings Papers in Microeconomics* **2** (1993), 71–159.

Bairoch, P. and Levy-Leboyer, M. (eds.), *Disparities in Economic Development since the Industrial Revolution* (London: Macmillan, 1981).

Balassa, B., 'Whither French Planning', *Quarterly Journal of Economics* **179** (1965), 537–54.

Balbin, P. F., 'Spain: Industrial Policy under Authoritarian Politics', in J. Foreman-Peck and G. Federico (eds.), *European Industrial Policy: The Twentieth Century Experience* (Oxford University Press, 1999), 233–67.

Balfour Committee on Industry and Trade, *Further Factors in Industrial and Commercial Efficiency*, Parliamentary Papers, 1928/9, XXX.

Balzani, R. and Giuntini, A., 'Urban Infrastructure and the Hygiene Question in Liberal Italy (1880–1915)', Paper presented to International Economic History Congress, Madrid, 1998.

Bannister, D., 'Bus Deregulation in the UK', in J. McConville (ed.), *Transport Regulation Matters* (London: Pinter, 1997), 31–51.

Barker, T. S. and Savage, C. I., *An Economic History of Transport* (London: Heinemann, 1974).

Baron, J. and Villeneuve. C., 'Le Problème du déficits des entreprises publique', *Problèmes Economique* April 13 (1977), 2–7.

Bauer, J. M. and Latzer, M., 'Telecommunications in Austria', in J. Foreman-Peck and J. Mueller (eds.), *European Telecommunications Organisation* (Baden-Baden: Nomosverlagsgesellschaft, 1988), 53–85.

Baum, W. C., *The French Economy and the State* (Princeton University Press, 1958).

Bayliss, B. T., 'Transport in the European Communities', *Journal of Transport Economics and Policy* **13** (1979), 28–43.

Baxter, R. D., 'Railway Extension and its Results', *Journal of the Royal Statistical Society of London* **29** (1866), 549–95.

Beesley, M. E. and Evans, T., 'The British Experience: The Case of British Rail', in R. Vernon and Y. Aharoni (eds.), *State-Owned Enterprise in Western Economies* (London: Croom Helm, 1981), 117–32.

Beesley, M. and Littlechild, S., 'Privatisation: Principles, Problems and Priorities', *Lloyds Bank Review* 149 (1983), 1–20, reproduced in J. Kay, C. Mayer and D. Thompson (eds.), *Privatisation and Regulation: The UK Experience* (Oxford: Clarendon Press, 1986), 78–93.

Bell, F. and Millward, R., 'Public Health Expenditures and Mortality in England and Wales 1870–1914', *Continuity and Change* 13(2) (1998), 221–49.

Bell, P. and Clarke, P., 'Regulation and Control of Transport in Britain', in P. Bell and P. Clarke (eds.), *Deregulation and Transport: Market Forces in the Modern World* (London: David Fulton Publishers, 1990), 28–52.

Benson, J., 'Coal Mining', in C. Wrigley (ed.), *A History of British Industrial Relations 1875–1913* (Hassocks, Sussex: Harvester Press, 1982), 187–208.

Bergman, L., et al., *Europe's Network Industries* (London: Centre for Economic Policy and Research, 1998).

Behrendt, G., 'Ownership Policy in the Federal Republic of Germany', *German Economic Review* 3 (1965), 281–9.

Berg, H., 'The Municipalisation of the Cinema in Norway', *Annals of Collective Economy* 3 (1927), 130–3.

Bertho-Lavenir, C., 'The Telephone in France 1879–1979: National Characteristics and International Influences', in R. Maintz and T. P. Hughes (eds.), *The Development of Large Technical Systems* (Boulder, Colo.: Frankfurt and Westview Press, 1978), 155–73.

Bhagwati, J. N., 'Splintering and Disembodiment of Services and Developing Nations', *World Economy* 7(2) (1984), 133–43.

Bianchi, F., 'The IRI in Italy: Strategic Role and Political Constraints', *West European Politics* 10(2) (1987), 269–90.

Bijker, W. E., Hughes, T. P. and Pinch, T., *The Social Construction of Technological Systems* (Cambridge, Mass.: MIT Press, 1987).

Blanchard, M., 'The Railway Policy of the Second Empire', in F. Crouzet, W. Chaloner and W. Stern (eds.), *Essays in European Economic History 1789–1914* (London: Arnold, 1969), 98–111.

Blankart, C. B., 'Strategies of Regulatory Reform: An Economic Analysis with Some Remarks on Germany', in G. Majone (ed.), *De-Regulation or Re-Regulation?: Regulation in Europe and the United States* (London: Pinter, 1990), 211–22.

Blum, J., *Lord and Peasant in Russia: From the Ninth to the Nineteenth Century* (Princeton University Press, 1961).

Bohlin, J., 'Sweden: The Rise and Fall of the Swedish Model', in J. Foreman-Peck and G. Federico (eds.), *European Industrial Policy: The Twentieth Century Experience* (Oxford University Press, 1999), 152–76.

Boiteux, M., 'La Tarification des demandes en pointe: Application de la théorie de la vente au coût marginal', *Revue Générale de l'Eléctricité* 58(8) (1949), 321–40, reprinted in English in *Journal of Business* 33 (1960), 157–29 and as chapter 4 of J. R. Nelson (ed.), *Marginal Cost Pricing in Practice* (Englewood Cliffs, N. J.: Prentice-Hall, 1964).

'La Vente au coût marginal', *Revue Française de l'Energie* **81** (1956), 113–17, reproduced in English as chapter 3 of J. R. Nelson (ed.), *Marginal Cost Pricing in Practice* (Englewood Cliffs, N. J.: Prentice-Hall, 1964).

'Le Tarif vert d'Electricité de France', *Revue Française de l'Energie* **82** (1957), 137–51, reprinted in English as chapter 6 of J. R. Nelson (ed.), *Marginal Cost Pricing in Practice* (Englewood Cliffs, N. J.: Prentice-Hall, 1964).

Boiteux, M. and Stasi, P., 'The Determination of the Costs of Expansion of an Inter-connected System of Production and Distribution of Electricity', in J. R. Nelson (ed.), *Marginal Cost Pricing in Practice* (Englewood Cliffs, N. J.: Prentice-Hall, 1964), 91–126.

Bonelli, F., 'The Origins of Public Corporations in Italy', in V. Zamagni (ed.), *Origins and Development of Publicly Owned Enterprises* (University of Florence, Ninth International Economic History Conference, Section B111, 1986), 20–7.

Bongaerts, J. C., 'Financing Railways in the German States 1840–60: A Preliminary View', *Journal of European Economic History* **14** (1985), 331–45.

Bonnard, J. J., 'Planning and Industry in France', in J. Hayward and M. Watson (eds.), *Planning, Politics and Public Policy* (Cambridge University Press, 1975), 93–110.

Bös, D., 'Privatisation in Europe: A Comparison of Approaches', *Oxford Review of Economic Policy* **9**(1) (1993), 95–111.

Bressler, H. J., 'The French Railway Problem', *Political Science Quarterly* **37** (1922), 211–28.

Bristow, J. A., 'State Enterprise in the Republic of Ireland', *Annals of Public and Collective Economy* **37** (1966), 25–42.

British Railways Board, *The Reshaping of British Railways* (the Beeching Report) (London: HMSO, 1963).

Broadberry, S. N., 'The Impact of the World Wars on the Long Run Economic Performance of the British Economy', *Oxford Review of Economic Policy* **4**(1) (1988), 25–36.

'Manufacturing and the Convergence Hypothesis: What the Long-Run Data Show', *Journal of Economic History* **53**(4) (1993), 772–95.

'Anglo-German Productivity Differences 1870–1990: A Sectoral Analysis', *European Review of Economic History* **1**(2) (1997), 247–68.

'How Did the US and Germany Overtake Britain: A Sectoral Analysis of Comparative Productivity Levels', *Journal of Economic History* **58** (1998), 275–407.

'Britain's Productivity Performance in International Perspective 1870–1990', in R. Barrell, G. Mason and M. O'Mahony (eds.), *Productivity, Innovation and Economic Performance* (Cambridge University Press, 2000), 38–57.

Broadberry, S. N., and Ghosal, S., 'From the Counting House to the Modern Office: Explaining Comparative Productivity Performance in Services since 1870', *Journal of Economic History* **62**(4) (2002), 967–98.

Broadberry, S. N. and Howlett, P., 'The UK: Victory at All Costs', in M. Harrison (ed.), *The Economics of World War II: Six Great Powers in International Comparison* (Cambridge University Press, 1998), 43–80.

Broadberry, S. N. and Howlett, P., 'The UK during World War I: Business as Usual?', Paper Presented at Warwick University Economic History Workshop, July 2002.

Brondel, G., 'The Sources of Energy', in C. Cipolla (ed.), *The Fontana Economic History of Europe: The Twentieth Century* (Glasgow: Fontana/Collins, 1973), 219–300.

Brooks, B. C., 'Municipalisation of the Berlin Electrical Works', *Quarterly Journal of Economics* **30** (1916), 188–94.

Brooks, P. W., 'The Development of Air Transport', *Journal of Transport History* **1**(2) (1967), 164–83.

Brown, J. C., 'Coping with Crisis: The Diffusion of Waterworks in Late 19th Century German Towns', *Journal of Economic History* **48** (1988), 307–18.

  'Public Reform for Private Gain?: The Case of Investments in Sanitary Infrastructure 1880–1998', *Urban Studies* **26** (1989), 2–12.

  'Who Paid for the Sanitary City?: Issues and Evidence c. 1910', Paper presented to Session C7, Eleventh International Economic History Conference, Milan, 1994.

Bruno, G., 'L'Utilisation des resources hydroliques pour la production d'énergie électrique en Italie du Sud: 1895–1915', in F. Cardot (ed), *1880–1980: Une siècle de l'électricité dans le monde* (Paris: Presses Universitaires de France, 1987), 253–67.

Bucheim, C., 'Attempts at Controlling the Economy in Western Germany (1945–69)', in E. Aerts and A. S. Milward (eds.), *Economic Planning in the Post-War Period* (Leuven University Press, 1990), 24–33.

Bukow, W., 'Public Undertakings in the Federal Republic of Germany', *Annals of Public and Collective Economy* **36** (1965), 7–13.

Butschek, F., 'Planning for Social Strategy', in E. Aerts and A. S. Milward (eds.), *Economic Planning in the Post-War Period* (Leuven University Press, 1990), 34–41.

  'Were there Alternatives to Transition Policies in Eastern Europe? Some Lessons from the Post-War Reconstruction in Austria', *Journal of European Economic History* **28** (1999), 171–81.

Button, K. J. and Pitfield, D. C. (eds.), *International Railway Economics* (Aldershot: Gower, 1985).

Buxton, N. K., *The Economic Development of the British Coal Industry* (London: Batsford, 1978).

Cafagna, L., 'Italy 1830–1914', in C. Cipolla (ed.), *Fontana Economic History of Europe: The Emergence of Industrial Societies*, 2 parts (Glasgow: Fontana/Collins 1973), part 1, 279–328.

Cain, P. J., 'Private Enterprise or Public Utility? Output, Pricing and Investment in English Railways', *Journal of Transport History* **1** (1973), 9–28.

Cairncross, A., *Years of Recovery: British Economic Policy* (London: Methuen, 1985).

Calvo, A., 'El telefono en España antes de Telefonica (1877–1921)', *Revista de Historia Industria* **13** (1998), 59–80.

Cameron, R. E., *France and the Economic Development of Europe 1880–1914: Conquests of Peace and Seeds of War* (Princeton University Press, 1961).

Cameron, R. E. (ed.), *Essays in French Economic History* (Georgetown, Ontario: R. D. Irwin, 1970).

Cardot, F. (ed.), *1880–1980: Une siècle de l'électricité dans le monde* (Paris: Presses Universitaires de France, 1978).

Carlin, W., 'West German Growth and Institutions 1945–90', in N. Crafts and G. Toniolo (eds.), *Economic Growth in Europe since 1945* (Cambridge University Press, 1996), 455–97.

Caron, F., 'French Railway Investments 1850–1914', in R. Cameron (ed.), *Essays in French Economic History* (Georgetown, Ontario: R. D. Irwin, 1970), 315–40.

An Economic History of Modern France (London: Methuen, 1979).

'France', in P. O'Brien, *Transport and the Economic Development of Europe* (Oxford: Macmillan, 1983), 28–48.

'The Evolution of the Technical System of Railways in France', in R. Maintz and T. P. Hughes (eds.), *The Development of Large Technical Systems* (Boulder, Colo.: Frankfurt and Westview Press, 1987), 69–103.

Caron, F. and Cardot, F. (eds.), *Histoire générale de l'électricité en France. I. 1881–1918: Espoirs et conquêtes* (Paris: L'Association pour l'Histoire de l'Electricité en France, Fayard, 1991).

Carreras, A., Giuntini, A. and Merger, M. (eds.), *European Networks 19th–20th Centuries: New Approaches to the Formation of a Transnational Transport and Communications System* (Milan: Universita Bocconi, Proceedings Eleventh International Economic History Congress, Session B8, 1994).

Carreras, A., Tafunell, X. and Torres, E., 'The Rise and Decline of Spanish State-Owned Firms', in P. A. Toninelli (ed.), *The Rise and Fall of State Owned Enterprise in the Western World* (Cambridge University Press, 2000), 208–36.

Castronovo, V. (ed.), *Storia dell'industria elettrica in Italia. IV. Daldopoguerra alla nazionalizzazione 1945–62* (Roma-Bari: Laterza & Figli, 1994).

Cavalcanti, J., 'Economic Aspects of the Provision and Development of Water Supply in Nineteenth Century Britain', PhD thesis, University of Manchester, 1991.

Centre Européen de l'Entreprise Publique (CEEP), *Les entreprise publiques dans la Communauté Européenne* (Paris: Dunod, 1967).

The Evolution of Public Enterprises in the Community of the Nine (London: CEEP English Editions, 1973).

The Financing of Public Enterprises in the Countries of the European Community (London: CEEP English Editions, 1978).

Public Enterprises in the European Community (London: CEEP English Editions, 1978).

Cerny, P. and Schain, M. (eds.), *Socialism, the State and Public Policy in France* (London: Frances Pinter, 1985).

Chadeau, E., 'Early Nationalisations in France in Long Term Perspective', in V. Zamagni (ed.), *Origins and Development of Publicly Owned Enterprises* (University of Florence, Ninth International Economic History Conference, Section B11, 1986), 28–33.

'The Rise and Decline of State-Owned Industry in Twentieth Century France', in P. A. Toninelli (ed.), *The Rise and Fall of State Owned Enterprise in the Western World* (Cambridge University Press, 2000), 185–207.

Chadwick, E., *Report on the Sanitary Conditions of the Labouring Population of Great Britain: 1842* (ed. M. W. Flinn, Edinburgh University Press, 1965).

'Results of Different Principles of Legislation and Administration in Europe: Of Competition for the Field, as Compared with Competition within the Field, of Service', *Journal of the Royal Statistical Society* 22 (1859), 381–420.

Chantler, P., *The British Gas Industry: An Economic Study* (Manchester University Press, 1938).

Chatterton, D. A., 'State Control of Public Utilities in the Nineteenth Century: The London Gas Industry', *Business History* 14 (2) (1972), 166–78.

Chandler, A. D. and Daems, H. (ed.), *Managerial Hierarchies* (Cambridge, Mass.: Harvard University Press, 1980).

Chester, Sir N., *The Nationalisation of British Industry 1945–51* (London: HMSO, 1975).

Chevrier, J., 'The French Electricity Supply Company: The First Ten Years', *Annals of Collective Economy* 28 (1957), 284–300.

Chick, M., 'Nationalisation, Privatisation and Regulation', in M. W. Kirby and M. B. Rose (eds.), *Business Enterprise in Modern Britain* (London: Routledge, 1994), 315–38.

Industrial Policy in Britain 1945–51: Economic Planning, Nationalisation and the Labour Governments (Cambridge University Press, 1998).

'Le Tarif vert retrouvé: The Marginal Cost Concept and the Pricing of Electricity in Britain and France 1945–73', *Energy Journal* 23(1) (2002), 97–116.

Ciocca, P. and Toniolo, G., 'Industry and Finance in Italy, 1918–40', *Journal of European Economic History* 13 (1984), 113–36.

Clapham, J. H., *The Economic Development of France and Germany 1815–1914* (Cambridge University Press, 1921).

The Economic History of Britain: Vol. I (Cambridge University Press, 1964).

Clarke, J. G., 'The Nationalisation of War Industries in France, 1935–37: A Case Study', *Journal of Modern History* 49 (1977), 411–30.

Clifton, J., Comin, F. and Fuentes, D. D., *Privatisation in the European Union: Public Enterprises and Integration* (London: Kluwer, 2003).

Cohen, J. S., 'Was Italian Fascism a Developmental Dictatorship?', *Economic History Review* 41 (1988), 97–113.

Commissioners on the State of Large Towns and Populous Districts, *First Report 1844* (London: HMSO, 1844).

Second Report 1845 (London: HMSO, 1845).

Confraria, J., 'Portugal: Industrialisation and Backwardness', in J. Foreman-Peck and G. Federico (eds.), *European Industrial Policy: The Twentieth Century Experience* (Oxford University Press, 1999), 268–94.

Conti, F., 'The Creation of a Regional Electrical System: Selt Valdarno Group and the Electrification of Tuscany', in M. Trédé (ed.), *Electricité et électrification dans le monde 1880–1980* (Paris: Association pour l'Histoire de l' Electricité en France, Presses Universitaires de France, 1990), 155–68.

Coombe, D., *State Enterprise: Business or Politics* (London: Allen and Unwin, 1972).

Corti, G., 'Perspectives on Public Corporations and Public Enterprises in Five Nations', *Annals of Collective Economy* 47 (1976), 47–86.

Costa-Gomes, M. and Tavares, J., 'Democracy and Business Cycles: Evidence from Portuguese Economic History', *European Review of Economic History* **3**(3) (1999), 295–322.

Court, W. H. B., 'Problems of the British Coal Industry between the Wars', *Economic History Review* **15**(1) (1945), 1–24.

Coustel, J-P., 'Telecommunications Services in France: The Regulatory Movement and the Challenge of Competition', *Telecommunications Policy* **10** (1986), 229–43.

Craeybeckx, J., 'The Beginnings of the Industrial Revolution in Belgium', in R. Cameron (ed.), *Essays in French Economic History* (Georgetown, Ontario: R. D. Irwin, 1970), 187–99.

Crafts, N. F. R., *British Economic Growth during the Industrial Revolution* (Oxford: Clarendon Press, 1985).

'The Human Development Index and Changes in Standards of Living: Some Historical Comparisons', *European Review of Economic History* **1**(3) (1997), 299–322.

Crafts, N. and Toniolo, G. (eds.), *Economic Growth in Europe since 1945* (Cambridge University Press, 1996).

Crompton, G. W., ' " Efficient and economical working?": The Performance of the Railway Companies 1923–33', *Business History* **27** (2) (1985), 222–37.

'Squeezing the Pulpless Orange: Labour and Capital on the Railways in the Inter-War Period', *Business History* **31** (1989), 66–83.

'The Railway Companies and the Nationalisation Issue, 1920–50', in R. Millward and J. Singleton (eds.), *The Political Economy of Nationalisation in Britain 1920–50* (Cambridge University Press, 1995), 116–43.

Crouzet, F., Chaloner, W. and Stern, W. (eds.), *Essays in European Economic History 1789–1914* (London: Arnold, 1969).

Cubel, A. F., 'The Policy of Industrial Promotion in Spain, 1874–1973', Paper presented at the European Historical Economics Society Conference on *A Century of Industrial Policy in Europe*, Oxford, Worcester College, 1992.

Dakyns, A. L., 'The Water Supply of English Towns in 1846', *Manchester School* **2**(1) (1931), 21–5.

Daunton, M., 'Urban Britain', in T. R. Gourvish and A. O. Day (eds.), *Later Victorian Britain, 1867–1900* (London: Macmillan, 1988), 37–67.

Davids, M., 'The Relationship between the State Enterprises for Postal, Telegraph and Telephone Services and the State in the Netherlands: A Historical Perspective', *Business and Economic History* **24**(1) (1995), 194–205.

'The Dutch Way: Privatisation and Liberalisation of PTT', *Business History* **47** (April 2005).

Davids, M. and Zandem, J. L. van, 'A Reluctant State and its Enterprises: State-Owned Enterprises in the Netherlands in the "Long Run" 20th Century', in P. A. Toninelli (ed.), *The Rise and Fall of State Owned Enterprise in the Western World* (Cambridge University Press, 2000), 253–72.

Dawson, W. H., *Municipal Life and Local Germany* (London: Longmans, Green and Co., 1961).

Demsetz, H., 'Why Regulate Utilities?', *Journal of Law and Economics* **11** (1968), 55–65.

Department of Trade and Industry, *UK Energy Statistics 1972* (London: HMSO, 1972).

Digest of UK Energy Statistics 1999 (London: HMSO, 1999).

Despicht, N., 'Diversification and Expansion: The Creation of Modern Services', in S. Holland (ed.), *The State as Entrepreneur: New Dimensions for Public Enterprise: The IRI State Shareholding Formula* (White Plains, N.Y.: International Arts and Sciences Press, 1972), 127–64.

Dickinson, H. W., *The Water Supply of Greater London* (London: Courier Press, 1956).

Dieck, M., 'Collective Economy Undertakings in the Federal Republic of Germany', *Annals of Public and Collective Economy* **39** (1968), 225–49.

Dienel, H.-L., 'Lufthansa: Two German Airlines', in H.-L. Dienel and P. Lyth, *Flying the Flag: European Commercial Air Transport since 1945* (Basingstoke: Macmillan, 1998), 87–125.

Dienel, H.-L. and Lyth, P.J. (eds.), *Flying the Flag: European Commercial Air Transport since 1945* (Basingstoke: Macmillan, 1998).

Dierikx, M., 'KLM: An Airline Outgrowing its Flag', in H.-L. Dienel and P. Lyth, *Flying the Flag: European Commercial Air Transport since 1945* (Basingstoke: Macmillan, 1998), 126–58.

Dierikx, M. L. and Lyth, P. J., 'The Development of the European Scheduled Air Transport Network, 1920–1970: An Explanatory Model', in A. Carreras, A. Giuntini and M. Merger (eds.), *European Networks 19th–20th Centuries: New Approaches to the Formation of a Transnational Transport and Communications System* (Milan: Universita Bocconi, Proceedings Eleventh International Economic History Congress, Session B8, 1994).

Distenfass, F., 'Entrepreneurial Failure Reconsidered: The Case of the Inter-War British Coal Industry', *Business History Review* **62**(1) (1988), 1–34.

Divall, C. and Bond, W. (eds.), *Suburbanising the Masses: Public Transport and Urban Development in Historical Perspective* (Aldershot: Ashgate, 2003).

Dobbin, F., *Forging Industrial Policy: The United States, Britain and France in the Railway Age* (Cambridge University Press, 1994).

Dobson, A., 'Regulation or Competition?: Negotiating the Anglo-American Air Services Agreement of 1977', *Journal of Transport History* **15**(2) (1994), 144–64.

Donges, J.B., 'From an Autarchic towards a Cautious Outward Looking Industrialisation Policy', *Weltwirtschaftliches Archiv* **107** (1971), 33–72.

Dormois, J.-P., 'France: The Idiosyncrasies of *Voluntarisme*', in J. Foreman-Peck and G. Federico (eds.), *European Industrial Policy: The Twentieth Century Experience* (Oxford University Press, 1999), 58–97.

Dougall, H. H., 'Railway Rates and Rate Making in France since 1921', *Journal of Political Economy* **35** (1933), 289–333.

'The French Solution for the Railway Problem', *Journal of Political Economy* **36** (1934), 385–92.

'Railway Nationalisation and Transport Co-ordination in France', *Journal of Political Economy* **40** (1938), 218–28.

'Public and Private Operation of Railways in France', *Annals of the American Academy of Politics and Social Science* **201** (1939), 211–16.

Doukas, K., 'Ownership, Management and Regulation of Electric Undertakings in France', *The George Washington Law Review* **6**(2) (1938), 147–70 (January) and 282–312 (March).

'Armaments and the French Experience', *American Political Science Quarterly* **33** (1939), 279–91.

The French Railroads and the State (New York: Columbia Press, 1945).

Duchene, V., *150 jaar stadsgas te Leuven* (Deurne, 1995).

Dumke, R. H., 'Reassessing the Wirtschaftswunder: Reconstruction and Post War Growth in West Germany in an International Context', *Bulletin of Oxford University Institute of Statistics* **52** (1990), 451–71.

Dunham, A. L., 'How the First French Railways were Planned', *Journal of Economic History* **1** (1941), 12–25.

Dunlavy, C. N., *Politics and Industrialisation: Early Railroads in USA and Prussia* (Princeton University Press, 1992).

'Corporate Democracy: Stockholder Voting Rights in 19th Century USA and Prussian Railroad Corporations', in L. Andersson-Skog and O. Krantz (eds.), *Institutions and the Transport and Communications Industries* (Canton, Mass.: Science History Publications, Watson, 1999), 33–60.

Dupuy, G., 'Utility Networks and Territory in the Paris Region: The Case of Andresy', in J. A. Tarr and G. Dupuy (eds.), *Technology and the Rise of the Networked City in Europe* (Philadelphia: Temple University Press, 1988), 295–306.

Dyson, K., 'West European States and the Communications Revolution', in K. Dyson and P. Humphries (eds.), *The Politics of the Communications Revolution in Europe* (London: Cass, 1986), 10–55.

Dyson, K. and Humphries, P. (eds.), *The Politics of the Communications Revolution in Europe* (London: Cass, 1986).

Dyson, K. and Wilks, S. (eds.), *Industrial Crisis: A Comparative Study of the State and Industry* (New York: St. Martin's Press, 1988).

The Economist, 'Public Sector Enterprise: The State in the Market' (30 December 1978), 37–58.

Edelstein, M., *Overseas Investment in the Age of High Imperialism: The United Kingdom 1850–1914* (London: Methuen, 1982).

Einaudi, M., 'Nationalisation in France and Italy', *Social Research* **15**(1) (1948), 22–43.

'Nationalisation of Industry in Western Europe: Recent Literature and Debate', *The American Political Science Review* (March 1950), 177–91.

Einaudi, M., Byé, M. and Rossi, E., *Nationalisation in France and Italy* (Ithaca, N. Y.: Cornell University Press, 1955).

Eloranta, J., 'Beyond the Void: Interaction of Military Spending, Systematic Leadership and Economic Growth for Democracies and Transitional Regimes 1870–1938', Paper presented at European Historical Economics Society Conference, Merton College, Oxford, 2001.

'Re-assessing First World War Military Spending: The Role of the Great Powers in the International System 1870–1913', Paper presented at Warwick University Economic History Workshop, July 2002.

Espeli, H., 'From Dual Structure to State Monopoly in Norwegian Telephones, 1880–1924', Working Paper, Norwegian School of Management, Scandvika, Norway, January 2002.

Esser, J. E. and Fach, W. with K. Dyson, '"Social Market" and Modernisation Policy: West Germany', in K. Dyson and S. Wilks (eds.), *Industrial Crisis: A Comparative Study of the State and Industry* (Oxford: Blackwells, 1983), 102–27.

Estapé-Triay, S., 'Economic Nationalism, State Intervention and Foreign Multinationals: The Case of the Spanish Ford Subsidiary 1936–54', *Essays in Economic and Business History* **16** (1998), 41–56.

Estrin, P. and Holmes, P., *French Planning in Theory and Practice* (London: Allen and Unwin, 1983).

Estrin, P. and Pérotin, V., 'The Regulation of British and French Nationalised Industry', *European Economic Review* **31** (1987), 301–7.

Eurostat (Statistical Office of the European Communities), *Energy Statistics: Yearbook 1969–73* (Brussels: Eurostat, 1974).

Energy Yearly Statistics 1990 (Brussels: Eurostat, 1992).

Evans, P., Ruesehemeyer, D. and Skocpol, T., *Bringing the State Back in* (Cambridge University Press, 1985).

Evans, R. J., *Death in Hamburg: Society and Politics in the Cholera Years 1830–1910* (Oxford: Clarendon Press, 1990).

Falk, W. and Pittack, H., 'Publicly Owned Enterprises and Forms of Participation of the State in Private Enterprise in Germany before 1933', in V. Zamagni (ed.), *Origins and Development of Publicly Owned Enterprises* (University of Florence, Ninth International Economic History Conference, Section B111, 1986), 34–9.

Falkus, M. E., 'The British Gas Industry before 1850', *Economic History Review* **20** (1967), 494–508.

'The Development of Municipal Trading in the Nineteenth Century', *Business History* **19**(2) (1977), 134–61.

Fearon, P., 'The British Airframe Industry and the State 1918–35', *Economic History Review* **26** (1974), 236–51.

Federal Ministry of Transport and Nationalised Undertakings, 'The Nationalisation of Austria's Basic Industries', *Annals of Collective Economy* **23** (1952), 1–39.

Federation of British Industry, *The Next Five Years* (London: FBI, 1960).

Federico, G. and Giannetti, R., 'Italy: Stalling and Surpassing', in J. Foreman-Peck and G. Federico (eds.), *European Industrial Policy: The Twentieth Century Experience* (Oxford University Press, 1999), 124–51.

Federico, G. and Tena, A., 'Was Italy a Protected Country', *European Review of Economic History* **2**(1) (1998), 73–98.

Feinstein, C. H. and Pollard, S. (eds.), *Studies in Capital Formation in the UK, 1750–1920* (Oxford University Press, 1988).

Fenoaltea, S., 'Railroads and Italian Industrial Growth 1861–1913', *Explorations in Economic History* **9** (1972), 323–51.

'The Growth of the Utility Industries in Italy 1861–1913', *Journal of Economic History* **42** (1982), 601–28.

'Italy', in P. O'Brien (ed.), *Railways and the Economic Development of Europe* (Oxford: Macmillan, 1983), 48–120.

Feldenkirchen, W., 'Germany: The Invention of Interventionism', in J. Foreman-Peck and G. Federico (eds.), *European Industrial Policy: The Twentieth Century Experience* (Oxford University Press, 1999), 98–123.

Fernandez, A., 'Production and Distribution of Electricity in Bordeaux, 1887–1956: Private and Public Operation', *Contemporary European History* 5(2) (1996), 159–70.

Economie et politique de l'électricité à Bordeaux (1887–1956) (Talence: Sciences PO Bordeaux, Presses Universitaires de Bordeaux, 1998).

'Les Lumières de la ville: L'Administration municipale à l'épreuve de l'électrification', *Vingtième Siècle Revue d'Histoire* 62 (1999), 107–22.

Fine, B., 'Economies of Scale and a Feather-Bedding Cartel?: A Reconsideration of the Inter-War British Coal Industry', *Economic History Review* 43(3) (1990), 438–49.

Finer, H., *Municipal Trading* (London: Allen and Unwin, 1941).

Florio, M., 'The Privatisation of British Telecom', *Economia Pubblica*, 3(2) (2003), 187–220 (in Italian).

The Great Divestiture: Evaluating the Welfare Effects of British Privatisation (Cambridge, Mass.: MIT Press, 2004).

Fontana, J. and Nadal, J., 'Spain 1914–70', in C. Cipolla (ed.), *Fontana Economic History of Europe: Contemporary Economies* 2 parts (Glasgow: Fontana/Collins, 1976), Part 2, 460–529.

Fohlen, C., 'France 1920–70', in C. Cipolla (ed.), *The Fontana Economic History of Europe: Contemporary Economies* 2 parts (Glasgow: Fontana/Collins, 1976), Part 1, 72–127.

Foreman-Peck, J., 'Competition and Performance in the UK Telecommunications Industry', *Telecommunications Policy* 9 (1985), 215–27.

'Natural Monopoly and Railway Policy in the 19th Century', *Oxford Economic Papers* 39 (1987), 699–718.

'Competition, Cooperation and Nationalisation in the Early Telegraph Network', *Business History* 31(3) (1989), 81–102.

'L'Etat et le développement du réseau de télécommunications en Europe à ses débuts', *Histoire, Economie, Société* 4 (1989), 383–402.

Foreman-Peck, J. and Federico, G. (eds.), *European Industrial Policy: The Twentieth Century Experience* (Oxford University Press, 1999).

Foreman-Peck, J. and Hannah, L., 'Britain: From Economic Liberalism to Socialism – and Back?', in J. Foreman-Peck and G. Federico (eds.), *European Industrial Policy: The Twentieth Century Experience* (Oxford University Press, 1999), 18–57.

Foreman-Peck, J. and Manning, D., 'Telecommunications in Italy', in J. Foreman-Peck and J. Mueller (eds.), *European Telecommunications Organisation* (Baden-Baden: Nomosverlagsgesellschaft, 1988), 181–201.

'Telecommunications in Norway', in J. Foreman-Peck and J. Muller (eds.), *European Telecommunications Organisation* (Baden-Baden: Nomosverlagsgesellschaft, 1988), 221–36.

'Telecommunications Policy in the United Kingdom', in J. Foreman-Peck and J. Mueller (eds.), *European Telecommunications Organisation* (Baden-Baden: Nomosverlagsgesellschaft, 1988), 257–78.

Foreman-Peck, J. and Millward, R., *Public and Private Ownership of British Industry 1820–1990* (Oxford University Press, 1994).

Foreman-Peck, J. and Mueller, J. (eds.), *European Telecommunications Organisation* (Baden-Baden: Nomosverlagsgesellschaft, 1988).

Foreman-Peck, J. and Waterson, M., 'The Comparative Efficiency of Public and Private Enterprise in Britain: Electricity Generation between the World Wars', *Economic Journal* 95 (Supplement) (1985), 83–95.

Fraenkel, G., 'Italian Industrial Policy in the Framework of Economic Planning', in J. Hayward and M. Watson (eds.), *Planning, Politics and Public Policy* (Cambridge University Press, 1975), 128–40.

Frankel, P. H., *Mattei: Oil and Politics* (London: Faber and Faber, 1966).

Fraser, H., 'Municipal Socialism and Social Policy', in R. J. Morris and R. Rodger (eds.), *The Victorian City: A Reader in British Urban History: 1820–1914* (London: Longman, 1993), 258–80.

Freedman, C. E., *The Conseil d'Etat in Modern France* (New York: Columbia University Press, 1961).

'Joint Stock Business Organisation in France 1807–67', *Business History Review* 39 (1965), 184–204.

Fremdling, R., 'Railroads and German Economic Growth: A Leading Sector Analysis with a Comparison to the USA and GB', *Journal of Economic History* 37 (1977), 583–604.

'Freight Rates and the State Budget: The Role of the Nationalised Prussian Railways 1880–1913', *Journal of European Economic History* 9(1) (1980), 21–39.

'Germany', in P. O'Brien (ed.), *Railways and the Economic Development of Europe* (Oxford: Macmillan, 1983), 121–47.

'The Prussian and Dutch Railway Regulaton in the 19th Century', in L. Andersson-Skog and O. Krantz (eds.), *Institutions and the Transport and Communications Industries* (Canton, Mass.: Science History Publications, Watson, 1999), 61–92.

Fremdling, R. and Knieps, G., 'Competition, Regulation and Nationalisation: The Prussian Railway System in the 19th Century', *Scandinavian Economic History Review* 41(1) (1993), 129–54.

Fridensen, P., 'Atouts et limites de la modernisation par en haut: Les Entreprises publiques facé à leurs critiques (1944–1986)', in P. Fridensen and A. Strauss (eds.) *Le capitalisme française* (Paris: Librairie Arthème, Fayard, 1987), 169–88.

Fritz, M, 'Shipping in Sweden, 1850–1913', *Scandinavian Economic History Review* 28 (1980), 147–60.

'Post-War Planning in Sweden', in E. Aerts and A. S. Milward (eds.), *Economic Planning in the Post-War Period* (Leuven University Press, 1990), 43–51.

Frost, R. L., 'The Flood of "Progress": Technocrats and Peasants at Tignes (Savoy), 1946–52', *French Historical Studies* 14 (1985), 117–40.

Alternating Currents: Nationalised Power in France 1946–70 (Ithaca, N. Y.: Cornell University Press, 1991).

Fullerton, B., 'Deregulation in a European Context – The Case of Sweden', in
P. Bell and P. Clarke, *Deregulation and Transport: Market Forces in the Modern
World* (London: David Fulton Publishers, 1990), 125–40.

Galasso, G., (ed.), *Storia dell'industria elettrica in Italia. III. Expansiove e oligopolio.
1926–45* (Roma-Bari: Laterza & Figli, 1993).

Galessi, F. L., 'Hanging off the Windowsill: Italy at War 1915–18', Paper presented at Warwick University Economic History Workshop, July 2002.

Geiger, R., 'Planning the French Canals: The Becquez Plan of 1820–1922',
Journal of Economic History **44** (1984), 329–39.

General Board of Health, *Report on the Supply of Water to the Metropolis* (London:
HMSO, 1850).

Gershenkron, A., *Economic Backwardness in Historical Perspective* (Cambridge,
Mass., Harvard University Press, 1967).

Giannetti, R., 'Resources, Firms and Public Policy in the Growth of the Italian
Electrical Industry from the Beginnings to the 1930s', in F. Cardot (ed.),
1880–1980: Une siècle de l'électricité dans le monde (Paris: Presses Universitaires
de France, 1987), 41–50.

'Dinamica della demanda e delle tariffe', in G. Galasso (ed.), *Storia dell'industria elettrica in Italia. III. Expansiove e oligopolio. 1926–45* (Roma-Bari: Laterza
& Figli, 1993), 269–324.

Gillet, M., 'The Coal Age and the Rise of Coalfields of the North and the
Pas de Calais', in F. Crouzet, W. Chaloner and W. Stern (eds.), *Essays
in European Economic History 1789–1914* (London: Arnold, 1969),
179–202.

Giterman, M, 'The Long Distance Gas Supply in Germany', *Annals of Collective
Economy* **5** (1929), 166–90.

Giuntini, A., 'Inland Navigation in Italy in the 19th Century', in A. Kunz and
J. Armstrong (eds.), *Inland Navigation and Economic Development in 19th
Century Europe* (Mainz: Verlag Philipp von Zabern, 1995), 147–57.

'La modernizzazione della infrastrutture e dei servizi urbani in Italia: Termi,
risultali e objettivi della ricerca storica', Mimeo, 2001.

Gjolberg, O., 'The Substitution of Steam for Sail in Norwegian Ocean Shipping,
1866–1914: A Study in the Economics of Diffusion', *Scandinavian Economic
History Review* **28** (1980), 135–46.

Glachant, J.-M., *Competition in European Electricity Markets: A Cross-Country
Comparison* (Cheltenham: Edward Elgar, 2003).

Gomez-Mendoza, A., 'Spain', in P. O'Brien (ed.), *Railways and the Economic
Development of Europe* (Oxford: Macmillan, 1983), 148–69.

'Europe's Cinderella: Inland Navigation in 19th century Spain' in A. Kunz and
J. Armstrong (ed.), *Inland Navigation and Economic Development in 19th
Century Europe* (Mainz: Verlag Philipp von Zabem, 1995), 131–45.

'Competition between Private and Public Enterprise in Spain, 1939–59: An
Alternative View', *Business and Economic History* **26**(2) (1997), 696–708.

'Along Broad Lines: The Economic History of Spanish Railways, 1973–96',
Journal of Transport History **19**(1) (1998), 1–17.

'Motor Cars and Railways in Inter-War Spain: Regulation vis à vis
De-regulation', in L. Andersson-Skog and O. Krantz (eds.), *Institutions and*

the Transport and Communications Industries (Canton, Mass.: Science History Publications, Watson, 1999), 199–216.

Gordon, R., 'Comment', on M. Baily, 'Competition, Regulation and Efficiency in Service Industries', *Brookings Papers in Microeconomics* 2(1993), 131–44.

Goubert, J.-P., 'The Development of Water and Sewerage Systems in France 1850–1950', in J. A. Tarr and G. Dupuy (eds.), *Technology and the Rise of the Networked City in Europe* (Philadelphia: Temple University Press, 1988), 116–36.

The Conquest of Water: The Advent of Health in the Industrial Age (Princeton University Press, 1989).

Gournay, C. de, 'Telephone Networks in France and Great Britain', in J. A. Tarr and G. Dupuy (eds.), *Technology and the Rise of the Networked City in Europe* (Philadelphia: Temple University Press, 1988), 322–38.

Gourvish, T., *British Railways 1948–73: A Business History* (Cambridge University Press, 1986).

'The Regulation of Britain's Railways', in J. McConville (ed.), *Transport Regulation Matters* (London: Pinter, 1997), 3–15.

British Railways: 1974–97: From Integration to Privatisation (Oxford University Press, 2002).

Grassini, F. A., 'The Italian Experience: The Political Constraints', in R. Vernon and Y. Aharoni (eds.), *State-Owned Enterprise in Western Economies* (London: Croom Helm, 1981), 70–84.

Greasley, D., 'Fifty Years of Coal Mining Productivity: The Record of the British Coal Industry before 1939', *Journal of Economic History* 50(4) (1990), 877–902.

'The Coal Industry: Images and Realities on the Road to Nationalisation', in R. Millward and J. Singleton (eds.), *The Political Economy of Nationalisation in Britain 1920–50* (Cambridge University Press, 1995), 37–64.

Green, D., 'Strategic Management and the State: France', in K. Dyson and S. Wilks (eds.), *Industrial Crisis: A Comparative Study of the State and Industry* (New York: St Martin's Press, 1988), 161–92.

Griffiths, R. T., 'Macroeconomic Planning in the Netherlands (1945–1958)', in E. Aerts and A. S. Milward (eds.), *Economic Planning in the Post-War Period* (Leuven University Press, 1990), 52–60.

Groupe de Travail du Comité Interministériel des Entreprises Publiques (Nora Report), *Rapport sur les entreprises publiques* (Paris: La Documentation Française, Editions de Secrétariat Général de Gouvernment, Direction de la Documentation, April 1967).

Guellec, J. Le, 'The French Gas Company, 1946–56', *Annals of Collective Economy* 28 (1957), 264–83.

Guillerme, A., 'The Genesis of Water Supply, Distribution and Sewerage Systems in France 1800–1850', in J. A. Tarr and G. Dupuy (eds.), *Technology and the Rise of the Networked City in Europe* (Philadelphia: Temple University Press, 1988), 91–136.

Gunston, W. H., 'Telephone Development of the World at the End of 1932', *The Telegraph and Telephone Journal* 56 (1933), 56–8.

Hackett, J. and Hackett, A., *Economic Planning in France* (Cambridge, Mass.: Harvard University Press, 1963).

Haid, A. and Mueller, J., 'Telecommunications in the Federal Republic of Germany', in J. Foreman-Peck and J. Mueller (eds.), *European Telecommunications Organisation* (Baden-Baden: Nomosverlagsgesellschaft, 1988), 155–80.

Hall, P. A., *Governing the Economy: The Politics of State Intervention in Britain and France* (New York: Oxford University Press, 1986).

Hamlin, P. A., 'Muddling in Bumbledom: On the Enormity of Large Sanitary Improvements in Four British Towns, 1855–1885', *Victorian Studies* **32**(1) (1988), 57–81.

Hannah, L., 'A Pioneer of Public Enterprise: The Central Electricity Generating Board and the National Grid', in B. Supple (ed.), *Essays in British Business History* (Oxford: Clarendon Press, 1977), 207–26.

Electricity before Nationalisation (London: Macmillan, 1979).

'Public Policy and the Advent of Large Scale Industry: The Case of Electricity Supply in the U.S.A., Germany and Britain', in N. Horn and K. Kocka (eds.), *Recht und Entwicklung der Grossunternehmen im 19. und frühen 20. Jahrhundert* (Göttingen: Vandenhoeck and Ruprecht, 1979), 577–89.

Engineers, Managers and Politicians: The First Fifteen Years of Nationalised Electricity Supply in Britain (London: Macmillan, 1982).

'A Failed Experiment: The State Ownership of Industry', in R. Floud and P. Johnson (eds.), *The Cambridge Economic History of Modern Britain: Structural Change and Growth 1939–2000* (Cambridge University Press, 2004), 84–111.

Harcavi, G., 'Nationalisation of the French Railways', *Annals of the American Academy of Political and Social Science* **190** (1939), 217–26.

Hardach, K., 'Germany', in C. Cipolla (ed.), *The Fontana Economic History of Europe: Contemporary Economies*, 2 parts (Glasgow: Fontana/Collins, 1976), Part 1, 180–265.

Harris, J., 'Society and the State in Twentieth Century Britain', in F. M. L. Thompson (ed.), *The Cambridge Social History of Britain 1750–1850. III. Social Agencies and Institutions* (Cambridge University Press, 1990), 63–118.

Harrison, M., (ed.), *The Economics of World War II: Six Great Powers in International Comparison* (Cambridge University Press, 1998).

Harrison, R. J., *An Economic History of Modern Spain* (Manchester University Press, 1978).

Hassan, J. A., 'The Growth and Impact of the British Water Industry in the Nineteenth Century', *Economic History Review* **38**(4) (1985), 531–47.

'The Water Industry: A Failure of Public Policy?', in R. Millward and J. Singleton (eds.), *The Political Economy of Nationalisation in Britain 1920–50* (Cambridge University Press, 1995).

A History of Water in Modern England and Wales (Manchester University Press, 1998).

Hawke, G. R., 'Pricing Policy of Railways in England and Wales before 1881', in M. C. Reed, *Railways in the Victorian Economy: Studies in Finance and Economic Growth* (Newton Abbott: David and Charles, 1969), 76–110.

Hazlewood, A., 'The Origin of the State Telephone in Britain', *Oxford Economic Papers* **5** (1953), 13–25.

Hedin, L.-E., 'Some Notes on the Financing of the Swedish Railways 1860–1914', *Economy and History* **10** (1967), 3–37.

Hefeker, C., 'The Agony of Central Power: Fiscal Federalism in the German Reich', *European Review of Economic History* **5**(1) (2001), 119–42.

Heinze, C. W. and Kill, H. K., 'The Development of the German Railroad System', in R. Maintz and T. P. Hughes (eds.), *The Development of Large Technical Systems* (Boulder Colo.: Frankfurt and Westview Press, 1978), 105–34.

Hennock, E. P., 'Finance and Politics in Urban Local Government in England 1835–1900', *Historical Journal* **6**(2) (1963), 212–25.

'The Urban Sanitary Movement in England and Germany 1838–1914: A Comparison', *Continuity and Change* **15**(2) (2000), 269–96.

Henriksen, M., Juning, L. and Stymne, J., 'Economic Growth and the Swedish Model', in N. Crafts and G. Toniolo (eds.), *Economic Growth in Europe since 1945* (Cambridge University Press, 1996), 240–89.

Hens, L. and Solar, P., 'Belgium: Liberalism by Default', in J. Foreman-Peck and G. Federico (eds.), *European Industrial Policy: The Twentieth Century Experience* (Oxford University Press, 1999), 194–214.

Hentenryk, G. Kurgen-van, 'Les Chemins de fer belges ou les ambiguités de l'éntreprise publiques en économie capitaliste au XIX siècle', in V. Zamagni (ed.), *Origins and Development of Publicly Owned Enterprises* (University of Florence, Ninth International Economic History Conference, Section B111, 1986), 47–53.

'La Régime économique de l'industrie électrique belge depuis la fin du XIX siècle', in F. Cardot (ed.), *1880–1980: Une siècle de l'électricité dans le monde* (Paris: Presses Universitaires de France, 1987), 121–33.

Herten, B. van der, 'Belgian Inland Shipping 1831–1939: An Estimate of Total Output', in A. Kunz and J. Armstrong (eds.), *Inland Navigation and Economic Development in 19th Century Europe (Mainz: Verlag Philipp von Zabem, 1995), 30–45.*

Hietalla, M., *Services and Urbanisation at the Turn of the Century: The Diffusion of Innovations*, Studia Historica 23 (Helsinki: Finnish Historical Society, 1987).

Higginson, M., 'Introduction to International Transport Deregulation', in P. Bell and P. Clarke, *Deregulation and Transport: Market Forces in the Modern World* (London: David Fulton Publishers, 1990), 52–64.

Hirschfield, A., 'The Role of Public Enterprise in the French Economy', *Annals of Public and Collective Economy* **44** (1973), 225–69.

Hochmuth, M. S., 'Aerospace', in R. Vernon, *Big Business and the State* (Cambridge, Mass.: Harvard University Press, 1974), 145–69.

Hoffman, S., 'The Effects of World War II on French Society and Politics', *French Historical Studies* **2** (1961), 28–63.

Holcombe, A. N., 'The Telephone in Britain', *Quarterly Journal of Economics* **21**(1) (1906), 96–135.

Public Ownership of Telephones on the Continent of Europe (Cambridge, Mass: Harvard University Press, 1911).

Holland, S., (ed.), *The State as Entrepreneur: New Dimensions for Public Enterprise: The IRI State Shareholding Formula* (White Plains, N. Y.: International Arts and Sciences Press, 1972).

Holter, D. W., 'Mineworkers and Nationalisation in France: Insights into the Concept of State Theory', *Politics and Society* **11**(1) (1982), 2–21.

Hook, J. van, 'From Socialisation to Co-Determination: The US, Britain, Germany and Public Ownership in the Ruhr', *Historical Journal* **45** (2002), 179–93.

Horn, N., and Kocka, K., (eds.), *Recht und Entwicklung der Grossunternehmen im 19. und frühen 20. Jahrhundert* (Göttingen: Vandenhoeck and Ruprecht, 1979).

Hornby, O. and Nilsson, C. A., 'The Transition from Sail to Steam in the Danish Merchant Fleet, 1865–1910', *Scandinavian Economic History Review* **28**(2) (1980), 109–34.

Houpt, S., 'More than Ore: Modern Spanish Steel', Paper presented at European Historical Economics Society Conference, Merton College, Oxford, 2001.

Howe, F., *European Cities at Work* (New York: Charles Scribner's Sons, 1913).

Howlett, P., 'British Business and the State during the Second World War', in J. Sakudo and T. Shiba (eds.), *World War II and the Transformation of Business Systems* (Tokyo University Press, 1994), 133–53.

Hughes, T. P., 'Technological Momentum in History: Hydrogenation in Germany 1898–1933', *Past and Present* **44** (1969), 106–32.

'Technology as a Force for Change in History: The Effort to Form a Unified Electric Power System in Weimar Germany', in H. Mommsen (ed.), *Industrielles System und politische Entwicklung in der Weimarer Republik* (Düsseldorf: Droste Verlag, 1977), 153–66.

Networks of Power: Electrification in Western Society 1880–1930 (Baltimore: Johns Hopkins Press, 1983).

Hughes, T. P. and T. Pinch, *The Social Construction of Technological Systems* (Cambridge, Mass.: MIT Press, 1987), 51–82.

Humphreys, B. K., 'Nationalisation and the Independent Airlines in the United Kingdom 1945–51', *Journal of Transport History* **3** (1976), 265–81.

Humphries, P., 'Legitimising the Communications Revolution: Government, Parties and Trade Unions in Britain, France and West Germany', in K. Dyson and P. Humphries (eds.), *The Politics of the Communications Revolution in Europe* (London: Cass, 1986), 163–94.

Hyldtoft, O., *Den lysende gas: Etablerinjen af det danske gassystem 1800–1890* (Herning, Denmark: Systimes Teknologihistorie, European Educational Publishers Group, 1994) (English summary 173–190).

'Modern Theories of Regulation: An Old Story: Danish Gasworks in the 19th Century', *Scandinavian Economic History Review* **42** (1) (1994), 29–53.

'Making Gas: The Establishment of the Nordic Gas Systems, 1800–1870', in A. Kaijser and M. Hedin (eds.), *Nordic Energy Systems: Historical Perspectives and Current Issues* (Canton, Mass.: Science History Publications, 1995), 76–99.

Hymans, M., ' "Air France" – A National Company', *Annals of Collective Economy* **28** (1957), 311–21.

Iordanoglou, C. F., *Public Enterprise Revisited: A Closer Look at the 1954–79 UK Labour Productivity Record* (Cheltenham: Edward Elgar, 2001).

Jakobsson, E., 'Industrialised Rivers: The Development of Swedish Hydropower', in A. Kaijser and M. Hedin (eds.), *Nordic Energy Systems: Historical Perspectives and Current Issues* (Canton, Mass.: Science History Publications, 1995), 55–74.

Jeding, J.,'Liberalisation and Control: Instruments and Strategy in the Regulation of reform of Swedish Telecommunications', in L. Magnusson and J. Ottosson, *Evolutionary Economics and Path Dependence* (Cheltenham: Edward Elgar, 1997), 166–82.

Jeding, J., Ottosson, J. and Magnusson, L., 'Regulatory Change and International Co-operation: The Scandinavian Telecommunications Agreements, 1900–1960', *Scandinavian Economic History Review* **47** (2) (1999), 63–77.

Jeppson, S. E., Paulsen, K. G. and Schneider, F., 'Telecommunications Services in Denmark', in J. Foreman-Peck and J. Muller (eds.), *European Telecommunications Organisation* (Baden-Baden: Nomosverlagsgesellschaft, 1988), 109–29.

Johansen, H. C., *Danish Historical Statistics* (Copenhagen: Nordisk Forlag, 1985).

Joint Select Committee of the House of Lords and the House of Commons, *Report on Municipal Trading*, Parliamentary Papers 1900 VII and 1903 VII (London: HMSO).

Jolly, P., 'Public Utilities in France', *Harvard Business Review* **9**(4) (1931), 409–16.

Jones, L. J., 'Public Pursuit and Private Profit: Liberal Businessmen and Municipal Politics in Birmingham, 1845–1900', *Business History* **25**(3) (1983), 240–59.

Jorberg, L. and Krantz, O., 'Scandinavia 1914–70' in C. Cipolla (ed.), *Fontana Economic History of Europe: Contemporary Economies* 2 parts (Glasgow Fontana/Collins, 1976), Part 2, 377–450.

'Economic and Social Policy in Sweden' in P. Mathias and S. Pollard (eds.), *Cambridge Economic History of Europe. VIII. The Industrial Economies: The Development of Economic and Social Policy* (Cambridge University Press, 1989), 1048–105.

Jouhaux, L., 'Nationalisation in France', *Annals of Collective Economy* **20** (1949), 215–21.

Kaijser, A., 'From Local Networks to National Systems: A Comparison of the Emergence of Electricity and Telephony in Sweden', in F. Cardot (ed.), *1880–1980: Une siècle de l'électricité dans le monde* (Paris: Presses Universitaires de France, 1987), 7–22.

'Controlling the Grid: The Development of High Tension Power Lines in the Nordic Countries', in A. Kaijser and M. Hedin (eds.), *Nordic Energy Systems: Historical Perspectives and Current Issues* (Canton, Mass.: Science History Publications, 1995), 31–53.

'The Helping Hand: In Search of a Swedish Institutional Regime for Infrastructure Systems', in L. Andersson-Skog and O. Krantz (eds.), *Institutions and the Transport and Communications Industries* (Canton, Mass.: Science History Publications,Watson, 1999), 223–44.

Kaijser, A. and Hedin, M. (eds.), *Nordic Energy Systems: Historical Perspectives and Current Issues* (Canton, Mass.: Science History Publications, 1995).

Kay, J., Mayer, C. and Thompson, D. (eds.), *Privatisation and Regulation: The UK Experience* (Oxford: Clarendon Press, 1986).

Kelf-Cohen, R., *Nationalisation in Britain: The End of a Dogma* (London: Macmillan, 1958).

Keller, M., 'Public Policy and Large Enterprises: Comparative Historical Perspective', in N. Horn and K. Kocka (eds.), *Recht und Entwicklung der Grossunternehmen im 19. und frühen 20. Jahrhundert* (Göttingen: Vandenhoeck and Ruprecht, 1979), 515–34.

Regulation and the New Economy: Public Policy and Economic Change in America 1900–1933 (Cambridge, Mass.: Harvard University Press, 1990).

Kemp, T., 'The French Economy under the Franc Poincare', *Economic History Review* 24(1) (1971), 80–99.

'Economic and Social Policy in France', in P. Mathias and S. Pollard (eds.), *Cambridge Economic History of Europe. VIII. The Industrial Economies: The Development of Economic and Social Policy* (Cambridge University Press, 1989), 691–751.

'The Proposals for the Reorganisation of the Industrial Assets Owned by the Federal German Government', *Annals of Public and Collective Economy* 42 (1971), 347–68.

'The Vereinigte Industrie-Unternehmen AG: A German Public Enterprise', *Annals of Public and Collective Economy* 42 (1971), 305–46.

Kieve, J. C., *The Electric Telegraph: A Social and Economic History* (Newton Abbott: David and Charles, 1973).

Kirby, M. W., *The British Coal Mining Industry 1870–1946* (London: Macmillan, 1977).

'The Politics of State Coercion in Inter-War Britain: The Mines Department of the Board of Trade', *Historical Journal* 22(2) (1979), 373–96.

Knieps, G., 'De-Regulation in Europe: Telecommunications and Transportation', in G. Majone (ed.), *De-Regulation or Re-Regulation?: Regulation in Europe and the United States* (London: Pinter, 1990), 72–100.

Knoop, D., *Principles and Methods of Municipal Trading* (London: Macmillan, 1912).

Knox, V., 'The Economic Effects of the Tramways Act of 1870', *Economic Journal* 11 (1901), 492–510.

Kocha, J., 'The Rise of the Modern Industrial Enterprise in Germany', in A. D. Chandler and H. Daems (eds.), *Managerial Hierarchies* (Cambridge, Mass.: Harvard University Press, 1980), 77–116.

Koebel, P., 'De-Regulation in the Telecommunications Sector: A Movement in Line with Recent Technological Advances', in G. Majone (ed.), *De-Regulation or Re-Regulation?: Regulation in Europe and the United States* (London: Pinter, 1990), 110–23.

Krantz, O., 'Inland Navigation and Economic Growth in Sweden in the 19th Century', in A. Kunz and J. Armstrong (eds.), *Inland Navigation and Economic Development in 19th Century Europe* (Mainz: Verlag Philipp von Zabem, 1995).

Kreuzberger, H., 'Oil in Austria', *Annals of Public and Collective Economy* 32 (1961), 190–203.

Kriele, M., 'Public Enterprise and the Pursuit of Strategic Management: Italy', in K. Dyson and S. Wilks (eds.), *Industrial Crisis: A Comparative Study of the State and Industry* (New York: St. Martin's Press 1988), 192–219.

Kuhl, U., 'Le Débat sur le socialisme municipal en allemagne avant 1914 et la municipalisation de l'électricité', in A. Kuhl (ed.), *Der Munizipalsozialismus in Europa* (Munich: Oldenberg Verlag, 2002), 81–100.

Kuisel, R. F., 'The Legend of the Vichy Synarchy', *French Historical Studies* **6** (1970), 385–98.

'Technocrats and Public Economic Policy: From the 3rd to the 4th Republic', *Journal of European Economic History* **2** (1973), 53–99.

Capitalism and the State in Modern France (Cambridge University Press, 1981).

Kunz, A., 'Steamship Companies in Industrialising Germany: A Contribution to a Sectoral Analysis of the German Inland Shipping Industry during the Nineteenth Century', in L. Andersson-Skog and O. Krantz (eds.), *Institutions and the Transport and Communications Industries* (Canton, Mass.: Science History Publications, Watson, 1999), 173–98.

Kunz, A. and Armstrong, J. (eds.), *Inland Navigation and Economic Development in 19th Century Europe* (Mainz: Verlag Philipp von Zabem, 1995).

Kuster, G. H., 'Germany', in R. Vernon (ed.), *Big Business and the State* (Cambridge, Mass.: Harvard University Press, 1974), 64–86.

Labour Party, *Let us Face the Future: A Declaration of Labour Policy for the Consideration of the Nation* (London: Labour Party, 1945).

Laffut, M., 'Belgium' in P. O'Brien (ed.), *Railways and the Economic Development of Europe* (Oxford: Macmillan, 1983), 203–26.

Landes, D. S., 'French Entrepreneurs and Industrial Growth in the 19th Century', *Journal of European Economic History* **9** (1949), 45–61.

'French Business and the Businessman: A Social and Cultural Analysis', in E. Earle (ed.), *Modern France* (Princeton University Press, 1950), 334–53.

Lane, T., 'Globalisation, Deregulation and Crew Competence in World Shipping', in J. McConville (ed.), *Transport Regulation Matters* (London: Pinter, 1997), 98–125.

Langer, E., 'The Economic Importance of Public Enterprise in Belgium', *Annals of Public and Collective Economy* **37** (1966), 65–76.

Lanthier, P., 'Les Dirigeants de grands entreprises électrique en France 1911–73', in M. Levy-Leboyer (ed.), *Le Patronal de la seconde industrialisation* (Paris: Les Editions Ouvrières, 1979), 107–36.

'The Relationship between State and Private Electric Industry, France 1880–1920', in N. Horn and Jorgen Kocha (eds.), *Recht und Entwicklung der Grossunternehmen im 19. Und Fruhen 20. Jahrhundert* (Göttingen: Vandenhoek & Ruprecht, 1979), 590–603.

Larroque, D., 'Economic Aspects of Public Transit in the Parisian Area', in J. A. Tarr and G. Dupuy (eds.), *Technology and the Rise of the Networked City in Europe* (Philadelphia: Temple University Press, 1988), 40–66.

Lauterbach, A., 'Managerial Attitudes in Private, Public and Co-operative Enterprise in Western Europe', *Annals of Public and Collective Economy* **26** (1955), 236–42.

Lebaron, F., 'The State and the Market: The Rise of the Economic Rationale', *Contemporary European History* **9**(3) (2000), 463–73.

Le Besnerois, 'The National Railroad Company and the Financial Amendement of the French Railroads', *Annals of Collective Economy* **18** (1947), 29–33.

Lebois, R., 'Charbonnages de France', *Annals of Collective Economy* **28** (1957), 256–64.

Lee, W. R., 'Tax Structure and Economic Growth in Germany 1750–1850', *Journal of European Economic History* **4**(1) (1975), 153–78.

'Economic Development and the State in 19th Century Germany', *Economic History Review* **41**(3) (1988), 346–67.

Lee, W. R. (ed.), *German Industry and German Industrialisation* (London: Routledge, 1991).

Lefranc, G., 'The French Railroads 1823–42', *Journal of Economic and Business History* **2** (1929/30), 299–331.

Levey, J., 'George Valois and the Faisceau', *French Historical Studies* **8**(2) (1973), 279–304.

Levy, P., 'The Railroads in France', *Annals of the American Academy of Politics and Social Science* **187** (1936), 184–92.

Levy-Leboyer, M., 'The French Electrical Power System: An Inter-Country Comparison', in R. Maintz and T. P. Hughes (eds.), *The Development of Large Technical Systems* (Boulder, Colo.: Frankfurt and Westview Press, 1978), 245–62.

'The Large Corporation in Modern France', in A. D. Chandler and H. Daems (eds.), *Managerial Hierarchies* (Cambridge, Mass.: Harvard University Press, 1980), 117–57.

'Introduction', 'Panorama de l'électrification: De la Grande Guerre à la nationalisation' and 'Une réussite inachevée', in M. Levy-Leboyer and H. Morsel (eds.), *Histoire de l'électricité en France. II. L'interconnection et le marché, 1919–46* (Paris: L'Association pour l'Histoire de l'Electricité en France, Fayard, 1994), 13–25, 27–127, 1357–70.

Lewis, E. G., 'Parliamentary Control of Nationalised Industry in France', *American Political Science Review* **51** (1953), 669–83.

Leyen, A. von der, 'The German Federal Railway Company', *Annals of Collective Economy* **2** (1926), 321–45.

Liebermann, S., *The Growth of European Mixed Economies 1945–70* (Cambridge University Press, 1977).

'The Ideological Foundations of Western European Economic Planning', *Journal of European Economic History* **10**(2) (1981).

Little, D. J., 'Twenty Years of Turmoil: ITT, The State Department, and Spain, 1924–44', *Business History Review* **53**(4) (1979), 449–72.

Littlechild, S., 'The Effect of Ownership on Telephone Concentration', *Telecommunications Policy* **7** (1983), 246–7.

Lowe, R., 'The Erosion of State Intervention in Britain 1917–24', *Economic History Review* **31** (1978), 270–86.

Lowell Field, G., 'Forms of Organisation of Italian Public Undertakings', *Annals of Collective Economy* **10** (1934), 1–47.

Lucas, N., *Western European Energy Policies* (Oxford: Clarendon Press, 1985).

Lundmark, K., 'Welfare State and Employment Policy', in K. Dyson and S. Wilks (eds.), *Industrial Crisis: A Comparative Study of the State and Industry* (New York: St. Martin's Press 1988), 220–44.

Lutz, V., *Italy: A Study in Economic Development* (London: Royal Institute of International Affairs and Oxford University Press, 1962).

French Planning (Washington: American Enterprise Institute for Public Policy Research, 1965).

Lynch, F., 'Resolving the Paradox in the Monnet Plan: National and International Planning in French Reconstruction', *Economic History Review* **37**(2) (1984), 229–43.

Lyth, P. J., 'A Multiplicity of Instruments: The 1946 Decision to Create a Separate British European Airline and its Effects on Airline Productivity', *Journal of Transport History* **11**(2) (1990), 1–17.

'The History of Commercial Air Transport: A Progress Report', *Journal of Transport History* **14**(2) (1993), 166–80.

'The Changing Role of Government in British Civil Aviation', in R. Millward and J. Singleton (eds.), *The Political Economy of Nationalisation in Britain 1920–50* (Cambridge University Press, 1995), 65–87.

'Institutional Change and European Air Transport 1910–85', in L. Magnusson and J. Ottosson (eds.), *Evolutionary Economics and Path Dependence* (Cheltenham: Edward Elgar, 1996), 168–85.

'Experiencing Turbulence: Regulation and De-Regulation in the International Air Transport Industry 1930–90', in J. McConville (ed.), *Transport Regulation Matters* (London: Pinter, 1997), 154–74.

'Chosen Instruments: The Evolution of British Airways', in H.-L. Dienel and P. Lyth, *Flying the Flag: European Commercial Air Transport since 1945* (Basingstoke, UK: Macmillan, 1998), 50–86.

'Sky Wars: Conflicting Approaches to Air Transport Regulation in Europe and the United States 1920–90', in L. Andersson-Skog and O. Krantz (eds.), *Institutions and the Transport and Communications Industries* (Canton, Mass.: Science History Publications,Watson, 1999), 93–112.

Lyth, P. J. and Dierikx, M. L., 'From Privilege to Popularity: The Growth of Leisure Air Travel', *Journal of Transport History* **15**(2) (1994), 97–116.

Mackay, J. P., *Tramways and Trolleys: The Rise of Urban Transport in Europe* (Princeton University Press, 1976).

'Comparative Perspectives on Transit in Europe and the USA 1850–1914', in J. A. Tarr and G. Dupuy (eds.), *Technology and the Rise of the Networked City in Europe* (Philadelphia: Temple University Press, 1988), 3–21.

MacMahon, A. W. and Dittmar, W. R., 'Autonomous Public Enterprise – The German Railways', *Political Science Quarterly*, Part I, **54** (December 1939), 481–513, Part II, **55** (March 1940), 25–52, Part III, **56** (June 1940), 176–98.

Maddison, A., *Dynamic Forces in Capitalist Development* (Oxford University Press, 1991).

Monitoring the World Economy 1820–1992 (Paris: Organisation for Economic Cooperation and Development, 1995).

Magee, L., 'Electricity Railway Practice in Germany', *Street Railway Journal* **19** (1899), 647–62.

Magnusson, L. and Ottosson, J., *Evolutionary Economics and Path Dependence* (Cheltenham: Edward Elgar 1997).

The State, Regulation and the Economy: An Historical Perspective (Cheltenham: Edward Elgar 2001).

Maintz, R. and Hughes, T. P. (eds.), *The Development of Large Technical Systems* (Boulder, Colo.: Frankfurt and Westview Press, 1978).

Majone, G. (ed.), *De-Regulation or Re-Regulation? Regulation in Europe and the United States* (London: Pinter, 1990).

Maltbie, M. R., 'Gas Lighting in Great Britain', *Municipal Affairs* 4 (1900), 538–73.

Manning, D., 'Telecommunications in Spain', in J. Foreman-Peck and J. Mueller (eds.), *European Telecommunications Organisation* (Baden-Baden: Nomosver-lagsgsellschaft, 1988), 237–55.

Mantegazza, A., 'Alitalia and Commercial Aviation in Italy', in H.-L. Dienel and P. Lyth, *Flying the Flag: European Commercial Air Transport since 1945* (Basingstoke, UK: Macmillan, 1998), 158–94.

Marel, J. H. van der, 'Some Considerations on Costs, Tariffs and Finance in the Netherlands State-Operated P.T.T', *Annals of Public and Collective Economy* 26 (1955), 508–14.

Margairaz, M., 'Companies under Public Control in France 1900–50', in N. Whiteside and R. Salais (eds.), *Governance and Labour Markets in Britain and France* (London: Routledge 1998), 25–51.

Martinelli, A., 'The Italian Experience: A Historical Perspective', in R. Vernon and Y. Aharoni (eds.), *State-Owned Enterprise in Western Economies* (London: Croom Helm, 1981), 85–98.

Mason, E. S., 'Saint Simonism and the Rationalisation of Industry', *Quarterly Journal of Economics* 45 (1931), 640–83.

Massard-Guilbaurd, G., 'French Local Authorities and the Challenge of Industrial Pollution', in R. J. Morris and R. H. Trainor (eds.), *Urban Governance: Britain and Beyond since 1750* (Aldershot: Ashgate, 2000), 150–64.

Massé, P., ' "Electricité de France" Faces Expansion Problems', *Annals of Public and Collective Economy* 26 (1955), 40–58.

Matthews, D., 'Rogues, Speculators and Competing Monopolies: The Early London Gas Companies, 1812–1860', *The London Journal* 2 (1985), 39–50.

'Laissez-faire and the London Gas Industry in the Nineteenth Century: Another Look', *Economic History Review* 39(2) (1986), 244–63.

'Technology Transfer in the Late 19th Century Gas Industry', *Journal of Economic History* 47(4) (1987), 967–80.

Mazzolini, R., 'European Government-Controlled Enterprises: Explaining International Strategic and Policy Decisions', *Journal of International Business Studies* 10(3) (1979), 16–27.

McConville, J., 'The United Kingdom Shipping Industry and International Deregulation', in J. McConville (ed.), *Transport Regulation Matters* (London: Pinter, 1997), 78–97.

McGowan Report, *Report of the Committee on Electricity Distribution* (London: Ministry of Transport, 1936).

Meadows, P., 'Planning', in F. Blackaby (ed.), *British Economic Policy 1960–74* (Cambridge University Press, 1978), 402–17.

Megginson, W. N. and Netter, J. M., 'From State to Market: A Survey of Empirical Studies on Privatisation', *Journal of Economic Literature* **39** (2001), 321–89.

Merger, M., 'The Economic Performance of Inland Navigation in France: The Lower Seine and the Paris–Lens Route in a Comparative Perspective, 1740–1914', in A. Kunz and J. Armstrong (ed.), *Inland Navigation and Economic Development in 19th Century Europe* (Mainz: Verlag Philipp von Zabem, 1995), 181–211.

Messager, R., 'Municipalities and Managers: Heat Networks in Germany', in J. A. Tarr and G. Dupuy (eds.), *Technology and the Rise of the Networked City in Europe* (Philadelphia: Temple University Press, 1988), 282–93.

Meyer, B. H., 'The Administration of Prussian Railroads', *Annals of the American Academy of Political Science* **10** (1897), 77–111.

Meyer, H. R., 'Municipal Ownership in Germany', *Journal of Political Economy* **14** (1906), 553–67.

'The Prussian Railway Department and the Berlin Milk Supply', *Journal of Political Economy* **15** (1907), 299–307.

Michalat, C. A., 'France', in R. Vernon (ed.), *Big Business and the State* (Cambridge, Mass.: Harvard University Press, 1974), 105–29.

Midttun, A., '(Mis)understanding Change: Electricity Liberalisation Policies in Norway and Sweden' in A. Kaijser and M. Hedin (eds.), *Nordic Energy Systems: Historical Perspectives and Current Issues* (Canton, Mass.: Science History Publications, 1995), 141–67.

Mierzejewski, A. C., 'The Deutsche Reichsbahn and Germany's Supply of Coal, 1939–45', *Journal of Transport History* **8** (1987), 111–25.

'The German National Railway Company between the World Wars: Modernisation or Preparation for War?', *Journal of Transport History* **11** (1990), 40–60.

'The German National Railway Company 1924–32: Between Public and Private Enterprise', *Business History Review* **67** (1993), 406–38.

'Accounting Reforms at the German National Railway Company 1924–32', *Business and Economic History* **23** (1994), 406–38.

'Payment and Profits: The German National Railway Company and Reparations 1924–32', *German Studies Review* **18** (1995), 65–85.

'The German National Railway Company Confronts its Competitors 1920–39', *Business and Economic History* **25** (1996), 89–102.

'The Reich Association of German Industry's Proposal to Privatise the German National Railway Company 1921–2', *Business and Economic History* **27** (1998), 477–85.

The Most Valuable Asset of the Reich: A History of the German National Railway Company, 2 vols. (Chapel Hill: University of North Carolina Press, 1999), volume I 1920–32, volume II 1932–45.

Milhaud, E., 'The Nationalisation of the Aeronautical Industry in France and its Immediate Consequences', *Annals of Collective Economy* **15** (1939), 223–51.

Miliband, R., *The State in Capitalist Society* (London: Quartet Books, 1973).

Millward, R., 'The Comparative Performance of Public and Private Ownership', in J. Kay, C. Mayer and D. Thompson (eds.), *Privatisation and Regulation: The UK Experience* (Oxford: Clarendon Press, 1986), 119–44.

'Privatisation in Historical Perspective: The UK Water Industry', in D. Cobham, R. Harrington and G. Zis (eds.), *Money, Trade and Payments* (Manchester University Press, 1989).

'Productivity in the UK Services Sector: Historical Trends 1856–1985 and Comparison with USA 1950–85', *Oxford Bulletin of Economics and Statistics* **52**(4) (1990), 423–36.

'The Market Behaviour of Local Utilities in Pre-World War I Britain: The Case of Gas', *Economic History Review* **44** (1991), 102–27.

'The Emergence of Gas and Water Monopolies in Nineteenth Century Britain: Contested Markets and Public Control', in J. Foreman-Peck (ed.), *New Perspectives on the Late Victorian Economy* (Cambridge University Press, 1993), 96–124.

'The 1940s Nationalisations in Britain: Means of Production or Means to an End?', *Economic History Review*, **50** (2) (1997), 209–34.

'The Political Economy of Urban Utilities in Britain 1840–1950', in M. Daunton (ed.), *The Cambridge Urban History of Britain*, III (Cambridge University Press, 2000), 315–49.

'State Enterprise in Britain in the Twentieth Century', in P. Toninelli (ed.), *The Rise and Fall of State Owned Enterprise in the Western World* (Cambridge University Press, 2000).

'The British Privatisation Programme: A Long Term Perspective', *Economia Pubblica* **33**(2) (2003), 155–68 (in Italian).

'The Economic Organisation and Development of Electricity Supply in Britain in the 20th Century', in A. Giuntini and G. Paoloni (eds.), *La Citta elettrica: Esperienze di elettrificazione urbana in Italia e in Europa fra ottocento e novecento* (Rome: Gius, Laterza & Figli and ENEL, 2003), 99–124 (in Italian).

'The Economic Development and Impact of the Urban Infrastructure in Victorian Britain', in A. Giuntini, P. Hertner and G. Nunez (eds.), *The Urban Infrastructure in Europe 1850–1950* (University of Granada Press, 2004).

'Regulation and Ownership of Public Services in Europe: An Historical Perspective c.1830–1950', *Economia Pubblica* **34** (2) (2004), 25–38 (in Italian).

'The Rise of the Service Sector', in R. Floud and P. Johnson (eds.), *The Economic History of Britain since 1700*. III. *Structural Change and Growth, 1939–2000* (Cambridge University Press, 3rd edn, 2004), 238–66.

'Urban Water Supplies c.1820–1950: The Dilemma of the Private Companies', *Histoire, Economie, Société* (forthcoming 2005).

Millward, R. and Sheard, S., 'The Urban Fiscal Problem 1870–1914; Government Expenditure and Finances in England and Wales', *Economic History Review* **48**(3) (1995), 501–35.

Millward, R. and Singleton, J. (eds.), *The Political Economy of Nationalisation in Britain 1920–50* (Cambridge University Press, 1995).

Millward, R. and Ward, R., 'The Costs of Public and Private Gas Enterprises in Late Nineteenth Century Britain', *Oxford Economic Papers* **39** (1987), 719–37.

'From Private to Public Ownership of Gas Undertakings in England and Wales, 1851–1947: Chronology, Incidence and Causes', *Business History* **35**(3) (1993), 1–21.

Milward, A. S., *The New Order and the French Economy* (Oxford University Press, 1970).

Milward, A. S. and Saul, S. B., *The Development of the Economies of Continental Europe 1850–1914* (Cambridge, Mass.: Harvard University Press, 1977).

The Economic Development of Continental Europe 1780–1870 (London: Allen and Unwin, 1979).

Ministry of Power, *Digest of Energy Statistics 1978* (London: HMSO, 1978).

Mitchell, B. R., 'The Coming of the Railway and UK Economic Growth', *Journal of Economic History* **24** (1964), 315–36.

British Historical Statistics (Cambridge University Press, 1988).

International Historical Statistics: Europe 1750–1993 (London: Macmillan, 3rd edn, 1998).

International Historical Statistics: The Americas: 1750–1993 (London: Macmillan, 4th edn, 1998).

Moch, J., 'Thoughts on the Nationalisation of Enterprises', *Annals of Collective Economy* **14** (1938), 308–27.

'Nationalisation in France', *Annals of Collective Economy* **24** (1953), 97–111.

Molinas, C. and Prados de la Escosura, L., 'Was Spain Different: Spanish Historical Backwardness Revisited', *Explorations in Economic History* **26** (1989), 385–402.

Moore, J., 'Why Privatise?', in J. Kay, C. Mayer and D. Thompson (eds.), *Privatisation and Regulation: The UK Experience* (Oxford: Clarendon Press, 1986), 78–93.

Morgan, K. and Webber, D., 'Divergent Paths: Political Strategies for Tele-communications in Britain, France and West Germany', in K. Dyson and P. Humphries (eds.), *The Politics of the Communications Revolution in Europe* (London: Cass, 1986), 56–79.

Morsel, H., 'L'Hydro-électricité en France: Du patronal disperse à la direction nationale (1902–46)', in P. Fridensen and A. Strauss (eds.), *Le Capitalisme française* (Paris: Librairie Arthème, Fayard, 1987), 381–97.

'Etude comparée des nationalisations de l'électricité en Europe occidentale apres la deuxième guerre mondiale', in M. Trédé (ed.), *Electricité et électrification dans le monde 1880–1980* (Paris: Association pour l'Histoire de l'Electricité en France, Presses Universitaires de France, 1990), 443–57.

'Reflexions sur le nationalisation de l'électricité', in M. Levy-Leboyer and H. Morsel (eds.), *Histoire de l'électricité en France. II. L'Interconnection et le marché, 1919–46* (Paris: L'Association pour l'Histoire de l'Electricité en France, Fayard, 1994), 1334–54.

Morsel, H., (ed.), *Histoire générale de l'électricité en France. III. Une œuvre nationale: L'Equipement, la croissance de la demande, le nucléaire (1946–87)* (Paris: L'Association pour l'Histoire de l'Electricité en France, Fayard, 1996).

Motes, M. de, 'L'Electricité, facteur de développement économique en Espagne: 1930–36', in F. Cardot (ed.), *1880–1980: Une siècle de l'électricité dans le monde* (Paris: Presses Universitaires de France, 1987), 57–67.

Mueller, J., 'Telecommunications in Belgium', in J. Foreman-Peck and J. Mueller (eds.), *European Telecommunications Organisation* (Baden-Baden: Nomosverlagsgesellschaft, 1988), 83–107.

Mulert, O., 'The Economic Activities of German Municipalities', *Annals of Collective Economy* 5 (1929), 209–67.

Muller, K.-J., 'French Fascism and Modernisation', *Journal of Contemporary History* 11(4) (1976), 75–107.

Müller-Armack, A., 'The Principles of the Social Market Economy', *German Economic Review* 3 (1965), 89–104.

Myers, M. R., 'The Nationalisation of Banks in France', *Political Science Quarterly* 64 (1949), 189–210.

Nadal, J., 'Spain 1830–1914', in C. Cipolla (ed.), *Fontana Economic History of Europe: The Emergence of Industrial Societies*, 2 parts (Glasgow: Fontana/ Collins, 1973), part 2, 532–626.

Nash, C., 'European Railway Comparisons – What Can we Learn?', in K. J. Button and D. C. Pitfield (eds.), *International Railway Economics* (Aldershot: Gower, 1985), 237–69.

National Economic Development Office, *A Study of UK Nationalised Industries* (London: HMSO, 1976).

Nelson, J. R. (ed.), *Marginal Cost Pricing in Practice* (Englewood Cliffs, N. J.: Prentice-Hall, 1964).

Neumann, K. H. and Wieland, B., 'Competition and Social Objectives: The Case of West German Telecommunications', *Telecommunications Policy*, 10 (1986), 121–31.

Newbery, D., *Privatisation, Restructuring and Regulation of Network Industries* (Cambridge. Mass.: MIT Press, 1999).

Newton, C., 'The Sterling Crisis of 1947 and the British Response to the Marshall Plan', *Economic History Review* 37(3) (1984), 391–408.

Nguyen, G. D., 'Telecommunications: A Challenge to the Old Order', in M. Sharp (ed.), *Europe and the New Technologies: Six Case Studies in Innovation and Adjustment* (London: Pinter, 1985), 87–133.

'Telecommunications in France', in J. Foreman-Peck and J. Mueller (eds.), *European Telecommunications Organisation* (Baden-Baden: Nomosverlagsgesellschaft, 1988), 131–54.

Nichols, A. J., *Freedom with Responsibility: The Social Market Economy in Germany 1918–43* (Oxford: Clarendon Press, 1994).

Niemeijer, A. F. J., 'Waterways and the Dutch Economy in the 19th Century', in A. Kunz and J. Armstrong (eds.), *Inland Navigation and Economic Development in 19th Century Europe* (Mainz: Verlag Philipp von Zabem, 1995), 213–15.

Niertz, N., 'Air France: An Elephant in an Evening Suit', in H.-L. Dienel and P. Lyth, *Flying the Flag: European Commercial Air Transport since 1945* (Basingstoke, UK: Macmillan, 1998), 18–49.

Niskanen, W. A., *Bureaucracy and Representative Government* (New York: Aldine-Atherton, 1971).

Noam, E., *Telecommunications in Europe* (New York: Oxford University Press, 1992).

Noreng, Ø., 'State-Owned Oil Companies: Western Europe', in R. Vernon and Y. Aharoni (eds.), *State-Owned Enterprise in Western Economies* (London: Croom Helm, 1981), 133–44.

Nunez, G., 'Développement et intégration régionale de l'industrie électrique en Andalousie jusqu'en 1935', in M. Trédé (ed.), *Electricité et électrification dans le monde 1880–1980* (Paris: Association pour l'Histoire de l'Electricité en France, Presses Universitaires de France, 1990), 169–201.

'Local Life and Municipal Services in Spain at the Beginning of the 20th Century', Paper presented at International Economic History Congress, Madrid, 1998.

'Spanish Cities in a Forgotten Modernising Process', in M. Morner and G. Tortella (eds.), *Different Paths to Modernisation* (University of Lund, forthcoming).

O'Brien, P., *Railways and the Economic Development of Europe* (Oxford: Macmillan, 1983).

Oeftering, H., 'The Participation of the German Federal State in Economic Enterprises', *Annals of Collective Economy* 24 (1953), 271–88.

Ohlin, G., 'Sweden', in R. Vernon (ed.), *Big Business and the State* (Cambridge, Mass.: Harvard University Press, 1974), 126–41.

Olivares, J. V. and Ortunez, P. P., 'The Internationalisation of Ownership of the Spanish Railway Companies', *Business History* 44 (4) (2002), 29–54.

Olivier, J.-P., 'Public and Collective Economy in Sweden', *Annals of Public and Collective Economy* 40 (1969), 435–53.

O'Mahony, M., *Britain's Productivity Performance: An International Perspective* (London: National Institute of Economic and Social Research, 1999).

O'Mahony, M., Oulton, N., and Vass, J., 'Market Services: Productivity Benchmarks for the UK', *Oxford Bulletin of Economics and Statistics*, **60** (1998), 529–51.

O'Mahony, M. and Vecchi, M., 'The Electricity Supply Industry: A Study of an Industry in Transition', *National Institute Economic Review* **177** (2001), 85–99.

Opie, R., 'Economic Planning and Growth', in C. Feinstein (ed.), *The Managed Economy* (Oxford University Press, 1983), 147–68.

Organisation for European Co-operation and Development (OECD), *Energy Statistics of OECD Countries 1960–75* (Paris: International Energy Agency, 1991).

Organisation for European Co-operation and Development (OECD), *Energy Statistics of OECD Countries 2000–1* (Paris: International Energy Agency, 2003).

Ostergaard, G. N., 'Labour and the Development of the Public Corporation', *Manchester School* 22 (1954), 192–226.

Ott, H., 'History of Electricity in Germany', in F. Cardot (ed.), *1880–1980: Une siècle de l'électricité dans le monde* (Paris: Presses Universitaires de France, 1987), 135–50.

Ottosson, J., 'Path Dependence and Institutional Evolution – The Case of the Nationalisation of Private Railways in Inter-War Sweden', in L. Magnusson and J. Ottosson, *Evolutionary Economics and Path Dependence* (Cheltenham: Edward Elgar, 1997), 186–96.

'The Making of a Scandinavian Airline Company: Private Actors and Public Interests', in L. Andersson-Skog and O. Krantz (eds.), *Institutions and the Transport and Communications Industries* (Canton, Mass.: Science History Publications, Watson, 1999), 267–80.

'The State and Regulatory Orders in Early European Civil Aviation', in L. Magnusson and J. Ottosson, *The State, Regulation and the Economy: An Historical Perspective* (Cheltenham: Edward Elgar, 2001), 148–65.

Overy, R., *War and Economy in the Third Reich* (Oxford: Clarendon Press, 1994).

Parker, W.N., 'National States and National Development: French and German Ore Mining in the Late 19th Century', in H. G. J. Aitken, (ed.), *The State and Economic Growth* (New York: SSSRC, 1959), 201–12.

Parris, H., Pestieau, P. and Saynor, P. (eds.), *Public Enterprise in Western Europe* (Lund: Croom Helm, 1987).

Pasquino, G. and Pecchini, U., 'The National Context: Italy', in J. Hayward and M. Watson (eds.), *Planning, Politics and Public Policy* (Cambridge University Press, 1975), 70–92.

Perry, C. R., 'The British Experience 1876–1912: The Impact of the Telephone during the Years of Delay', in I. de Sola Pool (ed.), *The Social Impact of the Telephone* (Cambridge, Mass., MIT Press, 1977), 69–96.

Peters, L., 'Managing Competition in German Coal 1893–1913', *Journal of Economic History* **49** (1989), 419–32.

Petersen, H. J. S., 'Diffusion of Coal Gas Technology in Denmark, 1850–1920', *Technological Forecasting and Social Change* **38**(1) (1990), 37–48.

Petterson, T., 'From Informal Practice to Formal Policy: Path Dependence and the Case of Swedish Transport Aid', in L. Magnusson and J. Ottosson, *Evolutionary Economics and Path Dependence* (Cheltenham: Edward Elgar, 1997), 183–96.

'Institutional Rigidity and Economic Change: A Comparison between Swedish Transport Subsidies', in L. Andersson-Skog and O. Krantz (eds.), *Institutions and the Transport and Communications Industries* (Canton, Mass.: Science History Publications, Watson, 1999), 281–300.

Picard, J.-F., Beltran, A. and Bungener, M., *Histoire de l'EDF* (Paris: Dunod, 1985).

Pinkney, D. H., 'Nationalisation of Key Industries and Credit in France after the Liberation', *Political Science Quarterly* **62** (1947), 368–80.

'The French Experiment in Nationalisation, 1944–50', in E. M. Earle, *Modern France* (Princeton University Press, 1951), 354–67.

'Money and Politics in the Rebuilding of Paris 1860–1870', *Journal of Economic History* **17** (1957), 45–61.

Polanyi, G. and Polanyi, P., *Failing the Nation: The Record of the Nationalised Industries* (London: Fraser Ansbacher, 1974).

Political and Economic Planning (PEP), *Growth in the British Economy* (London: Allen and Unwin, 1960).

Pontusson, J., 'The Triumph of Pragmatism: Nationalisation and Privatisation in Sweden', *West European Politics* **11**(4) (1988), 129–40.

Posner, M. V. and Woolf, S. J., *Italian Public Enterprise* (London: Duckworth, 1967).

Prados de la Escosura, L., 'International Comparisons of Real Product 1820–1990: An Alternative Data Set', *Explorations in Economic History* 27 (2000), 1–41.

Primeaux, V. J., 'An Assessment of X-Efficiency Gained through competition', *Review of Economics and Statistics* 59 (1977), 105–8.

Prodi, R., 'Italy', in R. Vernon (ed.), *Big Business and the State* (Cambridge, Mass.: Harvard University Press, 1974), 45–63.

Pryke, R., *Public Enterprise in Practice* (London: McKibbon and Kee, 1971).

Radcliffe, B., 'The Origins of the Paris-Saint Germain Railway', *Journal of Transport History* 1(4) (1972), 197–219.

'The Building of the Paris-Saint Germain Railway', *Journal of Transport History* 2(1) (1973), 20–40.

'Railway Imperialism: The Example of the Pereires' Paris-St. Germain Company', *Business History* 18 (1976), 66–84.

'Economic Impact of the Saint Simonians: Myth or Reality?', *Proceedings of the Annual Meeting of the Western Society for French History* 5 (1978), 252–62.

Ramunni, G., 'L'Elaboration du réseau électrique française: Un débat technique de l'entre-deux-guerres', in F. Cardot (ed.), *1880–1980: Une siècle de l'électricité dans le monde* (Paris: Presses Universitaires de France, 1987), 269–81.

Rawson, R. W., 'On Railways in Belgium', *Journal of the Royal Statistical Society of London* 2 (1839), 47–62.

Richardson, J., 'Policy, Politics and the Communications Revolution in Sweden', in K. Dyson and P. Humphries (eds.), *The Politics of the Communications Revolution in Europe* (London: Cass, 1986), 80–97.

Ricossa, S., 'Italy 1920–70', in C. Cipolla (ed), *Fontana Economic History of Europe: Contemporary Economies*, 2 parts (Glasgow: Fontana/Collins, 1976), part 1, 262–324.

Ritschl, A., 'The Pity of Peace: German Economy at War 1914–18', Paper presented at Warwick University Economic History Workshop, July 2002.

Robson, W. A., 'The Public Utility Services', in H. J. Laski, W. I. Jennings and W. A. Robson (eds.), *A Century of Municipal Progress: The Last One Hundred Years* (London: Allen and Unwin, 1935), 316–19.

Rogissart, G. and Dumoulin, A., 'Problems of Public Undertakings within the Common Market', *Annals of Public and Collective Economy* 33 (1962), 232–50.

Rollings, N., ' "The Reichstag Method of Governing"?: The Attlee Governments and Permanent Economic Controls', in H. Mercer, N. Rollings and J. Tomlinson (eds.), *The 1945 Labour Government and Private Industry* (Edinburgh University Press, 1992), 15–36.

Roman, E. S. and Sudria, C., 'Synthetic Fuels in Spain: 1942–66: The Failure of Franco's Autarkic Dream', *Business History* 45(4) (2003), 1175–88.

Rosa, L. de, 'Economics and Nationalism in Italy', *Journal of European Economic History* 11 (1982), 537–74.

Roses, J. and Sanchez-Alonso, B., 'Regional Wage Convergences in Spain 1850–1936', Paper presented at European Historical Economics Society Conference, Merton College, Oxford, 2001.

Royal Commission on Water Supply, *Report of the Commissioners* (London: HMSO, 1869).

Royal Sanitary Commission, *Report* (London: HMSO, 1871).

Ruggles, N., 'The Welfare Basis of the Marginal Cost Pricing Principle', *Review of Economic Studies* 17(1) (1949/50), 29–46.

Sanchez, R. Myro, 'Public Enterprise in the Spanish Economy 1940–1985', in V. Zamagni (ed.), *Origins and Development of Publicly Owned Enterprises* (University of Florence, Ninth International Economic History Conference, Section B111, 1986), 54–9.

Sark, R., 'Fascist Modernisation in Italy: Tradition or Revolution?', *American Historical Review* 74(4) (1970), 1029–45.

Sauer, W., 'National Socialism: Totalitarianism or Fascism?', *American Historical Review* 73(1) (1967), 404–24.

Savage, C. I., *An Economic History of Transport* (London: Allen and Unwin, 1966).

Sawyer, M. and O'Donnell, K., *A Future for Public Ownership* (London: Lawrence Wishart, 1999).

Schiavi, A., 'Municipal Services in Italy', *Annals of Collective Economy* 5 (1929), 350–8.

'Municipal Undertakings in Italy', *Annals of Collective Economy* 7 (1931), 228–53.

Schneider, H. K. and Schultz, W., 'Market Structure and Market Organisation in the Electricity and Gas Public Utilities of the Federal Republic of Germany', in W. J. Baumol (ed.), *Public and Private Enterprise in the Mixed Economy* (New York: Macmillan, 1980), 71–96.

Schott, D., 'Power for Industry: Electrification and its Strategic Use for Industrial Promotion. The Case of Mannheim', in. D. Schott (ed.), *Energy and the City in Europe: From Preindustrial Wood-Shortages to the Oil Crisis of the 1970s* (Stuttgart: Franz Steiner Verlag, 1997), 169–93.

'Electrifying German Cities: Investment in Energy Technology and Public Transport and their Impact on Urban Development 1880–1914', Paper presented to the International Economic History Conference, Madrid, 1998.

'Remodeling Father Rhine: The Case of Mannheim 1825–1914', in S. Anderson and B. H. Tabb (eds.), *Water, Culture and Politics in Germany and the American West* (New York: Peter Lang, 2000), 203–25.

'From Gas Light to Comprehensive Energy Supply: The Evolution of Gas Industry in Three German Cities: Darmstadt–Mannheim–Mainz 1850–1970', and 'The Significance of Gas for Urban Enterprises in Late 19th Century German Cities', in S. Paquier and J.-P. Williot (eds.), *Naissance et développement de l'industrie gazière en Europe (XIXe–XXe siècles)* (Berne: Peter Lang, forthcoming).

Schram, A., *Railways and the State in the 19th Century* (Cambridge University Press, 1997).

Schremmer, D.E., 'Taxation and Public Finance: Britain, France and Germany', in P. Mathias and S. Pollard (eds.), *Cambridge Economic History of Europe*. VIII. *The Industrial Economies: The Development of Economic and Social Policy* (Cambridge University Press, 1989), 315–494.

Schultze, A., 'The Financial Significance of the Gainful Activities of German Municipalities', *Annals of Collective Economy* 7 (1931), 183–94.

Schwob, P., 'Relations between the State and the Electric Power Industry in France', *Harvard Business Review* 13(1) (1934), 82–95.

Segreto, L., 'Aspetti e problemi dell'industria elettrica in Europa tra le due guerre', in G. Galasso (ed.), *Storia dell'industria elettrica in Italia. III. Expansiove e oligopolio. 1926–45* (Roma-Bari: Laterza & Figli, 1993), 325–98.

Select Committee on the Health of Towns, *Report* (London: HMSO, 1840).

Sembenelli, A., 'Investimenti, strategie e vincoli fininziari', in G. Zanetti (ed.), *Storia dell'industria elettrica in Italia. V. Glisviluppi dell ENEL. 1963–1990* (Roma-Bari: Laterza & Figli, 1994), 733–74.

Shackleton, J. R., 'Privatisation: The Case Examined', *National Westminster Bank Review* (May 1984), 59–71.

Sharp, M. (ed.), *Europe and the New Technologies: Six Case Studies in Innovation and Adjustment* (London: Pinter, 1985).

Shaw, A., 'Glasgow: A Municipal Study', *Century*, 39 (1890), 721–36.

Municipal Government in Continental Europe (New York: Fisher Unwin, 1895).

Sheahan, J. M., *Promotion and Control of Industry in Post-War France* (Cambridge, Mass.: Harvard University Press, 1963).

'Experience with Public Enterprise in France and Italy', in W. G. Shepherd (ed.), *Public Enterprise: Economic Analysis in Theory and Practice* (London: Heath & Co., 1976), 123–83.

Sheail, J., 'Planning, Water Supplies and Ministerial Power in Inter-War Britain', *Public Administration* 61 (1983), 386–95.

Sherman, D., 'Government Responses to Economic Modernisation in mid 19th Century France', *Journal of European Economic History* 6 (1977), 717–36.

Sherratt, W., 'Water Supply to Large Towns', *Journal of the Manchester Geographical Society* 4 (1888), 58–71.

Shonfield, A., *Modern Capitalism: The Changing Balance of Public and Private Power* (Oxford University Press, 1956).

Silva, A. F. da, 'Running for Money: Urban Infrastructure Finance and Municipalisation in Lisbon (1850–1914)', Paper presented at International Economic History Congress, Madrid, 1998.

Silverthorne, A., *London and Provincial Water Supplies* (London: Crosby, Lockwood & Co., 1884).

Simson, J. von, 'Water Supply and Sewerage in Berlin, London and Paris: Developments in the 19th Century', in H. T. Teuteberg (ed.), *Urbanisierung im 19. um 20. Jahrhundert* (Cologne: Bohlau Verlag, 1983), 429–40.

Singleton, J., 'Labour, the Conservatives and Nationalisation', in R. Millward and J. Singleton (eds.), *The Political Economy of Nationalisation in Britain 1920–50* (Cambridge University Press, 1995), 13–33.

Sleeman, J. F. L., 'Municipal Gas Costs and Revenue', *Manchester School* 18 (1950), 31–53.

Smart, W., 'Glasgow and its Municipal Industries', *Quarterly Journal of Economics* 9(2) (1895), 188–94.

Smith, C. O., Jr, 'The Longest Run: Public Engineering and Planning in France', *American Historical Review* 95 (1990), 657–92.

Soderlund, E. F., 'The Placing of the First Swedish Railway Loan', *Scandinavian Economic History Review* **11** (1963), 43–59.

Sola Pool, I. de (ed.), *The Social Impact of the Telephone* (Cambridge, Mass.: MIT Press, 1977).

Solomon, J. H., 'Telecommunications Evolution in the UK', *Telecommunications Policy* **10** (1986), 86–92.

Splawn, W. M. W., *Government Ownership and Operation of Railways* (New York: Macmillan, 1928).

Stahl, P., 'Les Débats politiques sur l'électricité dans les années trentes', *Bulletin de l'Histoire de l'électricité* **7** (1986), 93–106.

Statens Statistiscke Bureau, *Statistick aarbog* (Copenhagen: Thieles Bogtrykle, 1897, 1912).

Stefani, G., 'Public Undertakings in Italy and the Prospects for Economic Programming', *Annals of Public and Collective Economy* **37** (1966), 41–63.

Stephens, R., 'The Evolution of Privatisation as an Electoral Policy, c.1970–1990', *Contemporary British History* **18**(2) (2004), 47–75.

Stern, W. M., 'Water Supply in Britain: Development of a Public Service', *Royal Sanitary Institute Journal* **74** (1954), 998–1004.

Stiefel, D., 'Fifty Years of State Owned Enterprise in Austria 1946–96', in P. A. Toninelli (ed.), *The Rise and Fall of State Owned Enterprise in the Western World* (Cambridge University Press, 2000), 237–52.

Stolper, G. F., Hauser, K. and Borschadt, K., *The German Economy: 1870 to the Present* (London: Wiedenfeld and Nicholson, 1967).

Storaci, M. and Tattara, G., 'The External Financing of Italian Electric Companies in the Inter-War Years', *European Economic History Review* **2**(3) (1998), 345–75.

Sturmthal, A., 'The Study of Nationalised Enterprises in France', *Political Science Quarterly* **67** (1952), 357–77.

Sudria, C., 'Notas sobre la implantacion y el desarrollo de la industria del gas en España 1840–1901', *Revista de Historia Economica* **1**(2) (1983), 97–118.

'Les Restrictions de la consummation de l'électricité en Espagne pendant l'après guerre 1944–54', in F. Cardot (ed.), *1880–1980: Une siècle de l'électricité dans le monde* (Paris: Presses Universitaires de France, 1987), 425–35.

Summers, R., 'Services in the International Economy', in R. P. Inman (ed.), *Managing the Service Economy* (Cambridge University Press, 1985), 27–48.

Summerton, J., 'Coalitions and Conflicts: Swedish Municipal Energy Companies on the Eve of De-Regulation', in A. Kaijser and M. Hedin (eds.), *Nordic Energy Systems: Historical Perspectives and Current Issues* (Canton, Mass.: Science History Publications, 1995), 169–85.

Supple, B., 'Ideology or Pragmatism?: The Nationalisation of Coal 1916–46', in N. McKendrick and R. B. Outhwaite (eds.), *Business Life and Public Policy: Essays in Honour of D. C. Coleman* (Cambridge University Press, 1986), 228–50.

The History of the Coal Industry. IV. 1913–46: The Political Economy of Decline (Oxford: Clarendon Press, 1987).

Sutcliffe, A., *The Autumn of Central Paris: The Defeat of Town Planning 1850–1970* (Montreal: McGill-Queens University Press, 1971).

'Street Transport in the Second Half of the 19th Century: Mechanisation Delayed?', in J. A. Tarr and G. Dupuy (eds.), *Technology and the Rise of the Networked City in Europe* (Philadelphia: Temple University Press, 1988), 22–39.

Towards the Planned City: Services in Britain, USA and France 1790–1914 (Oxford University Press, 1991).

Tarr, J. A. and Dupuy, G., 'Sewers and Cities: France and the US Compared', *Journal of the Environmental Engineering Division, Proceedings of the American Society of Civil Engineers* **108** (1982), 327–38.

Taylor, J., 'Private Property, Public Interest and the Rise of the State in Nineteenth Century Britain: The Case of the Lighthouse', *Historical Journal* **44** (2001), 749–71.

Thomas, F., 'The Politics of Growth: The German Telephone System', in R. Maintz and T. P. Hughes (eds.), *The Development of Large Technical Systems* (Boulder, Colo.: Frankfurt and Westview Press, 1978), 179–213.

Thompson, C. D., *Public Ownership: A Survey of Public Enterprises* (New York: T. W. Crowell, 1925).

Thue, L., 'The State and the Dual Structure of the Power Supply Industry in Norway, 1890–1940', in M. Trédé (ed.), *Electricité et électrification dans le monde 1880–1980* (Paris: Association pour l'Histoire de l'Electricité en France, Presses Universitaires de France, 1990), 227–34.

'Electricity Rules: The Formation and Development of the Nordic Electricity Regions', in A. Kaijser and M. Hedin (eds.), *Nordic Energy Systems: Historical Perspectives and Current Issues* (Canton, Mass.: Science History Publications, 1995), 11–29.

Tilly, R., 'The Political Economy of Public Finance and Prussian Industrialisation 1815–60', *Journal of Economic History* **26** (1966), 484–97.

'Municipal Socialism and Municipal Enterprise in Germany 1890–1914', Paper presented to ESRC Quantitative Economic History Conference, Edinburgh, September 1991.

'Municipal Enterprise, Tax Burden and Municipal Socialism in German Cities 1870–1914', Paper presented to International Economic History Congress, Milan, 1994.

Tipton, F. B., 'Government Policy and Economic Development in Germany and Japan: A Sceptical Re-evaluation', *Journal of Economic History* **41** (1981), 139–50.

Tipton, F. B., Brech-Maksvylin, M. and Newell, S., 'Bureaucracy and the Railways in Germany and Japan', in L. Andersson-Skog and O. Krantz (eds.), *Institutions and the Transport and Communications Industries* (Canton, Mass.: Science History Publications, Watson, 1999), 5–32.

Tomlinson, J., 'Labour's Management of the National Economy 1945–51: Survey and Speculations', *Economy and Society* **18**(1) (1989), 1–24.

Public Policy and the Economy Since 1900 (Oxford: Clarendon Press, 1990).

Government and the Enterprise since 1900 (Oxford: Clarendon Press, 1994).

Toninelli, P. A. (ed.), *The Rise and Fall of State Owned Enterprise in the Western World* (Cambridge University Press, 2000).

Tortella, G., *The Development of Modern Spain* (Cambridge. Mass.: Harvard University Press, 2000).

Treasury, H. M., *The Financial and Economic Objectives of the Nationalised Industries*, Command 1337 (London: HMSO, 1961).

Nationalised Industries: A Review of Financial and Economic Objectives, Command 3437 (London: HMSO, 1967).

Trédé, M. (ed.), *Electricité et électrification dans le monde 1880–1980* (Paris: Association pour l'Histoire de l'Electricité en France, Presses Universitaires de France, 1990).

Turnbull, P. and Wass, V., 'Dockers and Deregulation in the International Port Transport Industry', in J. McConville (ed.) *Transport Regulation Matters* (London: Pinter, 1997), 126–53.

Ullmo, Y., 'The National Context: France', in J. Hayward and M. Watson (eds.), *Planning, Politics and Public Policy* (Cambridge University Press, 1975), 22–51.

Ungerer, H., 'Comments on Telecommunications Reform in the European Community', in G. Majone (ed.), *De-Regulation or Re-Regulation?: Regulation in Europe and the United States* (London: Pinter, 1990), 108–9.

United Nations, *World Energy Supplies 1950–74* (New York: Statistical Office, Department of Economic and Social Affairs, Series J 19, 1976).

Vagts, D., 'Railroads, Private Enterprise and Public Policy – Germany and the Unter State', in N. Horn and K. Kocka (eds.), *Recht und Entwicklung der Grossunternehmen im 19. und frühen 20. Jahrhundert* (Göttingen: Vandenhoeck and Ruprecht, 1979), 604–17.

Valdaliso, J. M., 'The Diffusion of Technological Change in the Spanish Merchant Fleet during the Twentieth Century: Available Alternatives and Conditioning Factors', *Journal of Transport History* 12(2) (1996), 1–17.

Verney, D. V., *Public Enterprise in Sweden* (Liverpool University Press, 1959).

Vernon, R., 'The International Aspects of State-Owned Enterprises', *Journal of International Business Studies* 10(3) (1979), 7–15.

Vernon, R. and Aharoni, Y. (eds.), *State-Owned Enterprise in Western Economies* (London: Croom Helm, 1981).

Vinck, F. and Boursin, J., 'The Development of the Public and Private Sectors of the Coal Mining Industry in Europe: A Comparative Study', *Annals of Public and Collective Economy* 33 (1962), 385–491.

Vos, M. de, 'The Belgian National Railways (S.C.N.B.)', *Annals of Public and Collective Economy* 26 (1955), 523–9.

Votaw, D., *The Six-Legged Dog: Mattei and ENI – A Study in Power* (Berkeley: University of California Press, 1964).

Vries, J. de, 'Benelux 1920–70', in C. Cipolla (ed.), *The Fontana Economic History of Europe: Contemporary Economies*, 2 parts (Glasgow: Fontana/Collins, 1976), part 1, 1–71.

Walker, G., *Road and Rail* (London: Allen and Unwin, 1947).

'Transport Policy before and after 1953', *Oxford Economic Papers* 5 (1953), 90–116.

Walkland, S. A., 'Economic Planning and Dysfunctional Politics in Britain 1945–83', in A. M. Gamble and S. A. Walkland (eds.), *The British Party System and Economic Policy: 1945–1983: Studies in Adversary Politics* (Oxford: Clarendon Press, 1984), 92–151.

Wallsten, S., 'Ringing in the 20th Century: The Effects of State Monopolies, Private Ownership and Operating Licences on Telecommunications in Europe 1892–1913', Paper presented at Annual Conference of the Economic History Society, University of Birmingham, April 2002.

Walters, R. D. and Morrison, R. J., 'State Owned Business Abroad: New Competitive Threat', *Harvard Business Review* **57** (1979), 161–70.

Ward, B. T., 'National Economic Planning and Policy in 20th Century Europe', in C. Cipolla (ed.), *Fontana Economic History of Europe: The Twentieth Century*, 2 parts (Glasgow: Fontana/Collins, 1973), part 2, 698–738.

Webb, M. G., 'Energy Pricing in the UK', *Energy Economics* **2**(4) (1980), 194–98.

Webb, M. G. and Ricketts, M. J., *The Economics of Energy* (London: Macmillan, 1980).

Weber, F., 'Austrian Nationalised Industry 1845–85', in V. Zamagni (ed.), *Origins and Development of Publicly Owned Enterprises* (University of Florence, Ninth International Economic History Conference, Section B111, 1986), 71–5.

Weir Committee, *Report of a Committee Appointed by the Board of Trade to Review the National Problem of the Supply of Electricity Energy* (London: Board of Trade, 1926).

Wellisz, S., 'Economic Planning in the Netherlands, France and Italy', *Journal of Political Economy* **68**(3) (1960), 252–83.

Wengenroth, U., 'The Electrification of the Workshop', in F. Cardot (ed.), *1880–1980: Une siècle de l'électricité dans le monde* (Paris: Presses Universitaires de France, 1987), 357–66.

'The Rise and Fall of State Owned Enterprise in Germany', in P. A. Toninelli (ed.), *The Rise and Fall of State Owned Enterprise in the Western World* (Cambridge University Press, 2000), 103–27.

Weyman-Jones, T., *The Economics of Energy Policy* (Aldershot: Gower, 1986).

Whitaker and Sons, *Whitaker's Almanack* (London: Whitaker and Sons, 1911).

Whitelegg, J., *Transport Policy in the EEC* (London: Routledge, 1988).

Whiteman, T., 'North Sea Oil', in D. Morris (ed.), *The Economic System in the UK* (Oxford University Press, 1985), 229–50.

Wickham, S., 'Development of French Railways under the French Four Year Plans', *Bulletin of the Oxford University Institute of Statistics* **24**(1) (1962), 167–84.

Wieland, B., 'Telecommunications in the Netherlands' in J. Foreman-Peck and J. Mueller (eds.), *European Telecommunications Organisation* (Baden-Baden: Nomosverlagsgesellschaft, 1988), 203–19.

Williamson Committee, *Report of a Committee Appointed by the Board of Trade to Consider the Question of Electric Power Supply*, Command 9062, Parliamentary Papers 1918, vi (London: HMSO, 1918).

Wilson, J. F., 'The Finance of Municipal Capital Expenditure in England and Wales', 1870–1914', *Financial History Review* **4** (1997), 31–50.

Wingate, A., 'Railway Building in Italy before Unification', Centre for the Advanced Study of Italian Society, Occasional Papers no. 3, Reading: Department of Italian Studies, University of Reading, 1970.

Wright, V., *Privatisation in Western Europe* (London: Pinter, 1994).

Yago, G., *The Decline of Transit: Urban Transportation in German and US Cities 1900–70* (Cambridge University Press, 1984).

Yarrow, G., 'Privatisation in Theory and Practice', *Economic Policy* **2** (1980), 232–64.

Young, S., 'A Comparison of the Industrial Experience', in J. Hayward and M. Watson (eds.), *Planning, Politics and Public Policy* (Cambridge University Press, 1975), 141–54.

Zamagni, V., *The Economic History of Italy 1860–1990* (Oxford: Clarendon Press, 1993).

'Italy: How to Lose the War and Win the Peace', in M. Harrison (ed.), *The Economics of World War II* (Cambridge University Press, 1998), 177–223.

Zamagni, V. (ed.), *Origins and Development of Publicly Owned Enterprises* (University of Florence, Ninth International Economic History Conference, Section B111, 1986, some of which was reproduced in *Annali di Storia dell Impresa*, 1987).

Zamdem, J. L. van, 'The Netherlands: The History of an Empty Box', in J. Foreman-Peck and G. Federico (eds.), *European Industrial Policy: The Twentieth Century Experience* (Oxford University Press, 1999), 177–93.

Zanetti, G. (ed.), *Storia dell'industria elettrica in Italia. V. Glisviluppi dell ENEL. 1963–1990* (Roma-Bari: Laterza & Figli, 1994).

Index

Made in the USA
Las Vegas, NV
04 November 2021